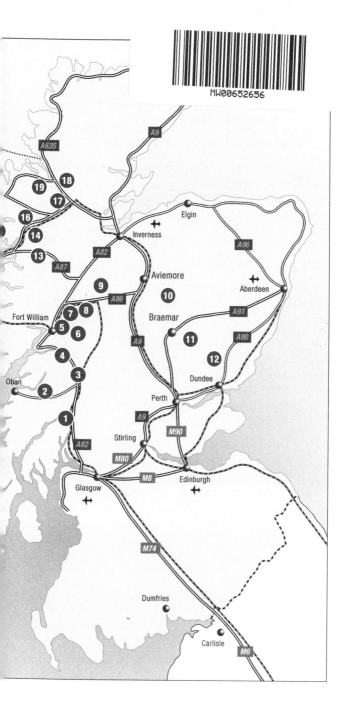

MW00652656

A835

A9

Elgin

A96

Inverness

Aberdeen

A82

Aviemore

19
18
17
16
14
13   A87

9   A86

7   8
5   6
Fort William

4

3

Oban

2

1

A82

A82

10

Braemar

11

12

A93

A90

A9

Dundee

Perth

A9

Stirling

M90

M80

M8   Edinburgh

Glasgow

M74

Dumfries

Carlisle   M6

SCOTTISH WINTER CLIMBS

SCOTTISH WINTER CLIMBS

Andy Nisbet
Rab Anderson
Simon Richardson

Series Editor: Brian Davison

SCOTTISH MOUNTAINEERING CLUB
CLIMBERS' GUIDE

Published in Great Britain by The Scottish Mountaineering Trust, 2008

ISBN 978-0-907521-98-3

A catalogue record for this book is available from the British Library

Front Cover: The Wand, V,5, Creag Meagaidh. Climber Blair Fyffe
(photo Cubby Images)

Frontispiece: The Curtain, IV,5, Ben Nevis (photo Cubby Images)

Route descriptions of climbs in this guide, together with their grades
and any references to in situ or natural protection are made in good
faith, based on past or first ascent descriptions, checked and
substantiated where possible by the authors.
However, climbs lose holds and are altered by rockfall, rock becomes
dirty and loose and in situ protection deteriorates. Even minor
alterations can have a dramatic effect on a climb's grade or
seriousness. Therefore, it is essential that climbers judge the
condition of any route for themselves, before they start climbing.
The authors, editors, friends and assistants involved in the
publication of this guide, the Scottish Mountaineering Club, the
Scottish Mountaineering Trust and Scottish Mountaineering Trust
(Publications) Ltd, can therefore accept no liability whatever for
damage to property, nor for personal injury or death, arising
directly or indirectly from the use of this publication.

This guidebook is compiled from the most recent information and
experience provided by members of the Scottish Mountaineering
Club and other contributors. The book is published by the Scottish
Mountaineering Trust, which is a charitable trust.
Revenue from the sale of books published by the Trust is used for the
continuation of its publishing programme and for charitable
purposes associated with Scottish mountains and mountaineering.

Design concept: Curious Oranj, Glasgow
Production: Scottish Mountaineering Trust (Publications) Ltd
Typesetting: Ken Crocket
Diagram and map graphics: Andy Nisbet, Tom Prentice
Colour separations: Core Image Ltd, East Kilbride
Printed & bound by Elkar, Bilbao

Distributed by Cordee Ltd, 11 Jacknell Road,
Dodwells Industrial Estate, Hinkley. LE10 3BS
(t) 01455 611185   (e) sales@cordee.co.uk

For details of other SMC guidebooks see inside rear endpaper

Contents

Diagrams & Maps

Introduction & Acknowledgements

Scottish winter climbing is now an activity of international importance, with visitors arriving from not only south of the border and from all over the world This rise in popularity is easily explained by the very special climbing conditions that are readily produced by the alternation of the influences of moist maritime and cold polar air masses. The frequent freeze-thaw cycles and high precipitation creates snow, ice and 'mixed' conditions which can be a joy to climb, often in remote and impressive surroundings. However, the very factors which produce these unique climbing conditions are themselves a problem for the climber; the weather may be poor, even hostile, and the rapidly changing conditions may make one crag a bad choice, while another nearby is excellent. For a first-time or occasional visitor these problems can be frustrating and this book aims to overcome the frustrations by describing a selection of the best winter climbs throughout mainland Scotland, with notes on how to judge weather and climbing conditions to select the best option for the day.

In recent times, global warming has produced a more unsettled weather pattern, with even more rapid temperature changes. Heavy snowfall followed by freeze-thaw on the high cliffs is increasingly common, with good ice potentially available at any time of the season, but the long cold high pressure producing frozen waterfalls on the low crags has become rare. Rocky mixed climbs have become the most reliable, and the intricacy of torquing cracks plus improved axes for twisting and hooking has increased interest in this style. A few grades have been raised due to loss of turf on the most popular routes and also because the two-tier grading system is settling down. But ice grades are generally the same despite better tools and ice-screws; hopefully this keeps the styles comparable and benefits the ego. The 'ethics police' are continuously critical of winter climbing. The key thing is to enjoy it but don't spoil things for future parties. Placement of bolts on mountain cliffs and climbing on unfrozen turf are two elements which must be resisted.

This edition has many more routes than the last, and they are concentrated on the high cliffs, while cliffs of the lowest altitude have been deleted. The emphasis on lower grades has been maintained but the average has been raised to reflect the increase in standards. The changeable weather has made the choice of cliff more difficult and crucial, but more than matched by increased communication, mostly on the Internet. The only disadvantage is a concentration of folk on the popular areas where recent pictures have been seen. We hope that this book may encourage climbers to venture from the well known climbing areas (excellent though they are) so that they may discover the wealth of opportunity that lies elsewhere, along with the joy of mountaineering in magnificent scenery. Suffice to say that there are many other excellent climbs and crags in Scotland that have not been described in this book, so if your appetite has been whetted you can obtain fully comprehensive coverage in the SMC Climbers' Guides Series.

Andy Nisbet, Rab Anderson, Simon Richardson
Autumn 2008

Almost everyone in the climbing scene has had some input, although fewer named individuals than for the comprehensive guides. Thanks to all who took the time to become involved. The authors of this book are often the same as for the comprehensive guides, but they have kept their eye on comments made personally, sent to discussions on winter grades and posted on web-sites like UK Climbing.

The editing team of Brian Davison for text and Grahame Nicoll for photographs have made this guide both accurate and attractive. The whole series of Scottish guidebooks has been very well received largely due to the design and production management of Tom Prentice.

ENVIRONMENT

Access

Part 1 of the Land Reform (Scotland) Act 2003 gives you the right to be on most land and inland water for recreation, education and for going from place to place, providing you act responsibly. This includes climbing, hillwalking, cycling and wild camping. These access rights and responsibilities are explained in the Scottish Outdoor Access Code. The key elements are:

- Take personal responsibility for your own actions and act safely.
- Respect people's privacy and peace of mind.
- Help land managers and others to work safely and effectively.
- Care for the environment and take your litter home.
- Keep your dog under proper control.
- Take extra care if you're organising an event or running a business.

If you're managing the outdoors:

- Respect access rights;
- Act reasonably when asking people to avoid land management operations;
- Work with your local authority and other bodies to help integrate access and land management;
- Respect rights of way and customary access.

Find out more by visiting <www.outdooraccess-scotland.com> or phoning your local Scottish Natural Heritage office.

Footpath Erosion

Part of the revenue from the sale of this and other Scottish Mountaineering Club books is granted by the Scottish Mountaineering Trust as financial assistance towards the repair and maintenance of hill paths in Scotland. However, it is our responsibility to minimise our erosive effect, for the enjoyment of future climbers.

Litter & Pollution

Do not leave litter of any sort anywhere, and take it down from the hill or crag in your rucksack. Do not cause pollution, and bury human waste carefully out of sight far away from any habitation or water supply. Avoid burying rubbish as this may also pollute the environment.

Cairns

The proliferation of navigation cairns detracts from the feeling of wildness, and may be confusing rather than helpful as regards route-finding. The indiscriminate building of cairns on the hills should be discouraged.

Cars & Bicycles

Use bicycles instead of driving along private roads. Although the use of bicycles can often be helpful for reaching remote hills and crags, they can cause severe erosion and damage when used 'off road' on soft footpaths and open hillsides. Bicycles should only be used on hard tracks such as vehicular or forest tracks.

General Privacy

Respect for personal privacy near people's homes is nothing less than good manners

Mountaineering Council of Scotland

The MCofS is the representative body for climbers and walkers in Scotland. One of its primary concerns is the continued free access to the hills and crags. Information about bird restrictions, stalking and general access issues can be obtained from the MCofS. Should you encounter problems regarding access you should contact the MCofS, whose current address is: The Old Granary, West Mill Street, Perth PH1 5QP, tel (01738 638 227), fax (01738 442 095), email <info@mountaineering-scotland.org.uk>, website <www.mcofs.org.uk>.

Astral Highway, VI,5, Orion Face, Ben Nevis. Climber William Sim

VENUE, WINTER TACTICS & RISK

Participation

"Climbing and mountaineering are activities with a danger of personal injury or death. Participants in these activities should be aware of and accept these risks and be responsible for their own actions and involvement."
UIAA participation statement.

Liabilities

You are responsible for your own actions and should not hold landowners liable for an accident, even if it happens while climbing over a fence or dyke. It is up to the individual climber to assess the reliability of bolts, pegs, slings or old nuts, which may have deteriorated over time and therefore fail.

Choice of Venue

Scottish weather and conditions are very variable, so flexible plans are the key to success. The ideal is to decide the destination area a day or two before departure, and the particular cliff the day before, reviewed in the morning. Any plans made ahead of a weather forecast (say 5 days) are a gamble to be avoided if possible. Those who can go climbing midweek at short notice have a big advantage. The general weather rule is to let the wind cross as much land as possible to find the least snow-fall and mist. If the weather is cold (and has been for a few days), stay low; if mild, go high. Avoid visiting a cliff for the first time in mist. If it is thawing at all levels, perhaps go home. If there is a blizzard, perhaps go home. It is crucial to be keen, but don't push your luck in deteriorating weather or on potential avalanche slopes.

The Hoarmaster, VI,6, Coire an Lochain, Cairngorms. Climber Alasdair Buchanan

Prediction of good conditions is harder, particularly in relation to the thickness of ice which is determined by the weather during the previous weeks. Years of experience will help accurate prediction, but the word from someone who's been there recently will always be better. Generally speaking, a long spell of cold weather without thaws means thicker ice, although not on Ben Nevis and parts of the Cairngorms, where temporary thaws are required. Conditions for turf and rock mixed climbing are less critical, but try to avoid deep powder or unfrozen turf. Early in the season, remember that the turf will freeze more rapidly if it is not insulated by a thick layer of fresh snow.

There is a lot of information about conditions on the Internet. This is both from individual climbers on sites like <ukclimbing.com> and from providers of winter courses who provide information as a means of attracting you to their business website. These are all very useful but should not be taken as totally reliable. Conditions may change overnight so the weather forecast is important. Opinions about quality will vary according to the enthusiasm of the individual and providers of courses are guaranteed to be optimistic. But if a route has been climbed, that is a fact and pictures don't lie (much). Put a number of options on your "Favourites" and keep track of conditions throughout a winter. The Scottish Avalanche Information Service <www.sais.gov uk> run blogs on snow conditions for four of their five areas (see below), often showing specific pictures of the main cliffs. There are webcams for many of the mountain areas. <www.visit-fortwilliam.co.uk/webcam/index.html> gives a view of Ben Nevis.

Arrochar & Southern Highlands: The climbing here is mostly turfy, but some ice forms if it is cold. Many of the cliffs are relatively low, and so they are very prone to thaw in tropical maritime winds. Avoid in late season, but turf conditions can be excellent after heavy frosts and light snow early on.

Glen Coe: There is a wide variety of options here. Cold conditions are required for good ice, which can be quickly stripped by thaw, so it is not generally a good late season venue. Northerly or easterly winds bode well.

Aonachs: Aonach Mòr is good in early season but the Gondola has a closed spell. January to March is very reliable. A big build-up of snow blows in, so beware of cornices and avalanches, but as a result the gullies can survive big thaws. The buttresses are often poor due to sun in March.

Ben Nevis: This is the best venue for snow-ice, so conditions can be wonderful or awful; look for reports on conditions and don't miss out when at their best. Go mid to late season, after thaws and a re-freeze. The Ben is useless and dangerous under deep powder. Early season mixed climbing is slowly catching on, but involves a long approach in short daylight.

Creag Meagaidh: Ice climbing predominates here, which requires good conditions, both for safety on the routes and the long approach. It is a place to avoid under powder or spindrift, and February or March is usually best. The climbing is excellent when the weather is cold enough.

Cairngorms: The longest season. Mixed climbing on the high cliffs is often in condition at times during November and December. January to April continues reliable for all styles, although good ice conditions have been patchy in recent years due to occasional big thaws. The weather is drier and colder than the west during the prevailing westerly winds, but prone to wind and spindrift. Northerly or easterly winds often cause poor conditions.

Northern Highlands: Due to their lower altitude, January to March is the most likely. Showery polar maritime winds bring heavy snow while tropical maritime winds bring quick thaw. There are a wide variety of venues if it is cold enough. Note that it is further to drive, information on conditions may be harder to obtain, and the weather can be different to everywhere else.

Summary of best season

Nov – Dec	Cairngorms
Jan	Southern Highlands & Arrochar, Glen Coe, Northern Highlands
Feb	Creag Meaghaidh, Glen Coe, Northern Highlands, Aonach Mor, higher venues during a mild winter
March	Cairngorms, Ben Nevis, high areas of Glen Coe, Northern Highlands
April	Ben Nevis

Weather Forecasts

The weather forecast is one of the key factors in choice of venue. Obviously it may not be correct, especially for more than two days ahead, although better than your best guess. Once committed (i.e. after arrival), the best information is found by looking out the window. The other problem is interpreting a ground level forecast into a mountain forecast, particularly one relevant to your intended route. This takes much practice; cliff altitude, aspect and location, and wind strength and direction are all important factors. Obviously the temperature is crucial, but this is not always easily predicted from the valley. While it is true that it usually gets colder the higher one goes, the rate at which this happens (the lapse rate) depends of the origin and humidity of the air mass. As a general rule, the lapse rate is lower in moist maritime air than in showery polar air. Hence, if it is mild and drizzly (say 8 to 10 degrees C) in the valley it will probably be soggy on most cliffs, while the same valley temperature in a north-westerly airflow may cause crisp and sparkling neve high up. Another exception is in periods of settled high pressure, when temperature inversions keep the valleys cold (and sometimes dull) while the crags may be basking in sunshine above a blanket of cloud. Those climbing for one or two days can obtain the forecast before leaving home; those with a longer time in the hills are advised to update their information. The four choices are radio, TV, newspaper or telephone recorded messages.

Radio: Radio 4 gives the most concise forecasts, although often lacking detail for Scotland. Radio Scotland forecasts are also good. The best combination is the Shipping Forecast on Radio 4 (17.54 pm) giving sea winds which are relevant to mountain winds, followed by the weather forecast (17.57 pm) with other details, particularly rain, snow and timing of fronts. On the Shipping Forecast, Malin (west; Fort William and south), Hebrides (north-west) and Cromarty (east) are relevant. A Radio Scotland forecast then follows at 17.58pm, but usually doesn't overlap. The Shipping Forecast can also be found on <www.bbc.co.uk/weather/coast/shipping>. An Outdoor Conditions forecast is on at 17.13pm on Radio Scotland and another weather forecast at 20.58pm.

Newspapers: Newspaper forecasts are poor compared to the information on TV, radio and internet.

Television: The BBC offers a better and more detailed chart than ITV. The Reporting Scotland forecast at approx. 18.55pm Monday to Friday is the best daily one, available all day on BBCi on an updated loop with 24hr and 5day forecast maps.

Internet: Use of the Internet has led to the withdrawal of good telephone forecasts. There are a wide variety of forecasts on the Internet (in 2008), including:

<www.mwis.org.uk> is the best mountain forecast. A mountain forecast is also available on <www.metoffice.gov.uk/loutdoor/mountainsafety>, with East and West Highland options.

<www.metcheck.com> gives a huge range of information including long range forecasts.
<www.bbc.co.uk/weather> and <www.metoffice.co.uk> give reliable forecasts.

<www.wetterzentrale.de> gives 10 day synoptic pressure and temperature charts (speculative), and is the best access to a huge amount of technical information.

<www.weatheronline.co.uk/GreatBritain/CairngormMt.htm> gives summit temperatures on Cairn Gorm (1200m).

<www.weatheronline.co.uk/GreatBritain/BenNevis.htm> gives 1130m temperatures on Aonach Mor.

<www.phy.hw.ac.uk/resrev/weather.htm> gives summit temperatures and wind on Cairn Gorm.

Winter Tactics

Having decided where to climb, a number of other factors must be considered to produce a successful day.

Accommodation

The early starts required for the normal winter day mean that convenience takes precedent over comfortable accommodation, although for longer trips the latter is also a necessity. Those lucky enough to live in Scotland can often climb for a single day by leaving home very early in the morning, which avoids the problem. However, for longer trips in terms of both time and distance, somewhere to spend the night must be found. To maximise use of daylight, it is best to stay as close as possible to the point of departure from the road. Many have found that sleeping in their car or van is best for one night. Short-term camping is also a possibility, but putting a tent up in the dark in a blizzard after a long drive is not something that many people take pleasure in. Except for the most remote cliffs, camping above valley level is rarely advantageous and many tents have been destroyed by wind.

These temporary accommodation tactics must be modified for longer trips. Clothing and equipment is likely to be wet after a day on the hill, and unless drying facilities are available, a complete second set of clothes is a good precaution for the second day of a weekend. Similarly, a spare rope is worth considering because frozen ropes are difficult to handle and possibly dangerous. So, after a day on the hill many teams will welcome somewhere warm to spend the evening, have a comfortable night, and dry clothes and equipment. A selection of potential indoor accommodation, club huts and hostels, is listed in the introduction to each chapter. Information on these and alternatives like hotels and B&B, is available either through the climbing magazines, Internet or the local Tourist Information Office (see chapter introductions). All these options of comfortable indoor accommodation reduce flexibility because of the pre-booking that may be required, and the fixed location. Therefore, a willingness to drive to other areas from these bases is important.

Smith's Route, V,5, Icicle Variation, Ben Nevis

Tourist Offices are the best source of general information and listed in the chapter introductions. <www.visitscotland.com/aboutscotland> gives links to regional tourist websites. Mountaineering Huts are unwardened and privately owned by mountaineering clubs. These are usually only available to members of clubs affiliated to the MCofS or BMC. Addresses and phone numbers of current hut custodians can be obtained through your club or for huts of Scottish Clubs, by contacting the MCofS (01738 493942), or their website <www.mcofs.org.uk/huts>. There are a limited number of petrol stations in the Highlands; an indication of opening times is given in the chapter introduction. There are many hotels in the Highlands but some are closed in the winter. Most serve bar meals.

Starting Times
Early starts are more or less essential in winter, especially in December and January when daylight is limited. Accordingly, except for the more convenient cliffs, be prepared to start the approach walk in the dark. The longer climbs are probably best climbed later in the season if possible, when the days become luxuriously longer. It is best to aim to get to the top of the cliff and past the most awkward part of the descent before darkness falls, as once it becomes dark, anything technical will take at least twice as long (half an hour in the morning can save two hours or more at the end of the day). Therefore try to calculate your starting time by estimating the timing backwards from this point. Although some famous heroes of the past seemed to thrive on late starts and climbing through the night, do not attempt to emulate them unless you enjoy being frightened and uncomfortable.

Equipment
A basic knowledge of winter hillwalking is assumed, indeed a prerequisite for winter climbing. The following notes may be found helpful by those starting the winter climbing game.
Helmet: This is absolutely essential. Put it on below the approach slopes and make

sure it is big enough to go over a balaclava.

Harness: It should be possible to put your harness on while wearing crampons, so a nappy-style design or adjustable leg loops are better than fixed leg loops.

Axe and hammer: Banana pick axes are better for ice or technical routes, while curved picks are equally good for easier routes and better for ice-axe breaking. Some of the axes that are designed specifically for thick water ice may not be suitable for general Scottish use as contact with rock may ruin them. Sharp axes work immeasurably better than blunt ones on ice. The bent shaft is great for technical moves but very poor on steep snow and therefore lower grades. Climbing leashless is a definite advantage on hard technical sections but requires practice to place protection and needless to say a big disadvantage if you drop a tool! Whether it will become popular on the classic climbs is uncertain.

Crampons: For lower grade climbs, the make or design matters less than you might think, as long as they fit your boots.

Rucksack: This should be quite big, 50-60 litres, so that all clothing and equipment can be stowed inside to be kept dry during the approach.

Boots: Rigid soled leather boots are the current favourite. They are more comfortable than plastic boots but not as warm. Both work equally well on the climb. If using plastic boots, have them loosely laced for the approach, then tighten them up at the foot of the climb. Leather boots are normally laced quite tightly on the approach but you need to think flexibly and adjust tightness if necessary before damage to your feet is done.

Hardware: This will vary according to the climb being attempted. Harder mixed routes need a plentiful supply of rock gear. Usually take a supply of rock pegs.

Waterproofs and principal clothing: Staying warm is the key. Often this means waterproofs and a flexible number of layers underneath, but some prefer a single pile/pertex layer with zips for ventilation (often thermals underneath).

Gloves: The problem here is maintaining both warmth and utility. Large insulated mitts can be clumsy, but if they are large enough and have restraining straps, thin fingered gloves may be worn underneath to allow removal of the mitt when necessary. Dachsteins are the best for warmth and recommended for hillwalking but clumsy for climbing. For harder routes, wear as thin as your circulation allows. It is wise to have a warm pair of gloves in reserve just in case.

Headtorch: Another absolutely essential piece of equipment. LED torches have taken over, being lighter and with a longer battery life. If climbing, one with a halogen bulb option is worthwhile. One of the authors can confirm that it is very cold sitting on a ledge throughout the night because of a forgotten headtorch.

Spare clothing: While sound mountaineering principle requires a spare jacket (or duvet) to be carried, in practice the climber needs to wear sufficient clothing to remain warm while belaying in cold and windy conditions for perhaps hours at a stretch. Therefore, additional clothing is not really required. A belay jacket shared between leader and second is a good solution. Some climbers carry a spare base layer and change into this after the walk-in when gearing-up. A bivouac sac is a good precaution.

Food and drink: A thermos flask is perhaps not worth the extra weight, but this is a matter of personal preference. However, take some liquid to replace that lost during the sweaty approach, and take enough calories to keep you going. Don't overdo it; you need less liquid than in the summer.

Other items: A map and a compass should be carried by both climbers (what happens if your mate falls through a cornice with the only set?), and a small First Aid kit. An increasing number of people take mobile phones. While they have undoubtedly been of great use in some cases, they have also been abused and may give a false sense of security, as batteries can run out and they don't work in some locations. Ski-goggles can be useful in wind-driven snow.

Maps & Navigation

A surprising number of winter accidents and incidents involve a navigation error. The relevant map and a compass are essential items of equipment; learn how to use them. An altimeter can also be useful, especially in poor visibility. GPS units offer pin point grid reference location and reasonable altitude. This is very useful when in an uncertain position, either when finishing a route or having difficulty with navigation. At present they are less useful for bearings, but features like on-screen Ordnance Survey maps may change this; digital mapping software on your computer and careful pre-programming will be necessary. But they should not be taken as a substitute, since there is always the risk of battery failure and they may be impossible to use in the worst conditions.

In general, the O1:50000 series of Maps is best for Scotland, partly because the extra detail of 1:25000 may be buried under snow and partly because so many of the larger scale maps would be required to cover all the cliffs.

Place names and map references have in general been taken from the Ordnance Survey 1:50000 Landranger maps. The specific OS 1:50000 Landranger (L) and 1:25000 Explorer (E) maps are listed in the introduction to the relevant chapter, as well as the Harvey Superwalker (1:25000) maps and Harvey 'all weather' Mountain Maps (1:40000).

Symbols are used on the sketch maps to indicate different categories of summit. Tops are not marked on the maps in this guide:

Munro – black triangle
Corbett – black circle
Graham – black diamond
Other – crossed circle

Books

The following SMC and SMT publications, *The Munros*, *The Corbetts*, *Scottish Hill Names*, *Scottish Hill Tracks*, *Hostile Habitats – Scotland's Mountain Environment*, and *A Chance in a Million? – Scottish Avalanches* are useful for hill walking routes and general mountain interest in this area. For more information and to order SMC and SMT publications, visit the SMC website <www.smc.org.uk>. See also the publications list at the end of this guide.

Risks

Scottish winter climbing is a potentially dangerous sport, but part of the challenge is reduction of the risk to an acceptable level. The following are common causes of accidents:

Deteriorating Weather

The number of fine days in the winter is small, so you must climb in poor weather if you want to get anything done! But there is a big difference between poor and stormy weather. Stormy weather in the morning is less of a problem, because a change of plans is obvious. A fine start with a rapid deterioration to wind and blowing snow can be a trap. It is hard for the inexperienced to realise just how bad the weather can get; ferocious winds with blowing snow can make walking and navigation almost impossible, preventing descent. This can and does prove fatal; it happens every year. The only answer is to have flexible plans when the forecast is poor. A quick easy route ahead of the bad weather is still fun, but have the courage to turn back if it seems prudent. Remember that the weather on top is likely to be much worse than in the relative shelter of the cliff.

Basic Mountaineering Skills

The importance of proficiency in ice axe braking, walking in crampons, and navigation, and sufficient fitness, can be underestimated by climbers who are not hill walkers or mountaineers. In fact, the experienced winter hill walker is more likely to be a safer first season winter climber than a technical rock climber, who has much to learn. These skills apply to the unroped part of the day, but this is normally the longer part. Don't relax at the top of the route; maintain concentration and a sense of urgency until the road is reached. Many of Scotland's best winter climbers started with an instructional course, and this is recommended.

Approaching the cornice on Stirling Bridge, VI,7, Aonach Mòr. Climber Graeme Ettle

Avalanches

The possibility of avalanches should always be considered unless all the snow is hard or there is only a dusting. An awareness that avalanches are common coupled with some knowledge of how they occur is half the battle. This includes a flexibility with route choice, because normally there are safe options, even if the grade is easier than planned (even bagging a peak instead of a Grade I climb). The other half of the battle, deciding whether a potential risk is real, is anything but easy and even experienced climbers get avalanched, although excessive enthusiasm in poor conditions is usually their problem.

By far the commonest cause of avalanches in Scotland is windslab, which is wind-blown snow settling in an unstable layer, usually on lee slopes. The greater the amount of snow, the higher the risk. A sudden increase in wind after a heavy snowfall during light winds, for example when the centre of a low pressure area moves away, can cause the largest volume of blown snow and both the worst weather and highest avalanche risk. But a wind change can redistribute snow and produce the same result even if no fresh snow has fallen.

On meeting snow of dubious stability, climbers should dig a snow pit and examine the snow profile, looking especially for different layers of snow with different degrees of bonding. Slab avalanches are caused when a surface layer of snow is insufficiently attached to layers below and often when a climber triggers the slide. A simple snow pit can be dug very quickly, so there is no excuse. The test is to determine how well the top layer is bonded to layers below. The method is to excavate a vertical wall exposing the layers of snow, then a quick examination followed by a practical test of increasing pressure to see how easily the top layer will slide off. If you've never seen a "snow pit", get someone to show you. Literature is useful, but nothing beats practical experience.

Consider the following questions and principles:

1. Before leaving your accommodation, before leaving the road and as you approach the cliff, consider whether the choice of cliff is sensible in terms of windslab accumulation. Is snow being blown (or has it been recently) and collecting above, on, or below the cliff? Unfortunately for climber comfort, snow

collects in sheltered spots, so the windy cliff is safer.

2. Having looked at conditions and thought of a route, is it possible to reach the route safely? Is there a fresh layer of snow (as against isolated patches) of sufficient depth to avalanche (about 15cm)? If in doubt, dig a pit but remember that any dangerous layer will deepen approaching the cliff base. So assess the depth of the top layer as you proceed. Other factors are often observed and can aid decision. Convex slopes are more dangerous (the snow is less supported from below). Protruding rocks help to anchor a slope. Even a thin crust (starting to freeze after a thaw) stabilises a slope.

3. Having reached it, is the route safe? Ridges are much safer than gullies, but only assuming they continue as ridges to the top.

4. Is the finish, particularly the cornice, safe? Snow, freshly blown over a cliff-top, tends to accumulate on the cornice itself and the slope immediately below. On a big cliff it is easy to underestimate the amount of snow collecting so far away. While the slope below a cliff tends to avalanche when triggered by a climber, cornice slopes tend to avalanche spontaneously and funnel down gullies. The consequences of an avalanche at the top are more serious.

5. Once you are on or below the slope, you are committed!

6. However much you know, no-one knows everything. There will be many exceptions to the above generalisations. For example, windslab has been known to become more dangerous with time (instead of the normal consolidation) due to vapourisation inside the snowpack.

7. Avalanche reports are informative, but slopes can stabilise or become dangerous even before the tester reaches the valley, let alone you reading it. Your own assessment at the cliff is crucial.

8. Other avalanche types also occur. Old wet snow (crystalline) is usually safe, with rare exceptions where the snow is lying on a smooth ground layer. Fresh wet snow is not safe, nor are wet cornices. Fresh snow in the sun can avalanche from a single point spreading out, but this is rarely serious unless on steep ground (but it is extremely dangerous in the Alps).

If avalanched, try to jump free or ice axe brake. The chances of escaping may be quite good if the avalanche is a small volume, or you are near the edge or top. If swept down in a large volume on a slope, try to stay on the surface. Keep your mouth closed, especially in powder, and as the snow slows down try to create a breathing space in front of your mouth. Wet snow avalanches harden rapidly on settling, so try to break free just before the debris stops. If trapped, try to stay calm, which will reduce oxygen demand.

If you are an uninjured companion or witness to an avalanche, it is vital to start a search immediately; don't go immediately for help. And remember, the same slope will not avalanche again. Sometimes there is an arm, leg or piece of equipment visible even if the head is under the snow. If buried, victims will often be alive at first but their chances of survival lessen rapidly. Unless severely injured, some 80% may live if found immediately, but only 10% after a three hour delay (the minimum time for a rescue team to arrive). Listen for any sound, look carefully for any visual clue and mark the burial site if it can be guessed, or at least the line of fall. Search for a considerable time, ideally until rescue arrives (if someone else has summoned them). A working knowledge of First Aid is important, as many victims may have stopped breathing.

A Chance in a Million? by Bob Barton and Blyth Wright, published by the SMC, is the classic work on Scottish avalanches (see Books, below).

While the ability to make your own assessment of risk is vital to anyone venturing into an area, avalanche predictions for the major winter climbing areas, produced by the Scottish Avalanche Information Service, or <www.sais.gov uk> are readily available during the winter. As well as on the website, these can be found at police stations, outdoor shops, tourist information centres and on display boards in climbing areas. Specific forecasts are available for the Northern Cairngorms (Northern Corries and Loch Avon Basin), Southern Cairngorms (Lochnagar and Glen Shee), Creag Meagaidh, Lochaber (mostly Ben Nevis and

Aonach Mòr) and Glen Coe. Climbers in the Northern and Southern Highlands will have to make their own assessments, and snow conditions are often different. Remember when reading them in the morning that this is a forecast made the previous day and that avalanche conditions may be worse or better than the forecast says. And while the risk may be great on one aspect of slope, a different aspect may be safe.

Protection
In most cases, protection on winter pitches is poorer than summer. Even mixed routes classified as safe involve more risk of injury after a fall than the average rock climb. The consequences of a fall in winter, particularly in a remote place in poor weather, are more serious. Ice routes are more serious again and on some, particularly the thinly iced slabs of Ben Nevis, a fall might be fatal. Impatience in the searching for runners and belays has to be resisted. Their quality may still be poorer, in particular camming devices in icy cracks close to useless, as are dead men in shallow snow. Despite recent disapproval of pegs placed on popular rock climbs, they should always be carried in case icy cracks make them the only safe option. Most winter climbs follow vegetated or gully lines and scarring by pegs will not offend. On popular rock climbs, one should try to limit their use, remembering that a nut is quicker to place and remove.

Descents
Some of the descents described involve snow slopes of up to 45 degrees (Grade I). At this angle of icy snow, there is no guarantee that an ice-axe brake will be effective, especially after some speed has been built up. Choose your route carefully, remove clogged snow from your crampons as necessary and don't trip up.

Rescue Proceedure
Despite the utmost care, winter climbing has its dangers and you may be faced with looking after an injured partner. The key decision for the standard climbing party of two is whether you should stay with the casualty, leave them and go for help, or struggle to assist them down towards shelter and safety. Clearly, the decision depends on circumstances, of which there are endless variations. Remember that a helicopter might arrive 2hrs after your call for help, but in bad weather when helicopters cannot operate (mist or wind, unfortunately common), it might be 4-6 hours before a rescue team can arrive on the scene. If the decision is to go down, then the aim is to reach a phone as soon as possible and dial 999 for the Police, who coordinate mountain rescue. Public phones are marked on the OS maps. Minutes making decisions and longer making your partner comfortable are time well spent when the arrival of a rescue may take hours.

TECHNICAL
Winter Grades
Routes are graded for on-sight ascents, using the two-tier system. The technical grades, which are shown by the Arabic numbers, apply to the hardest move or crux sequence of a route, while the Roman numeral gives an indication of the overall dificulty of the climb. The combination of the two grades makes the system work in a similar way to how the E grades and the numerical grades are used in summer.

In this way a V.4 would normally be a serious ice route and V.5 would be a classic ice route with adequate protection, V.6 would be a classic mixed route and V.7 would indicate a technically difficult but well protected mixed route. Each route has the same overall difficulty (Grade V) but with differing degrees of seriousness and technical difficulty. Both parts of the grading system are open-ended.

As a rough guideline to technical grades on ice, 3 = 60 degrees, 4 = 70 degrees, 5 = 80 degrees or vertical steps, 6 = vertical, 7 = hanging icicles or overhangs.

    Grade I – Uncomplicated, average-angled snow climbs normally having no pitches. They may, however, have cornice difficulties or long run-outs.

    Grade II – Gullies which contain either individual or minor pitches, or high-angled snow with difficult cornice exits. The easiest buttresses under winter conditions.

Grade III – Gullies which contain ice in quantity. There will normally be at least one substantial pitch and possibly several lesser ones. Sustained buttress climbs, but only technical in short sections.

Grade IV – Steeper and more technical with short, near vertical sections found on ice climbs. Mixed routes will require a good repertoire of techniques.

Grade V – Climbs which are difficult, sustained and serious. If on ice, long sustained ice pitches are to be expected; mixed routes will require a degree of rock climbing ability and the use of axe torquing and hooking and similar winter techniques.

Grade VI – Thin and tenuous ice routes or those with long vertical sections. Mixed routes will include all that has gone before but more of it.

Grade VII – Usually mixed routes which are very sustained or technically extreme. Also sustained routes on thin or vertical ice.

Grade VIII – Very hard and sustained mixed routes.

Grade IX – Now well established as the next level of difficulty, often sustained on vertical or overhanging ground with little for the feet.

Grade X – the system is open ended!

Winter Conditions

Many of the routes described here would be easier without snow, but this is not the Scottish tradition. Many definitions have been proposed but none work perfectly. The ideal is to fulfil the following:

• Routes should be wintry in appearance
• Routes should be easier climbed with crampons and axes
• On rocky mixed climbs the rock should not be wet (i.e. the ground is frozen)
• Any turf should be frozen. This is largely to protect the turf, because unfrozen turf is harder to climb

Pegs and Bolts

Scotland has a tradition of climbs with leader placed protection. Pegs are acceptable in winter if necessary but other protection is quicker to place and should be preferred, particularly on popular summer lines. Bolts are considered unacceptable on mountain cliffs.

Left and Right

The terms refer to a climber facing the cliff. If the terms are used in descent, then the direction is specified. Routes are described from left to right and this should be assumed, unless the cliff is always approached from the right, when right to left may be used and indicated in the text.

Diagrams

If a route has been numbered, this indicates that there is a diagram depicting the cliff, which will be found close to the relevant text. The numbers of the climbs in the text correspond to the numbers on the diagrams.

Recommended Routes

A star quality system has been used. No star routes are still worthwhile, or they would not have been included.

* Good climbing, but the route may lack line, situation or balance.
** A route of the highest quality, but lacking one of the features of a three star route, while having similar quality of climbing.
*** A route of the highest quality, combining superb climbing with line, character and situation.
**** The best climbs of their class in Scotland.

Quality will vary with conditions. Stars, like grades, are applied for the conditions in which the route will commonly be climbed. In the best conditions the routes may justify more stars.

SOUTHERN HIGHLANDS

There are three main areas of interest to the winter climber in the Southern Highlands; the Arrochar Alps, Ben Cruachan and the Bridge of Orchy hills. All are generally approached by the A82 Glasgow to Fort William road which runs through Crianlarich and Tyndrum.

Most of the climbing in this area has a comparatively recent history, which is surprising considering the quality of the routes and the accessibility of the cliffs. Winter climbing on the island of Arran has not been included since the area is remote from the rest of the climbing areas and awkward to get to for weekends. Those wishing to visit this fickle venue will no doubt not mind having to acquire the comprehensive guide.

Weather and Conditions: Due to their southerly latitude, parts of this area can often escape the worst effects of frontal systems ravaging across the hills further north. However, when combined with the relatively low altitude of the cliffs this means that they are severely affected by mid-season thaws and are often stripped bare. Despite this, the cliffs are in condition more often than one might think. The climbing is on metamorphic rock, mainly schist, which tends to be vegetated, with frozen turf and moss an important factor on many climbs.

Another point worth bearing in mind, is that if the weather is poor in Fort William or Glen Coe it is only a short drive south to the cliffs of the Southern Highlands. When the cliffs in the areas further north are under threat of high avalanche condition it should be possible, with a bit of due care and attention, to find safe climbs in the Southern Highlands. For those facing a long weekend return drive, the cliffs of this area can offer a convenient second days climbing.

Arrochar Alps

These rather romantically named hills are situated around the head of Loch Long, overlooking the village of Arrochar, some 65km north of Glasgow. There are a number of cliffs of interest, however only the main climbing area of The Cobbler and two other cliffs with classic climbs on Beinn Ìme and Beinn an Lochain are covered.

Maps: OS L56 (Inverary & Loch Lomond Area) and E364 (Glen Coe & Glen Etive). Harvey Superwalker 1:25000 (Arrochar Alps).

SMC Climbers' Guide: *Arran, Arrochar and the Southern Highlands* (1997)

Public Transport: Train from Glasgow to Fort William (4 p/day, 1 on Sunday) to Tarbert 1km from Arrochar. Bus from Glasgow to Fort William (4 p/day) passes through Tarbert and the Glasgow to Oban bus (3 p/day) passes through Arrochar.

Tourist Information: Loch Lomond TIC (08707 200631). Tarbert TIC is closed during the winter.

SYHA Youth Hostels: Loch Lomond (NS 368 834) <www.syha.org.uk>

Amenities: The village of Arrochar has shops, cafes, hotels and petrol.

Weather and Conditions: The climbing is generally on turf and snowed-up rock, only requiring a freeze with a dump of snow. The South Face of The Cobbler's North Peak does hoar but without cloud cover it is quickly stripped. Since the rock is fairly soft in nature, care should be taken with axes, crampons and especially pegs, since The Cobbler is a popular rock climbing venue.

THE COBBLER

(NN 259 058)   Alt 884m

Although it has higher neighbours, The Cobbler forms the centrepiece of the Arrochar Alps with its superb trio of jagged peaks, South, Central and North, holding a fine corrie. The Cobbler's rocky skyline is instantly recognisable rising above Loch Long just before entering Arrochar, a short distance along the A83 after leaving the A82 at Tarbert on Loch Lomond. Due to its proximity to Glasgow the hill is very popular with winter walkers.

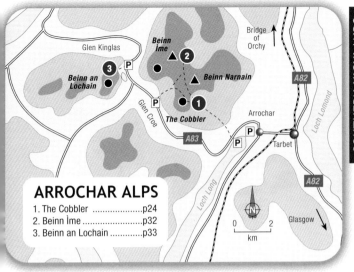

ARROCHAR ALPS

Approach: The most scenic approach, recommended for the first time visitor on a clear day, is also the longest. This starts from the shores of Loch Long a short way beyond Arrochar village, just past the head of the loch, at a large car park (NN 294 049). Opposite the car park entrance, the main signposted path zigzags up the hillside passing a communications aerial to reach a small dam in 45mins. The traditional route climbs directly up a steep path on the right to join a concrete slabbed ramp which leads to a path which contours leftwards to the dam. With The Cobbler now in sight follow the Allt a' Bhalachain (Buttermilk Burn) past the two Narnain Boulders and cross the burn higher up. Head up under the rocks of the North Peak towards the col between the North and Central Peaks. (4.5km, 2hrs).

A less scenic but much quicker 'back door' route starts from a small lay-by on the Rest and be Thankful road, at a bridge (NN 243 060). There is another lay-by a short distance further up the road. Follow the left side of the burn which descends from the col between Beinn Ìme and Beinn Narnain to reach a small dam at (NN 253 067). On the other side, a vague path leads up the slope to the col between the North and Central Peaks following the left bank of the stream descending from the col. (2.5kms, 1hr 15mins). There are two cols a short distance apart, the right-hand one leads to beneath Central Peak Buttress and the left-hand one is where the main path comes up under the North Peak. For climbs on the South Peak it is perhaps best to go up over the Central Peak and descend from the col on the other side.

Descent: The descent from the top of the South Peak is north-west to the col between it and the Centre Peak. This involves some awkward down climbing and route finding, made easier by dropping down a short way before making a short abseil off big flakes to reach the col. The summit crest of the Centre Peak gives easy walking to either of the cols to join the line of the approach. The descent from the North Peak is north to north-west, taking care of the cliffs which cut in, there is one short slabby section.

Layout: The Matterhorn like South Peak lies to the left, with its North Face overlooking the corrie. The Centre Peak lies in the middle with easy slopes leading to the summit block and a steeper, more continuous face on the right above a shallow gully which leads to a col. The North Peak is on the right, with the impressive brows of its South Face jutting out towards the corrie. Climbs are described from left to right.

Gibber Crack, V,7, The Cobbler South Peak. Climber Dave McGimpsey

SOUTH PEAK - NORTH FACE

(NN 261 058)   Alt 770m   North facing   Diagram p28, 29

The left-hand skyline if formed by a prominent edge between the South and North Faces. Due to its aspect and the nature of the climbing the routes on the North Face are regularly climbable.

1 South-East Ridge and The Arete   200m   III **

This is a traverse of the South and Centre Peaks with good exposure and impressive scenery. Start at the foot of the prominent skyline ridge, on a ledge just left of the lowest rocks, and climb the ridge. Variations are possible and these become harder to the right, towards the corrie edge. **Jughandle** (105m IV,5) starts some 20m around to the right from the lower part of the ridge and climbs a corner-crack to gain the ridge.

Descent to the col is either by a tricky down climb, or more usually by a short down climb, then an abseil. The South Ridge of the Centre Peak now follows. Climb a 15m crack and follow the arete to the summit block. Descend carefully and thread the hole from left to right.

2 Aeonoclast   70m   VI,6 **

C.Stewart, T.Prentice   12 Jan 1995

A fine and varied route. Start at the lowest rocks at a big vegetated groove topped by an overhang.

1. 15m The groove leads to a belay in a corner below the overhang.

2. 25m Climb the corner to a good spike, traverse left and climb a steep turfy crack in the wall (poor protection) followed by the steep, shallow chimney splitting the second overhang. Belay on the left.

3. 30m Move up and left with difficulty to climb a thin crack in the slabby wall in a superb position. Finish up walls and turf, keeping to the left edge of the finishing groove of **Grassy Traverse** (60m III) which arrives here from the base of **Sesame Groove** (30m IV,6) to the right.

North Wall Groove   100m   V,6 ***
N.Muir, A.Paul   16 Feb 1977
The conspicuous groove which cleaves the upper part of the North Face gives a first rate outing, only requiring a sprinkling of snow and a decent freeze. Start where a ledge leads up left to an obvious groove in the lower section; Sesame Groove.
1. 10m Move easily up left to the foot of the groove.
2. 50m Climb the groove to its end under steep rock, then make a hard pull out right to easier ground; low is technical, high is intimidating. Hollow block and possible belay. Climb steep turfy steps to enter the groove, which leads to a flake-crack below the upper groove. A direct alternative follows the edge just right of the rib (IV,6).
3. 35m Continue up the groove until delicate moves right across a thin slab gain clumps of turf in an exposed position. Move up to a belay.
4. 5m Continue steeply to finish.

Deadman's Groove   130m   VI,7 ***
R.Anderson, R.Milne   28 Jan 1990
A steep and intimidating route up the left-hand groove in the wall left of North Wall Groove, gained by climbing most of the first two pitches of that climb. **McLean's Folly** (90m VIII,8), climbs the right-hand groove above the start of pitch 3.
1. 10m Move easily up left to the foot of Sesame Groove.
2. 40m Climb the groove to its end under steep rock, then pull out right to easier ground and a hollow block. Turfy walls lead to a stance at the right end of a small roof; thread.
3. 20m Move up right for 3m, then back across above the belay to gain the groove which leads over a steepening with hollow flakes to a fine perch in the upper groove beside the overhanging left arete.
3. 20m Continue up the groove to its top.
4. 40m Move left and find easy ground leading to the summit.

North Wall Traverse   140m   IV,5 **
W. Skidmore, P.McKenzie   Jan 1961
The right-slanting traverse from the foot of the upper groove of North Wall Groove. The initial big pitch provides the crux and on pitch 3, 'drive-ins' are useful for the turf.
1. and 2. 60m Climb North Wall Groove, or the variation to its right (IV,6) and belay at the flake below the upper groove.
3. 40m Traverse up and right across turf and snowy slabs to beneath the blocky arete forming the right edge of the face.
4. 40m Right of the arete, short cracks, corners and large ledges lead to the top.

Gibber Crack   110m   V,7 *
R.Anderson, R.Milne   25 Nov 1990
An obvious line up the open corner-groove at the right side of the face. Start in a bay at the foot of the groove.
1. 10m Go up rightwards to a ledge.
2. 20m Climb the corner-groove to gain a crack in the right wall and climb this, then move right at a bulge to belay on its top.
3. 40m Climb a short crack above, then move up right and follow easier ground to belay on a ledge on the crest.
4. 40m Climb the flake-crack directly above, move right, go up a short crack to a edge, then move right again to climb to a larger ledge. Although it is possible to escape here, it is better to climb to the top via the second corner-crack right of the arete.

THE COBBLER
South Peak
North Face

2. Aeonoclast	VI,6	**
3. North Wall Groove	V,6	***
4. Deadman's Groove	VI,7	***
5. North Wall Traverse	IV,5	**
6. Gibber Crack	V,7	*
GT. Grassy Traverse	III	

CENTRE PEAK - EAST FACE

(NN 261 059)   Alt 800m   East and North-East facing

The reasons behind the adopted name for this hill become clear on viewing the summit block. An ascent of this summit block is made by going through the hole from north to south, then scrambling around to the top, a rope might be required. The climbing is on Centre Peak Buttress, which lies towards the right side of the Centre Peak and is gained by descending the gully between it and the North Peak. A cave like recess is obvious and is home to **Cathedral** (70m X,11).

7 Centre Gully   80m   II/III

The steep and narrow gully towards the left end of the buttress can vary according to conditions. A bulge at 50m is avoidable to the right. It is occasionally corniced.

8 Cave Route   130m   III,4 **

Good scenery with a sensationally exposed last pitch. Descend the gully past an obvious snow traverse, to a ramp like groove near the lowest part of the buttress.
1. 40m Either climb a groove directly to the base of a deep gully, or use the easier snow traverse higher up.
2. and 3. 65m Follow the narrow gully and exit right at the top. A steeper section

THE COBBLER

South Peak · Centre Peak · North Peak

1. SE Ridge and Arete III **
3. North Wall Groove V,6 ***
7. Centre Gully II/III
8. Cave Route III,4 **
9. Chimney Route V,7 *
15. Great Gully II

19. Chockstone Gully II *

A. Centre Peak Buttress
B. Great Gully Buttress
a. approach

25m above gains an open groove then a cave.
3. 25m Traverse delicately right round a bulge to gain a chimney and follow it to another cave. A window at the top offers an exit but most will avoid this by an awkward exit right to finish up the chimney.

Chimney Route   70m   V,7 *
T.Prentice, P.Beaumont 2 Jan 1994
This is the obvious corner system above and right of the cave like recess on the North Face. Start in the gully just down from the col where turfy ledges lead to the corner. It holds snow longer than most routes.
1. 10m Follow turf up left to the base of the first corner.
2. 20m Climb the short, technical corner to a large ledge and continue up the easier corner above to another ledge.
3. 15m Ascend to a higher grass ledge and traverse right, then step down to beneath a chimney.
4. 25m Climb the chimney, then walls, taking a large jutting block on the left.

NORTH PEAK - SOUTH FACE

(NN 262 060)   Alt 770m   South facing   Diagram p31

The steep walls and jutting overhangs of this peak provide impressive surroundings in winter. Unfortunately, the downside to the pleasant southerly aspect means that routes strip off pretty fast when there is little cloud cover. The initial part of the crag rises above a terrace gained from a short distance above the col; the final pitch of Right-Angled Gully takes the obvious corner just to the right. The described routes all start further down the path from the col. Ramshead Ridge descends from the upper terrace here and care should be taken when rounding its base to avoid the pothole of The Cobbler Cave.

Ramshead Ridge / Right-Angled Gully Direct   80m   V,6 **
H.Raeburn, W.Tough 31 Oct 1896; S.M.Richardson, C.Cartwright 30 Dec 1990
A good combination with a long history, which also involves reputed ascents in the

Great Gully Groove, IV,6, The Cobbler North Peak. Climber Rob Milne

1930s by H.Hamilton as well as W.H.Murray.
1. 45m Climb Ramshead Ridge by a wide crack and steep corner in the crest to reach the terrace. **Right-Angled Groove** (35m V,7) is directly ahead but rarely in acceptable condition.
2. 35m The obvious large corner on the left is Right-Angled Gully and is climbed directly to the top passing a ledge off to the right. At the end of this ledge a short undercut groove enables the route to be climbed at (IV,5).

11 Ramshead Gully   60m   IV,5 *
The obvious narrow chimney-gully rising from the back of the snow bay right of Ramshead Ridge.

12 Recess Route   85m   V,6 ***
A Cobbler classic taking the left-hand chimney-line in the buttress right of the bay leading to Ramshead Gully. Either start at the lowest rocks at a cracked slab just left of a small overhung recess, or up to its left at a groove.
1. 20m Climb from either start to reach a belay in the chimney.
2. 30m Continue up the chimney to Halfway Terrace and traverse right.
3. 10m Step into a steep groove, The Fold, and climb this to a cave.
4. 25m Climb the overhang above and continue to the top by a final chimney.

13 Fold Direct   85m   V,7 *
R.Anderson, T.Prentice 9 Dec 1990
The obvious line just right of Recess Route, starting left of a steep corner capped by an overhang. Awkwardly climb a short, steep recess corner, then go up and right to the base of a chimney-scoop. Enter the scoop with difficulty then climb it and the ensuing chimney-line to Halfway Terrace and finish as for Recess Route.

14 Maclay's Crack   70m   III,4 **
A good route with fine positions. Start round the edge of the buttress within the lower reaches of Great Gully below an obvious groove.
1. 20m Climb the crack-groove.

2. 10m Continue up the left branch to a small ledge on the left edge.
3. 40m A short corner leads to a wider ledge. Follow this for 3m, then climb a shallow groove in the wall above to easy ground.

5 Great Gully 60m II
The obvious gully near the right-hand end of the peak, left of Great Gully Buttress. Although the gully can bank out there will often be an initial tricky section through and around some large chockstones and an awkward rock step at mid-height. A short climb gains the exposed summit of North Peak, take care in misty conditions!

6 North Rib Route 90m V,7 **
R.Anderson, C.Anderson, R.Milne, D.McCallum   4 Jan 1994
This lies on Great Gully Buttress, which tends to hold snow longer than climbs further left. There are a number of routes with interchangeable pitches; this climb takes the left-hand rib, left of a prominent groove. Start 5m right of the entrance to Great Gully at a shallow, steep recess.
1. 15m Climb the recess and a groove to belay on a ledge right of a bay.
2. 35m Move up into the bay, pull into the prominent groove and stand on a block, then traverse out left to climb the rib and ensuing slabby ground.
3. 40m Move right, climb a short step via a nose, then go right and follow a steep crack up the right side of a huge block to finish up a shallow groove.

7 Great Gully Groove 95m IV,6 *
R.Milne, R.Anderson   27 Dec 1994
The prominent groove running up the left side of Great Gully Buttress, start 10m

THE COBBLER - North Peak
South Face & Great Gully Buttress

10. Ramshead Ridge /		
Right-Angled Gully Direct	V,6 **	
11. Ramshead Gully	IV,5 *	
12. Recess Route	V,6 ***	
13. Fold Direct	V,7 *
14. Maclay's Crack	III,4 **
15. Great Gully	II
16. North Rib Route	V,7 **
17. Great Gully Groove	IV,6 *
18. Heart Buttress	III *

BEINN ÌME
Fan Gully Buttress

BEINN AN LOCHAN
Monolith Buttress

1. Ben's Fault   IV,5 ***

1. Monolith Grooves   IV,5 ***
2. Purple Blaze   V,6 **

right of North Rib Route.
1. 20m Climb up and slightly left to the right side of a bay.
2. 35m Enter the bay and climb the groove on the left. North Rib Route goes out left and **Lulu** (95m IV,6) goes out right. Near the top of the groove swing out left around a roof and continue up a crack to a ledge.
3. 40m Move left, climb the left side of a huge block and finish up a shallow groove.

18 Heart Buttress   100m   III *
K.V.Crocket, T.Weir   14 Feb 1987
Just right of Great Gully Groove follow turf to a large ledge. Further turf, short walls and grooves lead sinuously up, out right and up to a short gully. Exit out right to finish on a prow.

19 Chockstone Gully   100m   II *
K.V.Crocket, A.Walker   Dec 1983
This lies well right of Great Gully and lower down, around on the north face of the North Peak. Leave the last steep section of the corrie approach path at about one-third height and traverse easy ledges right and up for about 200m to gain the gully edge. Two or three pitches lead to an impressive arch formed by a giant chockstone, exit by a narrow squeeze on the left or thin slab on right. The climb finishes below Great Gully Buttress.

BEINN ÌME

(NN 255 085)   Alt 1011m   Map p25

Lying to the north of The Cobbler, the grassy western slopes of Beinn Ìme, the highest hill in the Arrochar Alps, reveal little of the large crag on its eastern flanks.

EAST FACE - FAN GULLY BUTTRESS

(NN 262 081)   Alt 750m   East Facing

Weather and Conditions: Due to the height, aspect and type of climbing, the cliff can come into condition rapidly. The only problem is the approach, since westerlies build cornices and deposit large accumulations of snow above and across the approach traverse. Massive collapses and avalanches have occurred, so due care should be exercised.

Approach: As for the back door route up The Cobbler from (NN 243 060) by the path up the left side of the stream, passing the dam to reach the Bealach a' Mhaim. Move onto the East Face and with a watchful eye for any danger, make a long horizontal traverse along the line of least resistance.

Descent: By the hillwalkers route down the south ridge to the Bealach.

Ben's Fault   185m   IV,5 ***
A traditional route of great character taking the deep fault left of centre on the buttress. It can be climbed in a variety of conditions but will be harder when lean.
1. 50m A short corner and crack which can bank out lead to the fault and a belay higher up.
2. 40m Climb to a cave, step left and continue to a chimney.
3. 20m Squirm up the chimney and the one after to a chockstone where the fault becomes a vertical slot.
4. 25m Enter the slot and burrow past a wedged Damoclean flake to a widening below the final obstacle.
5. 50m Bridge the open groove, then continue to a cave and exit left on turf to easier ground.

BEINN AN LOCHAIN

(NN 218 080)   Alt 901m   Map p25

This fine mountain stands in a commanding position above Loch Restil at the head of the Rest and be Thankful pass, a short distance North-West of The Cobbler. The corrie on the North Face just below the summit holds a fine buttress, The Monolith, which is home to a classic Cold Climbs route and a more recent companion.

NORTH FACE - THE MONOLITH

(NN 218 081)   Alt 750m   North facing

Weather and Conditions: Due to the height, aspect and type of climbing, the cliff comes into condition rapidly, as long as the turf is frozen.

Approach: The North-East Ridge of the mountain is obvious and is used to access the North Face. Park just beyond Loch Restil at (NN 234 089) where the road begins to descend. Cross the burn, gain the ridge and climb it with an occasionally awkward section at mid-height passing an initial wall of crags (Kinglas Crag), to reach the upper open corrie beneath the summit. There are two crags here with the right side being dominated by the impressively steep two-tiered buttress of The Monolith.

Descent: To the summit, then down the exposed North-East Ridge to join the upward route, taking great care with the section above Kinglas Crag.

Monolith Grooves   130m   IV,5   ***
J.R.Mackenzie, B.Clarke   16 Jan 1977
A tremendous mountaineering route, offering a variety of pitches in exciting situations with a fine crux at the top. Start below the impressive hidden cleft on the left side of The Monolith.
1. 20m A shallow gully-groove leads to good rock belays on the left.

Purple Blaze, V,6, Beinn an Lochain. Climber Tom Prentice

2. 30m Traverse right into the cleft and follow it until a steeper section leads to a superb cave.

3. 10m Move delicately right onto the exposed arete and commit to the groove above. Belay on a snowy ledge, The Table.

4. 30m At the top left edge of The Table is a large block. Traverse left below it and follow a line of exposed turf ledges up and left, above the cleft of pitch 2. Belay below a short chimney in the upper wall.

5. 40m Climb the constricted chimney, the more snow at the start the easier, then follow easier ground to a ledge. The open groove on the right leads via hanging turf and icy walls to a short snow ramp, then the top.

2 Purple Blaze 120m V,6 **
T.Prentice, A.Fraser, D.McGimpsey (pitch 2) 10 Feb 1994; T.Prentice, R.Anderson, R.Milne complete 2 Jan 1997

A fine and varied route with an atmospheric top pitch up the overhanging corners and hanging slab right of the top pitch of Monolith Grooves. Start as for Monolith Grooves.

1. 20m A shallow gully-groove leads to good rock belays on the left.

2. 50m Some 10m left of the gully of Monolith Grooves is a narrow steep chimney with an overhanging chockstone. Climb the chimney with difficulty, then traverse right under steep rock for 6m. Follow the grooves above to the terrace and traverse right to belay below a fault leading to a steep corner on the broken arete of the upper buttress.

3. 50m Gain the corner with difficulty and climb it to a grass ledge. Traverse the hanging ledge to the left and pull awkwardly round to the left to reach the base of a slab. Continue to a snowy recess from where a thin crack fortuitously leads to the upper grass ledge. Traverse this up and right with poor protection and increasing exposure to finish on the very edge of the buttress.

Ben Cruachan & Bridge of Orchy Hills

This section describes the climbing on an assortment of peaks, all easily accessed from the A82 and A85, when travelling north from Loch Lomond and the Arrochar area to Glen Coe and Ben Nevis.

Ben Cruachan is the most westerly, lying above Loch Awe and the A85 road to Oban. Ben Lui and Beinn Chuirn lie further east, close by the A82 near Tyndrum. A short way down Glen Orchy just to the north, is the pure ice climbing offered by Beinn Udlaidh's Coire Daimh.

Further north on the A82 is the main area in this section, the extensive and popular cliffs of Beinn an Dòthaidh and Beinn Dòrain above Bridge of Orchy. Further north again, almost within sight of Glen Coe lies Stob Gabhar above Loch Tulla. The cliffs in this section offer a tremendous mix of climbing on all of the different mediums and as long as there is some snow with a fairly low freezing level, there should always be some routes in condition.

Maps OS L50 (Glen Orchy & Glen Etive) and E377 (Glen Orchy & Loch Etive).

SMC Climbers' Guide: *Arran, Arrochar and the Southern Highlands (1997).*

Public Transport: The train from Glasgow to Fort William (4 p/day, 1 on Sunday) stops at Bridge of Orchy Station within walking distance for some cliffs. This train stops at Tyndrum for the climbs here and splits for Oban, passing beneath Ben Cruachan, the closest halts being at Loch Awe and Taynuilt. The bus from Glasgow to Fort William (4 p/day) passes through the area on the A82 and the bus from Glasgow to Oban (3 p/day) passing through Arrochar goes along the foot of Cruachan.

Tourist Information: Tyndrum TIC is closed during the winter. See other sections for other TICs.

Mountaineering Huts: Inverardran Cottage, Crianlarich (Ochils MC) and Clashgour (Glasgow Uni), Bridge of Orchy. See also Glen Coe section and <www.mcofs.org.uk>

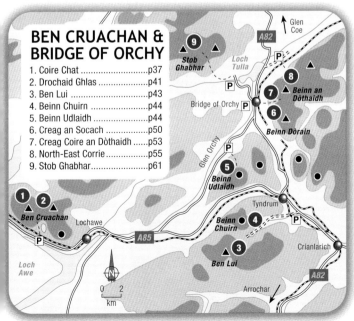

BEN CRUACHAN & BRIDGE OF ORCHY

1. Coire Chat p37
2. Drochaid Ghlas p41
3. Ben Lui p43
4. Beinn Chuirn p44
5. Beinn Udlaidh p44
6. Creag an Socach p50
7. Creag Coire an Dòthaidh p53
8. North-East Corrie p55
9. Stob Ghabhar p61

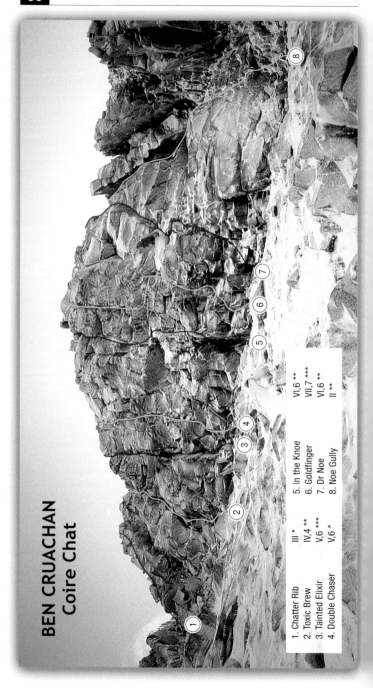

36

BEN CRUACHAN
Coire Chat

1. Chatter Rib	III *	5. In the Knoe	VI,6 **
2. Toxic Brew	IV,4 **	6. Goldfinger	VII,7 ***
3. Tainted Elixir	V,6 ***	7. Dr Noe	VI,6 **
4. Double Chaser	V,6 *	8. Noe Gully	II **

Independent Hostels: West Highland Way Sleeper, Bridge of Orchy (013838 408548). Bridge of Orchy Hotel Bunkhouse <www.bridgeoforchy.co.uk> Also see Glen Coe section. Further details at <www.hostel-scotland.co.uk> and <www.mcofs.org.uk>

Amenities: Tyndrum has shops, cafes hotels and petrol (7days p/wk 8am – 9pm). Bridge of Orchy has a hotel. Closer to Ben Cruachan, Dalmally, Lochawe & Taynuilt have everything between them.

BEN CRUACHAN

(NN 070 305)   Alt 1126m   Map p35

This lies 32km west of Tyndrum and the Bridge of Orchy area, on the A85 to Oban. Ben Cruachan is a splendid six topped mountain, the round of which is a classic winter hillwalking expedition; the Cruachan Horseshoe.

COIRE CHAT

(NN 067 306)   Alt 950m   North facing   Map p35

There are several winter cliffs on Ben Cruachan, but the finest climbing lies on two compact granite buttresses that nestle into the north side of Coire Chat, just west of the main summit. It is not possible to see the cliffs from above, and they remained untouched until 2002. This is a superb venue for technical mixed climbing – think Coire an Lochain in the Northern Corries of Cairn Gorm with no people and a stunning view. Although the routes are short (typically 70 to 80m), they are continuously sustained from the first move to the very top of the crag. The granite is fractured into clean vertical crack-lines, and the blocky rock provides good nicks for frontpoints.

Weather and Conditions: The cliff is reliably in condition during cold spells from November until March. It needs to be frozen with some snow, and the climbing is on rock and turf.

Approach: The cliff is best approached by starting from laybys east of the Cruachan Power Station on the A85 Tyndrum to Oban road. Take the track on the west side of the Cruachan reservoir to its end and climb to the summit of Cruachan. From here, descend west for 250m, over one small rise, to the short East Gully, which lies at the eastern end of the crag, 3hrs.

Descent: East Gully provides a straightforward descent to the cliff base and enables more than one route to be climbed in a day.

Layout: Coire Chat lies on the north side of the ridge running west from Cruachan's summit. The climbing is divided between two main buttresses. The steep Chatter Buttress, runs westwards from East Gully to the prominent Noe Gully, and the easier angled Noe Buttress lies to the right. The routes are described from left to right from the foot of East Gully.

Chatter Rib   50m   III *
S.M.Richardson, C.Cartwright   23 Nov 2003
A pleasant route up the obvious rib defining the left-hand side of Chatter Buttress, and a good option for the second route of the day. Start at the left-hand toe of the buttress.
1. 25m Climb the left edge of the buttress for 15m then trend slightly right to belay in an obvious recess.
2. 25m Step right from belay, surmount some large blocks, and continue up grooves to the top.

**Toxic Brew   60m   IV,4 ** **
C.Cartwright, S.M.Richardson   23 Nov 2003
An excellent introduction to the cliff. Start below the line of shallow icy chimneys and grooves that lie 20m right of **Quickfire** 45m III, the prominent recessed gully

Tainted Elixir, V,6, Coire Chat, Ben Cruachan. Climber Chris Cartwright

just right of Chatter Rib.
1. 30m Climb the initial groove to a steep wall barring access to the continuation chimney. Surmount the wall and bridge the chimney until a belay on the left.
2. 30m Follow the right-trending groove to the top.

3 Tainted Elixir   70m   V,6 ***
C.Cartwright, S.M.Richardson   14 Dec 2003
The wall right of Toxic Brew is cut by three parallel, left-leaning crack systems. The leftmost is the most prominent and starts with a right-facing corner. A must do route with continuously sustained climbing and a puzzling crux.
1. 25m Climb up between the corner and a large perched block. Continue up the bulging corner to a belay on the left.
2. 25m Surmount the cracked wall above and continue with interest to an over-hanging barrier wall split by a tapered slot. Pull up and into the slot, then go left to belay overlooking Toxic Brew. An excellent pitch.
3. 20m Step into the Toxic Brew groove and follow this to the top.

4 Double Chaser   65m   V,6 *
I.Small, C.Cartwright   25 Jan 2004
A slightly harder companion to Tainted Elixir, taking the central of the three parallel crack-lines.
1. 30m Start 3m right of Tainted Elixir and climb the intermittent double crack system by a series of ever steepening steps to a bulging crux. Contemplate the left

and right options, choose the right and step awkwardly up on to a small ledge. Reach high for a right tool placement then make a committing pull up and left to easier ground and a belay.
2. 35m Immediately above the belay is a wide, overhanging chimney. Bridge spectacularly up this to easier ground. Step left to a short right-facing corner and crack and follow this to the top.

In the Knoe   85m   VI,6 **
I.Small, C.Cartwright   12 Feb 2003
The first hard route added to the cliff, and still one of the best. It takes the prominent fault-line cleaving the central section of the cliff, and requires some build-up of ice and is high in the grade.
1. 30m The fault-line starts up an overhanging left-facing corner. Climb the steep right wall of the corner via a turfy crack and continue straight up to belay on a good ledge below and right of the continuation chimney.
2. 40m Step left 2m, surmount a short wall and slab to enter the chimney. Climb the chimney to an impasse, make a steep move to exit out right and continue up the steep left-facing groove to below a deep, wide corner-crack (visible from the ground). Spectacular bridging leads to a good belay.
3. 15m Easy ground leads to the top.

Goldfinger   85m   VII,7 ***
C.Cartwright, S.M.Richardson   29 Dec 2003
The showpiece of the crag with continuously sustained climbing in an outstanding position. It takes an uncompromising line up the bulging wall to the right of In the Knoe, and the primary feature is an apparent off-width crack splitting the clean wall high on the buttress. Belay at a slightly raised platform 3m right of the corner of In the Knoe.
1. 30m Climb a short wall with twin cracks into a small niche, then step up and right into a short left-facing corner. Surmount this, then step right onto a sloping ledge and into a fault-line. Climb the bulging wall above via the fault and work up and slightly left to a ledge with a recess on the left. Climb the right-trending, off-

Goldfinger, VII,7, Coire Chat, Ben Cruachan. Climber Chris Cartwright

width groove to the belay ledge of In the Knoe.

2. 35m From the left end of the belay ledge climb the left-facing corner directly above and pull right onto a ledge (possible belay). Continue up the cracked corner-groove until it runs into the head wall. Make a hard move up to a horizontal break, then commit rightwards and step up into the apparent off-width, which thankfully turns out to be a short shallow right-facing corner. Climb the corner then a bulge to easier ground. Continue to a belay on the left overlooking In The Knoe.

3. 20m Continue above trending right then back left, and pull through a final steep bulge to the top.

7 Dr Noe   85m   VI,6 **
S.M.Richardson, C.Cartwright   4 Jan 2004

Another sustained and intricate route taking the stepped ramp-line running left to right up to a point overlooking Noe Gully.

1. 35m Stat as for Goldfinger and move right from the belay over to the base of an obvious fault-line that is taken higher up by Goldfinger. Climb up and right into the start of the ramp-line. Step right, then up and left, and follow the ramp-line via a series of steps to an obvious belay ledge.

2. 35m Continue along the ramp-line by a series of ever steepening steps to the crux step, an awkward right-facing corner with an off-width crack. Pull out right from the top of this and continue until a final pull onto a ledge and belay over-looking Noe Gully.

3. 15m Step down and right from the belay onto the left wall of Noe Gully. Make a couple of steep moves directly up the wall to easier ground before a final awkward move leads to the top.

8 Noe Gully   70m   II **
D.Ritchie, M.Shaw   9 Feb 2002

An impressive, freestanding, square-cut fin of rock marks the right-hand end of Chatter Buttress. The Noe Fin is defined by this distinct gully on its left-hand side, and the deep **Thunderbolt Chimney** (70m IV,5) on its right. Climb the gully via a narrowing to the base of the Fin then continue up the narrow left-hand gully.

9 Noe Buttress   70m   IV,4 *
D.Ritchie, M.Shaw   9 Feb 2002

The original mixed route on the cliff taking the left wall of Noe Buttress. Start 30m up from the lowest toe of the buttress in Noe Gully.

1. 50m Move onto the left-hand edge of the buttress and climb mixed ground above to gain a shallow right-slanting chimney. At its top turn the rock nose on its right side, climb a groove followed by a right-slanting fault to easier ground.

2. 50m Follow the buttress crest more easily to finish.

10 Noe Buttress Direct   120m   VI,6 **
I.Small, A.Hume   27 Jan 2004

The longest route on the cliff giving intricate technical climbing up the front face of Noe Buttress.

1. 40m Start at the lowest point of the buttress and climb slabs to a right-facing corner. Climb the corner and pull out left onto a ledge. Take a small icy corner and strenuously pass a small flake to an overlap and ledge above. Move left up a flake then back right across a steep wall to gain a slabby recess. Exit this to an easier groove and move up rightwards to a huge flake belay.

2. 50m From the flake climb a left-slanting ramp to below a monstrous perched block. Swing right to gain the wide crack behind it and climb to the top and the crest of the buttress. Continue up the buttress crest as for Noe Buttress.

3. 30m Finish easily to the top.

11 Cooper Cleft   100m   IV,4 *
S.M.Richardson, C.Cartwright   30 Jan 2005

The narrow gully just right of Noe Buttress.

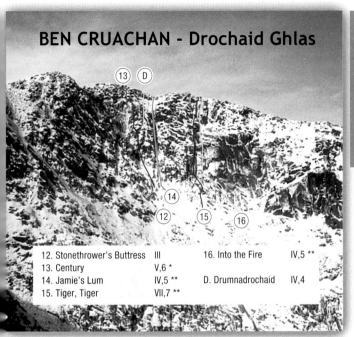

BEN CRUACHAN - Drochaid Ghlas

12. Stonethrower's Buttress	III	16. Into the Fire	IV,5 **
13. Century	V,6 *		
14. Jamie's Lum	IV,5 **	D. Drumnadrochaid	IV,4
15. Tiger, Tiger	VII,7 **		

1. 50m Follow the gully up to where it steepens and narrows. Climb the chimney and exit rightwards, then follow the continuation groove.
2. 50m Climb easily upwards to enter a broad easy angled scoop, and head rightwards for a col.

DROCHAID GHLAS

(NN 083 306)   Alt 850m   East facing   Map p35

The other reliable winter climbing venue on Ben Cruachan lies on the east side of the north ridge of the Munro Top of Drochaid Ghlas. The rock is good quality granite and the cliff is well vegetated making for good mixed climbing. Later in the season the crag can form ice, which is helpful for the drainage lines of Jamie's Lum and Tiger, Tiger. The climbs are not as sustained as those in Coire Chat, but the crag has a shorter walk and sees more visits.

Weather and Conditions: The cliff is in condition during cold spells from December until early March, but it is not as reliable a venue as Coire Chat, and is more vulnerable to thaw. The approach slopes are avalanche prone and the crag should be avoided after a heavy snowfall.

Approach: Start as for Coire Chat to the end of the track north of the Cruachan reservoir, then go straight up the hillside to reach the main ridge at the col between Drochaid Ghlas and Stob Diamh. Descend to the crag from a point about 100m east of the summit of Drochaid Ghlas, then contour under the north side of the cliff (tricky in poor snow conditions) to reach the climbs, 2hrs 30mins.

Layout: Stonethrower's Buttress extends north from the summit of Drochaid Ghlas and is separated from the main cliff by a deep Grade I gully. The majority of routes lie on the granite wall to the right of this gully, which is split by the prominent square-cut gully of Jamie's Lum.

12 Stonethrower's Buttress 100m III
S.M.Richardson, R.D.Everett 24 Feb 1990
The low angle buttress to the left of the obvious easy gully provides a worthwhile consolation route if the climbs on the main crag are not in condition. Start at the lowest rocks and follow easy snow up a small gully in the centre of the buttress. At the first steepening, step right into a continuation deeper gully. Follow this to a huge jammed block, pass this on the left and continue up easy snow to the summit cairn.

13 Century 100m V,6 *
C.Cartwright, S.M.Richardson 20 Feb 2000
An interesting mixed climb taking the wall to the left of Jamie's Lum. Start just left of parallel grooves taken by **Drumnadrochaid** (85m IV,4) below a groove with a prominent 3m finger of rock on its left side.
1. 30m Pull up a small wall into the groove and climb it exiting right at the top. Follow a ramp up and left to a good stance at its end.
2. 35m Climb up to the steep headwall which is cut by a prominent slot. Move up the wall to a roof, step left into the slot and climb it to a terrace.
3. 35m Trend left up snow and finish up the easy left-facing corner above to reach the summit ridge.

14 Jamie's Lum 85m IV,5 **
I.Blackwood, S.Kennedy, D.Ritchie 13 Feb 1994
This fine line takes the central chimney-groove splitting the left side of the crag. It requires icy conditions so is not climbed as often as the other routes on the face.
1. 25m Climb a short ice pitch into a snow bay below the chimney and belay on the right.
2 and 3. 60m Continue up the chimney using ice on the left wall, climb the continuation wall and finish up easy ground above.

15 Tiger, Tiger 130m VII,7 **
C.Cartwright, S.M.Richardson 7 Mar 1999
A superb mixed route taking the compelling corner to the left of Into the Fire. The base of the groove is guarded by blank bulging slabs, so start 10m right of the corner below a left-trending ramp.
1. 20m Ascend turf for 5m then move left across a bulging wall to gain the ramp. Follow this to a good stance at the base of the corner.
2. 40m Climb the corner on thin ice and frozen turf to a good platform where the angle eases. A sustained and intricate pitch.
3. and 4. 70m Continue up the wall directly behind the belay, move up and right to gain easier ground and finish up the easy chimney of Into the Fire.

16 Into the Fire 130m IV,5 **
S.M.Richardson, R.D.Everett 4 Mar 1990
This excellent mixed climb takes a left-slanting line across the highest part of the face, and is the first to come into condition on the crag. Start 20m right of an obvious groove system, at a left-slanting ramp beneath smooth steep slabs.
1. 35m Follow the ramp over several steep steps to belay at the foot of a groove.
2. 25m Climb the groove for 15m to a huge spike on the left. Swing down left round the arete to a commodious ledge.
3. 40m Step left, climb the left wall of the corner-groove for 5m, then swing right across the groove. Traverse right around the arete, then continue straight up to belay below a chimney.
4. 30m Climb the chimney, then continue direct to the crest of the ridge
Variation: **Left-Hand Finish 40m IV,4 *
D.Ritchie, D.Sinclair, 18 Mar 1995
Follow the original route to the top of pitch 3, then continue trending up and left to finish up a chimney-groove and the open fault to the top.

Eas Anie, III/IV,4, Beinn Chùirn. Climber Mary Twomey

BEN LUI

(NN 265 263)   Alt 1130m   Map p35

The classical shape of this fine mountain, with the great slope of its north-east corrie falling in one great sweep from beneath its two tops, cannot fail to catch the eye of those travelling north on the A82 just before Tyndrum. In the early days of the railways, Tyndrum with its two stations was accessible by early morning trains from both Glasgow and Edinburgh and this made Ben Lui one of the most popular mountains with the Scottish mountaineering pioneers. The Central Gully of Ben Lui is one of the earliest winter climbs, albeit that it was climbed in descent prior to its first ascent.

Approach: The usual approach is from the Tyndrum side, either from Tyndrum Lower Station (NN 327 302), or from the car park at Dalrigh (NN 343 292) just south of Tyndrum. Both routes follow tracks that join short of Cononish Farm and continue past this to the track end at the Allt an Rund where the corrie lies directly ahead (about 8.5km; allow 2hrs 30mins). The shortest approach (4.5km) is from the west in Glen Lochy (NN 239 279) but the face remains hidden and a river crossing is involved, albeit that this is close to the car park and can be prepared for. There is also a bridge 1km downstream.

Descent: Although both ridges bounding the corrie face can be descended it is normally the Stob Garbh (NNE) ridge that is taken. If conditions are suitable the gully face itself can give a fine glissade once the cornice and steep upper slope have been negotiated. Glen Lochy is reached by the south-west ridge.

**Central Gully   200m   I ** **
W.W.Naismith,   W.R.Lester,   T.F.S.Campbell   Apr   1981   (descent);   A.E.Maylard,
W.Brunskill, W.Douglas, J.Mackay   Dec 1892 (ascent)

One of the classic Scottish snow climbs taking a direct line up the centre of the face of the north-east corrie. Initially the gully is enclosed and quite narrow but higher it opens into a wide and steep snowfield below the summit ridge. The finish can be heavily corniced, in which case bear left and climb directly to the summit cairn. Variations on the left and right are all of the same character and standard. The exception is the crescent shaped ridge on the left (II), which gives a good scramble with possibly some difficulty at the start. It ends on the east ridge of the mountain some distance below the summit. In mild weather, especially late season, there can be a hazard from cornice collapse.

BEINN CHÙIRN

(NN 281 293)   Alt 880m   Map p35

This hill sits to the north-east of Ben Lui and is passed on the approach to that mountain from Tyndrum.

EAST FACE

(NN 290 285)   Alt 500m   East facing

**Eas Anie   150m   III/IV,4 ** **
This is the waterfall on the east flank of the mountain above Cononish Farm. The start is only a few hundred metres from the gold mine workings. Given a freeze it does come into condition and provides continuous ice. The lower introductory gully is easier and has variations on the left and leads to a basin. Above, the left-hand option is steeper and a splendid ice wall can form, which provides two long pitches. The right-hand finish is easier and can have unusual ice flutings and an ascent through an ice cave, climbing an icicle to reach the upper gully.

The mixed face on the left is **Alchemist's Wall** (160m V,5). It should be possible to climb Eas Anie and Ben Lui's Central Gully in one day, as a short descent from the former leads to the Ben Lui path.

BEINN UDLAIDH

(NN 280 332)   Alt 840m   Map p35

This hill lies between the forks in the main Oban and Fort William roads just above and to the north-west of Tyndrum. Otherwise unremarkable, when seen from the north it has two unusual features. One is a quartzite dyke, which breaks its grassy slopes and is visible from afar. The other is the north facing corrie just to the west of its summit, where streams cascade over a steep cliff to form the highest concentration of easily accessible ice climbs in the country.

COIRE DAIMH

(NN 275 330)   Alt 650m   North facing   Diagrams p48, 49
The crescent shaped corrie overlooking Glen Orchy.

Weather and Conditions: The summit slopes of Beinn Udlaidh collect sufficient precipitation to feed a series of springs which flow over the cliff edge. In a good freeze, these quickly build-up impressive quantities of ice, giving many quality pure ice routes. Between the harder icefalls there are some more amenable gullies.

Approach: Leave the A82 1km south of Bridge of Orchy and take the B8074 road down Glen Orchy for 5km to Glen Orchy Farm, near where the Allt Daimh joins the River Orchy. Park on the left immediately before reaching the farm track; there is room for a few cars parked carefully. At the start of the farm track is a sign pointing

BEINN UDLAIDH - East Sector Left, Black Wall

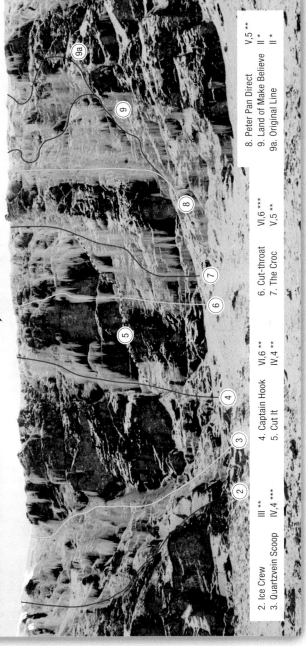

2. Ice Crew   III **
3. Quartzvein Scoop   IV,4 ***

4. Captain Hook   VI,6 **
5. Cut It   IV,4 **

6. Cut-throat   VI,6 ***
7. The Croc   V,5 **

8. Peter Pan Direct   V,5 **
9. Land of Make Believe   II *
9a. Original Line   II *

Quartzvein Scoop, IV,4, Beinn Udlaidh. Climber Chad Harrison

climbers across a field on the right to a rough track (marked as a path on the 1:50000 map). Follow this through the forest to open ground where it bends away right. Leave the track and head direct into the corrie, 1hr to the West Sector, 1hr 15mins to the East Sector.

Descent: Down either flank, taking care during icy conditions when desperate sheets of ice can form on otherwise easy slopes.

Layout: The West Sector, or right-hand side of the corrie, is the first encountered and includes all the climbs to the right of Central Gully, the prominent left-slanting gully in the middle. To its right is Central Buttress, then West Gully and finally West Wall. The East Sector lies over on the left-hand side and includes all the climbs to the left of Central Gully, a smaller lower cliff sits beneath its right side. This Sector is dominated by the ice draped Black Wall towards its left side. This is bordered on its right by South Gully of The Black Wall, then a square-cut buttress flanked by Ramshead Gully and finally Sunshine Gully, appearing from below as a left-sloping ramp. Routes are described from left to right starting with East Sector.

1 Zigzag Gully   90m   II *
A.Agnew, J.Jewel   14 Nov 1970
The gully starts at the leftmost edge of the corrie. It may include one ice pitch of 30m in the centre. From the top of this, traverse left into a shallow gully which leads to the top.

2 Ice Crew   90m   III **
I.Duckworth. N.Morrison   Feb 1980
A parallel route left of Quartzvein Scoop, finishing up a steep scoop.

3 Quartzvein Scoop   90m   IV,4 ***
D.Evans, A.Gray, A.Shepherd   Winter 1979
The line of icy grooves immediately left of the Black Wall gives an excellent route amidst impressive scenery.

4 Captain Hook   75m   VI,6 **
D.Cuthbertson, C.Calow   Jan 1980
The impressive funnel shaped icefall on the Black Wall trending right. The exit can be corniced and there may be unstable snow.

5 Cut It   75m   IV,4 **
D.MacLeod   28 Jan 1998
This cuts across the Black Wall utilising the big diagonal ledge running up and right. Start at Captain Hook, gain and follow the ramp to belay at the Cut-throat icicle. Continue right to the end of the ledge and finish up The Croc.

6 Cut-throat   75m   VI,6 ***
D.Cuthbertson, R.Duncan, R.Young, C.Calow   Jan 1980
The splendid icicle right of Captain Hook rarely forms.

7 The Croc   75m   V,5 **
A.Barton, D.Evans, J.G.Fraser   Jan 1979
The left-hand icefall on the right section of the Black Wall, via a rib.

8 Peter Pan Direct   75m   V,5 **
D.Claxton, I.Duckworth, A.Kay, N.Morrison   1 Jan 1982
The right-hand icefall forms more readily than its neighbours. Climb it directly to the top.

Cut-throat, VI,6, Beinn Udlaidh. Climber Dave MacLeod

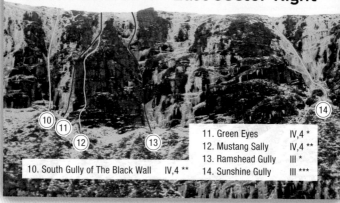

BEINN UDLAIDH - East Sector Right

11. Green Eyes   IV,4 *
12. Mustang Sally   IV,4 **
13. Ramshead Gully   III *
14. Sunshine Gully   III ***

10. South Gully of The Black Wall   IV,4 **

9 Land of Make Believe   90m   II *
N.Morrison, M.Orr   29 Dec 1979
An easy route through impressive scenery. Start below and right of Peter Pan
Direct. Climb up, trending right to a belay. Continue right to a small gully, then
move up and left to belay at its top. Traverse hard right to a block, step up and
continue directly to the top.

10 South Gully of The Black Wall   120m   IV,4 **
R.McGowan, G.Skelton   30 Nov 1969
The gully right of the Black Wall gives a good route which often has a large cornice.
A narrow chimney leads to easy ground, then a steep icefall which can be taken
direct.

11 Green Eyes   120m   IV,4 *
I.Duckworth, J.G.Fraser   29 Dec 1979
The icy corner up the left margin of the buttress right of South Gully. Finish right-
wards up a depression.

12 Mustang Sally   90m   IV,4 **
D.MacLeod, A.Weir   1 Mar 1998
This turfy line follows a corner system right of Green Eyes.

13 Ramshead Gully   120m   III *
G.H.Caplan, I.D.Crofton   4 Dec 1976
The next main gully to the right has a narrow chimney with an overhanging chock-
stone.

14 Sunshine Gully   90m   III ***
E.Fowler, F.Jack, R.McGowan, G.Skelton   14 Nov 1970
To the right of Ramshead Gully, mid-way between South Gully of the Black Wall
and Central Gully, this gully looks like a left-slanting ramp when seen from the
entrance to the corrie. It gives an interesting climb with much ice.

15 Blitz   45m   V,6 **
D.MacLeod   28 Jan 2001
The left-slanting fault through the steep buttress left of the upper part of Central
Gully gives good mixed climbing.

Central Gully   180m   II
J.Buchanan, J.Forbes, G.Skelton   2 Dec 1968
The left-slanting gully in the centre of the corrie may have four pitches, the second one being the hardest. It banks out later in the season.

Junior's Jaunt   80m   IV,5
P.Bilsborough, I.Duckworth, N.Morrison, W.Woods   24 Feb 1979
The icefall on the right, some 45m up the gully, has two steep pitches.

Doctor's Dilemma   180m   IV,4 **
I.Duckworth, M.Firth   Winter 1978
This very good route takes the obvious, wide central line of icefalls running the height of Central Buttress.

White Caterpillar   105m   III *
G.Skelton, W.Woods   30 Dec 1978
Start halfway up West Gully and break left up a wide ice ramp until a short gully leads right to another left-trending ramp. A direct line avoiding the short gully is IV,4.

West Gully   180m   III *
The obvious right-slanting gully can contain two enjoyable pitches, both short, leading to an easy angled groove and finish.

Organ-Pipe Wall   75m   V,5 *
R.Duncan, J.G.Fraser   27 Jan 1979
Gain the obvious icefall high on the cliff to the right of West Gully via an easy, deep-cut chimney. Climb the icefall directly, following a groove and wall up the middle.

The Smirk   90m   V,5 ***
R.Duncan, J.G.Fraser   27 Jan 1979
The very steep and obvious chimney-gully towards the right-hand side of the West Wall gives a superb climb but it is slow to come into condition. The left fork is the normal route but a more direct finish is possible.

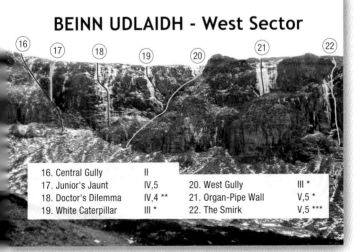

BEINN UDLAIDH - West Sector

16. Central Gully	II		
17. Junior's Jaunt	IV,5	20. West Gully	III *
18. Doctor's Dilemma	IV,4 **	21. Organ-Pipe Wall	V,5 *
19. White Caterpillar	III *	22. The Smirk	V,5 ***

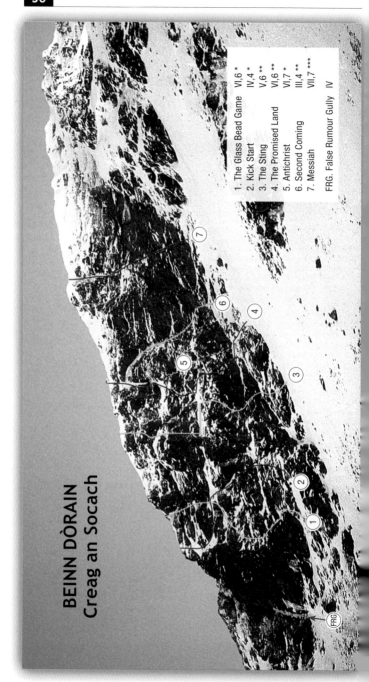

BEINN DÒRAIN
Creag an Socach

1. The Glass Bead Game   VI,6 *
2. Kick Start   IV,4 *
3. The Sting   V,6 **
4. The Promised Land   VI,6 **
5. Antichrist   VI,7 *
6. Second Coming   III,4 **
7. Messiah   VII,7 ***

FRG. False Rumour Gully   IV

SOUTHERN HIGHLANDS

BEINN DÒRAIN & BEINN AN DÒTHAIDH

(NN 326 379, NN 332 409) Alt 1076m, 1004m Map p35

These hills contain three areas of climbing. Between the two hills is a west facing corrie, Coire an Dòthaidh, with a cliff on either side, one on each mountain. The col between the hills is obvious above Bridge of Orchy station, as are the cliffs. On the other side of Beinn an Dòthaidh is the North-East Corrie, which has the most reliable conditions.

COIRE AN DÒTHAIDH

Approach: From the Bridge of Orchy station car park, go under the railway and follow a path up the right side of the Allt Coire an Dòthaidh towards the col between the two hills. For Creag an Socach break off right where the path crosses the burn and head up to the crag (2.5km, 1hr). For Creag Coire an Dòthaidh, cross the burn, climb a short steep section, then go left on a terrace (2.5km, 1hr).

Creag an Socach

(NN 321 394) Alt 750m North-West facing Map p35

This steep crag contains a number of mixed routes of a high technical standard.

Weather and Conditions: Ice is usually limited and too much snow is a disadvantage. The compact schist can make protection difficult to arrange at times

Descent: Head north, then follow a burn steeply down into the corrie.

The Glass Bead Game 120m VI,6 *
R.Carchrie, K.V.Crocket, R.Duncan, G.McEwan, A.Walker 13 Dec 1987
A wide ledge runs out right from below the steep chimney of **False Rumour Gully** (60m IV) at the left end of the crag. Start at a point where the ledge curves round the toe of the buttress; the ledge continues on round and up for another 10 to 15m. Climb a corner, pull out left and go up a groove to a ledge and belay. Step left round an exposed edge, then go up and left to a ledge and block belay. Step onto a slabby wall directly above the block and make a rising traverse right, aiming for small spike right of a steep wall. Gain the slab above the spike and belay above (sustained and technical). Go hard right passing a corner to gain a ramp and follow this to a short, overhanging chimney. Climb the chimney over a roof and continue to a belay above. Easy ground leads to the top.

Kick Start 120m IV,4 *
N.Morrison, R.Stewart 21 Dec 1980
At the lowest point of the cliff a curving chimney-groove leads to a horizontal ledge cutting across the cliff at half-height. Start about 10m right of The Glass Bead Game, below vegetatious slabs. Climb up and right to enter the chimney-groove. Follow this to gain the ledge and traverse left along this, crossing The Glass Bead Game below its overhanging chimney, to a groove which leads onto a rock ramp and the top.

The Sting 120m V,6 **
G.E.Little, K.Howett 19 Jan 1991
To the right of the previous route is an area of dark, clean bulging rock low down on the face. A narrow rock ramp cuts across its right flank. Start at a fan of slabs below the bulging rock.
1. 30m Move up, then go left across slabs to a block with a horizontal crack. Take a snow ramp trending right until it is possible to climb up to a small rock bay at the base of the narrow rock ramp.
2. 25m Climb the ramp, then go directly up steep ground to the right end of the central snow ledge.

The Sting, V,6, Creag an Socach, Beinn Dòrain. Climber Kevin Howett

3. 10m Cross to the left end of the ledge to below a slim corner.
4. 15m Climb the superb corner-crack (large hexentrics useful) to its top, then make an interesting move left to a ledge.
5. 40m Climb to the base of a vague, wide rock rib, move slightly left, then sur-mount a short difficult wall and trend right up steepening ground to the top. A groove on the right of the rock rib would give an alternative.

4 The Promised Land   120m   VI,6 **

G.E.Little, D.Saddler   29 Mar 1987

Start about 20m down from Second Coming, well right of the lowest point of the cliff. This route needs a good ice build-up on the second pitch, which can be assessed from below.

1. 45m Move up to a snow ledge, then traverse left to its termination at flakes. Ascend very steep rock, then move right into a snow bay below a groove, flake runner. Traverse hard left for 8m, then go up to gain a large snow ledge and belay below an ice scoop, right of an obvious corner.
2. 35m Climb the ice scoop, exiting right by short awkward wall, then go up to below an ice chimney.
3. 40m Climb the left wall of the chimney on thin ice to gain an ice groove, then climb directly up to the top by a second ice groove above, common to Second Coming.

Antichrist   120m   VI,7 *
S.M.Richardson, R.D.Everett   15 Mar 1992

A good route taking the groove system between Promised Land and Second Coming. It was originally climbed in lean conditions and might be even harder if smothered in hoar. Start next to Promised Land.

1. 15m Climb easily up to the rake.
2. 25m Climb the awkward wall 5m right of the flakes of Promised Land and enter the groove, which leads to a good stance.
3. 40m Continue up the fault-line, trending left to an overhang. Climb this, then traverse right onto the lip of the overhanging wall on the right. Move up in a spectacularly exposed position to reach the terrace 5m up and right of the ice chimney of Promised Land.
4. 20m Continue up the impending wall above, starting on the right arete, then moving left to reach a hairline crack. A series of steep moves on widely spaced tufts (not visible from below) lead to a ledge.
5. 20m The final ice groove of Second Coming leads to the top.

Second Coming   95m   III,4 **
I.Fulton, C.D.Grant   Winter 1978

High in the centre of the cliff is an obvious curving ramp-line which forms the demarcation between the very steep clean wall on the right and the more slabby, vegetated face on the left. Start to the right of a steep turfy groove that drops from the ramp but does not reach the base of the crag.

1. 50m Ascend the steepening, then broken ground to a ledge. Hand-traverse a sharp flake leftwards to gain ledges which lead to the groove. This leads to a corner below steep ice.
2. 45m Climb the ice, or the little chimney on the left, traverse left along a snow ramp, then go up an icy groove to the top.

Messiah   85m   VII,7 ***
G.E.Little, R.Reid   28 Jan 1988

The face right of Second Coming is intimidatingly steep and ledgeless. The only apparent breach is an open corner, low down, leading to a thin groove. This sustained and technical route is one of the finest lines in the Southern Highlands.

1. 30m Climb the corner to a niche below overhanging rock. Move up and hand-traverse hard left to below a groove. Gain this and go up to a small ledge.
2. 10m Climb a short corner, then move directly up to the base of a vertical ice filled groove. (Linking the first two pitches would cause serious rope drag).
3. 45m Climb the groove into a continuation gully and follow this to the top.

Creag Coire an Dòthaidh

(NN 325 403)   Alt 750m   West facing   Map p35   Diagram p54

This is the vegetatious crag on the left side of the corrie.

Weather and Conditions: Some of the climbs are fed by springs and require a few days hard freeze to come into condition. On clear days there may be a risk of falling ice from the effects of the thawing sun, particularly on Fahrenheit 451. The rock is compact schist with protection often in the form of drive-ins into frozen turf.

Descent: Head south to the col between Beinn an Dòthaidh and Beinn Dòrain. The descent from the col is steep at first.

Layout: The two most obvious lines are Salamander Gully on the left, with an ice-fall high up, and the series of icefalls on the right taken by Fahrenheit 451. Routes are described from left to right.

Salamander Gully   150m   III,4 **
K.V.Crocket, J.A.P.Hutchinson   25 Jan 1976

Near the left end of the cliff is an obvious gully leading to an icefall. This gives a

54

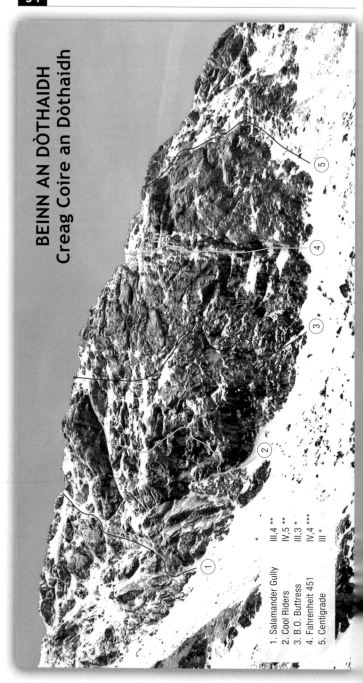

BEINN AN DÒTHAIDH
Creag Coire an Dòthaidh

1. Salamander Gully   III,4 **
2. Cool Riders   IV,5 **
3. B.O. Buttress   III,3 *
4. Fahrenheit 451   IV,4 ***
5. Centigrade   III *

scenic and enjoyable route. Climb the gully to the icefall, which is crossed by a ledge, possible escape left following the gully continuation. The easiest line up the ice takes a groove on the left which leads to a right traverse across the icefall and a belay below a bulging icefall. Climb this up and left, where an ice slab leads to a small ice pitch and so to the top.

Cool Riders   170m   IV,5 **

D.MacLeod, D.Redpath   Feb 2003

An amenable line up the steeper left-hand central section of the cliff. Start beneath a large, easy left-slanting ramp, directly below a band of roofs high above.

1. 60m   Climb the ramp for 8m, then break out right to a flake. Step down and traverse awkwardly round a nose to gain a turfy bay. Move diagonally right to climb a line of turfy grooves until level with the big roof on the left. Traverse left over a nose to a short, steep corner.

2. 30m   Bridge up the corner (crux) and follow a ledge-ramp system leftwards past an awkward step to gain a large expanse of easy angled slabs.

3. 60m   Climb directly up the slabs to the headwall.

4. 30m   Walk off right along a big ramp.

B.O. Buttress   165m   III,3 *

C.J. Gilmore, C.D.Grant   25 Jan 1976

This lies just right of the centre of the buttress, bypassing steep rock walls in the lower part by short traverses. The climbing is mainly on frozen turf and rock. Start just right of the middle of crag at a broad scoop right of ill-defined rocks. Above is a prominent red wall. The route has a big face atmosphere at an easy grade.

1. 30m   Climb mixed ground up and left to belay at foot of the red wall.

2. 40m   Traverse right, climb a short corner, then go up and left to a ledge below a short wall.

3. 35m   Go right to the end of the ledge, then work back left and go up to a belay.

4. and 5. 60m   Continue directly to the top.

Fahrenheit 451   135m   IV,4 ***

K.V.Crocket, I.Fulton   Feb 1976

A first rate climb. Near the right end of the face a prominent icefall builds up, requiring at least a week of good freeze. An initial gully leads to ice walls, corners, short traverses, and huge sheets of water ice.

Centigrade   105m   III *

D.Baker, R.Howard   30 Jan 1983

A pleasant, varied route. Start below a large, protruding rock, 15m right of Fahrenheit 451.

1. 45m   Climb diagonally right under a wall for 20m, then up an ice groove to a belay.

2. 45m   Ascend the ramp above, move left on ice, then go up and right to the foot of a scoop.

3. 15m   Climb directly out of the scoop.

NORTH-EAST CORRIE

(NN 327 413)   Alt 750m   North facing   Map p35   Diagram p57

This is located around on the north side of Beinn an Dòthaidh.

Weather and Conditions: A fairly reliable venue and since there is little ice it comes into condition fairly quickly following a fall of snow.

Approach: From the Achallader Farm car park (NN 321 443). Walk around the barn opposite the house, then go through a gate to reach the moor. Above the farm cross the railway by a bridge. Follow the west bank of the Allt Coire Achaladair for about 1hr towards Coire Daingean, then head diagonally right to pass under the end of the north ridge, aiming for a small cone shaped hillock. Enter

Taxus, III, Beinn an Dòthaidh North-East Corrie. Climber David Bell

the subsidiary corrie under the cliffs (4km, 1hr 30mins).

Descent: This can be by the West Gully, given safe snow, although it is often corniced, or more reliably by continuing west behind the cliff edge and dropping down to the col before the North Ridge. An easy descent then leads into the subsidiary corrie.

Layout: To the left of the corrie entrance are several easy gullies (I) on the north face leading to the plateau close to the col between the summit and the West Top. The obvious, wide gully above and just inside the subsidiary corrie is the West Gully, a useful landmark in misty conditions. Most of the climbing, and certainly all of the steeper and more technical routes, is found in the right-hand, or subsidiary corrie. The two large buttresses here are North Buttress on the left and the West Buttresses further right, which are separated by the obvious West Gully.

1 Femme Fatale 90m IV,5 **
E.W.Brunskill, P.Greene, S.Archer   18 Feb 1995

A direct route which climbs the obvious central groove and corner-line in North Buttress, the lowest of the steep buttress in the corrie. It is steeper than it appears from below and passes right of an icicle fringe. Start in the top right corner of a square shaped snow bay, above and to the left of the lowest rocks.
1. 20m Climb a short steep step on the right to enter the groove-line and climb this until it becomes a right-facing corner.
2. 30m Climb the corner through a bulge (crux) to a small ledge and continue up steep icy corners to a snowfield.
3. 40m Continue in the same line, up chimneys and grooves to reach a terrace. Either climb the easy buttress above to join Taxus or traverse off left to descend.

BEINN AN DÒTHAIDH

North-East Corrie

1. Femme Fatale	IV,6 **
2. Circean	V,6 **
3. Taxus	III ***
3a. Icefall Finish	IV,4 **
4. The Upper Circle	III *
5. West Gully	I *

6. Stairway to Heaven	III *
7. The Skraeling	IV,5 *
8. Haar	III *
9. West Buttress	IV,6
10. Splitting The Difference	IV,6

11. Pas de Deux	V,6 ***
12. Cirrus	IV,4 ***
13. Coup De Grace	V,7 *
14. Menage a Trois	V,6 **
15. Clonus	IV,4 *

2 Circean 100m V,6 **
E.W.Brunskill, P.Greene 16 Mar 1995
A fine, harder companion route to Femme Fatale. Below and right of the square shaped snow bay the buttress descends in a series of easier angled slabs. Belay at the start of the slabs, at the lowest point of the buttress and below an obvious left-facing corner 10m right of Femme Fatale.
1. 25m Climb the slabs, difficult if thinly iced, trending left to below the corner.
2. 25m Enter and climb the sustained and poorly protected corner above until it ends at a small ledge. Above and left is a fine small cave with a good belay.
3. 50m Climb an undercut blocky wall on the left to reach a snowfield and finish as for Femme Fatale up chimneys and grooves.

3 Taxus 240m III ***
A.W.Ewing, A.J.Trees 8 Mar 1969
The gully line branching left out of West Gully gives a long classic route with a satisfying finish on the summit. The initial section provides two short steep ice pitches. These bank out to steep snow in the best conditions when the route becomes Grade II. Above, snow leads to the bifurcation. Follow the left branch to a snow ridge and follow it until an easy leftward traverse gains a narrow gully leading to the summit.
Variation: **Icefall Finish** 90m IV,4 **
J.Crawford, D.Dawson, J.Madden, W.Skidmore 25 Jan 1976
The best finish when icy, but feels slightly artificial. Climb the buttress above the bifurcation, a mixture of ice and icy turf, to an obvious recess on the right. Climb steeply on its left to an easy finish to the summit crest.

4 The Upper Circle 200m III *
S.Kennedy, N.Morrison, A.Nisbet 10 Jan 1981
On the left wall of West Gully, beyond the start of Taxus, is a prominent ramp, guarded by a steep wall. Gain the ramp by a short hard corner, then follow the ramp in three pitches, going right at the top of the third pitch to gain a platform. To avoid a short vertical wall, traverse down and left round a corner into a small gully which leads back right to a saddle. Finish by a choice of lines.

5 West Gully 300m I *
Prof.W.Ramsay, W.Ramsay Jnr, F.Campbell, C.C.B.Moss 26 Mar 1894
The uncomplicated snow gully cutting up between North and West Buttresses gives an easy climb with good scenery.

WEST BUTTRESSES

The rocks right of West Gully are divided by fault lines into three buttresses; North-West, West and Far West. All the routes except the first two start from a sloping terrace gained from a small corrie under the buttresses, which is best approached from the right.

6 Stairway to Heaven 135m III *
D.Evans, A.Kay Winter 1982
Leave West Gully where Taxus starts and climb the left edge of North-West Buttress by walls and ramps. There are two rocky steps, with one good pitch at half-height on the second step. A useful climb in poor conditions.

7 The Skraeling 270m IV,5 *
I.Fulton, J.Hutchinson Feb 1976
A good climb following a natural line up North-West Buttress.
1. and 2. 80m Start up rocks right of the foot of West Gully and climb easily to gain a broad terrace. Alternatively, gain the terrace from the right via the corrie and traverse left to gain the same point. Belay under an obvious roof.
3. 40m Above is an obvious corner, move down and left for 10m, then follow turf up the wall to gain the left edge of the main corner. Climb 20m up the corner to

Pas de Deux, V,6, Beinn an Dòthaidh West Buttress. Climber Graham Little

beneath a small roof.
4. 25m Climb the upper section of the corner, well protected crux, moving left below the roof to gain the upper grooves.
5. etc 125m Several easier pitches in the upper grooves lead to the top.

Haar   135m   III *
M.H.Moar, C.Walmsley   12 Mar 1972
The obvious gully dividing North-West and West Buttresses. Start on a terrace below the cliff, below a square-cut recess. A short ice pitch leads up into the left corner of the recess (belay). On the right the crux ice pitch leads to the gully proper. Above, normally straightforward snow leads to the top. The icefall on the right is **Valhalla** (150m IV,5).

West Buttress   120m   III *
J.Crawford, D.Dawson, W.Skidmore   1 Feb 1976
A good turf climb, requiring a minimum of snow in a hard freeze. Start from the terrace below the main cliff about halfway between the gully of Haar and the next gully right, Cirrus, where a tapering shelf leads left above an undercut section to a series of chimney-grooves. Gain this system using the shelf and zigzag up using the grooves to gain easier ground above.

10 Splitting The Difference   155m   IV,6
G.Little, C.Bonington   16 Mar 1989
Start about 5m left of the cleft of Cirrus.
1. and 2. 55m Go up left to belay in a snow bay, then move up right to an over-hanging corner and follow a ramp leftwards to a wide triangular corner.
3. 30m Climb the corner by interesting wide bridging, then continue up the groove above.
4. 35m Continue up the turfy groove, immediately left of a clean rock tower, to gain easy broken ground.
5. 35m Climb easy ground to the top.

11 Pas de Deux   165m   V,6 ***
G.E.Little, D.Saddler   17 Feb 1986
This neo-classic provides varied and exciting climbing as it weaves an intriguing way up the challenging and unlikely looking barrel front of West Buttress. Start below and left of the foot of Cirrus at a short groove leading to a ramp on the left wall.
1. 35m Climb the ramp with increasing difficulty to gain a good ledge, then move right to beneath a short, open corner.
2. 50m Climb the awkward corner. Traverse a ledge rightwards until it narrows, then go up short wall to gain a right-trending zigzag line leading to a thread belay overlooking Cirrus. This is below and right of a striking tower of clean rock, seen from below.
3. 30m Climb the left side of a slot, past an icicle fringe, to spacious ledges below the overhanging face of the tower. Climb the short but steep corner on the right of the tower, exiting steeply right to easy ground.
4. 50m A snow ramp trends left leading to the top.

12 Cirrus   135m   IV,4 ***
J.Crawford, J.Gillespie, W.Skidmore   24 Mar 1974
A good line, testing if lean. The obvious deep cleft dividing the West and Far West Buttresses normally provides a steep 10m ice pitch at about mid-height and several other short pitches.

13 Coup De Grace   120m   V,7 *
S.M.Richardson, A.Robertson   28 Feb 1993
A good technical mixed route taking the bulging groove line left of Menage a Trois. Start directly below the groove.
1. 40m Climb a short wall and continue up turf and snow to belay at the top of a chimney.
2. 20m Climb a crack, pull round the bulge and move up a turfy depression to below a second bulge.
3. 20m Make a difficult series of moves up the smooth vertical wall above, step right onto the arete and bridge up the impending corner; a fine pitch.
4. 40m Traverse left for 10m to the foot of a right-slanting turfy ramp and follow this to the top.

14 Menage a Trois   105m   V,6 **
G.E.Little, D.Saddler, S.Visser   14 Feb 1987
Some 10m to the left of the obvious corner of Clonus is a steep, parallel corner, facing right at mid-height on the face. Start below this corner. A popular climb.
1. 35m Climb a steep wall to a snow bay (alternate belay which gives a longer second pitch), then go up awkwardly to gain a ramp leading rightwards into the base of the corner. Belay on the right.
2. 35m Climb the corner, technical but well protected, then break out right near the top to gain a wide ledge.
3. 35m Step right and follow a groove to the top.

15 Clonus   115m   IV,4 *
D.Hodgson, W.Skidmore   26 Dec 1976

This is the right-facing corner about 30m right of Cirrus.
1. 35m Climb the corner and iced slabs to a good stance above a small slot.
2. 40m Climb slabs to an overhanging barrier pitch in the corner. Climb the groove right of the corner for 5m with some difficulty, then gain a ledge and traverse left across the top of the corner to easy snow. A rising right traverse leads back into the corner. This can be climbed direct at (V,5). Escape is possible below the crux via a snow shelf to the right.
3. 40m Continue up the corner, now almost a gully, to the top.

STOB GHABHAR

(NN 230 455)   Alt 1090m   Map p35

Heading south across Rannoch Moor, this hill with its east facing summit corrie and cliff can be seen high in the south-west corner of the massive corrie of The Blackmount as one drops downhill and heads along the straight before Loch Bà. The approach is from the other side.

Approach: Leave the A82 at Bridge of Orchy and follow the A8005 round Loch Tulla to Victoria Bridge (5.5kms, parking just before the bridge). From Forest Lodge take the track west along the river as far as the small, corrugated metal hut belonging to Glasgow University MC (Clashgour, distinct from the farm at Clashgour further west). At the hut turn up to follow the good stalker's path north into Coire Toaig, following the Allt Toaig to reach the col between Stob Ghabhar and Stob a'Choire Odhair. Contour west over rough ground, rising gently to enter Coirein Lochain, the small north-east corrie of Stob Ghabhar, with the cliffs and the Upper Couloir ahead. Avoid a lower tier of easy rock on the left and go up and right to the upper buttress. The final section of the approach is avalanche prone and careful recognition of the prevailing conditions should be made before making the traverse towards the routes (6km, 2hrs 30mins).

Descent: From the summit follow the south-east ridge, descending to reach easy ground west of the Allt Toaig. Cross this to regain the approach track. If the burn is in spate continue along its bank to gain the track from Clashgour Farm.

Hircine Rib   130m   VI,7 *
S.M.Richardson, G.Dudley   30 Dec 1989
A fine mixed route up the buttress left of the couloir. Start just right of the lowest rocks below a left-slanting groove.
1. 10m Gain the groove by a steep, wall (bold) leading to a ledge.
2. 20m Climb the groove, stepping left after a vertical section to gain an icy runnel leading to a belay on the right arete.
3. 25m A steep friable rib is bounded on its left by a slabby groove. Climb this to half-height, then traverse across the slab to gain a ledge on the left arete. Continue right up the vertical continuation corner to an exposed stance.
4. and 5. 75m Follow groove for 5m, then step left to easier ground leading to the top.

The Upper Couloir   90m   II **
A.E.Maylard, Professor and Mrs Adamson, Miss Weiss   May 1897
This veritable classic up the obvious couloir is normally a straightforward snow gully, with one ice pitch in the middle of up to 10m in height and 70 degrees angle. In very lean conditions there may be an impassable chockstone pitch.

Upper Couloir Keyhole   90m   III *
C.L.Donaldson, G.J.F.Dutton   Mar 1952
A short distance right of the Upper Couloir, a narrow deep-cut gully rises from the left corner of a rock bay. Climb steep snow and the icy chimney above to a thread belay (35m). Steep snow leads to the right bounding rib of The Upper Couloir and ice arete, up which a finish is made.

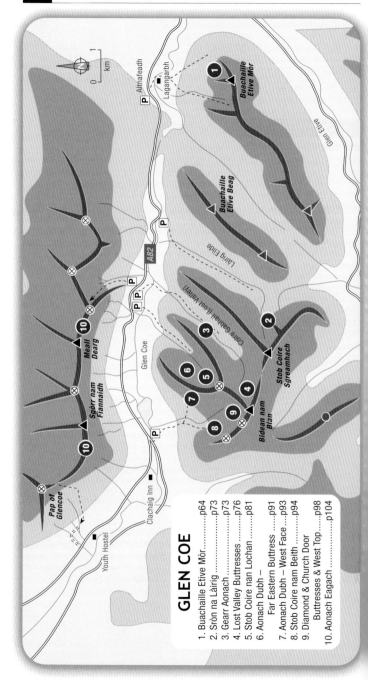

0 1 km

Althafeadh

Lagangarbh

Buachaille Etive Mòr

Glen Etive

Buachaille Etive Beag

Làirig Eilde

Coire Gabhail (Lost Valley)

Stob Coire Sgreamhach

A82

Glen Coe

Meall Dearg

Sgòrr nam Fiannaidh

Bidean nam Bian

Pap of Glencoe

Clachaig Inn

Youth Hostel

GLEN COE

GLEN COE

As one of Scotland's premier winter venues, Glen Coe offers a huge variety of rewarding climbs, of all grades and on all types of terrain. The topography of the surrounding hills with its distinctive peaks and narrow ridges gives Glen Coe a certain Alpine grandeur. The backdrop to the climbing is superb and on a clear winter's day the scenery is breathtaking. Added to this is the fact that the 'Coe' is richly steeped in climbing history with a past stretching back over 100 years.

The main A82 passes through the Glen on the way to Fort William some 30km distant and it can be used as a base for those also wishing to climb on Ben Nevis.

Glen Coe is justly popular but this can create problems by increasing the number of people vying for places to park and routes to climb. Parking is in roadside lay-bys and on a good day these soon fill up, so please park considerately. It may be necessary to queue for certain routes, especially for one of the Coe's many classics and it is a good idea to have alternative plans just in case.

Maps: OS Ben Nevis (Fort William & Glen Coe) L41, Glen Coe & Glen Etive E384. Harvey 'all weather' Mountain Map Ben Nevis & Glen Coe (1:40000), Harvey Superwalker Glen Coe 1:25000.

SMC Climbers' Guide: *Glen Coe* (2001)

Public Transport: Train from Glasgow to Fort William (4 p/day, 1 on Sunday) followed by bus to Kinlochleven, which passes through Glencoe village (10 p/day, none on Sunday). Bus from Glasgow to Fort William (4 p/day) which passes through Glen Coe.

Tourist Information: The nearest Tourist Information Centre is in Ballachulish at the Visitor Centre, open all year, <www.glencoetourism.co.uk> (01855 811286).

Mountaineering Huts: Alex McIntyre Memorial Hut (BMC/MCofS), Lagangarbh (SMC), Blackrock Cottage (LSCC), Inbhirfhaolain (Grampian Club), The Smiddy (Forventure), Waters Cottage (FRCC), Manse Barn (Lomond MC). For details go to <www.mcofs.org.uk>, or 'Google' the names..

SYHA Youth Hostels: Glen Coe (NN 118 577), <www.syha.org.uk>

Independent Hostels: Glencoe Independent Hostel (01855 811906), Inchree Hostel (01855 821287), Blackwater Hostel (01855 831253). Details at <www.hostel-scotland.co.uk> and <www.mcofs.org.uk>

Camping: <www.redsquirrelcampsite.com> (NN 120 573).

Amenities: Glen Coe is well served by visitor facilities and Fort William (see Ben Nevis section) is fairly close, though the road is slow and often busy. There is plenty of accommodation on offer and the two main climber's hostelries, The Kingshouse and The Clachaig, at opposite ends of the glen act as traditional magnets for the thirsty after a hard winter days toil. Glencoe village and Ballachulish lie nearby and have pubs, cafes and shops. Petrol can be obtained locally at Glen Coe and Onich (not 24 hours) and various places in Fort William (24 hours).

Climbing Shops: The Ice Factor (see below) & Fort William.

Climbing Walls: The Ice Factor (01855 831100) <www.ice-factor.co.uk>

Weather and Conditions: Glen Coe's proximity to the West Coast means that the weather is at times influenced by the Gulf Stream and as a result conditions can be somewhat fickle. Atlantic fronts can track across the area with monotonous regularity, combining fluctuating temperatures with a rapidly changing and often ferocious weather pattern. Snow does disappear quickly from many of the cliffs and although there should always be some routes in condition, catching snow on the harder routes can be a problem since the hoar associated with the Cairngorms is not so reliable here. On the other hand, polar highs can bring the remarkably cold clear, and still weather that remind you why the winter experience can be such an enjoyable one.

This rapidly changing weather pattern, combined with the complex nature of the terrain, often complicates approach to and descent from the routes. For this reason it is best to be prepared for navigation in poor weather and before venturing onto the hills it is best to familiarise oneself well with the terrain and the descent.

Climate change has definitely affected conditions in this area and a number of relatively low lying climbs that used to form regularly, now form rarely, if at all. For this reason a number of outstanding climbs have had to be omitted from this guide. Due to the weather and the terrain, there are few areas that are free from potential danger of avalanche. When routes catch the long awaited snow, the approaches and descents become more prone to avalanche. Frozen meltwater on paths presents another hazard typical of the area – there are many who have injured themselves after a simple slip on an icy path.

BUACHAILLE ETIVE MÒR - STOB DEARG

(NN 222 542)   Alt 1022m (summit)   Map p62

This iconic mountain watches over the eastern entrance to Glen Coe, rising gracefully in the angle between Glen Coe and Glen Etive and presents an inspiring sight to those approaching across the wild flat expanse of Rannoch Moor. It is actually a mountain massif of five tops, whose main summit crowns a complex array of buttresses, ridges and gullies that are thrown down onto the moor below to form the well-kent conical shape that is in fact Stob Dearg, to which the main massif name is generally applied. There are few finer sights in the country than the spectacle of the 'Buchal' in its full winter raiment. Before setting foot on the mountain it is worth familiarising oneself with its complex layout.

Weather and Conditions: Due to the relatively low altitude of the climbs on the Buachaille, when compared to those of the Bidean massif, the conditions are not so reliable. However, there are some deep nooks and crannies that hold snow and ice, as well as some classics that just need a dusting.

Approach: There is one main starting point for approaches to the frontal faces of the Buachaille and that is from the western side, close to the white SMC hut at Lagangarbh, since the descent from the summit brings one back to here. This approach leaves the A82 at Altnafeadh (NN 221 563) where there is ample parking. Follow the track down to the bridge across the River Coupall, then to just beyond the white cottage of Lagangarbh where the path splits. The right fork goes straight on into Coire na Tulaich and is the simplest way to and from the summit. Take the left branch and follow this diagonally beneath the western buttresses. After about 20mins the path crosses the great slabby rift of Great Gully, although generally unmistakable, in thick mist this can sometimes be confused with easier gullies further west. Now there are a number of choices:

(i) For Raven's Gully and the Great Gully Amphitheatre, follow the path steeply up the slopes on the left side of Great Gully and continue to the upper of two rowan trees. Break off and follow a rake up right beneath small walls to emerge beneath Slime Wall. This takes about 50mins.

(ii) For climbs on the North Buttress and Crowberry Basin areas, follow the path steeply up the slopes on the left side of Great Gully heading towards some prominent boulders. A rising left traverse leads across the broken lower rocks of North Buttress. Ahead the rocks steepen to form the main frontal mass of North Buttress. A little higher and to the left, a broad ledge at the foot of the East Face of North Buttress is gained by a gully and leads easily into Crowberry Gully, which can be crossed to reach the lowest part of Crowberry Ridge and Curved Ridge.

(iii) From Great Gully the traverse path continues to join a path which comes straight up the hillside from Jacksonville, the Creag Dubh MC hut. The paths meet below the prominent Waterslide from where the route zigzags up towards the foot of D Gully Buttress, then makes a rising traverse to the right, staying close under the lowest rocks of Curved Ridge to emerge at the bottom of a gully system below Crowberry Ridge. This is Crowberry Basin, the start of Curved Ridge, with Easy Gully above and Crowberry Gully further right. It is important to note that the whole area leading up to, and including Crowberry Basin, is subject to avalanche in deep soft snow.

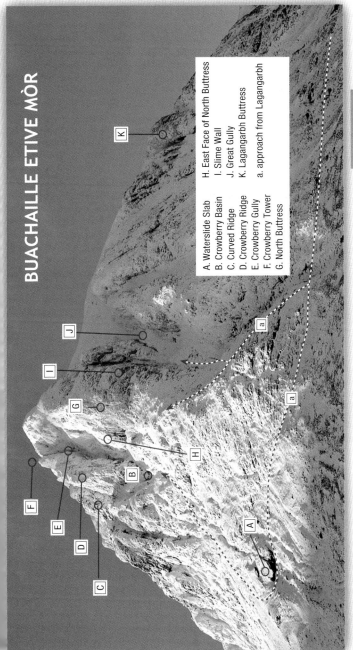

BUACHAILLE ETIVE MÒR

A. Waterslide Slab
B. Crowberry Basin
C. Curved Ridge
D. Crowberry Ridge
E. Crowberry Gully
F. Crowberry Tower
G. North Buttress
H. East Face of North Buttress
I. Slime Wall
J. Great Gully
K. Lagangarbh Buttress
a. approach from Lagangarbh

Descent: There is only one sure descent route and that is from the summit. Other possibilities will be mentioned in the appropriate sections. From the summit, follow the fairly level ridge south-west on a bearing of 250 grid for about 400m, then go due west on a bearing of 270 grid for about 300m down uncomplicated slopes to reach a flat, cairned col at 870m (NN 216 542); the head of Coire na Tulaich. Navigation on this section can be difficult in a white-out and it may be necessary to remain roped.

The most common mistake is to continue too far south-west and descend into Glen Etive, relatively safe but rather inconvenient. However, great care should be taken not to stray too far north, or west, or to turn west too early, as there are large cliffs at the head of Coire na Tulaich. From the col, turn north watching out for the cornice and go down a narrow steep gully leading into the corrie. This often icy slope has been the scene of many accidents and crampons may be a necessity, together with a rope. The lower part of the corrie leads easily down to Lagangarbh. This descent takes one through some potentially avalanche prone areas.

If there is any doubt over snow conditions following heavy snowfall and thaw, then from the col ascend to point 902m (NN 214 542) and descend by the ridge on the west side of Coire na Tulaich. There are some large outcrops here, in particular Dwindle Wall, but these can be avoided by moving left to go down and around them, staying on the ridge until below the lower funnel exiting from the corrie.

NORTH & NORTH-WEST FACES

Layout: This aspect of the Buachaille includes all the cliffs to the right of North Buttress, which naturally fall into two regions; the Lagangarbh Group, the first rock met on the approach, and the Great Gully Group. The Lagangarbh Group consists of from right to left: Lagangarbh Buttress; the distinctive, stepped Staircase Buttress; Broad Gully; Broad Buttress (split by a deep groove higher up) and finally, Narrow Gully (an obvious, trench like gully). The gullies provide pleasant (I/II) climbs, but they can be avalanche prone.

The Great Gully group consists of, from right to left: Great Gully Buttress and Great Gully Upper Buttress; Great Gully; Cuneiform Buttress; the obvious gash of Raven's Gully and Slime Wall.

Descent: In appropriate conditions, it is possible to descend from above Slime Wall by traversing right immediately above the finish of Raven's Gully into Great Gully, then to descend this, keeping close under Cuneiform Buttress, to join the ascent route below Slime Wall. In potential avalanche conditions Great Gully should be avoided at all costs. If in any doubt, go to the top of the mountain and descend by Coire na Tulaich, see above.

1 Lagangarbh Chimney 60m III *
This route lies on Lagangarbh Buttress, the most westerly of the North Face Buttresses and is good for a short day. Approach by climbing up to it well before reaching the outflow from Great Gully. A prominent feature on the front face of the buttress is a chimney-line on the right, which starts about halfway up the gully. It often contains ice and the last 15m is the crux. Descend by gullies on either side of the buttress, or into Coire na Tulaich.

2 Great Gully 360m II *
N.Collie 1894
The massive gully that dominates the north side of the Buachaille can provide a scenic route to the summit. Early in the season several pitches of water-ice may provide sport (III), but these generally bank out later to give a straightforward snow climb. There is usually a pitch where the gully kinks right under Cuneiform Buttress. Great Gully is a notorious avalanche trap and it should only be climbed after a settled spell. Avoid it at all costs should there be any chance of unstable snow.

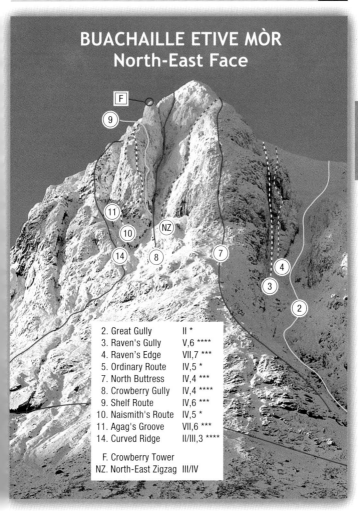

BUACHAILLE ETIVE MÒR
North-East Face

2. Great Gully	II *	
3. Raven's Gully	V,6 ****	
4. Raven's Edge	VII,7 ***	
5. Ordinary Route	IV,5 *	
7. North Buttress	IV,4 ***	
8. Crowberry Gully	IV,4 ****	
9. Shelf Route	IV,6 ***	
10. Naismith's Route	IV,5 *	
11. Agag's Groove	VII,6 ***	
14. Curved Ridge	II/III,3 ****	
F. Crowberry Tower		
NZ. North-East Zigzag	III/IV	

Raven's Gully   135m   V,6 ****
H.MacInnes, C. Bonington   14 Feb 1953
A magnificent climb up the dark and compelling cleft between Slime Wall and Cuneiform Buttress. Normally there is an easy pitch leading to a cave belay beneath a huge chockstone whose left wall provides considerable entertainment. Snow leads to a narrowing of the gully with a chockstone above. Another two difficult pitches lead to the gully fork. Now move left round a rib and climb snow and ice grooves to a platform on the gully edge. Climb the chimney on the right, sometimes hard, or traverse left and finish up icy grooves.
Variation: **Direct Finish   50m   VI,6 ******
Y.Chouinard, D.Tompkins   Feb 1970
A stunning finish if caught in condition. From the fork continue straight up with much bridging and interest.

Raven's Edge, VII,7, Buachaille Etive Mòr. Climber Rob Milne

4 Raven's Edge   170m   VII,7 ***

B.Sprunt, R.Allen   21 Jan 1984l; complete R.Anderson, R.Milne   30 Mar 1996

An atmospheric and splendidly situated climb up the edge of Cuneiform Buttress overlooking Raven's Gully, the most obvious feature of which is a big open book corner. Start at the foot of the gully.

1. 55m Move right and climb a line of weakness just right of the edge overlooking the gully. Move left around a projecting rib and belay at the top of a shallow left-facing corner.

2. 15m Move up left, then step down and follow a thin traverse line into the base of the corner some 6m above the gully. Belay a short way above.

3. 35m Climb to a roof, step down and traverse across the wall to a spike runner, then go back up left into the base of the 'open book' corner. Climb the corner and pull over onto a large shelf at its top.

4. 35m Follow the corner above to its top and traverse left to a thread runner beneath a roof, then continue left around the edge to a cramped but better placed thread belay.

5. 30m Move up left and climb the deep crack to a platform on the buttress crest.

6. A final short step gains easy ground leading to the top of the buttress.

Variation: **Pitch 2**

Belay 5m higher at the end of pitch 1, at a block on a platform, then climb a wall and traverse left past the spike runner to belay at the foot of the open book corner.

5 Ordinary Route   135m   IV,5 *

J.R.Marshall, D.N.Mill, G.J.Ritchie   15 Dec 1957

Start at the lowest rocks near the foot of Raven's Gully. Follow the line of least resistance to a broad grassy terrace. From its right end climb a short but steep pitch to grassy grooves which lead to another broad ledge under the vertical upper third of the buttress. Traverse right round an exposed edge onto the west face. Climb an obvious shelf, then turn towards the centre of the cliff and climb to the top.

6 The Long Chimney   135m   IV,5 *

R.Smith, D.Leaver 15 Dec 1957

Follow Ordinary Route to the broad grassy terrace, then traverses hard right to climb the obvious, long shallow chimney.

NORTH-EAST FACE

Diagrams   p65, 67, 70

Layout: This aspect of the Buachaille comprises from right to left: the broad and massive North Buttress, with the East Face on its left; Crowberry Gully; Crowberry Ridge and the Rannoch Wall, then Easy Gully and Curved Ridge with D Gully Buttress below.

Approach: See p64

7 North Buttress   300m   IV,4 ***
This splendid climb with its superb outlook can be climbed under almost any condition and will always provide interest. The route takes the prominent, continuous line of shallow chimneys that split the steeper mid-section of the buttress in the centre of the mountain. These are normally climbed in four pitches. On the third pitch there is width for two possibilities; the narrow chimney on the left being harder than the option to its right. At the top of the chimney system the left exit up a tricky slab is harder than the right exit and subsequent traverse. Easy ground ensues and higher, a pleasant crest can be followed to the summit.

8 Crowberry Gully   300m   IV,4 ****
H.Raeburn, E.W.Green   Apr 1909
The continuous deep-set gully between North Buttress and Crowberry Ridge provides a magnificent climb of great character and beauty. Conditions vary enormously depending on the build-up of snow. There are seldom more than five distinct pitches, most of which can be obliterated by heavy snow. Ideal conditions are not frequent and the gully can be very dangerous due to avalanche.

From Crowberry Basin, snow pitches lead to the narrows and the first chockstone pitch. More snow pitches lead to the first hard pitch, the Thincrack Chimney, which may give 10m of steep iced slabs but often forms no more than a few awkward steps. The junction is now reached where a steep rib divides the two forks. Here, a rising right traverse is made across slabs on which a firm cover is desirable, this may be hard if the ice is thin. Another snow pitch, or two leads to the Cave Pitch which is nearly always the crux and can be climbed by an impressive curtain of ice on the right wall. Snow leads to the finish not far below the summit.
Variation: **Left Fork   35m   IV,5 ****
C.M.G.Smith, R.J.Taunton, I.C.Robertson   Mar 1949
A deep and narrow, iced chimney leads to a great capstone. Climbed by ice on its left wall, this is hard but short and well protected. Easy snow leads to Crowberry Gap.

Should Crowberry Gully be in dangerous condition, or fully occupied, both common, then alternatives exist. Naismith's Route (route 10) is on Crowberry Ridge to the left. North Buttress (route 7) can be gained by a traverse to the right beneath the East Face. Another good alternative is **North-East Zigzag** (85m III/IV) which takes the line of least resistance up the left side of the East Face and is open to much variation.

CROWBERRY RIDGE & RANNOCH WALL

Diagrams p65, 67, 70

Approach: See p64

Descent: For the five routes that end on the ridge beneath Crowberry Tower, either climb the tower and descend its right side to Crowberry Gap, or traverse its left side to reach Curved Ridge a little lower. Finish up this to the summit.

Shelf Route   210m   IV,6 ***
W.M.Mackenzie, W.H.Murray   Mar 1937
The right flank of Crowberry Ridge overlooking Crowberry Gully is cut by two long,

BUACHAILLE ETIVE MÒR
Curved Ridge &
Crowberry Area

7. North Buttress	IV,4 ***	14. Curved Ridge	II/III,3 ****
8. Crowberry Gully	IV,4 ****		
11. Agag's Groove	VII,6 ***	I. Slime Wall	
12. Route I	V,6 **	NZ. North-East Zigzag	III/IV
13. Chuckle Brothers	VI,7 **		

parallel ribs with shallow gullies on their left. Shelf Route follows the lower line and Naismith's Route the upper. When in condition the former provides a very fine and exposed mixed climb with the crux high on the route. Start from the narrows at the foot of Crowberry Gully by a traverse of steeply shelving snow to reach a bay. If there is not enough snow, this point can be reached as for Naismith's Route. Climb the right wall and rib of the middle of three chimneys and follow the trough in the shelf for several pitches. The trough steepens to a scoop in the angle between the left wall and a small pinnacle on the right. Climb to a point where the scoop merges into the face beneath a small rectangular tower and move right to gain a square recess under the pinnacle. The pinnacle is usually climbed on the right by an awkward traverse. Above, a long groove leads to the crest below Crowberry Tower, see above.

10 Naismith's Route   210m   IV,5 *
Harder than North Buttress but the easiest line up Crowberry Ridge. A 6m chimney

at the far left side of ridge allows the First Platform to be traversed to its right end. Climb a groove up the left side of a 15m pinnacle to Pinnacle Ledge, then move right to the leftmost of three chimneys in a bay. Depending on the amount of snow, this point can also be gained from the narrows at the foot of Crowberry Gully as for Shelf Route. Climb the chimney, which becomes a long shallow gully with a series of short pitches. In the upper section, continue up a gully until it ends on a wide sloping slab. From the top of the slab climb the short left wall, which overhangs and is hard, to gain the crest. Failing this, traverse onto the crest from the bottom of the slab. Follow the crest to beneath Crowberry Tower, see above.

The crest of Crowberry Ridge is taken by the famous **Direct Route** (225m VII,6) which continues above Pinnacle Ledge to Abraham's Ledge then goes left and up the crest with difficulty. Around to the left of the crest is The Rannoch Wall, with Curved Ridge and Easy Gully on its left running up to meet the termination of Crowberry Ridge.

Agag's Groove   105m   VII,6 ***
H.MacInnes, C.Bonington, K.MacPhail, G.McIntosh   8 Feb 1953
This follows the obvious well defined corner-ramp rising diagonally across the Rannoch Wall. Due to its iconic summer status this is a route that should only be undertaken when in suitable winter condition. Start behind a large detached, rectangular block at the extreme right edge of the face.
1. 35m Climb a crack, which develops into a groove and leads to a block belay at the start of a ramp.
2. 25m Follow the ramp up and left to a large block belay.
3. 25m Continue up the ramp then move left to climb a hidden crack and narrow groove in the exposed nose. Go up and left to a block belay.
4. 20m Move left and continue quite boldly to the top.

Route I   70m   V,6 **
H.MacInnes and partner   Feb 1972
A fine, exposed mixed climb up the vegetated line of weakness in the middle of Rannoch Wall, which slants left and develops into an obvious groove. Start some 15m above the pitch in Easy Gully, at a short vegetated chimney. Climb the chimney to belay at some more open rocks (15m). Trend right, then take a long slant up a narrow shelf, which ends at an awkward stance, where two sloping slabs are topped by a 4m wall. Climb the wall, crux, and finish by the long upper groove.

Chuckle Brothers   50m   VI,7 **
M.Garthwaite, R.Anderson   4 Mar 2000
A good climb lying high on the left side of Rannoch Wall above the final pitch in Easy Gully, best gained by an abseil-in from high on Curved Ridge. Start beneath the main feature in the upper half of the face, a trough like corner-groove.
1. 25m Climb a ribbon of ice, or the turf and rock beneath it, and move right into a sentry box at the base of the corner-groove.
2. 25m Climb the corner to its top and follow a steep crack through a roof on the right to gain a ledge. Easy ground leads to the crest of Crowberry Ridge.

Curved Ridge   240m   II/III,3 ****
G.T.Glover, R.G.Napier   11 Apr 1898
Gracefully curving up and under the Rannoch Wall, through some impressive rock scenery, Curved Ridge provides one of the finest winter excursions in Glen Coe. It is climbable under most conditions although it can be arduous in deep snow. If any avalanche hazard exists great care should be taken around Crowberry Basin, the exposed slopes under Crowberry Tower and the final summit slopes. Curved Ridge is not a descent route.
    Most parties rope up for the traverse into Crowberry Basin, which can be icy. From Crowberry Basin, short steps lead to the bottom right-hand corner of the ridge where the climbing proper begins. Two mixed pitches up the right edge gain

Curved Ridge, II/III,3, Buachaille Etive Mòr

a spacious platform. The first ice pitch in Easy Gully lies just to the right. This section is normally the crux. More difficult variations exist further left. A shallow gully on the crest leads in two or three pitches to another good stopping place.

Above, gain a parallel chimney-gully and either climb this, or break out left beneath it and aim for a prominent tower on the crest. This is climbed via a short awkward wall to gain a platform. Continue up the ridge to emerge on a small ledge beneath a flat rib, which is climbed to reach a cairn on the shoulder.

The best route from here works up and under the lower rocks of Crowberry Tower, normally an easy left rising traverse. This is followed by a straightforward gully going back right to Crowberry Tower Gap at the head of the Left Fork of Crowberry Gully. A good little diversion is to climb Crowberry Tower by moving up a short corner, stepping left onto a ledge and traversing left to the edge before spiralling round to the top (15m). Reverse to descend. Above Crowberry Tower Gap, climb a ramp on the left to a block, then go back right to reach the summit slopes above the finish to Crowberry Gully.

BIDEAN NAM BIAN MASSIF

Map p62

Bidean nam Bian (1150m) is the highest point of a large and complex massif of eight mountains. From east to west, the major peaks are: Stob Coire Sgreamhach; Bidean itself with Stob Coire nan Lochan jutting out in front of it to the north; Stob Coire nam Beith; and finally An t-Sròn.

Emanating northwards from these peaks are three long ridges which terminate abruptly in steep faces overlooking the glen. These are the Three Sisters; Beinn Fhada, Gearr Aonach and Aonach Dubh. Three principal corries are formed by these ridges. From east to west these are Coire Gabhail (known as The Lost Valley), Coire nan Lochan and Coire nam Beitheach. With the exception of one route, Sròn na Làirig, all climbs are on the faces and hillsides around these three corries.

The ridges and peaks of the Bidean massif offer some rewarding high level winter mountaineering. Suggested starting routes to gain some of these ridges are Sròn na Làirig (II) on Stob Coire Sgreamhach, The Zigzags (I) on Gearr Aonach, Broad Gully (I) on Stob Coire nan Lochan, Dinnertime Buttress (I) on Aonach Dubh and Summit Gully (II) on Stob Coire nam Beith.

STOB COIRE SGREAMHACH

(NN 155 537)   Alt 1072m   Map p62

This pyramidal peak forms the south-eastern corner of the massif and is connected to Bidean nam Bian by the main ridge running over the Lost Valley Buttresses. The splendid Beinn Fhada ridge (I/II) runs north-east to Glen Coe, whilst a shorter ridge drops south-east into Glen Etive. There are some winter cliffs overlooking the Lost Valley, not described here, and the main pyramidal face itself has an alpine character with a number of pleasant routes at (I/II) and one at (III) taking in all the obstacles. The Beinn Fhada face overlooking the Làirig Eilde to the east contains a number of icefalls that provide good sport with the most prominent being **The Bubble** (60m IV.4) which forms low down on the right side.

LÀIRIG EILDE FACE - NORTH-EAST RIDGE

(NN 164 535)   Alt 700m   North-East facing
A ridge descends south-east from the summit to form the head of the Làirig Eilde. Part way down this ridge a prominent offshoot ridge drops north-east into the Làirig Eilde and provides the line for a fine climb.

Approach: Start from the car park (NN 188 563) on the Glen Coe side of the Làirig Eilde at a signposted footpath to Glen Etive. A long but easy walk of about 4km leads through the glen to the foot of the ridge.

Descent: Go south-east to a col (NN 164 529) and return into the Làirig Eilde. An alternative, is to continue to the summit of Stob Coire Sgreamhach and traverse the Beinn Fhada ridge for a splendid finish to the day. The descent off Sgreamhach is tricky (I/II); some blocks on the crest provide a belay from where a short drop gains a shelf going right (facing out) onto the east side where short steps, ledges and traverses lead to the bottom and a short traverse past a good belay to the col. Further along, the ridge can be descended at various points, including at its end, into the Làirig Eilde, taking care of small outcrops. Do not attempt to descend directly north into Glen Coe from the termination of the Beinn Fhada Ridge.

Sròn na Làirig   300m   II ***
P.D.Baird, Coulson, Allberry, Kendall, T.M.Wedderburn   Mar 1934
The prominent offshoot ridge gives an excellent outing with a remote and alpine feel. The broad lower part of the ridge is open to much variation at various levels of difficulty. It can also be avoided by a traverse-in from the left. Above this, a broad ledge girdles the ridge and the rocks above are generally climbed by a groove-line slanting up from the left side. Grooves continue to easier ground and a level section followed by further climbing up the left side of the ridge and an airy traverse around the head of a steep gully before the final ascent.

GEARR AONACH

Map p62

This is the north-east ridge of Stob Coire nan Lochan and the middle of the Three Sisters.

EAST FACE

(NN 163 555)   Alt 450m   East facing   Diagram p65

This face runs along the entire western side of Coire Gabhail, better known as the Lost Valley. Part of this face, the Mome Rath Face, sits above the flat section of the valley floor and is home to some stunning ice climbs. Unfortunately these have seldom come into condition in recent years and are not described.

Weather and Conditions: Due to its relatively low altitude the East Face of

Gearr Aonach does not readily come into condition. Given enough snow and cold weather, the sun provides a thaw-freeze cycle which can produce copious amounts of ice and it is recommended that if the face ever comes into condition, then the climbing should be experienced.

Approach: Park in the upper of the two large lay-bys in the middle of Glen Coe. Cross the River Coe by a footbridge (NN 173 564) just below the Meeting of Three Waters and follow a good path up the right side of the wooded gorge of the Allt Coire Gabhail. Just beyond a stile the path levels out at the deep-cut entrance to the main gorge and then traverses through it. At this point a path breaks off right up a rocky bluff towards the Zigzags on Gearr Aonach and an alternative route which is useful if the lower path is icy, is to ascend the bluff and follow the edge of the gorge to join up with the other path at a large boulder opposite the slabby Sentry Crag, where there can be vast sheets of climbable ice.

Ahead is a formidable barrier of jumbled boulders and trees formed by a huge landslip from Gearr Aonach. Cross the stream and by-pass the boulder field easily around its left side to a magnificent viewpoint of the Lost Valley. A short descent gains the flat valley floor. If this path is missed one is plunged into the midst of the boulder field. Entertaining though this may be, especially when breaking trail through deep snow in the dark, the chance of dropping down a hole is best avoided! However, it may be necessary if the stream is in spate. It is also possible to by-pass the boulder field up on the right. With the exception of The Zigzags, climbs are gained from the flat section of the Lost Valley.

Descent: The recommended descent is to head south along the ridge into Coire nan Lochan and to come down the east side of the waterfall issuing from the corrie. It is also possible to descend easy snow slopes into the Lost Valley at the southern end of the face.

Layout: Located just left of the frontal nose above the entrance to the Lost Valley lie The Zigzags. The East Face runs leftwards from here to merge into the slopes of Stob Coire nan Lochan and Bidean. Overlooking the flat valley floor the upper half of the main face is formed by a continuous steep wall, rising over 100m from a broad snow ledge to meet the summit ridge. This is the Mome Rath Face, which is defined by the long, left-trending gullies of Rev Ted's on the right and Lost Leeper on the left. Three further gullies lie just beyond the flat section. Under certain conditions all the gullies are avalanche prone.

1 The Zigzags 200m I *
The easiest approach to the Gearr Aonach ridge is by the broken ground between the nose on the right and the North-East Face on the left. Those of a nervous disposition may require a rope for the upper section. From the entrance to the lower gorge of the Lost Valley, a short distance beyond the stile, follow the path rightwards up a rocky bluff. Above this, move up leftwards to the lowest rocks of the North-East Face at the start of the broken ground.

Traverse up and right below overhanging rock walls. Go up past a tree, then back up left to the foot of the wall above and climb a short chimney step. Make a long traverse left beneath broken walls, then go up and back right to where the shelf opens out, small cairn. Go up, then left beneath a small wall to the ridge.

If used as a descent, reverse these directions. The way down may be difficult to locate. A small cairn marks the start, on the right when heading north, at the termination of the ridge. Due to the nature of the surrounding terrain there are no other alternatives here. Care should be taken, especially under heavy snow when the ledges can form windslab. It is not a recommended descent, especially for those without prior knowledge. If used, conditions may dictate that it be pitched. It will always be safer to descend via Coire nan Lochan.

2 Ingrid's Folly/Peregrine Gully 300m III **
Glencoe School of Winter Climbing Party 1960
This long, recessed gully system runs the full height of the face and is the first gully encountered on emerging from the boulder field; the second is **McArtney's Gully**

(155m III). It gives an entertaining combination of routes. Follow the gully of Ingrid's Folly with some amusement, including a through route, to the easier upper gully. An easy finish can be made up this but further fun can be obtained by traversing up left into the shallow fault of Peregrine Gully. This provides further pitches of caves and chockstones.

Rev Ted's Gully   300m   III **
H.MacInnes, Rev. Ted   Feb 1960

This is the obvious, long gully which slants left up the full height of the face. The lower reaches are straightforward and can be used to approach the Mome Rath Face. From the junction in the upper cliffs there are several options. Best is the iced chimney just left of an icefall, or the icefall direct. There is also an easy right branch leading to a bay and another steep chimney, interesting but awkward. An escape right can be made from the bay, reducing the entire route to (II).

Lost Leeper Gully   300m   III *
H.MacInnes, A.Gilbert, P.Debbage, D.Layne-Joynt, D.Allwright   13 Feb 1969

Rising from the end of the flat section of the Lost Valley, this shallow, indefinite gully bounds the left side of the Mome Rath Face. It provides interesting route finding with, higher up, the possibility of some ice pitches. Belays in the main part of the gully are poor.

Gully A (Right Fork)   245m   IV,4 *
H.MacInnes, D.Crabbe   Jan1964

This is the first gully encountered once the path starts to rise at the southern end of the Lost Valley. Gully B (II), then Gully C (I) lie to the left. A steep initial pitch leads to the bifurcation where the steep ice scoop on the right leads to easier climbing up the gully. An alternative from the bifurcation is the Central Branch (IV), which continues directly up a steep ice scoop. The Left Branch (IV) starts as a steep ice pitch slightly left of the main gully.

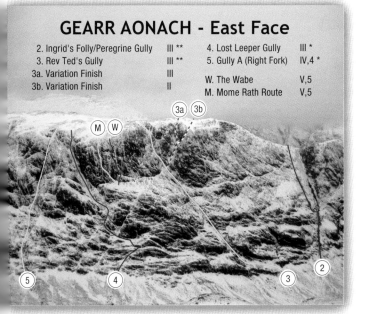

GEARR AONACH - East Face

2. Ingrid's Folly/Peregrine Gully	III **	4. Lost Leeper Gully	III *
3. Rev Ted's Gully	III **	5. Gully A (Right Fork)	IV,4 *
3a. Variation Finish	III		
3b. Variation Finish	II	W. The Wabe	V,5
		M. Mome Rath Route	V,5

GLEN COE

BIDEAN NAM BIAN - EAST

LOST VALLEY MINOR BUTTRESS

(NN 149 538)   Alt 900m   North-East facing   Map p62

This is the smaller and left-hand of the two conspicuous buttresses lying just right of the col at the head of the Lost Valley, on the summit ridge of Bidean. It provides a pleasant and less frequented middle grade venue.

Weather and Conditions: The buttress comes into condition regularly since much of the climbing is mixed in nature. The slopes leading to it can be prone to avalanche in certain conditions, so be wary of this.

Approach: Gain the Lost Valley (p74) and from the far end of the flat section, follow the higher of two paths rising up the side of the Upper Gorge to where the paths converge at a deeply-cut streamway dropping down from the right. Care should be taken at this point since the rift of the Upper Gorge lies directly below and should not be strayed into, especially in descent. Cross the stream, continue towards the obvious col at the head of the Lost Valley, then bear right to the buttress (allow 2hrs).

Descent: This is possible by either of the gullies left of the crag (I), which are separated by a rocky rib, or the gully to the right of the crag (I), which may have a large cornice. Alternatively follow the ridge east to the col, the Bealach Dearg, at the head of the Lost Valley (NN 151 537). There is likely to be a small cornice.

Layout: The cliff is split into two main facets by a central corner and ramp, the line of Right Edge, beneath which is a turfy snowfield. To the right there is a side wall overlooking the gully.

1 Chimney Route   80m   IV,4 *
J.R.Marshall, J.Moriarty   Jan 1959
The obvious chimney on the left side of the buttress provides several interesting chockstone problems.

2 Minor Issue   80m   IV,6 *
R.Anderson, G.Taylor   10 Jan 1988
The corner-groove line left of the buttress edge, between Chimney Route and Central Scoop.
1. 15m Climb the corner-groove to a ledge.
2. 20m Move left and climb a corner to a small block, step right and follow a groove to easy ground.
3. 45m Continue more easily to near the top.

3 Central Scoop   100m   IV,4 *
I.Clough, N.Clough   2 Mar 1969
The chimney-corner just up and right from Minor Issue chokes with ice and leads to the more open buttress.

4 Right Edge   130m   IV,4 **
J.R.Marshall, J.Stenhouse, D.Haston   Feb 1959
The main central corner and ramp-line leading up right beneath the headwall gives a fine varied route with good situations.
1. 40m Ascend the chimney past a chockstone, then go up an icy groove to a belay in the corner.
2. 45m Move up to the headwall, either via the corner, or by its slabby right wall, then traverse awkwardly up right to the edge. Take care in arranging protection.
3. 45m A shallow gully leads to easy snow slopes and the top.

5 Minor Adjustment   115m   IV,5 *
R.Anderson, C.Greaves   19 Feb 1989
This is the obvious groove and corner just up the gully from Right Edge, a direct

BIDEAN NAM BIAN - EAST
Lost Valley Minor Buttress

GLEN COE

1. Chimney Route	IV,4	*
2. Minor Issue	IV,6	*
3. Central Scoop	IV,4	*
4. Right Edge	IV,4	**
5. Minor Adjustment	IV,5	*
7. Right-hand Gully	I/II	

line joining that route after its upper traverse.

1. 45m Climb the steep groove to a small ledge and spike, then follow a ramp steeply up left around the edge to ledges. A short traverse right leads back to the corner; belay 3m higher.

2. 25m Continue up the corner, then move right and climb a short groove to step right below a small roof. Follow the snow ramp to a short, wide crack and climb this to a belay.

3. 45m Easier ground leads to the top.

Chimini Minor   75m   IV,6 *
R.Anderson, R.Milne   15 Nov 1998

A short way up right is a long, shallow left-facing corner-line, **Over the Influence** (90m IV,4). Immediately to the right is a narrow, chockstoned chimney-crack, then finally before the crag merges into the steepening gully, a left-facing slabby corner **Old Farts' Corner** (80m IV,5). The climbs vary in grade according to the amount of banking and ice.

1. 25m Climb the chimney-crack to a small ledge.

2. 50m Follow the groove to the top.

Right-hand Gully   I/II
The gully running up the right side of the crag gives a scenic route. The gully appears to end in a cul-de-sac but a long pitch where it steepens leads to the top from the foot of Old Farts' Corner.

LOST VALLEY BUTTRESS

(NN 148 540)   Alt 900m   North facing   Map p62

The larger and right-hand of the two buttresses is an excellent cliff with a splendid outlook. The buttress has a remote and serious feel to it, possibly due to the length of approach and relative lack of climbers.

Weather and Conditions: There are some great mixed climbs, which readily come into condition. The slopes leading to the cliff can be prone to avalanche under certain conditions.

Approach: Gain the Lost Valley (p74) and continue as for Lost Valley Minor Buttress (p76), then either traverse rightwards from that cliff or, from the top of the Upper Gorge, follow the right bank of the deeply-cut stream which descends from the col between Bidean and Stob Coire nan Lochain. This leads over two steepenings to a level section which continues to the slopes beneath the crag (allow 2hrs 30mins). The buttress can also be reached from the col between Bidean nam Bian and Stob Coire nan Lochan.

Descent: From the top of the buttress head west along the ridge a short way, passing the corniced top of Right-hand Gully (II) to reach Descent Gully (I) (NN 146 540). There is a convenient boulder which can be used if an abseil is required to break through the cornice. This gully accumulates snow. An alternative is the narrow buttress at the left end of the crag, which can be pitched, and another if no gear has been left below is to follow the ridge east, down to the col at the head of the Lost Valley (NN 151 537).

Layout: The buttress is divided by the great, central groove of Pterodactyl into an easier angled left half, which contains a prominent vertical corner, and set back at a higher level, the steeper right half, which contains a cave recess with a large corner above it.

8 Sabre Tooth   120m   IV,5 *
I.Clough, H.MacInnes   9 Feb 1969
Towards the right side of the left half of the buttress there is a prominent vertical corner, the alternative start (IV). Start up left from this corner. Climb to a snow bay, break out right, gain a terrace, then traverse left to a steep, shallow corner. This point can also be gained by a traverse from the left end of the crag. Climb the corner to a line of grooves which lead to the top.

9 Directosaur   160m   VI,7 **
G.Ettle, R.Anderson, R.Milne   Mar 1989
A good route taking a direct line up the right edge of the left half of the buttress. Start at the lowest rocks below the edge.
1. 45m Climb the shallow groove just left of the edge, step left and move up to a ledge leading back right to the edge. Ascend a steep flake-crack on the left, then follow easier ground to below a steep corner.
2. 30m Climb the corner, then follow grooves up the right side of a huge block-like feature and continue to its top.
3. 35m Move across right and climb a short groove to regain the crest. Snow grooves now lead to the upper rocks.
4. 50m Continue up the snow grooves to the final slopes.

10 Moonlighting   120m   V,6 **
R.Anderson, G.Taylor, N.West   27 Jan 1988
The obvious line splitting the buttress into its two distinct halves is Pterodactyl (V.6). Start just right of this, at the top of a bay beneath a groove.
1. 35m Climb the groove to a ledge at the foot of a wall.
2. 35m The steep flake-line up on the left leads to the edge overlooking Pterodactyl. Go up and right to a shallow groove leading to a short wall.
3. 50m The gully of Pterodactyl now leads to the top.

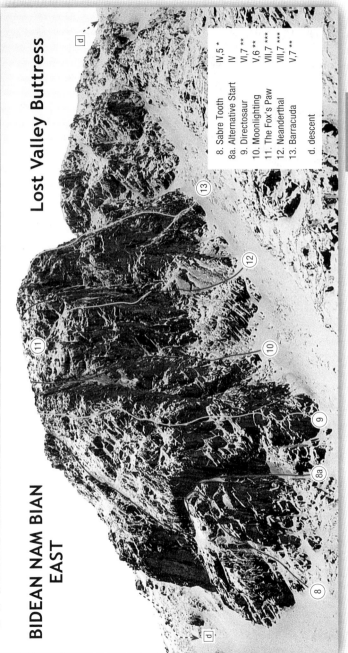

Lost Valley Buttress

BIDEAN NAM BIAN EAST

8. Sabre Tooth — IV,5 *
8a. Alternative Start — IV
9. Directosaur — VI,7 **
10. Moonlighting — V,6 **
11. The Fox's Paw — VII,7 ***
12. Neanderthal — VII,7 ***
13. Barracuda — V,7 **

d. descent

Neanderthal, VII,7, Lost Valley Buttress. Climber Ross Cowie

11 The Fox's Paw 115m VII,7 ***
C.Smith, I.Deans 6 Mar 1999
A stunning line immediately left of the Neanderthal corner, taking the iced groove and isolated icicle that run down the crag to terminate in steep ground above the left side of the cave recess.
1. 30m Climb Neanderthal and belay on the left just below the cave recess.
2. 20m Traverse left onto the rib below a steepening corner-groove. Levitate directly to belay below a square roof and an icicle fringe.
3. 30m Surmount the ice roof and ascend an ice smear to easy ground.
4. 30m The groove on the left leads to the top.

12 Neanderthal 120m VII,7 ***
R.Anderson, G.Nicol 14 Feb 1987
A superb climb in an impressive situation, taking a line through the cave recess right of Pterodactyl and on up the huge corner above.
1. 35m Easily up a gully, then its left wall to a ledge. Traverse right and climb a chute to belay in the cave recess.
3. 20m Move out right, then go up to the roof and gain the base of the corner. Climb the corner to a small ledge.
4. 25m Continue up the corner to the right side of a square roof, then move left beneath this to cracks in a recessed wall. Climb the cracks over a small roof and go through the final eaves by the narrow slot which is clearly visible from below, lurking on the skyline. Belay by large blocks a short way above.
5. 40m Climb a short corner to easy snow slopes and the top.

13 Barracuda 80m V,7 **
R.Anderson, R.Milne 16 Jan 1988
An obvious steep crack springs from the ramp which runs up leftwards from the right edge of the frontal face. This gives a short hard section followed by much easier climbing.
1. 10m Follow the ramp past a groove to belay beneath a crack.
2. 20m Climb the crack to the buttress edge and belay 5m higher in a shallow gully.
3. 50m Follow the gully over a steepening, to the top.

4 Barbarian   80m   V,6 *
R.McAllister, M.Gray   29 Dec 1995
Start just around the edge of the main face to the right of Barracuda.
1. 50m   Climb the groove of Dislocation for 3m, step left into the fault-line which runs parallel to and right of Barracuda and follow this to turfy climbing leading to the base of an obvious chimney.
2. 30m   The chimney leads to easy snow slopes and the top.

5 Dislocation   85m   III *
C.Bonington, F.Mitchell   1969
Start as for Barbarian and follow a groove trending slightly right to a snow patch, then finish up a shallow, broken chimney.

STOB COIRE NAN LOCHAN

(NN 149 549)   Alt 900m   North-East facing   Map p62   Diagrams p82, 85

Stob Coire nan Lochan (1115m) is undoubtedly the finest of Bidean's attendant peaks. From beneath its shapely summit, the long ridges of Gearr Aonach and Aonach Dubh run north to terminate abruptly in steep faces above the road through Glen Coe. Overlooking the tops of these ridges is a splendid high level corrie containing several tiny lochans backed by tall columnar cliffs and deeply cut gullies. 'Stob Coire', is an idyllic spot and the height of the corrie floor coupled with its northerly aspect, makes it the most reliable winter cliff in Glen Coe. There are a variety of excellent routes of all grades. However, it is a popular place and one may have to queue for certain climbs.

Weather and Conditions: With the cliffs taking little drainage there is not much ice and although a few routes do require a period of build-up, many can be done after a cold snap and a dump of snow. A number of the mixed routes hold little snow and it is best to catch them in hoared-up condition after they have been in the cloud and wind. Some of the easier routes are climbable through to April, though late season cornice collapse funnelling down the gullies should be watched out for. There are times when the slopes in the corrie accumulate large amounts of fresh snow and in such circumstances be wary of avalanche danger.

Approach: Start from either of two large lay-bys on the main road opposite the entrance to the corrie. After crossing the bridge over the River Coe (NN 167 566) a long, steady haul leads up a good path on the Gearr Aonach side of the glen.

Just above the bridge a shallow gully is crossed. This is **Avalanche Gully** (600m III/IV,4), which runs the full height of the hillside. Although it rarely comes into full condition, in a hard freeze the lower streamway provides good sport with 6 or 7 pitches on water ice from just above the path.

Opposite the rock walls of the East Face of Aonach Dubh the path runs beneath a series of rocky outcrops (frozen meltwater can cause problems here) and crosses the stream just before it disappears into a small ravine, into which a waterfall plummets (some sport here) from the floor of the corrie. Far Eastern Buttress (p91) is located just over on the right. Head towards its left side, then go up around a rocky outcrop to gain the corrie floor (1hr 30mins to 2hrs). Allow another 30mins to reach the routes.

Alternative approaches are via The Zigzags on Gearr Aonach, or Dinnertime Buttress on Aonach Dubh.

Descent: This is quickest by Broad Gully, straight ahead as one enters the corrie. However, a good, safe alternative is to follow the rim of the corrie northwards, taking care of the deeply cut gullies, to easy ground on Aonach Dubh where a short easy slope leads back into the corrie bowl. In poor weather care should be taken not to stray off left towards Stob Coire nam Beith, or the cliffs of Aonach Dubh.

Layout: The topography is straightforward. On the left, the bulk of Summit Buttress lies beneath the summit. To its right is the uncomplicated slope of Broad Gully, then Forked Gully, Twisting Gully, South, Central and North Buttresses and

STOB COIRE NAN LOCHAN - Left

1. Boomerang Gully — II *
2. Ordinary Route — IV,5 *
2a. Alternate Finish — V,6 **
3. Scabbard Chimney — V,6 ***

4. Spectre — V,6 *
5. Innuendo — V,6 *
6. Broad Gully — I *
7. Dorsal Arete — II ***
8. Forked Gully — I *
8a. F.G. Right Fork — II/III

finally Pinnacle Buttress. The buttresses are divided by narrow gullies, the most prominent being SC Gully between the tallest cliffs of South and Central Buttresses. Routes are described from left to right.

1 Boomerang Gully   210m   II *
W.H. Murray, J. Black, R.G. Donaldson   Jan 1949
This pleasant route follows the obvious curving gully immediately left of the steepest rocks of Summit Buttress. There is often an ice pitch where it bends back right. The left branch (II) moves onto the face here.

2 Ordinary Route   130m   IV,5 *
K.Spence & Party   Feb 1971
Start just left of Scabbard Chimney.
1. Climb straight up to a snow shelf and move left to a corner.
2. Climb the corner past a block, then follow a snow shelf up left beneath the main buttress. Easy escape to Boomerang Gully here.
3. On the steep wall to the right, gain then climb the obvious long, right-leaning grooved crack system and stepped ledges to the top.
Variation: **Alternate Finish   50m   V,6 ** **
A.Nisbet, M.Duff, N.Kekus   2 Jan 1986
An awkward short wall on the right leads to a ledge system. Traverse this rightwards, including a mantelshelf to a higher level, to a block belay in a sensational position. Climb the tapering groove above, sustained, then a short ramp and a blocky chimney leading back left to easier ground.

3 Scabbard Chimney   170m   V,6 ***
L.S.Lovat, J.R.Marshall, A.H.Hendry   12 Feb 1956
Although an excellent natural winter line, this superb climb is not likely to hold much ice. On the occasions it does, it becomes easier. Start beneath the most obvious feature of the buttress, a chimney slanting up right under the steep right flank.
1. 25m Climb a short chimney and its ensuing crack.
2. 25m Continue up the crack and corner-line to beneath a sentry box.
3. 40m The right-hand side of the sentry box has a crack which leads with some difficulty to the rib on right. Climb this, then return back left to easier ground which leads to a shoulder overlooking Broad Gully.
4. and 5. 80m An easy gully leads to the crest. A further 180m gains the top.

From a block below the easy gully a long abseil into Broad Gully gives a quick descent, or an approach to the following route. The sling can be collected on the way past.

Spectre   170m   V,6 *
K.Bryan, J.Simpson   12 Jan 1958
A good companion to Scabbard Chimney, taking the steep shelf about 10m to the right. Climb a broken wall to a point directly below the first true chimney section of Scabbard (20m). Above and to the right, a 10m slab leads to a ledge. Follow this to the right for 5m to where an awkward descent leads to the long shelf. Above, climb an icy bulge and an icy groove. Climb a steep slab and a bulge to an easing and continue to a broad ledge leading to the gully of Scabbard Chimney.

Innuendo   150m   V,6 *
H.MacInnes, R.Birch, P.Judge, R.O'Shea   1969
This is the obvious chimney-groove on the side wall overlooking Broad Gully, right of and below the final gully of Scabbard Chimney. A fine route, low in the grade. Start level with the foot of Dorsal Arete.
1. 35m Climb the chimney-groove to a ledge on the left.
2. Continue up to an overhung bay.
3. 25m Exit from the bay by an awkward chimney on the right and climb easily up rightwards to below the upper wall.

Dorsal Arete, II, Stob Coire nan Lochan. Climber Rosie Goolden

4. Traverse right beneath a hanging chimney until steep cracks lead back left into the chimney above the overhang. The chimney leads to easier ground.

6 Broad Gully   150m   I *
A popular ascent route, which also provides the main means of descent. There are times when the alternative descent may be safer.

7 Dorsal Arete   120m   II ***
J.Black, T.Shepherd, J.Allingham, J.Bradburn   28 Jan 1951
Starting from just inside Broad Gully, this excellent and popular route takes the rib between it and Forked Gully. Gain the slabby buttress, then climb a groove for two pitches, moving up right to where the arete narrows and becomes more defined with steep sides falling away on both flanks. The Arete Pitch follows and although it can be avoided by a rising traverse up its left side, it provides the highlight of the climb and should not be missed. An awkward, steep step with good holds gains the narrow and exposed crest where the confident will stand and walk, whilst others may prefer to climb 'a cheval'. The upper rocks are passed on their right side by a gully-groove. There are four other starts on the broad lower buttress at (III) to (IV).

STOB COIRE NAN LOCHAN
Right

9. Twisting Grooves	IV,5 **	13. Chimney Route	VI,6 ***
10. Twisting Gully	III,4 ****	14. Tilt	VI,7 ***
11. Twisting Gully R. Fork	IV,5 **	15. SC Gully	III ***
12. Moonshadow	IV,5 **	16. East Face Dir. Dir.	VII,7 ***

17. Central Grooves	VII,7 ****	20. Evening Citizen	V,7 **
18. Raeburn's Route	IV,4 ***	21. Intruder	V,7 *
19. NC Gully	II *	22. Crest Route	V,6 ***

Twisting Gully, III,4, Stob Coire nan Lochan

8 Forked Gully 140m I *

On the right side of the buttress with Dorsal Arete is another wide snow gully which slants slightly left. It is steeper than Broad Gully and also has a right fork with an ice pitch (Grade II/III).

9 Twisting Grooves 130m IV,5 **

W.Sproul, T.Carruthers 11 Mar 1962

A direct route up the groove-line in the left side of the frontal face of the small, narrow buttress to the left of the access cleft of Twisting Gully.

1. 50m Climb the long, tapering groove which steepens at the top to gain easier ground and continue to a belay just left of the short chimney of Twisting Gully.
2. 20m The chimney leads to a belay at the base of a fault in the upper buttress.
3. 50m Climb the fault, then a narrow chimney and continue up easy ground to belay at blocks on the crest.
4. 10m Climb to the top, the cornice is usually small.

10 Twisting Gully 140m III,4 ****

W.H Murray, D.Scott, J.Cortland-Simpson Dec 1946

One of the classic Scottish winter climbs, taking the gully running up the left side of South Buttress. Start at the foot of a small, narrow buttress.

1. 20m Climb up right into a deep recess and belay on the left wall below where the gully is split in two by a rib.
2. 35m Climb the chimney on the left to where it steepens, gain a ledge on the left wall (crux), then traverse left along this to the crest. Make an awkward mantelshelf and move easily up to belay beside a short chimney.
3. 40m Climb the chimney, then move up and right beneath a small buttress to the rocks beneath the final snow fan.
4. 45m If in doubt over the stability of the steep slope under the cornice, either curve around right and move over onto the rocks of South Buttress, or move up left onto the crest to break through the cornice.

Twisting Gully Right Fork   130m   IV,5 **
J.R.Marshall, I.D.Haig   Jan 1958

A splendid climb, which requires ice. Start from the belay on the left wall inside the gully recess.

1. 50m Move up right and climb the icefall to the right of the normal route, then follow easy ground to a point where Moonshadow breaks out right up a big corner.
2. 40m Continue over another steepening and go up to belay on the left of the entrance to a short, shallow chimney.
3. 40m Finish as for Twisting Gully.

Moonshadow   130m   IV,5 **
K.V.Crocket, C.Stead   30 Jan 1972

A good sustained combination, finishing up the prominent right-trending corner on the left flank of the buttress.

1. 50m As for Twisting Gully Right Fork.
2. 35m The corner starts on the right wall, and is climbed to a thread belay.
3. 45m Continue up the groove past a chockstone to the top.

Chimney Route   125m   VI,6 ***

The steep chimney overlooking the start of Twisting Gully gives a first-rate climb. The chimney can choke with ice making it difficult to protect.

1. 25m Climb steeply up the chimney.
2. 45m Continue up, then move slightly right on turfy ground to the left end of the Upper Terrace. On this pitch it would also be possible to head straight up into the wide chimney of Inclination, which is separated from the terrace by a huge fin of rock.
3. and 4. 55m Now follow Tilt, up its wall and V-groove.

Tilt   140m   VI,7 ***
M.Hamilton, K.Spence, A.Taylor   20 Jan 1980

Excellent sustained climbing. Start immediately left of the buttress crest at a line leading to a chimney some 20m up.

1. 40m Climb cracks and ledges to reach the chimney, then climb this to the crest.
2. 25m Follow the groove above and once above an overhang, move right onto the wall and climb to a huge flake.
3. 20m Climb grooves to the Upper Terrace.
4. 25m Move left along the terrace. Climb a wall to make an awkward entry into a V-groove and finish up this.
5. 30m Easy climbing leads to the top.

SC Gully   150m   III ***
P.D.Baird, E.Leslie, H.Fynes-Clinton   Mar 1934

Cleaving a line through impressive rock scenery between the tallest cliffs of South and Central Buttresses, this is one of the classic gully climbs of Glen Coe. Normally there is a short ice pitch near the start, avoidable by mixed climbing further left. A second pitch continues up steep snow in the narrowing gully to a cul-de-sac. The

SC Gully, III, Stob Coire nan Lochan. Climber Jo George

next pitch, the crux, takes the icefall curving its way up the right-hand corner. Reach this by an awkward right traverse to a ramp, then climb the icefall, which may be some 20m high, to the easy upper section of the gully. A long run-out may be required to reach a belay. More snow leads to a corniced exit. The route can be much harder in lean conditions.

16 East Face Direct Direct   110m   VII,7 ***

M.Hamilton, R.Anderson   20 Mar 1982; variations D.Kerr, I.Sharpe   26 Feb 2000; G Robertson, P.Benson   2005

A magnificent climb with a number of options depending on time and conditions. Overlooking the entrance to SC Gully, at mid-height on the side wall of Central Buttress are two, parallel, shallow chimney-gully systems rising either side of a lower chimney that ends at a shallow recess below a bulge. The left-hand one terminates at the headwall below a corner and the right-hand one continues to the crest. The direct line is the best but the right-hand line is easier and in climbable condition more often.

1. 20m Climb the chimney, then move left to a pedestal.

2. 15m Move back right and climb past the left end of a roof in the corner to good belays in a shallow recess. From here **East Face Route** (VI,7) offers a good route by moving right around the edge with difficulty to climb the right-hand, parallel chimney-gully.

3. 40m Move left and climb the main fault on steep ice (harder without) to

another recess and pull out of this with difficulty, then continue steeply to easier ground below the headwall. From here **East Face Direct** (VII,7) makes a tricky rising traverse rightwards to join Ordinary Route.

4. 35m The superb corner-crack provides a fitting finish.

7 Central Grooves   130m   VII,7 ****
K.Spence, J. McKenzie   Feb 1983

A brilliant and sustained route up the obvious diedre which springs from the toe of Central Buttress. One of the best winter climbs in Scotland.

1. 30m Climb the corner to small ledges.
2. 25m Continue up the corner to ledges on the crest.
3. 50m Follow the grooves above, passing left of a conspicuous overhang, to finish on a broad terrace.
4. 25m Easy climbing leads to the top.

8 Raeburn's Route   150m   IV,4 ***
H.Raeburn, Dr and Mrs C.Inglis Clark   Apr 1907

An excellent climb with fine situations. Start in the small bay some 10m right of the buttress crest, beneath a tapering chimney-fault, in the angle between the main face and the projecting spur on the right. Climb the chimney to a cul-de-sac and exit out right to reach easier ground leading to a short groove, then the crest. A long pitch. Another start takes the more open turfy face just to the right. The Tower lies a short way above and is climbed by a chimney up its back right-hand side. Climb the slabby wall above, awkward in deep snow, and continue to a steepening which is turned on the right. Go up and left to the crest and finish more easily by short stepped sections.

9 NC Gully   180m   II *

This gully splits Central and North Buttresses. It is normally a straightforward snow climb with a small cornice but it can sometimes form a short pitch.

10 Evening Citizen   95m   V,7 **
K.Spence, H.MacInnes, A.Thompson   1971

The obvious big groove running up the left side of the roofed pillar overlooking NC Gully on North Buttress.

1. 25m Start in the gully and climb grooves up and left to belay at a wall.

Raeburn's Route, IV,4, Stob Coire nan Lochan. Climber Rob Milne

Evening Citizen, V,7, Stob Coire nan Lochan. Climber Viv Scott

2. 25m A short corner leads to the main corner which is climbed to a belay.
3. 25m Continue to the top of the buttress.
4. 20m Breach a short wall at a number of places and climb to the top.

21 Intruder 100m V,7 *
R.Anderson, G.Nicoll   14 Feb 1988

This follows the slimmer right-hand groove, right of the roofed pillar, **Para Andy** (90m VI,7) is the groove to the left. Start at the lowest rocks.
1. 15m Move up left and climb to the base of the groove.
2. 25m Climb the groove to a flake, then continue to a ledge at the foot of a large flake.
3. 35m Gain the groove up on the left and climb this to the top of a pinnacle. Move up, then go right to climb a short groove and traverse right to belay by an obvious perched block.
4. 25m Easy climbing leads to the top.

22 Crest Route 110m V,6 ***
M.Hamilton, R.Anderson   24 Nov 1985

A little gem taking the crest on the right side of North Buttress, between the east

and north faces. Start at the lowest rocks.
1. 35m Move right, climb broken stepped ground to a short wall, then climb a crack to a pedestal.
2. 30m Climb the flake-crack above, then go right across a slab and climb a groove to the crest. Step left at a large spike to a ledge level with a pinnacle.
3. 20m Regain the groove-crack and follow this directly up the crest to belay by an obvious perched block. A variation returns left around the crest after regaining the groove to climb a thin crack just to its left. It is also possible to move left to climb the pinnacle and finish as for Intruder.
4. 25m Finish more easily.

AONACH DUBH

Map p62

This is the north-west ridge of Stob Coire nan Lochan and the right-hand of the Three Sisters.

EAST FACE - FAR EASTERN BUTTRESS

(NN 154 556)   Alt 690m   South-East facing

The East Face of Aonach Dubh overlooks the approach to Stob Coire nan Lochan and this slabby buttress lies high on the left side of the face, just right of the stream crossing, and is passed on the final ascent to the corrie floor of Stob Coire nan Lochan. It is useful for a short day, or when the higher cliffs are buried.

Approach: As for Stob Coire nan Lochan to the stream crossing (see p81), then easily up right.

Descent: Traverse across to the floor of Stob Coire nan Lochan.

Eastern Slant   120m   III,4 *
R.Anderson, C.Anderson, R.Milne   16 Feb 1992
The obvious corner-fault and rising traverse line in the angle between the steeper right-hand section and easier angled left-hand section.
1. 40m Climb the corner to a ledge on the right.
2. 40m Traverse left beneath the chimney, go around the edge, then pull up and left across a slab to a short corner. Pull out left and belay.
3. 40m Continue the left bias, up and across a fault-line, then climb a groove to finish up a short chimney.

AONACH DUBH - Far Eastern Buttress

1. Eastern Slant   III,4 *
2. Orient Express   IV,5 *

GLEN COE

Orient Express, IV,5, Aonach Dubh Far Eastern Buttress. Climber Rob Milne

2 Orient Express   85m   IV,5 *
R.Anderson, C.Anderson, R.Milne 2 Feb 1991
In the centre of the cliff, formed in the angle between the faces, is a thin iced chimney.
1. 40m Ice left of the corner leads to the belay of Eastern Slant.
2. 25m Move up left and climb the steep, iced chimney to a ledge.
3. 20m Continue to the top and a large boulder.

WEST FACE

(NN 145 555)   Alt 550m   West facing

The great West Face of Aonach Dubh flanks the entrance to Coire nam Beithach and dominates the lower reaches of Glen Coe above Loch Achtriochtan.

Weather and Conditions: The face does have some drainage lines, but the majority of the climbs require a build-up of snow and ice, so it can take time to come into ideal condition. Due to the low altitude of the face, in recent years some of the climbs have not formed and a number have not been described.

Approach: Begin where the main road crosses the River Coe (NN 138 566) at the junction of the main road and the old road leading to the Clachaig Inn. Parking is at a premium here so be considerate. Walk across the bridge, taking care of fast moving traffic, climb a stile and follow the path which gradually steepens as the prominent waterfalls are approached. The path zigzags its way up the right side of the falls heading towards Stob Coire nam Beith.
  Strike off left below the lowest waterfall, cross the stream and gain the lower slopes of Dinnertime Buttress. No.2 Gully is easily crossed at this point, giving access to the grassy lower tier of B Buttress, or any of the gullies further right.

Climbs on the right side of the face can be gained more directly from where the path levels out above the waterfalls.

Descent: (i) Safest is to cross over and descend via Coire nan Lochan, particularly in bad weather.
(ii) No.2 Gully. It is difficult to miss the gully since it has a wide re-entrant. When it steepens below Middle Ledge, traverse onto Dinnertime Buttress. The rocks of both gully and buttress are thereby avoided. The Rake provides an easy way left into No.2 Gully from some routes.
(iii) Traverse towards Stob Coire nam Beith and descend into the corrie.

Layout: The face is best seen from the old Glencoe road near the Clachaig Inn. It is a complex face, divided vertically by six gullies, forming distinct buttresses cut horizontally by two ledges. The lower, narrow ledge is Middle Ledge accessed from the left, while The Rake is the upper, broad ledge.

The gullies are numbered 1 to 6 from left to right with the most prominent being No.2 (I), which runs up the left side of the face to the col between Aonach Dubh and Stob Coire nan Lochan. To its left is Dinnertime Buttress (originally A Buttress) and to its right the buttresses continue B to F, divided by the gullies No.3 to No.6.

Dinnertime Buttress   335m   II *
The leftmost buttress between No.1 and No.2 Gullies provides a good poor weather route and an alternative approach to Stob Coire nan Lochan. Various options exist on reaching the final rocky section, which can become avalanche prone.

The Screen   75m   IV,5 **
D.Bathgate, J.Brumfitt   Feb 1965
The icefall which forms over the lowest tier right of No.3 Gully gives a good outing when combined with C-D Scoop or The Smear. It does not form as readily as it used to. Climb to an icicle recess, traverse right, then move left above the icicles to the final steep runnel.

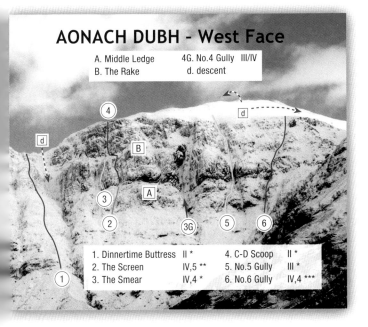

AONACH DUBH – West Face

A. Middle Ledge
B. The Rake

4G. No.4 Gully   III/IV
d. descent

1. Dinnertime Buttress	II *	4. C-D Scoop	II *
2. The Screen	IV,5 **	5. No.5 Gully	III *
3. The Smear	IV,4 *	6. No.6 Gully	IV,4 ***

GLEN COE

3 The Smear   75m   IV,4 *
I.Clough, I.Duckworth, F.Wells, R.York   26 Mar 1969
On C Buttress, just right of No.3 Gully where it cuts the middle tier, this icefall provides a continuation to The Screen.

4 C-D Scoop   150m   II *
D.Bathgate, J.Brumfitt   Feb 1965
The gully right of No.3 Gully, rising above Middle Ledge, can be climbed on its own, or following an ascent of The Screen. Two short ice pitches lead to The Rake. A good finish, giving one further pitch, is by the hidden right branch of the gully on the left, the continuation of No.3 Gully.

5 No.5 Gully   300m   III *
A. Fyffe, C. MacInnes, N. Clough   18th Feb 1969
Climb an obvious short, shallow, slanting gully to the left of the hanging icicle of **Elliot's Downfall** (105m VI,6) which now rarely forms. Where the gully steepens, move up right to a ridge left of the gully bed. Traverse right into the gully and climb an ice pitch to the easier upper section. There may be an easy angled 45m ice pitch here.

6 No.6 Gully   240m   IV,4 ***
D. Munro, P. Smith   30th Mar 1951
The rightmost gully on the face is a classic. Normally, two ice pitches lead to the crux, a large icefall at the level of Middle Ledge. There is a small stance about 15m up the icefall, otherwise a long pitch ensues. At the top of the gully there is a small bay and a choice of finishes. A traverse off right above steep ground gains the corrie beneath Stob Coire nam Beith.

STOB COIRE NAM BEITH

(NN139 546)   Alt 700m   North to North-East facing   Map p62

This shapely peak, the north-west top of Bidean, dominates the view from Glen Coe over Loch Achtriochtan. It is a huge, conical mass some 350m high, riven with buttresses and gullies.

Weather and Conditions: Fairly reliable but due to its snow holding capabilities large amounts do accumulate and in such circumstances care should be taken.

Approach: As for the West Face of Aonach Dubh to the waterfalls (see p92). Above these the path levels out and crosses a slabby section (if iced, it may be easier to descend to stream level) to reach a fork in the streams. Cross the right branch, head up the side of the vague central branch, then go around the top of a rocky bluff and left to the corrie floor (1hr 30mins). The vague central branch of the stream leads to Summit Gully.

The path following the right branch continues to the Bealach An t-Sròn, a col on the ridge between Stob Coire nam Beith and An t-Sròn. Lying at a height of 650m, the main corrie floor is occupied by some large boulders and old fence posts, a useful reference point in poor visibility.

Descent: Surest is to go down the cairned west ridge to the col between Stob Coire nam Beith and An t-Sròn. In poor visibility this descent can be confusing, especially when approached from Bidean nam Bian. From the summit cairn of Stob Coire nam Beith a ridge drops gently northwards, appearing to offer a descent. However, this actually heads off into the middle of the mountain. Instead, go west from the cairn around the broad head of Summit Gully (which is only some 5m from the summit) and descend the west ridge. The ridge levels off and becomes sharply defined where it curves around the head of the subsidiary corrie. Continue to the Bealach An t-Sròn, where a small hump separates the two lowest points (NN 135 547). From the col, head eastwards into the subsidiary corrie and go down to the main path.

Descent can also be made from the convergence of Buttresses 2 to 4 by heading towards Bidean nam Bian, contouring the upper easy part of Arch Gully, then

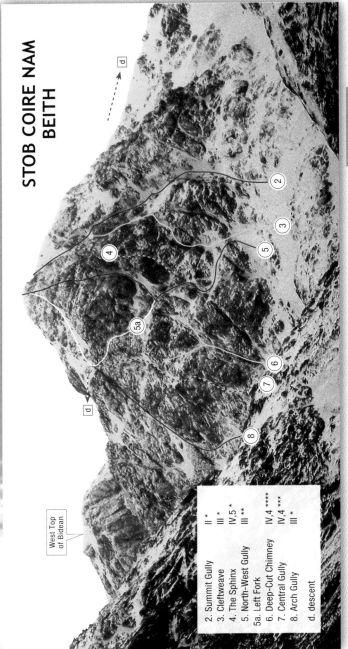

STOB COIRE NAM BEITH

West Top of Bidean

2. Summit Gully   II *
3. Cleftweave   III *
4. The Sphinx   IV,5 *
5. North-West Gully   III **
5a. Left Fork
6. Deep-Cut Chimney   IV,4 ****
7. Central Gully   IV,4 ***
8. Arch Gully   III *
d. descent

Deep-Cut Chimney, IV,4, Stob Coire nam Beith

crossing easy ground above No.1 Buttress and Zero Buttress, to drop into the basin beneath the West Top of Bidean nam Bian. Easy slopes lead back to the corrie. This is useful if time is pressing.

Layout: Approaching up the Allt Coire nam Beithach, the most obvious feature is Summit Gully, running up left of the right-hand skyline. On its right is West Buttress and on its left is a buttress formed by Pyramid and Sphinx Buttresses. Left of these, the shallow North-West Gully wanders up and left. Next is No.4 Buttress, with the prominent, Deep-Cut Chimney running up its left side. Left of this is No.3 Buttress, the highest and broadest on the mountain, whose principal feature is the shallow but continuous Central Gully. Beyond this and hidden from view is Arch Gully. Climbs are described from right to left, generally as met.

1 Hidden Gully   350m   IV,4 *
L.S.Lovat, W.J.R.Greaves   13 Feb 1955
A fine route taking the narrow, twisting gully up the right flank of the mountain. This is well up right from the lowest rocks, above a large rock island at the entrance to the subsidiary corrie on the right. The gully remains hidden until above the rock island. A 20m snow cone leads to a cave, then climb the icy left wall. Easy snow

for 30m leads to another cave; avoid this on the left by a very short ice pitch. Snow with occasional ice and a gradual increase in angle leads in 90m to a saddle above a rock rib in the middle of the gully. Beyond, the gully steepens and narrows, and 25m of snow leads to an overhang and a short chimney. A short distance above, a rock rib divides the very narrow gully into two narrower exits. Take the left-hand option, a long, slanting open chimney with a steep exit (35m). Finish in 150m or so by the right-bounding ridge of Summit Gully.

Summit Gully   450m   II *
This is the big gully which runs up left of the right-hand skyline and trends up left to a point just right of the summit cairn. It starts to the right of the ridge formed by the Pyramid and should not be (though it often is!) confused with North-West Gully on the left. From below, Summit Gully appears the only deep and obvious gully on the mountain. The vague central branch of the approach stream leads directly to it. The gully combines length with good scenery. There may be a short ice pitch near the foot and despite occasional forks the route is fairly obvious. High up, a cave pitch seems to bar the way and often provides a reasonable pitch, otherwise turn it on the right. Much higher, a prominent rock rib forms an island in the gully. Avalanche conditions can occur on this climb.

Cleftweave   390m   III *
B.Clarke, A.Strachan   1972
Start as for North-West Gully, then climb a series of gullies which wind up between the Pyramid and The Sphinx to a snowfield overlooking Summit Gully. Here, a short, steep ice wall on the left leads to another gully system. Follow this to a small amphitheatre, move into a short gully on the right where an ice pitch gains the summit slopes.

The Sphinx   135m   IV,5 *
J.R.Marshall, I.Douglas   12 Jan 1958
North-West Gully's right side is defined by two buttresses set one above the other forming the ridge left of Summit Gully. The lower, wedge like buttress is the Pyramid and the upper buttress is The Sphinx. Climb the lower part of North-West Gully and move right onto the upper buttress. About halfway up the buttress there is a cave. From a shattered wall below and slightly left of this, climb to a small basin under the cave and traverse right to a platform under the steep upper rocks. Climb walls for 20m to reach a chimney, then gain a little recess 3m up to the right where a pinnacle-flake on the right-hand edge gains a long easier climb to the top.

North-West Gully   450m   III **
G.T.Glover, Wordsell   Apr 1906
Sometimes mistaken for Summit Gully, this is the shallow gully which starts right of No.4 Buttress and just left of the ridge formed by the Pyramid. It wanders up and left to the convergence of the main buttresses well below the summit. The scenery is good and there is usually at least one pitch, even by the easiest line. Taking in the ice left of the normal start, can increase the grade to IV,4. From below the Pyramid go up and left into the gully where easy snow leads up past Sphinx Buttress to a fork. The left fork continues without difficulty to the convergence of the buttresses. The right fork leads in 80m to a second fork where the buttress splitting the gully is taken by **The Mummy** (60m IV,5). At this junction the left fork is better and may give a short pitch leading to the shoulder. A steep wall left of the shoulder gives the crux of the climb. Easier climbing above leads to the summit. Avalanche conditions can occur on this climb.

Deep-Cut Chimney   450m   IV,4 ****
W.M.Mackenzie, W.H.Murray   7 Apr 1939
The prominent, narrow chimney-gully dividing No.4 and No.3 Buttresses provides a classic climb. In its time, it was one of the hardest winter routes in the Central Highlands. The line proper ends 120m up, in a small amphitheatre, normally reached in three or four short ice pitches. The true line is then by the left fork, which

will be difficult if thinly iced. The right fork allows an escape to easier ground. Both routes join at the convergence of the buttress where some distance of easier calf burning ground leads to the summit for the full four star experience. This can be avoided by contouring the upper part of Arch Gully and traversing off left.

7 Central Gully   450m   IV,4 ***
J.Clarkson, J.Waddell   12 Jan 1958

One of the best winter climbs on the mountain, taking the shallow gully up the centre of No.3 Buttress. It is a natural ice trap and a large icefall can form at the start. From just left of the lowest rocks climb the left side of the icefall (the right side is an optional start) to gain the gully. Follow this with continual interest up several steep pitches to easier ground.

8 Arch Gully   240m   III *
J.H.B.Bell, C.M.Allen   Dec 1933

The gully running up the left side of the main mass of rock. It is set back and hidden until the lowest rocks have been turned. The Arch is a chockstone in the lower section, which generally banks out. Above, the gully narrows to form three chimney pitches, the first of which often banks out. Either traverse off left, or continue easily to the summit.

BIDEAN NAM BIAN - WEST

(NN 143 542)   Alt 1150m   North to North-West Facing   Map p62 Diagram p103

This west side of this majestic mountain has two distinctive buttresses, Diamond and Church Door, located just below its summit. A third and generally hidden cliff, the West Top, lies to their right.

Weather and Conditions. Due to the height and the mixed nature of the terrain conditions are fairly reliable although westerly winds and thaws can strip things surprisingly quickly.

Approach: From the corrie floor beneath Stob Coire nam Beith (see p94), follow the right side of the stream, go around a rocky spur to a shallow basin, then continue up slopes to another shallow basin. Diamond and Church Door Buttresses are directly ahead up the slope whilst up on the right, through a gateway formed by a rock sentinel and the shoulder of Stob Coire nam Beith, lie the slopes beneath the West Top. These highest buttresses are about 2hrs 30mins from the road.

Descent: (i) Carefully beneath Church Door Buttress from the col between Bidean nam Bian and its West Top.
(ii) The north-east ridge to the col (NN 146 545) between Bidean nam Bian and Stob Coire nan Lochan, then down into Coire nam Beith.
(iii) From the col (NN 140 543) between the West Top and Stob Coire nam Beith, then beneath the cliffs of the West Top into the corrie.
(iv) Continue over Stob Coire nam Beith and go down its west ridge to the col at the Bealach An t-Sròn (NN 135 547) where easy slopes lead into the corrie. In dangerous snow conditions this alternative is by far the safest. In poor visibility, refer to the more detailed description given on p94.

Layout: Diamond Buttress is the left-hand of the two buttress and Church Door Buttress is the impressive right-hand buttress. The buttresses are split by Central Gully, at the foot of which sits Collie's Pinnacle, beneath which there is normally a good gearing-up spot on a snow ledge. To the right is the West Top (NN 141 543) and a line of cliffs below this slants into Coire nam Beith below the slope running up under Church Door Buttress. The cliffs and the routes are described from left to right.

DIAMOND BUTTRESS

1 North Route Direct   210m   III
L.S.Lovat, W.Harrison   13 Mar 1955

BIDEAN NAM BIAN - WEST
Diamond & Church Door Buttresses

1. North Route Direct   III
2. Direct Route   V,6 **
3. Central Gully   I **
3a. Central Gully Variation   II

4. Un Poco Loco   VII,7 ***
6. Flake Route Right-hand   V,7 **
7. West Chimney   IV,6 ****

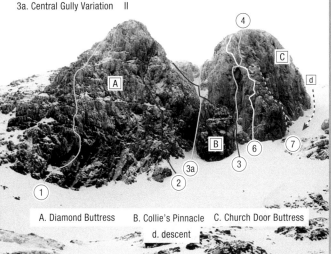

A. Diamond Buttress   B. Collie's Pinnacle   C. Church Door Buttress

d. descent

This follows the left edge of the buttress. Start below an obvious scoop at the lowest rocks at the left end of the buttress. The scoop swings up right onto the face and eventually overhangs where it splits a projecting spur. Climb the arete on the right, then make a short steep horizontal traverse round an edge into another scoop. Snow covered slabs and an awkward crack lead to a platform above the overhang of the first scoop. A long traverse left leads back to the crest, then follow this to the top. The original route (II) skirts around the left edge of the buttress by chimneys and scoops.

Direct Route   150m   V,6 **

J.McLean, M.Noon   Jan 1959

This route takes the obvious line on the right side of Diamond Buttress, a system of grooves leading up and right to the right end of the central girdling ledge. Continue by more grooves going up and right to emerge on the right-hand edge not far below the summit.

Central Gully   180m   I/II **

N.Collie, G.A.Solly, J.Collier   Mar 1894

The gully separating Diamond and Church Door Buttresses provides an interesting and scenic approach to the summit of Bidean. It is divided at its foot by a small buttress, Collie's Pinnacle. The easiest line (I) is by the right-hand start to the right of the pinnacle where a lack of snow can provide an awkward move, otherwise there should be no complications. Where the gully forks stay left. The more difficult line (II) is by the left-hand start, where a lack of build-up can provide more difficulty, then by the right fork about 75m above the pinnacle. Prone to avalanche at times.

Un Poco Loco Direct, VII,7, Church Door Buttress. Climber Es Tresidder

CHURCH DOOR BUTTRESS

4 Un Poco Loco 165m VII,7 ***
A.Cave, M.Duff Mar 1994; S.McFarlane, A.Clark 26 Feb 2006
Start at a groove with twin cracks, 6m left of Crypt Route.
1. 30m Climb the groove to a ledge on the right and continue by cracks to a belay 12m below the Arch.
2. 35m Step left, then go directly below The Arch by steep cracks to the left end of the span, swing into the groove on the left and climb to a ledge. Belay in the centre of The Arch. A direct variation climbs a shallow corner to thread the hole in The Arch.
3. 25m Climb directly above by a groove with a flake-crack, then trend gradually left.
4. 40m Climb more easily to the top.

5 Crypt Route 150m V,6 ***
H.MacInnes and party 1960
An atmospheric and entertaining route which finds a way up the very deep chimney in the alcove formed in the great gothic face overlooking Central Gully. Various subterranean alternatives are blocked and only one line remains. Climb Central Gully to beneath the chimney; the wide crack in the enormous flake to the right is taken by Flake Route.

1. 10m Gain the chimney.
2. 20m Climb it for 10m until it becomes smooth. Squeeze in leftwards behind a small chockstone and go along a passage (headtorch useful). Return back out above.
3. 30m Go up amongst chockstones, then inwards beyond a narrow chimney on the left until a strenuous move gains a second narrow chimney on the left. Chimney upwards to where a small hole provides a route outside (helmets and gear will have to be removed).
4. 20m Go up a smooth chimney to a ledge right of The Arch, then climb back left for 10m and belay on its top.
5. and 6. 70m Traverse left across The Arch and finish via 'Raeburn's Chimney', as for Flake Route and West Chimney.

5 Flake Route Right-hand   190m   V,7 **
G.R.Scott, F.W.Cope   18 Mar 1942; R.Anderson, R.Milne   26 Feb 2005
Climbs the right side of the huge flake overlooking Central Gully. Start at the toe of the buttress, at the entrance to the right-hand branch of the gully.
1. 40m Climb a short way up the gully and just below a chockstone climb a series of short, stepped corners on the right wall to snow ledges. The overall grade of this route could be brought in line with its neighbours by gaining this point from the gully on the left. Continue to a belay in the wide chimney where it forks.
2. 25m Climb the widening left fork over chockstones, then go beneath huge jammed blocks into a chimney behind the flake and emerge on the other side. Move up onto the top of the jammed blocks. **Flake Route** (130m IV,6) gains the same point by climbing the left side of the flake from further up the gully.

Crypt Route, V,6, Church Door Buttress. Climber Es Tresidder

West Chimney, IV,6, Church Door Buttress. Climber Rob Milne

3. 25m Step awkwardly up right, then go up rightwards across the top of a groove and belay over on the right where West Chimney emerges from its hole.
4. 30m Climb up left, take the crack in the sidewall, then continue to the jammed blocks at the start of the Arch and step down to belay.
5. and 6. 70m Finish up Raeburn's Chimney as for West Chimney.

7 West Chimney 170m IV,6 ****
A.Fyffe, H.MacInnes 8 Feb 1969
An immensely satisfying climb. Start up right from Central Gully, in a bay formed to the right of the spur projecting from the base of the buttress.
1. 45m Gain a ramp come chimney-line and follow it under a Damoclean chockstone, then climb over two more chockstones into a bay at a cul-de-sac.
2. 15m Find a tunnel up on the left, then burrow in and up to emerge mole like onto a ledge. This may expend considerable time and effort. Those of a masochistic nature may wish to wear their sac! It is possible to climb on the outside, but the tunnel is easier, more fun and shouldn't be missed, even if a little excavation is required.
3. 40m Move right, back to the chimney-line, then follow it up and under a chockstone to its top. Traverse left across ledges and boulders, then step down around the edge to a fine perch on the Arch – don't fall down the hole!
4. 30m Traverse the Arch, to the base of the shallow 'Raeburn's Chimney'. Some difficult moves entering the chimney are followed by some entertaining ones around its chockstone. Continue to ledges and move left.
5. 40m Shallow icy grooves lead to easier ground.

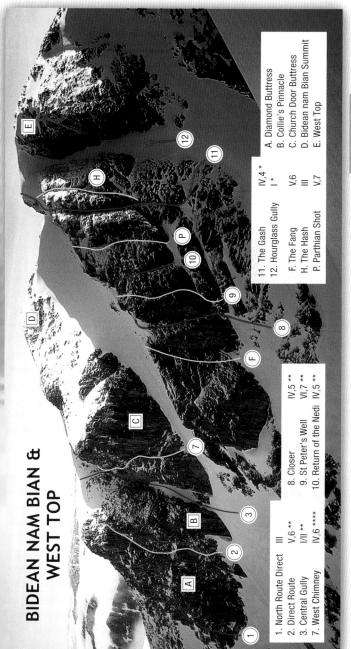

BIDEAN NAM BIAN & WEST TOP

1. North Route Direct   III
2. Direct Route   V,6 **
3. Central Gully   I/II **
7. West Chimney   IV,6 ****

8. Closer   IV,5 **
9. St Peter's Well   VI,7 **
10. Return of the Nedi   IV,5 **

11. The Gash   IV,4 *
12. Hourglass Gully   I *

F. The Fang   V,6
H. The Hash   III
P. Parthian Shot   V,7

A. Diamond Buttress
B. Collie's Pinnacle
C. Church Door Buttress
D. Bidean nam Bian Summit
E. West Top

WEST TOP

8 Closer 75m IV,5 **
C.Dale, A.Kassyk, D.Talbot 18 Feb 1982
The lowest rocks form a prominent, compact buttress, Bishop's Buttress. Right of which is a deep cleft, **The Fang** (75m V,6). This route takes the prominent steep chimney around to the right, with an icefall at its base. Climb the icefall to gain the chimney, then follow this over bulges and chockstones to a cave recess. Continue over bulges and chockstones to the top.

9 St Peter's Well 50m VI,7 **
B.Davison, S.Kennedy, D.Wilkinson 13 Jan 2001
This is the left-hand of three corner-lines on the steep wall right of Closer. Start by a short steep groove on the left (or from a ledge reached by a traverse in from the right). Climb the corner passing two distinct crux sections, one at half-height and the other at the exit from the corner. Finish up icy grooves.

10 Return of the Nedi 90m IV,5 **
S.Kennedy, A.Nelson 29 Dec 2000
A good sustained mixed route taking the prominent central corner 10m right of and slightly higher than St Peter's Well. The right-hand of the three corners is **Parthian Shot** (90m V,7). Gain a ledge from near The Gash, then traverse left to the start of the corner. Climb directly up the corner and continuation groove to easy ground. Finish up and right, close to the top of The Gash.

11 The Gash 120m IV,4 *
I.Clough, M.Hadley, M.Large 22 Mar 1959
Further up, left of Hourglass Gully, is an obvious V shape formed by two gullies. The right-hand one is **The Hash** (120m III). Gain the more prominent left-hand gully by a rising traverse from Hourglass Gully, or more directly from below. A ledge on the right provides a good stance. Climb the steep runnel over several bulges to a large overhanging chockstone, then turn this on the left to reach a cave below a second chockstone. A right traverse leads to easier ground or, if you are of a burrowing nature, find an intriguing through route in the back of the cave to a squeeze exit.

12 Hourglass Gully 120m I *
I.Clough and party Feb 1966
The gully splitting the cliffs below the top gives a steep but straightforward snow climb with perhaps one or two steps. **Dubiety** (110m IV,5) is an iced corner on the right wall.

AONACH EAGACH

Map p62
The distinctive notched ridge opposite the Bidean Massif contains the mountains Am Bodach (NN 168 580, 943m), Meall Dearg (NN 161 584, 953m) and Sgòrr nam Fiannaidh (NN 141 583, 967m), two are Munros. The lofty ridge that links them offers a superb traverse of Alpine proportions.

It is useful to arrange it so that there are two vehicles involved, one being left at the end of the ridge, unless the additional exercise is required! Another option is to possibly use the bus service from Glen Coe village (08.15, 11.50, 14.45 & 19.40, as of 2008) either at the start, or the finish of the traverse. After completion, this entails walking through Glencoe village to the bus stop on the main road, or the car park next to it. This is also a better place to hitch from while waiting for the bus.

Aonach Eagach Ridge 4km II/III ****
An exhilarating expedition in majestic surroundings. Speed is of the essence if a

Aonach Eagach Ridge, II/III

party is to avoid benightment; 5 to 8 hours seems fairly typical for an average party in good conditions. Where a competent party might happily solo, most would prefer to rope up and should certainly not feel embarrassed to do so. A large number of accidents have occurred here and the ridge should not be underestimated. It is certainly not a route for the winter hillwalker.

Start from a small parking area (NN 174 567) at a signpost, about 300m west of the white cottage of Allt-na-reigh. Space is limited here, so park with consideration. Either follow the broad ridge of Am Bodach directly, or go up and right into the corrie to the east, where easy slopes go up and left to the top of Am Bodach. The descent from here involves some tricky down-climbing where a step on the north side is made to move back south and down a short slabby, chimney-corner. Meall Dearg lies ahead and beyond this there is a narrow pinnacled section where there is an awkward slabby descent. The ridge carries on to Stob Coire Leith and then to the final summit, Sgòrr nam Fiannaidh.

Descent: There are no safe descent routes on the Glen Coe side of the ridge between the peaks of Am Bodach and Stob Coire Leith. If a party has run out of daylight it is better to complete, or reverse the traverse. The first reasonable descent route encountered on the traverse is the shallow corrie leading down to Loch Achtriochtan from Sgòrr nam Fiannaidh. The stream in this corrie has a steep pitch low down, avoided on the east. However, the slopes here are very steep, especially low down, and there is a risk of avalanche in soft snow conditions.

A descent directly to the Clachaig Inn, down the west side of the deep gorge of Clachaig Gully is commonly used. However, it is not recommended since great care has to be taken to avoid crags and the gully itself. The best line is difficult to locate from above, especially in poor visibility, and there are some steep and quite exposed sections. Although the lure of a well earned drink is tempting, by far the safest option is to drop down north-west, towards the col beside the Pap of Glencoe from where the road near the Youth Hostel can be gained. It is important that climbers should avoid the fenced off area above the Youth Hostel, which is used for livestock grazing.

BEN NEVIS

The icy North Face of Ben Nevis provides one extreme of the British mountain experience. Virtually the whole face can be plastered in ice to give the superb winter climbing so unique to Scotland. Climbing here is steeped in history, from the epic ascents of the great ridges in the early days, through heroic attempts on Point Five Gully and Zero Gully in the '50s, Smith and Marshall's blitzkrieg in the '60s, to the modern day playground. Here, step cutting became such an obvious limitation that front pointing and the use of curved picks produced an explosion of routes throughout the '70s, inspiring a revolution in Scottish ice climbing which has led to its international popularity.

Maps: OS L41, E392; Harvey Superwalker Ben Nevis; Harvey Mountain Map Ben Nevis (has a 1:12500 plan of the plateau and cliff with buttress names).

SMC Climbers' Guide: *Ben Nevis* (2002)

Mountaineering Huts: CIC Hut (NN 167 722, SMC) is at 680m altitude under the cliffs. The hut is privately owned by the Scottish Mountaineering Club, and bookings must be made well in advance through the hut custodian. Current contact details can be found on the SMC website <www.smc.org.uk>

Accommodation and Amenities: For other information see Lochaber p164.

BEN NEVIS

(NN 166 712)   Alt 1343m   Maps p108, 164

A fine selection of gully climbs contrast the face routes, which are long, bold and exposed, much dependent on conditions and exact choice of line. But also there are the buttresses, not only the classic ridges (which are without equal in Britain), but also mixed climbs in the modern idiom, snowed up rock routes with high technical difficulty. This feast of opportunities provides climbs of all styles at all grades, but if you just feel like a walk, the traverse of the Càrn Mòr Dearg Arete gives a stupendous view of it all.

A **Weather and Conditions:** As the highest massif in the British Isles, with the tallest and most extensive cliffs, it attracts some of the most severe winter weather. Proximity to the western seaboard results in large and frequent variations in temperature which, coupled with high precipitation, leaves even the steepest faces plastered white. Deep thaw followed by rapid freeze transforms the hoar and powder to climbable neve, with runnels of white ice filling the grooves and cracks. These are the famed Ben Nevis conditions, although the recent warming of the climate can produce excessive thaws and leave little left to freeze. So conditions have to be watched carefully, assisted by reports on the Internet which like weather forecasts, cannot always be taken literally.

The Ben has less turf than the Cairngorms or some of the crags on the nearby Aonachs, so early season climbing has been less practised. This is partly due to the long walk in and limited daylight, but some mixed routes are proving amenable under powder, and have better protection than in icier conditions. Optimum conditions for the face climbs that require freeze-thaw, may not occur until March or April. The ridges, however, can give enjoyable struggles on rocks plastered with powder as early as October. The altitude of the foot of the Orion Face is higher than the summits of most other Scottish mountains, and the whole of Indicator Wall and Gardyloo Buttress lie above 1200m. Once the major ice lines have formed, they are quite resilient to thaw and some high routes may remain in good condition into May. In contrast, some of the lower routes, particularly the ice smears around Càrn Dearg Buttress, require prolonged periods of frost to form, are most often in condition January or February and they disappear very rapidly during a thaw.

Often the weather should be the deciding factor whether to visit the Ben. Once into mid-season, there will normally be a suitable route in condition somewhere on the mountain, provided the weather is not too stormy and the temperature is below zero. Walking in with a specific target should be reserved for those with local knowledge.

The Ben is not a good choice if avalanches threaten, as there are no safe routes. Clearly some will be safer than others but folk have even been killed by a huge avalanche while walking up the Allt a' Mhuilinn. Despite the justified notoriety of the Castle Area, Observatory Gully is perhaps the commonest site for avalanches, but the upper part of Coire na Ciste is also bad and snow conditions should be monitored on approach. It is also worth mentioning that the approach slopes here are also of a scale not found elsewhere in Scotland, and a slip is likely to be disastrous. It is best to don crampons and helmet, and get out an axe, as soon as snow is reached after passing the CIC Hut.

Layout: The north-east face of Ben Nevis can be divided conveniently into four sectors by North-East Buttress (the skyline buttress on the approach), Tower Ridge (just above the CIC Hut) and Càrn Dearg Buttress (with its vertical rock face).

Sector 1: Beyond (above) North-East Buttress and unseen from the approach are Coire Leis and the Little Brenva Face.

Sector 2: Between Tower Ridge and North-East Buttress is the massive slope of Observatory Gully, with Tower and Gardyloo Gullies at its head. Observatory Ridge descending part way down the slope is flanked by Point Five and Zero Gullies. Left again is the huge Orion Face, with the Minus Gullies lower down.

Sector 3: Between Càrn Dearg Buttress and Tower Ridge is the expansive Coire na Ciste, with the Trident Buttresses on the right, Creag Coire na Ciste formed between Numbers Four and Three Gullies at the back and The Comb sheltering a subsidiary corrie around Number Two Gully at the back left.

Sector 4: Right of (below) Càrn Dearg Buttress is the Castle Ridge and Castle Gullies area.

Troubleshooting Summary: The following is a brief list of suggestions on what to do when the weather or conditions are poorer than expected, or if big thaws have stripped most of Scotland and the Ben is the last hope:

Poor weather or poor conditions options: Go for routes at a lower level that avoid the summit plateau, but even these may be threatened by avalanche. Slingsby's Chimney; Douglas Boulder and Douglas Gap West Gully; Vanishing Gully; Moonlight Gully Buttress; The Curtain; Macphee's Route.

In late season or after a big thaw and refreeze: Go high! The classic ridges are dependable, although their lower halves may be snow-free (alpine conditions!); Observatory Buttress; Tower Scoop; Good Friday Climb; Indicator Wall; Smith's Route; the easier gullies, assuming safe cornices; Raeburn's Wall; Number Three Gully Buttress area; Creag Coire na Ciste, although there may be huge cornices in late season.

Approach: Aim initially for the CIC Hut (NN 167 722), which is situated at 670m below The Douglas Boulder at the foot of Tower Ridge. The exception is the Castle Ridge and Castle Gullies area, where one would break off right below the Hut. The Hut is privately owned by the SMC, but its walls afford a little shelter and a convenient place for refreshment and gearing up. There are two possible approaches to the Hut from the valley:

1. North Face Car Park: Reach the car park by turning off the A82 at Torlundy (small sign to North Face Car Park), cross the railway bridge (traffic lights) then turn immediately right along a forestry road which leads to the car park (NN 144 763) after 800m. Follow a track from the north end of the car park across a bridge and after 100m take a path on the right to the top of a slope. Don't take the old path which traverses above the golf course, but take a new left branch uphill This is signposted, but having just been built, isn't on the maps. Follow this, with signposts at two forks, to a small dam (NN 147 751) and car park just beyond (access for those who pay a substantial charge, but no weekly payment available; this saves 30mins). Cross a stile and continue up the left bank of the Allt a' Mhuilinn on a fine new path to the Hut. Excellent views of the cliffs are obtained on this approach (2hrs).

2. Glen Nevis Approach via the Tourist Track: From Achintee (NN 126 730), or the Glen Nevis Youth Hostel (NN 128 718), follow the Tourist Track to the broad col between Meall an t-Suidhe and Càrn Dearg. Leave the track above Lochan Meall an t-Suidhe (known as the Halfway Lochan), and continue northwards,

BEN NEVIS

1. From the summit trig point follow 230° Grid for 150m.

2. Then follow 280° Grid for 800m to clear the plateau and gain the Tourist Track and Red Burn.

Plateau area

Grid North

N

CIC Hut

Allt a' Mhuilinn

Douglas Boulder

Observatory Ridge

Observatory Gully

North-East Buttress

Càrn Mòr Dearg Arête

Coire Leis

Coire Eoghainn

Summit to top of Gardyloo Gully

230° Grid

280° Grid

Gardyloo Gully to Tourist Track & Red Burn area

Number Two Gully

Coire na Ciste

Number Three Gully

Number Four Gully

Number Five Gully

North Castle Gully

South Castle Gully

Castle Ridge

Càrn Dearg NW Summit 1214m

Càrn Dearg 1221m

Five Finger Gully

Red Burn

Approximate Scale
0 metres 500

keeping almost level to the far slopes of the col. After descending 30m, bear north-east to contour under the North Wall of Càrn Dearg. Reach the Allt a' Mhuilinn and continue to the Hut (2hrs 30mins). This is not the best approach when there is blowing snow as the path is threatened by avalanches from Castle Corrie. The biggest advantage of this approach is the ease of the descent down the Tourist Path.

From the CIC Hut to the Climbs: It may take over an hour to reach the foot of some routes from the CIC Hut, and longer for Gardyloo Buttress and Indicator Wall, which are another 500m higher.

Coire Leis: Continue up the valley on a faint path.

Observatory Gully and Tower Ridge: Head diagonally up the hillside.

Coire na Ciste: Go over the domed rock east of the Hut, then negotiate a short vegetated wall at the foot of the main corrie. The approach to the buttresses in the region of Number Five Gully, and Càrn Dearg Buttress, starts up towards Coire na Ciste, then heads diagonally right below the short vegetated wall.

Castle Ridge, Castle Gullies, North Wall of Càrn Dearg: All easily reached from the foot of Càrn Dearg Buttress.

Descent: A navigation plan to the Tourist Path should be made before starting on a route in poor weather. A sensible decision is difficult if you arrive in the plateau in a storm, barely able to stand up or open your eyes. In poor weather, leave the rope on. It will only stop you falling over a cornice if your rope work is competent (apply techniques similar to Alpine glacier crossings), but at least it keeps the party in touch.

The summit plateau is a large area with two main tops (the summit and Càrn Dearg) linked by gentle slopes but it is bounded to the north by the cliffs and to the south by endless craggy ground which plummets into Glen Nevis. The only easy route off the plateau is taken by the Tourist Path, sandwiched between Five Finger Gully and the Red Burn. This conspires to make descent from the climbs a tricky business and many accidents have occurred in descent; a detailed map of the summit plateau and the descent routes is shown on the page opposite. A good idea of the configuration of the mountain can be gained from the diagram; put a sealed copy in your map pocket and remember that in the worst weather, you might not be able to read it!

Some routes finish near the summit and the best option may be to go there first. This particularly applies to the section to the east (near North-East Buttress and up to Point Five Gully). In a hard winter, the summit cairn and triangulation point can be completely buried by snow. However, the ruined Observatory, a few metres from the summit, is an unmistakable landmark, and it is topped by a survival shelter which can be used in an emergency.

1. Via the Tourist Path, near the Red Burn: This is the safest and easiest descent. From the summit follow a bearing of 230 degrees Grid for 150m (to a point just left of Gardyloo Gully), then continue downhill on a bearing of 280 degrees Grid to reach the Tourist Track and the Red Burn area (after 800m). If you can't remember the numbers, south-west (set precisely) for 150m, then west works fine. Continue on the same bearing down an easy slope for about 1km, then turn north towards Lochan Meall an t-Suidhe.

If parked at the North Face Car Park, follow a new path which goes to the north end of Lochan Meall an t-Suidhe. Keep right of its outflow and find posts which mark a mountain rescue vehicle track. Follow this and an old fence to the car park at the small dam. Alternatively, descend the Tourist Track to Glen Nevis from Lochan Meall an t-Suidhe.

It is essential to follow the bearings carefully, as there have been many accidents on this route in the vicinity of Five Finger Gully, when parties have been too cautious about keeping away from the cliff edge or headed towards Glen Nevis too early. The exact line of the Red Burn itself should be avoided in dubious conditions, as it can avalanche.

If completing a climb between Gardyloo Gully and Number Two Gully and the cornice edge is not visible (normal in the worst weather), then a modified version of navigation from the summit will be required. This involves a bearing directly away from the cliff edge for a short distance until the standard 280 degrees grid can be followed. The away leg will be between 100m and 200m south-west (225 degrees grid), away from the north-east facing cliff. The diagram of the plateau will help on choice of distance. From the top of Number Two or Number Three Gullies, a direct 280 degrees grid is correct (these gullies cut in furthest). From Number Four Gully, 270 degrees Grid leads directly to the Red Burn.

2. Number Four Gully: This descent is commonly used by those returning to the CIC Hut or the Allt a' Mhuilinn. Follow the line of the plateau, but only if the corniced edge can be distinguished, and remembering that Gardyloo and Tower Gullies are deeply incut, to reach the top of Number Four Gully. This is marked by a metal indicator post (NN 158 717) and is also just at the point where the ground starts rising again towards Càrn Dearg. Descend the gully into Coire na Ciste.

Sometimes the cornice is impassable, but it may be possible to gain the gully by descending steeper ground immediately to the north, or by abseiling from a bollard or even the marker post (but two ropes are required). For a change of plan, descend by the Tourist Path (270 degrees grid from the top of Number Four Gully) and contour round into the Allt a' Mhuilinn from Lochan Meall an t-Suidhe.

3. Càrn Mòr Dearg Arete: Although this descent is the fastest means of losing height from the summit, the navigation is tricky and there have been many fatalities; it is therefore not described.

COIRE LEIS

Coire Leis lies at the head of the Allt a' Mhuilinn, under the crescent shaped Càrn Mòr Dearg Arete, the well defined ridge extending from Càrn Mòr Dearg to Ben Nevis. On the east flank of North-East Buttress lies the Little Brenva Face, so-named due to its open alpine character.

Little Brenva Face

Alt 1000m   East facing   Map p108

The climbs here are not technically hard, but they are generally long and, if visibility is poor, route finding may be difficult, with the routes open to variation. The face is exposed to the sun so there is a risk of falling ice in mid to late season. Because of the sun, the routes are unlikely to be in condition come April. A good view of the face is obtained well back, so approach up the opposite side of the corrie, well away from the foot of North-East Buttress.

1 Bob Run   120m   II *
I.S.Clough, H.Fisher, B.Small, D.Pipes, J.Porter, F.Jones   10 Feb 1959
The leftmost gully on the face is its easiest route, often banked up with snow. Climb easy angled ice for 30m, then continue up snow to a bifurcation (30m). Either fork can be taken; each contains a short ice pitch. Finish up snow.

2 Moonwalk   260m   IV,3 *
K.Hughes J.Mothersele   Mar 1973
An interesting and varied icy mixed route up the open face right of Bob Run. Start just right of a small rocky spur (about 10m left of Cresta) below a short ice pitch. Climb this and continue up the snowslope above to the foot of an ice pitch formed by a rock corner (100m). Climb this (spike runners) to a snowslope (45m), then move up to a steep ice wall (45m). Surmount this (15m), then continue up an icy groove to another snowfield. Cross this trending right and belay below a steep rock wall. Traverse horizontally right below the wall until a steep rocky arete leads to the summit snowslopes.

3 Cresta   275m   III **
T.W.Patey, L.S.Lovat, A.G.Nicol   16 Feb 1957; Direct Finish: M.Slesser, N.Tennant   18 Feb 1957
This popular route is a climb of great character, and was the original route on the face. Conditions were excellent that week; Patey and Nicol, with MacInnes, climbed Zero Gully two days later. It follows a hanging snow gully which starts 90m up the cliff at a rocky spur. Start well right of this spur and climb a left-slanting ice shelf for 75m to gain the hanging gully. Continue up the gully for 150m to a large ice

BEN NEVIS - Little Brenva Face

1. Bob Run	II *	4. Route Major	IV,4 ***
2. Moonwalk	IV,3 *	4a. Frostbite	IV,4
3. Cresta	III **		
3a. Cresta Direct	IV,4		

BEN NEVIS

pitch, traverse right across steep rocks for 30m, then break through to easy ground above. **Cresta Direct** (270m IV,4) starts up ice to the left, climbs the hanging gully, then finishes straight up.

Route Major 300m IV,4 ***
I.S.Clough, H.McInnes 16 Feb 1969

A fine and sustained mountaineering route with difficult route finding, best climbed in good conditions. Start slightly left of the approach ramp to North-East Buttress, and climb mixed ground to the top right corner of a large snowfield. Go diagonally right towards a rocky spur. **Frostbite** (275m IV,4) crosses the spur and follows a shallow gully beyond. Stay left of the spur and follow a left-slanting gangway, broken by an awkward corner, into a snow bay (a distinctive feature high up on the face). Break out right to snow shelves near North-East Buttress, and follow these horizontally left for a short distance to reach a groove, which leads to the upper slopes.

North-East Buttress, the first of the great ridges of Ben Nevis, extends east-north-east from near the summit cairn and divides Coire Leis from Observatory Gully. The lower rocks of the front face of North-East Buttress form a subsidiary buttress topped by the First Platform. Above this, the crest of the buttress rises in a great sweep to the summit plateau.

North-East Buttress 300m IV,4 ****
W.W.Naismith, W.Brunskill, A.B.W.Kennedy, W.W.King, F.C.Squance 3 Apr 1896

This varied route is quite simply one of the finest mountaineering expeditions in the country. This was Willie Naismith's answer to the stealing of Tower Ridge by

Englishmen two years previously. Depending on conditions, all degrees of difficulty may be found, with success in the balance until past the Mantrap. The main difficulties are high up so, as with Tower Ridge, parties need to move fairly quickly in the lower part.

The start of the climb proper can be reached from Coire Leis by a rising traverse out right to the First Platform above the lowest buttress, or by an ascent of Slingsby's Chimney. After the First Platform, follow the easy ridge to a steepening of the buttress. Turn this by a shallow gully slanting up to the left, then trend right by steps and grooves to reach a snowfield on the left side of the ridge (90m). This is the Second Platform. Climb the Second Platform snowfield easily to its top, and continue to where the way is barred by an overhanging wall. Turn this on the right by a corner with large steps, and follow the ridge above to the notorious Mantrap. This can be extremely awkward when thinly iced, but it is short and well protected (metal handholds are often used!). Directly above, climb the '40ft Corner' to a final steepening, which is usually avoided by traversing left into a gully. The Mantrap can be avoided on the right by taking the Tough-Brown Variant, stepping down and moving right into a groove which leads up to the foot of the '40ft Corner'.

6 Slingsby's Chimney   125m   II *
C.Donaldson, J.Russell   Apr 1950
Bounding the right side of the lower buttress of North-East Buttress and facing the CIC Hut, this obvious gully provides an easy outing for a short day if combined with descent by the North-East Buttress approach ledge. However, it is often climbed as an alternative start to North-East Buttress. The lower gully gives a straightforward ascent on steep snow. The easiest line trends left where the gully fans out. If the top section is not snow- covered, it will provide a sustained mixed pitch (Grade III).

OBSERVATORY GULLY

Contained within this amphitheatre are some of the finest and most famous winter climbs in Scotland.

Minus Face

Alt 950m   North-West facing   Map p108   Diagrams p113, 120

The Minus Face is the impressive wall of slabby buttresses and long gullies between Slingsby's Chimney on the left and Minus One Gully on the right. Minus Three Buttress is the shortest buttress immediately right of Slingsby's Chimney, and is flanked on its right by Minus Three Gully, which has an overhanging right wall. Minus Two Buttress is easily identified by the huge undercut nose at about one-third height, and the gully to the right is Minus Two Gully. Minus One Buttress is the slim buttress between Minus Two Gully and the deeply-cut Minus One Gully. All the routes finish on North-East Buttress (below the Mantrap), which can be descended (Grade II in the good conditions required for the Minus Gullies to be in condition) or followed to the summit as desired.

7 Platforms Rib   130m   IV,5 **
H.MacInnes T.Sullivan M.White I.S.Clough   8 Mar 1959 (several PA)
A good climb, worth seeking out when the face is in condition. Technical 4 in good conditions. Start just left of Minus Three Gully and climb snow trending left to a short iced wall. Climb this, and continue by a series of grooves to the crest of North-East Buttress between the First and Second Platforms.

8 Minus Three Gully   150m   IV,5 **
R.Smith, J.R.Marshall   7 Feb 1960
The shallow gully close under the left flank of Minus Two Buttress. The right wall is overhung, but it is possible to escape to the left at several points to more broken ground on Platforms Rib. Climb to a deep cave (30m). Exit by a short icicle on the left (crux) to gain a groove. The groove holds a short difficult wall at 25m which

BEN NEVIS
Observatory Gully

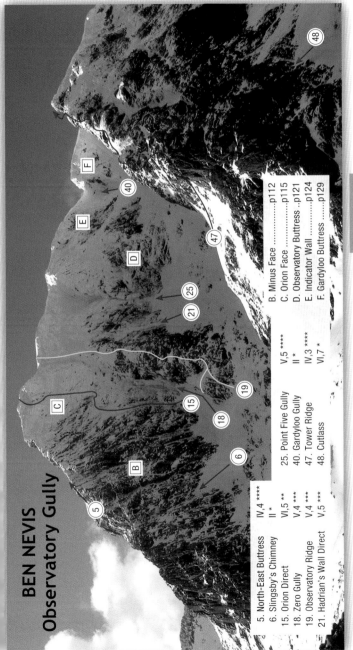

5. North-East Buttress	IV,4 ****	
6. Slingsby's Chimney	II *	
15. Orion Direct	VI,5 **	
18. Zero Gully	V,4 ***	
19. Observatory Ridge	V,4 ***	
21. Hadrian's Wall Direct	V,5 ***	
25. Point Five Gully	V,5 ****	
40. Gardyloo Gully	II *	
47. Tower Ridge	IV,3 ****	
48. Cutlass	VI,7 *	

Minus Two Gully, V,5. Climber Susan Jensen

can be turned on the left if not iced. This leads to an ice pitch and easier mixed climbing to the crest of North-East Buttress.

9 Left-Hand Route (Minus Two Buttress)   275m   VI,6 **

S.Docherty, N.Muir   30 Jan 1972 (a tension traverse)
The big left-facing corner system on the left of Minus Two Buttress gives a fine winter line up thinly iced slabs, which require a delicate touch. Climb the big corner next right of Number Three Gully (thin ice) until level with the overhangs on the right. Continue up the slab above, finding the best ice, until the difficulty eases at about half-height. Pick the easiest line to the crest of North-East Buttress.

10 Minus Two Gully   275m   V,5 ****

J.R.Marshall, J.Stenhouse, D.Haston   11 Feb 1959
A magnificent and classic climb – one of the finest of the Nevis gullies. Jimmy Marshall led the young Stenhouse and Haston up this prized line. Climb steep snow and ice to an overhang (45m). Turn the overhang by traversing left to enter the main chimney-line. Above is a steep ice pitch; turn this on the left, then continue more easily to where the gully forks. Climb the easy angled chimney on the left, or make a difficult step right to finish up the right-hand chimney.

11 Minus One Gully   275m   VI,6 ****

K.V.Crocket, C.Stead   23 Feb 1974
Another magnificent climb, the hardest of the Nevis gullies, which had survived many previous attempts. It is not often in condition and consequently it is a much prized route. The conspicuous overhang at one-third height is the crux. Enter the gully and climb easily to an awkward ice wall which leads to a cave below the overhang. Turn this on the left, then regain the gully above. Continue up steep ice

followed by a fine corner to reach a snow bay (the Meadow). A choice of two snowy grooves lies above. Either may be climbed, but the right-hand one is the more natural line. It leads to a groove which bears left to the final arete of Minus One Buttress.

Orion Face

Alt 1000m   North-West facing   Map p108   Diagrams p113, 120

Shaped like an inverted wedge, the Orion Face fans out from Minus One Gully on the left to Zero Gully on the right. The depression in the centre of the face is known as the Basin. It holds snow well into summer, and is a place of intersection for many routes on the face. The name Orion derives from a fancied resemblance of the original routes on the face to the configuration of the stars in the constellation Orion, with the Basin corresponding to Orion's belt. The short narrow chimney at the back left-hand corner of the Basin is **Epsilon Chimney**. The chimney, followed by a left-slanting line, gives the easiest exit from the Basin, and is also the best line for escape from the face in winter conditions (Grade IV,4).

2 Astronomy   300m   VI,5 **
A.Fyffe, H.MacInnes, K.Spence   Mar 1971 (1PA)
This first class winter route up the buttress right of Minus One Gully is never particularly hard, but it requires a good plastering of snow and ice, usually forming later in the season. Start just right of the toe of the buttress, immediately right of Minus One Gully. Climb up to twin cracks and onto sloping snow shelves slanting leftwards to a small snow bay. Climb up right by grooves to a large left-facing corner (the left-bounding corner of the Great Slab Rib). Follow the corner and exit right by a wide, shallow flake-chimney above the Great Slab Rib. Climb a thinly iced groove, then trend back left by walls and grooves until under the steep upper rocks near the top of the buttress. Make a short descent into the steep chimney at the top of Minus One Gully and climb this to the top.
Variation: **Direct Finish   120m   VI,5 *****
C.Fraser, M.Thompson   16 Feb 1986
This is a better finish, but less often in condition. At the top of the thinly iced groove, trend slightly right to a belay below the right-hand end of the steep upper section. Gain the crest of the buttress on the right, then continue up an iced slab trending right to reach a fine ice groove near the crest of the buttress. Follow this steeply to an easier arete which leads to North-East Buttress.

Smith-Holt Route   420m   V,5 *
R.Smith, R.K.Holt   Jan 1959
The first winter line on the face, a fine route with a different character from Orion Direct. Start at a right-facing corner about 15m left of the chimney at the start of Orion Direct. Climb the awkward corner on snow and ice to gain the left side of the Great Slab Rib (50m), which is turned on the left with difficulty. From here, follow Astronomy until above the Great Slab Rib. Now go up and right to the Basin. At the top left-hand corner of the Basin is the steep gully of Epsilon Chimney. Climb this and continue by grooves to the crest of North-East Buttress.

Astral Highway   240m   VI,5 **
C.Higgins, A.Kimber   28 Dec 1976
This excellent ice route takes a direct exit from the Basin up the steep line of grooves right of Epsilon Chimney. It is fairly often in condition and quite popular. The first of many of the thin face ice lines which were to be climbed in the good winters of the late '70s, and by a strong local team. Follow Orion Direct to the Basin and climb a shallow groove which trends left to the main groove line a few metres right of Epsilon Chimney. Climb the main groove over bulges (crux), then continue by grooves on the right to exit on the crest of North-East Buttress above the 40ft Corner.

15 Orion Direct 400m V,5 ****
J.R.Marshall, R.Smith 13 Feb 1960

One of the finest winter climbs in Scotland, with all the atmosphere of a major alpine face. This was the climax of a magnificent week's climbing by Jimmy Marshall and Robin Smith that has entered Scottish climbing legend. The route is sustained, open, and exposed, but in good conditions is nowhere technically difficult, although both belays and runners can be hard to find. Start left of Zero Gully, where a broad ledge leads to the foot of a prominent chimney-line leading up towards the Basin. Climb the chimney for two long pitches until a rising traverse right leads into the Basin. Traverse right across snow into a groove beside the Second Slab Rib, an obvious feature just right of the Basin. Descend a little, move round the right side of the rib, then climb up to and across a steep icy wall on the right (crux). Above, follow left-trending snow and ice grooves to the snow slope under the final tower. This is usually climbed by a steep icy chimney on the left to reach the plateau at the top of North-East Buttress. If conditions are poor on the upper section, it may be necessary to make a long traverse to the right in order to find a feasible route to the plateau near Slav Route.

Variation: **Long Climb Finish 240m VI,5 ** **
A.Cain R.Clothier Mar 1983

An excellent and steeper alternative finish to Orion Direct, which approximates to the upper section of The Long Climb. From the Basin climb a steep ice groove just left of the Second Slab Rib. Take a left-curving line up a series of icy grooves to finish on North-East Buttress.

16 Orion Directissima 375m VI,5 **
S.M.Richardson R.G.Webb 16 Apr 1994 (some pitches climbed before)

A sustained thin face climb starting to the right of Orion Direct and finishing up the prominent right-curving corner in the Orion headwall. A good alternative for those who have done Orion Direct. Although it requires good conditions to be fully iced, it is a logical line and the most direct way up the face. The groove of Long Climb finish is slow to ice and Orion Direct can be followed for a pitch; this is actually more direct. Start just left of Slav Route and climb a series of steep icy grooves to belay in a groove left of the Second Slab Rib (140m). Climb the steep ice groove above (as for Long Climb Finish), then move right across the snowfield and up to below the steep bow shaped corner on the right side of the headwall (140m). Climb the excellent corner to its top (45m). Finish easily up snow to the top (50m).

17 Slav Route 420m VI,5 **
D.F.Lang, N.W.Quinn 23 Mar 1974

This is one of the longest winter climbs of its standard in Scotland. It climbs a somewhat featureless section of cliff; in very snowy conditions it can be technically straightforward but very lonely for the leader who might not find runners or rock belays for long sections, possibly even the whole route. Indeed, the grade could be VI,4 apart from the steep lower icefall. In snowy but not icy conditions can sometimes be passed on the left near Orion Directissima. Climb a groove immediately left of Zero Gully, then move up right into an iced groove to belay below a steep icefall (50m). Climb the icefall (crux), or avoid it on the left (easier), then continue up grooves to a snowfield (50m). Move up and right and belay below a snow arete overlooking Zero Gully (50m). Continue by steps and grooves for four long pitches, keeping close to but left of Zero Gully, to emerge on a snow slope below a wide square-cut chimney immediately right of a steep buttress. Trend right initially, then finish by corners on the left to emerge at the top of North-East Buttress.

18 Zero Gully 300m V,4 ***
H.MacInnes, A.G.Nicol, T.W.Patey 18 Feb 1957

This historic route was the first Grade V gully on Ben Nevis. It had already received several attempts, the first being from Jim Bell in 1936; Hamish MacInnes roped in the Aberdonians at the CIC hut to overtake John Cunningham and Mick Noon's

Orion Direct, V,5. Climber Ian Grimshaw

imminent attempt in excellent conditions. It rarely achieves the character of a deep gully, being more of a great open groove. Although technically easy for the grade, it is a very serious climb with poor belays and it is exposed to spindrift. Only the first two or three pitches are difficult. Climb icy grooves on the left of the main gully to a poor belay below a steep wall. Traverse right into the gully and climb this steeply to gain the easy upper gully. The main gully can be climbed direct at the start; slightly harder.

Sickle, V,5. Climber Tony Moody

Observatory Ridge and West Face

Alt 1000m   North-West facing   Diagrams p113, 120, 123

Observatory Ridge is the prominent steep ridge between Zero and Point Five Gullies. Its west face, curving round to Point Five Gully, has the huge icefall of Hadrian's Wall Direct as its most obvious feature.

19 Observatory Ridge   450m   V,4 ***
H.Raeburn, F.S.Goggs, W.A.Mounsey   Apr 1920
This is the most difficult of the classic Nevis ridges. It gives a superb climb, which can be very awkward under powder and climbers frequently find it harder than the famous Grade V gullies either side! The last of the great ridges to be climbed in winter was also Harold Raeburn's last route on the Ben, on a par with his much earlier ascent of Green Gully. The easiest line starts up the shelf on the left flank and works up obliquely rightwards to the crest. The crest is hard (turn the difficulties on the right) but the upper ridge is normally straightforward, although it can be time consuming under heavy snow conditions. Many parties avoid it altogether and move left into the easier upper section of Zero Gully.

20 Vade Mecum   190m   V,5 **
D.Knowles, D.Wilson and party   Mar 1974
A superb ice climb and well worth ticking off when in condition. Start just left of the huge icefall of Hadrian's Wall Direct, and climb up to the base of twin ice grooves. Take the right-hand groove to a steep snow bay under the vertical upper wall. Belay to the left of a vertical ice pillar. Climb the pillar and continue more easily to the crest of the ridge.

21 Hadrian's Wall Direct   300m   V,5 ***
M.G.Geddes, G.E.Little   Apr 1971 (1PA)
This popular route is often the first major ice climb to come into condition on the mountain, and it remains reliably formed until late in the season. It takes the large prominent icefall on the right flank of Observatory Ridge. At the start of the '70s, Mike Geddes was one of the first to use front pointing exclusively. He had already repeated Point Five and this prominent target was soon to become one of the great

classics. Climb the ice smear, bulges and all, to a belay near steep rocks on the left. Continue very steeply for 10m, then trend slightly right on snow to a deep icy chimney, which leads to a snowfield. Continue more easily to finish by a scoop just right of Observatory Ridge (or by the ridge).

2 Sickle   300m   V,5 ***
M.G.Geddes, B.P.Hall   29 Dec 1977
This excellent ice route takes the curving slabby groove right of Hadrian's Wall Direct. It is quite often in condition, but the start can be thin. Start a few metres right of Hadrian's below a small icefall. Climb over a steep ice step to gain a groove leading up and left close to Hadrian's Wall Direct, then curve back right to a steep icy corner (90m). Follow the icy corner and exit right up grooves to reach a spike. This is sometimes used for a two pitch abseil descent but the second anchor is an ice thread. It is more satisfying to join Hadrian's for the snowy upper slopes.

3 Galactic Hitchhiker   300m   VI,5 ****
M.G.Geddes, C.Higgins   14 Apr 1978 (1PA)
This serious route starts up a shallow corner system in the ice glazed slabs between Sickle and Point Five Gully, then continues up the big right-trending and steepening corner system above. Geddes' finest contribution to Ben Nevis and one of the best

Hadrian's Wall Direct, V,5

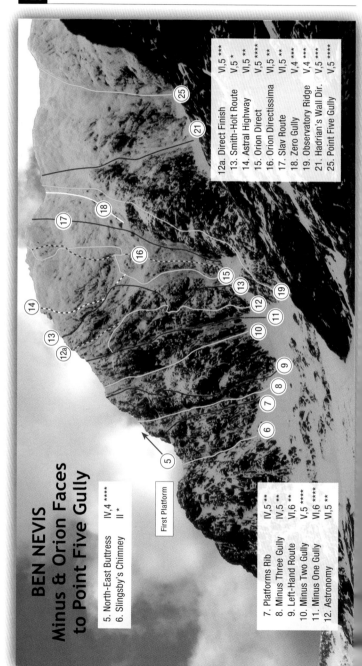

BEN NEVIS
Minus & Orion Faces
to Point Five Gully

5. North-East Buttress	IV,4 ****
6. Slingsby's Chimney	II *

7. Platforms Rib	IV,5 **
8. Minus Three Gully	IV,5 **
9. Left-Hand Route	VI,6 **
10. Minus Two Gully	V,5 ****
11. Minus One Gully	VI,6 ****
12. Astronomy	VI,5 **

12a. Direct Finish	VI,5 ***
13. Smith-Holt Route	V,5 *
14. Astral Highway	VI,5 **
15. Orion Direct	V,5 ****
16. Orion Directissima	VI,5 **
17. Slav Route	VI,5 **
18. Zero Gully	V,4 ***
19. Observatory Ridge	V,4 ***
21. Hadrian's Wall Dir.	V,5 ***
25. Point Five Gully	V,5 ****

First Platform

thin face routes on the mountain. Start 15m right of Sickle below an icy corner.

1. 50m Climb the corner for 10m, step into another on the right and follow this over thinly iced slabs to an overhang. Exit right to a belay at a nose.

2 and 3. 70m Climb the continuation of the corner and snow shelves to a snow bay up left, then traverse right past a distinctive pointed block to the base of the big corner (or reach this point by an icy corner on the right).

4. 45m Climb the iced wall right of the corner with difficulty, then move back into the next corner and follow it to easier ground and the Girdle Traverse ledge.

5 to 7. 135m Continue directly to the plateau.

Variation: **Left-Hand Start   100m   V,5**

This is easier than the original way and more often in condition. Climb slabs and grooves just right of Sickle, then traverse right to the pointed block.

**4 Pointless   330m   VII,6 ** **

N.Banks, G.Smith   19 Feb 1978

This serious thin face route, which follows slabs and an obvious corner trending left away from the base of Point Five, is guaranteed to provide a memorable experience! The climbing is hard and sustained, and protection is difficult to find; take care with this one! Gordon Smith was another of many talented climbers active on the Ben in the late '70s. Standards rose every year and this was probably the hardest of the thin face routes climbed that decade. Start below an icy slab some 5m left of Point Five Gully.

1. 50m Climb the slab to a groove, then break out right through a short overhang to reach the upper slab. Trend left across this to a large spike and peg belay. There is a variation nearer Point Five which goes higher across the upper slab.

2. 30m From the top of the spike (peg runner on the left wall), climb the difficult corner above (crux), then move right into a small alcove and spike belay.

3. 30m Climb an ice smear just to the left, and continue above to a narrow overhanging chimney.

4. 20m Follow the chimney to easy ground.

5. to 8. 200m Continue more easily to the plateau.

**Point Five Gully   325m   V,5 ** ** **

J.M.Alexander, I.S.Clough, D.Pipes, R.Shaw   16 Jan 1959 (six days, fixed ropes); First one day ascent: J.R.Marshall, R.Smith   10 Feb 1960

An outstanding climb, probably the most famous ice gully in the world! Belays are good and the route is often in condition. With the major difficulties concentrated in the first three pitches, the route is an excellent introduction to the Grade V classics and it is not uncommon for the gully to have several ropes of climbers stretching (often literally) from top to bottom. In windy conditions the route is best avoided. The upper funnel collects vast quantities of spindrift which causes mini avalanches to funnel down the lower narrow section.

1. 40m Climb easily up iced slabs to a steep ice wall, normally climbed on the left.

2. 45m Climb the narrow ice-choked chimney in two sections (possible belay between them).

3. 30m The Rogue Pitch. Continue up the gully and climb the bulging icy wall to the easier upper section.

4. etc. 210m Follow the gully past the occasional short pitch to the plateau. The cornice is normally avoided on the right.

Observatory Buttress

Alt 1050m   North facing   Map p108   Diagram p126

Observatory Buttress is the broad mass of rock extending from Point Five Gully on the left to Gardyloo Gully on the right. It rises steeply to a great ledge at half-height which narrows towards its left end. On the right, the ledge finishes at the foot of Gardyloo Gully at its junction with the top of Observatory Gully. The ledge is a useful but very exposed means of escape should conditions on the plateau make the prospect of a visit too daunting. Above the right end of the ledge and left of

Gardyloo Gully is Indicator Wall; it is possible to link the lower and harder part of the Observatory Buttress routes with a route on Indicator Wall.

The buttress is characterised by the open left-facing corner of Rubicon Wall, which separates the steep wall to the right of Point Five Gully from the easier angled spur of Observatory Buttress route on the right.

26 Left Edge Route   360m   V,5 ***
D.F.Lang, N.W.Quinn   9 Mar 1974; Direct Finish: D.Wilkinson, M.Burt   8 Mar 1980
A climb of great character, especially if followed by the Direct Finish. The team of Neil Quinn and Doug Lang from Dundee were one of the last to convert to front pointing but still continued to climb hard new routes (including Slav Route two weeks later). Start at the foot of Point Five Gully and climb its right bounding rib to a snow patch. From its right end, climb the left-hand of two grooves to a hidden traverse line leading right to beneath three parallel icefalls. Climb the left or central icefall to gain a large terrace. Either move right along the terrace and finish as for Observatory Buttress, or better if conditions suit, climb directly up a series of sustained icy grooves just right of the crest, overlooking the upper section of Point Five Gully.

27 Match Point   340m   VI,5 **
S.M.Richardson, E.Hart   29 Mar 1986
A good direct line between Left Edge Route and Rubicon Wall. Simon Richardson's first of many new routes on the Ben, an ice line which surprisingly had not been recorded before. Start below the right-hand of two left-facing corner systems.
1. 50m Climb the corner (good spike runner at 25m) to a steep snow patch.
2. 40m From the top of the snow patch, traverse left below an inverted triangular overhanging rock wall and climb an icicle fringe on its left-hand side. Belay on the snow terrace above.
3. 50m Take the central of the three parallel icefalls above to reach the large terrace.
4. to 7. 200m Continue as for the Direct Finish to Left Edge Route.

28 Rubicon Wall   340m   V,5 ***
N.Muir, A.Paul   14 Apr 1977
In good conditions a prominent icefall forms down the left-facing corner which divides centrally the smooth left side of the buttress from the spur on the right (about 20m from the left edge of the buttress). This had very quickly become a last great problem in 1977 after one particularly spectacular failure. Climb the icefall in three pitches to the large terrace. The icefall of Match Point is an alternative third pitch if formed better than the corner. Continue as for one of the other routes, or traverse right to Indicator Wall.

29 Observatory Buttress   340m   V,4 **
J.R.Marshall, R.Smith   9 Feb 1960
A fine and interesting climb, with one short harder section just before the chimney. Low in the grade. Start in the centre of the spur section, well right of Rubicon Wall, at an iced depression below a chimney. Climb a short snow runnel and continue on steep snow with short ice steps, following the shallow depression to the chimney (normally well choked with ice), then continue up an easier groove to the large terrace. It is possible to traverse right from here into Observatory Gully, but it is preferable to continue up and slightly left to the crest of the buttress, which leads with little difficulty to the plateau.

30 Never-Never Land   340m   VI,6 *
S.M.Richardson P.Takeda   9 Mar 1999
A good icy mixed climb taking the line of least resistance on the right side of the lower buttress before tackling the right side of the unlikely looking headwall above. Start 15m right of the initial snow runnel of Observatory Buttress.
1. 50m Climb mixed ground right of the runnel, then move left to reach the shallow depression of Observatory Buttress.
2. 45m From the top of the depression climb up then left to gain the line of snow ledges which cuts from right to left across the buttress. Follow this to the end and

BEN NEVIS - Point Five Gully & Observatory Buttress

20. Vade Mecum	V,5 **	
21. Hadrian's Wall Direct	V,5 ***	
22. Sickle	V,5 ***	
23. Galactic Hitchhiker	VII,6 **	

24. Pointless	VII,6 **	
25. Point Five Gully	V,5 ****	
26. Left Edge Route	V,5 ***	

27. Match Point	VI,5 **	
28. Rubicon Wall	V,5 ***	
29. Observatory Buttress	V,4 **	
30. Never-Never Land	VI,6 *	

Albatross, VI,5. Climber Brian Whitworth

belay below a short steep wall.
3. 40m Climb the wall, then instead of trending right (which is easier), climb straight up towards the headwall. Surmount another short steep wall, then move right to belay below the prominent right to left groove system which cuts through the headwall.
4. 35m Enter the groove from the right, and climb it pulling over a small roof at the top (crux). An excellent pitch in a superb position.
5. to 9. 170m Continue up easy ground to the large terrace and finish as for Observatory Buttress.

Indicator Wall

Alt 1200m   North-West facing   Map p108   Diagram p126

The steep slabby face at the top left corner of Observatory Gully extends from the narrow gully of Good Friday Climb on the left to the deep cleft of Gardyloo Gully on the right. The slabs become coated with a thin layer of ice and provide a number of excellent routes, which are mostly hard and can be serious with infrequent belays and limited protection unless ice screws are good. Good conditions require a build-up of heavy snow, then freeze-thaw. These are the highest ice climbs in the British Isles, and are often in condition late in the season.

Good Friday Climb   150m   III ***
G.G.Macphee, R.W.Lovel, H.R.Shepherd, D.Edwards   7 Apr 1939
This enjoyable and popular climb is especially good early in the winter before snow banks much of it out. It is also a reliable late season option, as sometimes it is the last route to remain iced at the end of the winter. From the foot of Gardyloo Gully, traverse left along the easy terrace to the foot of a narrow gully. Climb this for 60m to a steep rock wall. Traverse right on ice to a small gully, then climb up and slightly left to easier ground leading to a further small gully. Climb this for 15m, before moving up and right to the summit cornice. The indicator post no longer exists, but tradition still dictates taking the highest belay in the country, round the triangulation pillar on the summit!

Indicator Wall   140m   V,4 ***
G.Smith, T.King   Feb 1975
This excellent climb is often in condition, and takes the easier line up the prominent ice sheet on the left side of the face. Start the base of an icy chimney-groove 50m right of the gully of Good Friday Climb.
1. 30m Climb the icy chimney-groove to the right of a prominent rib, over ice bulges to a small snow scoop.
2. 30m Choose the best line through a steep ice bulge and ramp, then move up and right to the base of a short chimney.
3. 40m Climb the chimney and follow a line leading out left through bulges to the snow slope above.
4. 40m Climb straight up to the central of three short gullies above.

Indicator Right-Hand   140m   V,5 **
D.F.Lang, N.W.Quinn   Feb 1975
Steeper and more direct than the original route, but not so often in condition. Start below the steep groove 15m right of the normal start, and climb straight up to the bulging ice flow. Climb this either centrally or further right, to gain the snowslope above. Finish by the rightmost of the three gullies just left of a pronounced buttress, and turn the cornice on the right.

Riders on the Storm   140m   VI,5 **
D.Hawthorn E.Todd   11 Apr 1986
The prominent buttress to the right of Indicator Wall is cut by a bow shaped corner system on its left side. This corner gives a brilliant pitch on thin ice, but unfortunately it is slower to come into condition than other routes on the face.
1. 50m Start just left of the lowest point of the buttress. Climb the icy slab rightwards, then move left and up to gain the bow shaped corner. Climb this for 15m to a break in the right wall. Move right into the next groove, and climb this for 4m, where another break allows a similar move right into the next groove. Follow this to a stance.
2. 50m Climb the continuation groove to a stance.
3. 40m Climb right and up the prominent groove through the final buttress to the top.

Albatross   170m   VI,5 ***
M.G.Geddes, C.Higgins   21 Jan 1978
An excellent route up thinly iced slabs – a modern classic. Previously graded VII,6, but many ascents in good conditions have found it is no harder than Psychedelic Wall. This is perhaps not surprising, as the two routes were first climbed on consecutive days by rival local teams. The line follows the prominent shallow corner in the centre of the wall, which runs the full height of the crag. There are

**BEN NEVIS
Indicator Wall**

31. Good Friday Climb	III ***	34. Riders on the Storm	VI,5 **
32. Indicator Wall	V,4 ***	35. Albatross	VI,5 ***
33. Indicator Right-Hand	V,5 **		

36. Psychedelic Wall   VI,5 ***
37. Satanic Verses   VI,5 **
38. Shot in the Dark   V,5 *
39. Caledonia   V,5 **
40. Gardyloo Gully   II *

Simon Richardson

three separate starts, but the original central line is usually followed. Start left of centre of the open bay to the left of Psychedelic Wall, about 25m right of the rock spur on the left.

1. 30m Follow a shallow ramp trending up and right into the main line, which leads to a rock spike where the corner runs into an overlap.

2. 50m Climb the twinned groove above, and make an interesting move left onto the top of the overlap. Continue above on steep slabs, avoiding an overhang on the right, to a snow bay and belay.

3. 50m Exit the bay on the right by a ramp, then traverse left into a shallow corner, and follow this over an icy bulge to a snowfield below the cornice.

4. 40m Continue easily to the cornice.

36 Psychedelic Wall   165m   VI,5 ***
N.Muir, A.Paul   22 Jan 1978

A popular route, the established classic on the wall, which takes a direct line starting from the lowest rocks opposite the left edge of Gardyloo Buttress.

1. 50m Start up icy slabs to reach a snow bay, then continue up steeper ice to a left-trending snow ramp leading to a large plinth. Belay below and to the left.

2. 40m Climb slabs to an open corner which leads onto a large area of thinly iced slabs. Climb these slightly right to a corner high on the right.

3. 45m Continue up the corner and short chimney above, to below a steep wall. Step left through bulges and climb the rightmost of three corners to an easy snow slope.

4. 30m Follow the snow to the cornice, which is best breached on the left.

37 Satanic Verses   130m   VI,5 **
C.Cartwright, R.Clothier   7 Apr 1989

A superb ice route based on one of the four parallel ramp-lines that slant up right across the lower part of the wall and finishing up the big iced corner left of roofs near the top. Start immediately right of Psychedelic Wall.

1. 50m Take the furthest left ramp-line and follow this up and right to a snow patch. Continue up the next ramp to a second snow patch and belay.

2. 40m Climb straight up, then right to a small snow bay. Follow grooves to a large snow bay below the big corner.

3. 30m Climb the corner, mostly on its left wall, and continue directly up a groove to the cornice. If this is large, an exit can be made 15m to the left.

38 Shot in the Dark   140m   V,5 *
M.G.Geddes, A.Rouse   11 Feb 1978

The easiest climb on the wall, but a serious route nevertheless. Start a few metres right of Satanic Verses and climb the fourth (rightmost) ramp, or wherever the ice is thickest, aiming initially for a distant rectangular roof near the top of the face. Climb a short corner to where it forks, then climb a right-slanting snow ramp to below the rectangular roof. Traverse right crossing Caledonia and finish by a steep slab and short ridge some distance to the right of the rectangular roof.

39 Caledonia   110m   V,5 **
D.Gardner A.Paul   18 Feb 1978

A direct and therefore steeper line, cutting through Shot in the Dark and starting up the bulbous icefall some 60m right of Psychedelic Wall. Climb the icefall past a steep section to a snow bay (50m), then move up a right-trending snow ramp (common to Shot in the Dark). From its top, move right and finish up steep slabs, turning bulges on the right.

40 Gardyloo Gully   170m   II *
G.Hastings, E.L.W.Haskett-Smith   26 Apr 1896

Originally called Tin Can Gully, this deep cleft at the head of Observatory Gully was used as a rubbish chute for the old Observatory. The difficulty largely depends on the amount and condition of the snow. Start up a uniform snow slope above the narrows in Observatory Gully to reach an ice pitch. Climb this, and continue up

Psychedelic Wall, VI,5. Climber Jeremy Morris

steep snow to the cornice which can be very large, sometimes double and quite often impossible. The gully can almost totally bank out in a winter of heavy snow, but lying high on the mountain and being a natural drainage line, it is one of the first routes to freeze up. Under these conditions it provides an interesting passage under a huge chockstone to a steep ice pitch (III,4).

Gardyloo Buttress

Alt 1200m   North facing   Map p108   Diagram p130

This steep and compact buttress dominates the head of Observatory Gully, and consists of two ridges, with a shallow depression between them. The left-hand ridge is well defined, and the upper part of the depression opens out into a wide funnel. In winter the funnel takes the form of a snow chute, which drains into two icefalls. The most prominent by far is the left-slanting icefall of Smith's Route, and the steeper line to the left is taken by Kellett's Route.

Kellett's Route   125m   VI,6 ***
A.Paul, K.Leinster   1980
An excellent steep climb following the prominent icefall on the front face of the buttress. Start below the obvious right-facing corner, 30m left of Smith's Route.
1. 45m Climb the corner and step right over bulges to gain a shallow depression.
2. 30m Continue by an open groove on the right to belay at the foot of the final snow funnel.
3. 50m Climb the funnel to the top.
Variation: **Augean Alley Finish   50m   V,5 ***
K.Leinster, A.Paul, G.Reilly   Mar 1981
From the top of the second pitch, climb the ridge left of the snow funnel to the top. A superb pitch in a spectacular position.

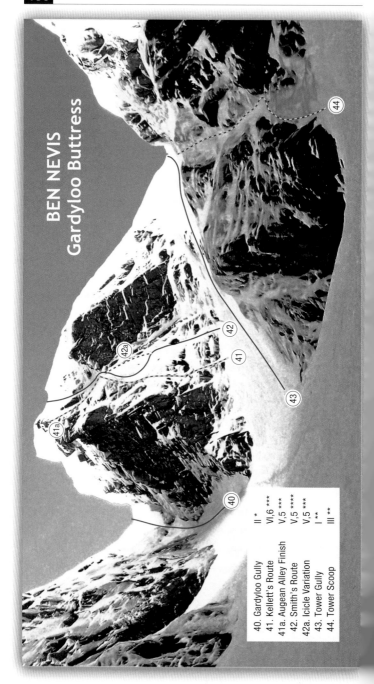

BEN NEVIS
Gardyloo Buttress

40. Gardyloo Gully — II *
41. Kellett's Route — VI,6 ***
41a. Augean Alley Finish — V,5 ***
42. Smith's Route — V,5 ****
42a. Icicle Variation — V,5 ***
43. Tower Gully — I **
44. Tower Scoop — III **

Smith's Route, V,5. Climbers Alastair Robertson and Stuart Allinson

Smith's Route   125m   V,5 ****
R.Smith, J.R.Marshall   8 Feb 1960
A very popular ice route. Although short, it is a sustained climb with impressive
exposure and is often in condition from December until May. Remember as you
make the exciting traverse on pitch 2 that it was first climbed by step cutting,
although by quite a strong team! The Icicle Variation is slightly easier and better
protected than the original route, but less often in condition. Start directly below
the lower end of the slanting grooves.
1. 30m Follow the ice groove to a good belay in the groove, below a roof.
2. 50m A serious pitch. Move up to below the icicle, then traverse out left to steep
grooves on the edge of the buttress. Break out right on steep ice to gain the left
edge of the upper funnel. Snow or ice belay.
3. 50m Continue easily up the gully above, and exit on the left.
Variation: **Icicle Variation   40m   V,5 *****
K.V.Crocket, C.Gilmore   February 1975
From the belay at the top of pitch 1, climb the icicle on its left side, then continue
up the brilliant ramp above into the funnel.

Tower Gully   120m   I **
G.Hastings, E.L.W.Haskett-Smith, W.P.Haskett-Smith   25 Apr 1897
This was renamed from Number One Gully, whether accidentally or not is
unknown. The gully defines the right flank of Gardyloo Buttress, and starts from the
broad hanging snowslope above the barrier wall (taken by Tower Scoop) at the
head of Observatory Gully. Climb the snow gully easily to a potentially large
cornice, which is usually passed on the right. The cornice is very variable, sometimes
non-existent and sometimes impossible. Depending on the cornice, this can be a
useful but exposed descent route down into Observatory Gully. Great care should

be taken to locate the top of the gully correctly, and a traverse right (facing down) is required below the level of Gardyloo Buttress to avoid the barrier wall.

Tower Ridge - East Face

44 Tower Scoop   65m   III **
I.S.Clough, G.Grandison   4 Jan 1961
This short and very popular ice route climbs the obvious icy scoop in the barrier wall halfway up Observatory Gully. It is almost always in condition, although not necessarily safe due to avalanche prone slopes above and below. It can be used as a good warm up on the way to the higher routes, if time allows. Climb an ice pitch to gain the scoop, and finish by an awkward corner to reach the terrace below Tower Gully. Some variation is possible depending on conditions.

45 Tower Cleft   75m   III *
C.Pratt, J.Francis   19 Feb 1949
This interesting route follows the deep cleft in the angle formed by the cliff containing Tower Scoop and the east flank of Tower Ridge. The difficulty depends largely on the quantity of snow present. Alternatively, climb the steep icy left wall to break out left to easy ground.

46 The Great Chimney   65m   IV,5 **
J.R.Marshall, R.Smith   6 Feb 1960 (sling for aid)
About halfway up the east flank of Tower Ridge is a huge recess, defined on the left by the impressively steep Echo Wall, and on its right by this conspicuous, deeply cut chimney which gives an atmospheric mixed route. The rock scenery in the chimney is impressive, and if little ice is present it can be an absorbing V,6. This route was the start of Marshall and Smith's amazing week of climbing in 1960 that climaxed with the first ascent of Orion Direct.
1. 30m Climb a steep snowslope into the icy chimney that leads to a belay under a vertical block.
2. 35m Climb the left crack on verglassed walls, followed by mixed snow and ice to the crest of the ridge.

Tower Ridge

Alt 800m   North-East facing   Map p108   Diagram p113

Probably the best known feature on Ben Nevis, Tower Ridge is the central of the great buttresses on the mountain.

47 Tower Ridge   800m   IV,3 ****
J.N.Collie, G.A.Sollie, J.Collier   30 Mar 1894
This provides perhaps the finest mountaineering expedition in Scotland. Collie was so pleased with the first ascent (climbed in 5hrs) that he climbed it again the following day. Depending on the conditions, all degrees of difficulty may be encountered, with many of the major obstacles being met high on the route. The Ridge has repulsed strong and experienced parties, and should not be under rated. Benightments occur with monotonous regularity and 6 to 10 hours should be allowed for an ascent. It is important to be quick on the easier lower sections; this may mean moving together in Alpine style. Early in the season, when coated in powder snow and verglas, the Ridge may be very time consuming.

Starting a short distance above the CIC Hut at a level of 700m, the ridge rises for 200m to the top of the Douglas Boulder, a gigantic rock pinnacle separated from the main ridge by the deep cleft of the Douglas Gap. The Gap has a gully either side with the East Gully on the left; this is the normal approach although the West Gully is a steeper alternative.

The chimney on the left leaving the Gap is tricky if iced. The ridge now narrows and after an almost level section, rises more steeply, then eases off. This second easier section leads to the Little Tower. It is important not to traverse left here, mistaking the Little Tower for the Great Tower; the Great Tower is unmistakeably

The Eastern Traverse on Tower Ridge, IV,3

vertical. In dry or good icy conditions the Little Tower is best climbed on the left, but a traverse right before climbing up is more normal. Above, easy but spectacular ground leads to the 30m barrier wall of the Great Tower.

The best route is to take the Eastern Traverse, a narrow ledge on the left which is sometimes banked out to an alarming angle. This leads to the (normally buried) fallen block chimney, above which tricky short walls lead to the top of the Great Tower. Follow the knife edge ridge to Tower Gap. The descent into the Gap involves a tricky move, but an in-situ sling often allows cheating. The climb out the other side is a little easier up a shallow corner on the left (the normal way) or a little harder if taken direct. Now the ridge eases until the final steepening, which is taken by a groove on its right-hand side.

If time, energy or proficiency run short, there are escape routes near Tower Gap, but not before the Eastern Traverse. The ascent of the Great Tower can be avoided by a rather devious continuation of the Eastern Traverse, with a tricky move at the start, which leads into Tower Gully close to Tower Gap. Alternatively, it is possible to escape into Tower Gully from Tower Gap (Grade II, or one abseil and a small traverse), but remember that the slopes leading across to Observatory Gully are steep (Grade I) and below them lie the cliffs of Tower Scoop.

Douglas Boulder

Diagram p113

The Douglas Boulder is often clear when the rest of the mountain is shrouded in mist. In winter there are a number of good mixed lines, which can provide absorbing climbing if there is avalanche risk after a heavy snowfall, or before the higher routes have come into condition. From the top of the Boulder, it is necessary to either down climb or abseil to reach the Douglas Gap. Route finding can be awkward, and it is easiest to descend to the right as one looks into the Gap.

Cutlass   200m   VI,7 *

A.Clarke, J.Main   23 Mar 1989

The clean-cut corner which lies some metres left of the South-West Ridge gives a good steep mixed climb, with a great crux pitch. It contains a surprising amount of turf and is especially good early in the season after a hard freeze and heavy snowfall.

1. 40m Climb easy slabs to the foot of the clean-cut corner.
2. 25m Climb the corner to a ledge (crux).
3. 30m Continue up the chimney above, followed by a cracked wall, to reach the South-West Ridge.
4. 40m Follow the crest to the top.

49 South-West Ridge   180m   IV,5 **

J.Y.MacDonald, H.W.Turnbull   Mar 1934

The crest of the well defined ridge overlooking West Gully is the easiest of the routes leading to the top of the Douglas Boulder. Grade III,4 in good conditions. It provides a great little climb, good value for money, with interest maintained throughout and fine situations and often at its best when other routes on the mountain are out of condition under deep snow. If conditions are lean the hardest section is starting up a short cracked wall to leave West Gully, although this can be avoided by moving a little further up the gully and climbing a vegetated groove.

50 Douglas Gap West Gully and Traverse   300m   I *

West Gully rises to the Douglas Gap from the Coire na Ciste side. It is a good snow gully with fine scenery, and it can be used as an alternative start to Tower Ridge. An interesting poor weather option is to climb the steeper West Gully to the Gap, then descend via East Gully.

COIRE NA CISTE

The large corrie bounded on the left by the West Flank of Tower Ridge and on the right by the Trident Buttresses leading down to Càrn Dearg Buttress. It includes The Comb and the numbered gullies and buttresses.

Secondary Tower Ridge

Alt 900m   North-West facing   Diagrams p135, 136

Secondary Tower Ridge lies on the west flank of Tower Ridge, some distance below its crest. For the most part it rarely attains the status of a distinct ridge but takes the form of a parallel slanting shelf, which is separated from the main ridge by a well defined depression which holds snow until late in the season and into which the routes finish.On completion of a route on this part of the mountain, one can ascend or descend Tower Ridge. Each route has a more direct descent, described under that route.

1 Vanishing Gully   200m   V,5 ***

R.Marshall, G.Tiso   15 Jan 1951

The next obvious gully well right of Douglas Gap West Gully gives a classic ice climb with good belays and protection. It can be combined with The Curtain to give a low-level ice day. It is deep and well defined in its upper reaches, but lower down it narrows, eventually becoming a crack before finally disappearing. It forms ice well, and under normal conditions it presents a steep ice runnel for the lower 70m. Lying low on the mountain however, it can be quickly stripped after a thaw. Gain and climb the deepening gully to belay in an ice cave. Continue above by the bulging ice wall to easier ground. Either continue up the easier upper gully to the crest of Tower Ridge, or if satisfied with the completion of the difficulties, traverse left and descend a shallow snow gully **1934 Route** (200m II) to reach snow slopes about 50m right of Douglas Gap West Gully. It has become quite common to abseil back down the route from the top of the difficulties, but be fair to parties below.

2 Italian Climb   180m   III *

J.R.Marshall, A.McCorquodale, G.J.Ritchie   Jan 1958

The deeply cut gully which defines the right flank of the steep two tiered buttress

BEN NEVIS - Coire na Ciste

| 18. Number Two Gully | II *** | 47. Number Four Gully | I * |
| 37. Number Three Gully | I ** | 59. Number Five Gully | I ** |

BEN NEVIS

right of Vanishing Gully provides a popular winter climb. This was Jimmy Marshall's first new route on the Ben. Care should be taken assessing snow conditions before attempting this route, since the large snowfield at the head of the gully lies on slabs, and is avalanche prone. The lower gully normally contains two good ice pitches, above which the angle eases to snow slopes and occasional ice, leading to the crest of Tower Ridge below the Little Tower. The alternatives are an abseil descent down Italian Right-Hand, from above its difficulties (see that route), or a descending traverse right from just before reaching Tower Ridge to gain Broad Gully (see diagram). Broad Gully leads down to the platform of Garadh na Ciste and a walk off right into Coire na Ciste.

Italian Right-Hand   IV,4 **
I.Fulton, S.Belk   Feb 1973
Better climbing than the original line, but harder. Follow the first pitch of the original route, climb the icefall on the right to a big thread, and rejoin the parent route shortly above on the easier upper section. A possible descent is to abseil from a thread above the difficulties, 60m or two shorter abseils, but this misses the easy upper section.

The Chute   220m   V,4 *
J.R.Marshall, R.N.Campbell, R.Holt   Feb 1965
This excellent route starts 30m right of Italian Climb and follows a prominent line of icy grooves directly up the face. Heavy snow conditions are required for the steep initial icefall to form. On the first ascent it was avoided by a rising traverse, first left then right, to gain entry to the grooves above (IV,4).
1. 30m Climb the icefall to the start of the grooves.

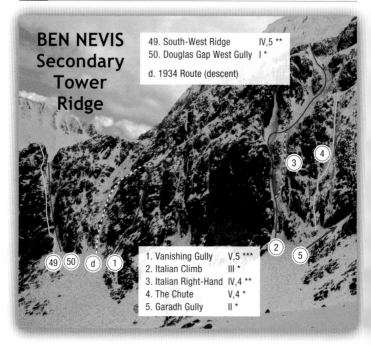

BEN NEVIS
Secondary
Tower
Ridge

49. South-West Ridge   IV,5 **
50. Douglas Gap West Gully I *

d. 1934 Route (descent)

1. Vanishing Gully   V,5 ***
2. Italian Climb   III *
3. Italian Right-Hand IV,4 **
4. The Chute   V,4 *
5. Garadh Gully   II *

2. 45m Move into an icy groove on the right and follow this to a horizontal ledge, which leads across a steep wall into a small gully.
3. 30m Traverse up and right to a stance below a steep ice wall.
4. 25m Climb the ice wall to the snow gully above.
5. and 6. 90m Continue above to a steep rock buttress and follow an easy snow shelf rightwards to the top of Broad Gully.

Garadh na Ciste

To the right of Italian Climb is a subsidiary buttress separated from the main mass of Tower Ridge by the wide Garadh Gully. The buttress is crowned by a spacious platform known as Garadh na Ciste.

5 Garadh Gully 95m II *
I.S.Clough, M.Bucke 16 Feb 1958
Although this gully is sometimes climbed for its own sake, it is often used as an interesting approach to routes starting higher up on the west flank of Tower Ridge (like Glover's Chimney). Under normal conditions the gully gives a straightforward climb with one or two short ice pitches. Later in the season it may bank out to a uniform snow slope.

Pinnacle Buttress of the Tower

Alt 1100m North-West facing Diagram p138

This well defined feature lies between Broad Gully and Glover's Chimney, and rises steeply to just below the Great Tower. The prominent crest of the buttress was unclimbed in winter until recently, but it now contains a superb mixed route. The buttress consists of two sections. A steep lower wall leads to a terrace that cuts across the buttress, and above this the buttress rears up as a steep prow. Above the prow, it is easiest to continue up an easy angled snow ridge and skirt round the left side of the Great Tower to gain Tower Ridge. If time permits, one of the Great Tower Variations such as **Recess Route** (45m IV,6) or **Cracked Slabs Route** (45m IV,5) makes a fine finish. Both start from the foot of the north-west arete and climb up to a broad platform. Recess Route steps off a large block into a chimney-recess above, and continues on good holds to the top of the Tower. Cracked Slabs Route climbs climb steep cracked slabs just to the right, followed by a shallow gully to the top.

6 Fatal Error   220m   IV,4 **

G.Dudley, S.M.Richardson   24 Mar 1996

This excellent mixed climb takes the prominent line of weakness just left of the steep crest of Pinnacle Buttress. The climbing is easier than it looks, but it is essential that the short slab at the start of pitch 2 is iced. The error, thankfully not fatal, occurred when Richardson dropped his axe high up on the route. Start by climbing Broad Gully for 50m to below a wide icy break in the right wall.

1. 50m A short ice step leads to a wide band of steep snow that trends up and right to the terrace. Belay below the prominent gully line that runs up left of the steep central section of the buttress.

2. 40m Climb a short icy slab to gain the gully and follow it for 35m to where it steepens, then move left along a short ramp to its top.

3. 45m Move awkwardly right along an upper ramp to gain the upper section of the gully. Climb this to its end, then traverse up and left below a smooth wall of slabs to reach the left edge of the buttress.

4. 35m Follow the buttress edge to a snow platform.

5. 50m Traverse easily left across snow to gain Tower Ridge about 30m below the Great Tower.

7 Stringfellow   230m   VI,6 ***

C.Cartwright, S.M.Richardson   11 Mar 1996

An outstanding icy mixed route up the crest of Pinnacle Buttress. One of the finest additions to the mountain in the '90s. Start in a snow bay below the upper prow and opposite the platform of Garadh na Ciste. At its top left is a shallow but well defined gully.

1. 50m Climb the gully, passing a steep section at half-height to reach the terrace. Cross this to below a slanting rake which cuts left to right through the lower part of the buttress.

2. 50m Follow the rake to its right end. Pull through a short steep wall and continue easily to a cave belay.

3. 25m Climb a shallow gully leading back left to a platform just left of the crest of the buttress.

4. 40m From the right end of the platform, climb a short icy wall cut by a vertical crack, and then move to the foot of steep twin grooves. Climb the right-hand groove, then move up to a block with a wide crack on its left side. Climb this and continue up the gully above to a large platform on the crest of the buttress. A difficult and sustained pitch.

5. 15m Climb up to the steep headwall, and move left to a notch. Swing up and left, the traverse left along an awkward narrow ledge to gain a prominent wide gap formed by a pinnacle.

6. 50m Follow the easy angled ridge to the foot of the Great Tower.

Pinnacle Buttress Direct   220m   V,5 **

R.Clothier, G.Armstrong   Mar 1989

This good ice route tackles the steep lower section of the buttress directly before taking a deep groove line on the right side of the front face of the buttress. Start at the right side of the snow bay directly below the upper groove, where a break in a barrier wall is found. Climb a ramp-line rightwards, then the icy wall above to enter the main groove line. Continue by the groove, with short ice bulges, moving left at the top to reach the foot of the Great Tower.

138

Pinnacle Buttress to Raeburn's Wall

BEN NEVIS

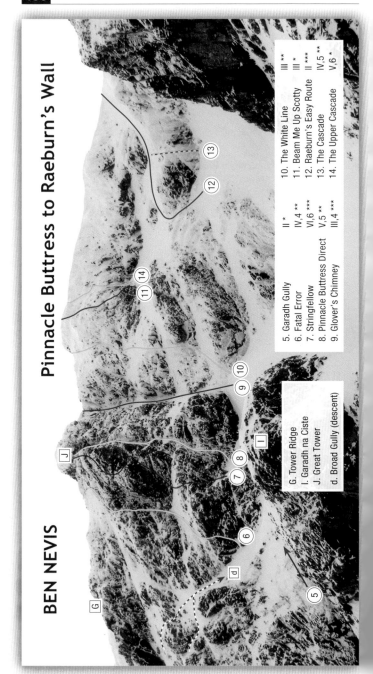

5. Garadh Gully	II *
6. Fatal Error	IV,4 **
7. Stringfellow	VI,6 ***
8. Pinnacle Buttress Direct	V,5 **
9. Glover's Chimney	III,4 ***

10. The White Line	III **
11. Beam Me Up Scotty	III *
12. Raeburn's Easy Route	II ***
13. The Cascade	IV,5 **
14. The Upper Cascade	V,6 *

G. Tower Ridge	
I. Garadh na Ciste	
J. Great Tower	
d. Broad Gully (descent)	

Raeburn's Wall

Alt 1100m   North-West facing   Map p108   Diagram p135, 138

This extends from Glover's Chimney, which leads up to the Tower Gap, across the west side of upper Tower Ridge and extending to the back wall of Coire na Ciste. The routes can be reached by skirting Garadh na Ciste to its right but it is more fun to climb Garadh Gully as a warm-up, which provides a more direct approach for the first two climbs.

9 Glover's Chimney   140m   III,4 *
G.G.Macphee, G.C.Williams, D.Henderson   17 Mar 1935
Dropping directly from Tower Gap to the right-hand end of Garadh na Ciste is a narrow gully which provides a fine and very popular winter route. This was one of the best routes by Graham Macphee who also repeated many of the routes while writing a new guidebook. Climb the initial icefall from left to right to a stance (35m), then take mixed snow and ice back left into the gully. Follow this easily on snow to the final chimney, and climb this to Tower Gap. This spectacular mixed pitch is seldom easy, but it is well protected.

0 The White Line   300m   III *
M.G.Geddes, H.Gillespie   18 Mar 1971
An excellent winter route. It comes into condition early and remains so throughout the season. Climb an icefall a few metres right of Glover's Chimney, cross a snow terrace and continue up a second icefall to gain a right-slanting snow ledge. A third icefall (sometimes difficult to start) leads to a snowfield. From the top of the snow-field, climb a short chimney, and then take a shallow gully, which leads left to open snowslopes, which finish at the top of Tower Ridge. The route is open to variation.

Beam Me Up Scotty   120m   III *
R.G.Reid, I.Crofton   Mar 1987
Interesting climbing up the line of grooves on the right side of the buttress formed between The White Line and the upper Cascade icefalls. Start in a narrow snow bay below the prominent icefall of The Upper Cascade itself.
1. 40m Climb the left-hand of two grooves on the left side of the bay until a steep section forces a move out left. Continue up to a ledge beneath a steep smooth wall.
2. 30m Follow a ramp-line diagonally right below the wall to gain an icy groove that leads straight up to more open mixed ground.
3. 50m Finish up snowslopes to the plateau.

Raeburn's Easy Route   250m   II *
SMC party, names not recorded   Apr 1920
The big but somewhat featureless wall between Tower Ridge and Number Two Gully holds ice very late in the season and provides this superb and reliable climb. Start 50m left of Number Two Gully and traverse left on snow to a large but easy angled icefall. Climb this for 30m to a snowslope which leads to a long right traverse below the upper wall. At its far end, gain the plateau by a shallow gully. The cornice is not usually too heavy at this point.

The Cascade   50m   IV,5 **
To the right of the icefall of Raeburn's Easy Route is a steep wall, containing a steep icefall. This provides a superb ice climb which is short but very sustained. Either finish up Raeburn's Easy Route or by The Upper Cascade.

The Upper Cascade   120m   V,6 *
G.Perroux, J.P.Destercke   Apr 1991
The steep curtain of ice on the left side of the upper wall. One of the first of many of Godefroy Perroux's icefall routes on the Ben. There are several steeper (and thinner!) icefalls further right. The icefall is vertical for the first 10m, but the angle then eases slightly (50m). Finish up snow to the cornice.

BEN NEVIS

Comb Gully Buttress, IV,5. Climber Colin Wells

Number Two Gully Buttress

Alt 1100m   North facing   Map p108   Diagram p135, 142

To the right of Raeburn's Wall is a scimitar shaped buttress, defined on the right by the wide and deeply cut Number Two Gully. This is Number Two Gully Buttress. There are several short but very worthwhile climbs here, which are often in good condition.

15 Five Finger Discount   135m   IV,4 *
M.G.Geddes, C.Higgins   4 Feb 1978
The right side of the smooth wall with Cascade forms a groove between it and Number Two Gully Buttress. The ice on the right side of the wall itself is **Rip Off** (120m IV,4).

16 Burrito's Groove   135m   IV,5 **
M.G.Geddes, C.Higgins   8 Apr 1978
This good climb takes a parallel groove about 20m right of Five Finger Discount. Climb the groove throughout, passing an overhang at 45m on the left, or continue straight up if it is well iced.

7 Number Two Gully Buttress   120m   III ★★
J.R.Marshall, L.S.Lovat, A.H.Hendry   23 Mar 1958
A popular and enjoyable route near the crest overlooking Number Two Gully. Climb easy angled mixed rock and ice to a large snowfield where the buttress steepens. About 20m left of the buttress crest, climb a steep ice groove for 20m, then trend right on snow and ice to reach the crest of the buttress a little below the plateau. A slightly harder variation climbs a groove close to the crest itself.

8 Number Two Gully   120m   II ★★★
J.Collier, G.Hastings, W.C.Slingsby   Apr 1896
This is the finest of the easy gullies on the mountain, passing through good scenery. The gully fills up well and is normally a steep snow slope with perhaps a short ice pitch at the narrows. The cornice is often large and difficult, and is best passed on the left. Early in the winter the route can be very interesting, and significantly harder (Grade III).

Comb Gully Buttress

Alt 1100m   North-East facing   Diagram p135, 142

This wedge shaped buttress between Number Two Gully and Comb Gully has an easy angled lower crest which leads to a broad middle snowfield topped by a steep headwall.

9 Comb Gully Buttress   125m   IV,5 ★★
I.S.Clough, J.M.Alexander   8 Jan 1960; Variation Finish: I.Fulton, D.Gardner   3 Jan 1971
This good route is normally combined with The Variation Finish which is more often in condition. Either start from just left of the lowest rocks and gain the central snowfield or, harder, climb directly up the lower chimney a little to the left (IV,4). Above the snowfield, follow a groove on the left edge of the buttress. The Original Route makes a rising traverse right to the foot of a chimney in the steep final rocks. This chimney is not so often in condition so the variation is usually followed. After the groove, go left to an ice column. Climb this to an ice filled groove which narrows and steepens and leads to the top.

Clough's Chimney   130m   VI,6 ★
S.M.Richardson, R.Clothier, R.Goolden   16 Apr 2000 (as described)
The prominent left-curving chimney splitting the centre of the steep headwall. Named in memory of Ian Clough who climbed the final pitch in 1960 during the original winter ascent of the buttress, after approaching from the left.
1. 50m Climb the easy lower section of the buttress and the snowfield to a belay right of the deep central chimney of Comb Gully Buttress.
2. 40m The chimney is undercut at its base. Make a difficult series of moves over the steep initial bulge and continue up the chimney to a good block belay.
3. 40m Continue up the left-curving chimney above to gain a snow ramp that leads to the flat top of Comb Gully Buttress just below the plateau rim.

Roaring Forties   130m   V,5 ★
D.F.Lang, C.Stead   28 Feb 1988
This superb looking line meets the challenge of the steep headwall by the striking right-curving icy V-groove.
1. 50m Climb the easy lower section of the buttress and snowfield to below a steep shallow gully 15m right of the deep central slot of Clough's Chimney.
2. 30m Continue up the gully to a ledge on the left.
3. 50m Traverse left for 6m and climb the long V-groove to the top.

Comb Gully   125m   IV,4 ★★★
F.G.Stangle, R.Morsley, P.A.Small   12 Apr 1938
The prominent gully which separates Comb Gully Buttress from The Comb provides a splendid climb which is in condition for most of the winter (but it is very hard in

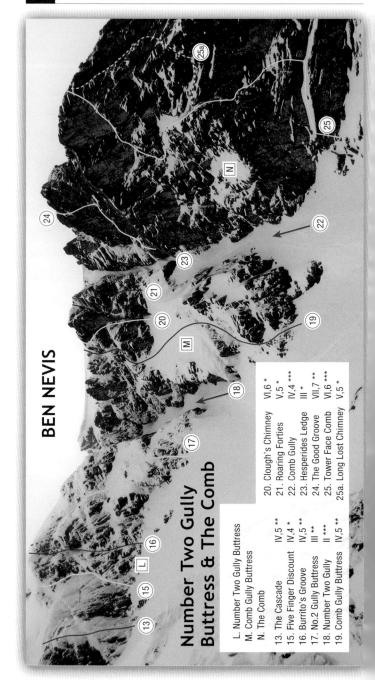

BEN NEVIS

Number Two Gully Buttress & The Comb

L. Number Two Gully Buttress
M. Comb Gully Buttress
N. The Comb

13. The Cascade	IV,5 **
15. Five Finger Discount	IV,4 *
16. Burrito's Groove	IV,5 **
17. No.2 Gully Buttress	III **
18. Number Two Gully	II ***
19. Comb Gully Buttress	IV,5 **

20. Clough's Chimney	VI,6 *
21. Roaring Forties	V,5 *
22. Comb Gully	IV,4 ***
23. Hesperides Ledge	III *
24. The Good Groove	VII,7 **
25. Tower Face Comb	VI,6 ***
25a. Long Lost Chimney	V,5 *

Comb Gully, IV,4. Climber Steve Elliott

early season when there is a cave pitch). The belays are good when found, but protection can be sparse. Follow easy snow to the narrows where a long pitch leads to a belay. Climb a short steep ice wall on the right (crux) to easy ground which leads to the top.

The Comb

Alt 1000m North facing Map p108 Diagrams p135, 142

This great wedge shaped buttress dominates the southerly part of Coire na Ciste. On each flank steep gullies define the buttress. To the left is Comb Gully and to the right, Green Gully, which separates The Comb from Number Three Gully Buttress. On the approach the buttress is dominated by a great overhanging wall facing Coire na Ciste. It is girdled by three prominent sloping fault-lines which rise from left to right. The lower fault, which is taken by **Pigott's Route** (200m V,6) runs up the base of the overhanging wall. The middle fault starts at the entrance to Comb Gully and crosses the buttress at one-third height. Initially it is a good ledge, but it soon disappears into a crack as it cuts through the top of the overhanging wall on the north side of the buttress. The upper fault, which is not visible from below, is known as Hesperides Ledge and runs up to the crest from the middle of Comb Gully. The routes on the Comb Gully side get the sun in late season, so are not likely to be in condition after the end of March.

Hesperides Ledge   200m   III *
J.R.Marshall, J.Stenhouse, D.Haston   12 Feb 1959
An exposed and exciting route taking the highest prominent shelf leading out right. Climb Comb Gully for 70m to an obvious snow ramp leading right onto the crest of the buttress. Follow this, with a difficult and exposed step, for two pitches to reach the crest. Continue up the crest in a fine position to the top.

The Good Groove   130m   VII,7 **
S.M.Richardson, R.D.Everett   27 Mar 1993 (1 peg rest); FFA: S.Halstead, J.Kuczera   6 Mar 2005
This excellent icy mixed climb takes the striking curving groove which cuts through the triangular headwall above Hesperides Ledge. Start by climbing Comb Gully for

70m to the beginning of Hesperides Ledge.

1. 30m The only line of weakness cutting the steep wall above Hesperides Ledge is a tiered ramp which slants up right then left. Climb delicately up to the start of the ramp, then move left with difficulty along the second narrow ramp into a corner. Follow this to a belay at the left end of the curving groove, just right of an icefall which is **The Comb, Left Flank** (100m IV,4).

2. 25m Follow the slab forming the right side of the groove up and right to a small stance below a steep tapering corner.

3. 25m Move up into the corner, and climb it with increasing difficulty to its top (crux). Continue up the following corner, then step left to a good platform.

4. 50m Climb the wall above the belay to gain a sharp horizontal ridge which leads to the plateau.

25 Tower Face of the Comb   250m   VI,6 ***
R.Smith, R.K.Holt   1 Jan 1959

One of the best mixed routes on the mountain. A great achievement by the young Edinburgh University team, the route was unrepeated for more than 25 years and acquired a huge reputation, but it now sees many ascents and has gained classic status. It is climbable throughout the season, but is best in icy conditions from late January onwards. Start just above the foot of Comb Gully where an obvious ledge cuts diagonally across the buttress at one-third height.

1. 40m From the left end of the ledge, climb a left-facing corner to reach a parallel ledge 10m higher. Move right until halfway along the ledge then climb a short steep wall and mixed ground to a good belay below the prominent left-facing groove that cuts through the steep lower section of the face.

2. 50m Climb the groove and continue up easier ground to belay below an impending wall. A fine and sustained pitch.

3. 45m Traverse left past a series of flakes and broken blocks then climb straight up turfy mixed ground to below a steep wall. Traverse right along a ledge to belay by a large flake which forms a window on the right.

4. 35m Move right to the end of the ledge, then climb a steep wall on the left before breaking out right to the crest.

5. and 6. 80m Continue more easily up the crest to the plateau.

Variation: **Long Lost Chimney   70m   V,5 ***
R.Everett, S.M.Richardson   31st March 1996

A worthwhile variation taking an elegant line up the crest of the buttress. Start from the top of the prominent groove on pitch 2.

1. 40m Traverse horizontally right for 10m then move up and right to climb the groove and chimney system on the crest of the buttress to a stance on the arete.

2. 30m Climb the arete (awkward) over a series of steep steps to where the angle eases and the original line comes in from the left at the end of pitch 4.

26 Mercury   150m   V,5 **
M.Hind, J.Christie   26 Jan 1985

A good ice route taking the furthest right of the four parallel grooves just left of Green Gully. The initial section is often thinly iced.

1. 30m Start just left of Green Gully and climb icy grooves to reach a chimney with a small chockstone (possible belay). Move left into the main groove and follow it to a small stance below a small overhang. If conditions are lean, it is possible to reach the chimney by climbing Green Gully for 10m then moving left around a rib.

2. 40m Move left and continue up the groove, which gradually eases, to belay on a big flake on the left.

3. and 4. 80m Climb the groove and continue over steep icy walls before trending left to the buttress crest. Follow this to the top.

27 Green Gully   180m   IV,4 ***
H.Raeburn, E.Phildius   Apr 1906

The prominent gully defining the right flank of The Comb is a popular classic and a fine companion to Comb Gully. This impressive ascent in 1906 by Harold Raeburn was unrecognised for many years. It is often in condition; a good choice

BEN NEVIS

Green Gully, IV.4. Climber Susan Jensen

early in the winter because, unlike Comb Gully, no surprises appear in thin conditions. Good climbers often say it is overgraded, but the ice pitches are quite long and the finish can be intimidating if the snow is soft. It has good belays, although they can be difficult to find on the central section of the route (but are sometimes in place). Climb a steep ice pitch (which can vary depending on the snow build-up) to a belay on the left wall (45m). Continue up the gully for two or three ice pitches. Above, the gully fans out and there are a choice of finishes. The easiest option is to trend left to the ridge at the top of The Comb. The best finish is straight up via a fine direct ice pitch, but a large cornice can make this problematical. A right finish is also often corniced.

Number Three Gully Buttress

Alt 1100m   North facing   Map p145   Diagram p135, 146

Number Three Gully Buttress extends rightwards from Green Gully, and presents first a broad slabby wall, then a very steep buttress. A huge open left-facing corner, taken by Quickstep, defines the junction of the two sections of the buttress. The buttress is bounded on its right edge by Number Three Gully.

Diana   190m   V,5 **
M.Duff, J.Tinker   16 Feb 1985
This route takes a direct line on ice, crossing Aphrodite. It provides a fine climb, but needs a good winter to come into condition. Start at the foot of the icefall to the right of Green Gully.
1. 50m Climb the icefall, then snow, to belay beneath a steep rock wall.
2. 45m Climb the chimney-groove in the centre of the steep wall. Pull over a large chockstone to reach another snow band and a huge block stance. Aphrodite crosses near here and finishes on the left.
3. 25m Follow corners to below a huge right-facing corner.
4. 45m Pull over an overlap onto the right wall and continue up steep thin ice to easier ground. The grade becomes V,4 if the ice is thick enough for solid placements.
5. 25m Follow the obvious line up snow to the top.

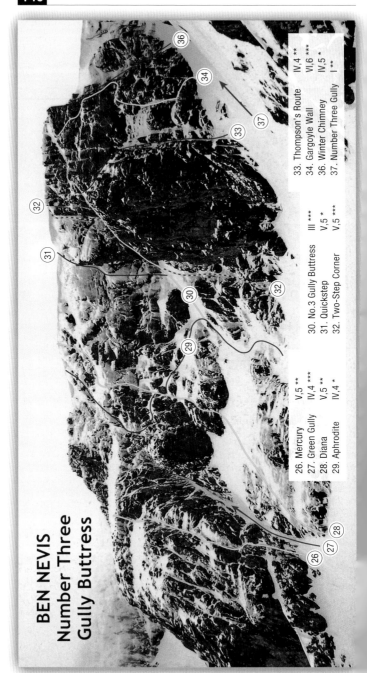

BEN NEVIS
Number Three
Gully Buttress

26. Mercury   V,5 **
27. Green Gully   IV,4 ***
28. Diana   V,5 **
29. Aphrodite   IV,4 *

30. No.3 Gully Buttress   III ***
31. Quickstep   V,5 *
32. Two-Step Corner   V,5 ***

33. Thompson's Route   IV,4 **
34. Gargoyle Wall   VI,6 ***
36. Winter Chimney   IV,5 *
37. Number Three Gully   I **

Quickstep, V,5. Climber Dave McGimpsey

BEN NEVIS

Aphrodite   200m   IV,4 *
M.G.Geddes, J.C.Higham   15 Mar 1971
This good but wandering route traverses left along the second snowy ledge system at half-height on the face to finish up mixed ground to the right of Green Gully. Start in a snowy depression just right of the centre of the base of the buttress (as for Number Three Gully Buttress). Climb to the foot of a slabby wall, then traverse up and left on snowy ledges until it is possible to make a hard move down and left to the foot of an open groove which is undercut by a large rock wall. Climb the groove and its continuation on the crest beside Green Gully. Move up right across snow to the cornice, which can sometimes be difficult.

Number Three Gully Buttress   160m   III ***
L.S.Lovat, D.J.Bennet   18 Feb 1957
One of the finest medium grade winter climbs on the mountain. The route is somewhat exposed in places, and the upper section can be time consuming if the snow is not consolidated. Start as for Aphrodite in a snowy bay just right of centre of the lower part of the buttress. Climb up to a snow shelf and follow it up to the right. From its highest point make a steep but short traverse right to a snowy platform. This traverse can either be on snow and ice, or mixed and still be Grade III. Go up to a rocky headwall. Either climb straight up the Chimney Variation, with a well protected move of technical 5 unless very icy, or follow the original line, which makes an exposed traverse right to gain icy slabs.

The large open slabby corner which splits the buttress into two distinct sections is interrupted by the traverse line of Number Three Gully Buttress. Quickstep follows the corner, and the obvious fault-line to the right is taken by Two-Step Corner.

Quickstep   150m   V,5 *
T.Bray, R.Townsend   26 Mar 1983
This excellent steep ice climb is based on the left of the two large left-facing corners. It is slightly harder than its Two Step companion. Start as for Number Three Gully Buttress to gain the corner. Move left to gain the icefall running down the left wall and climb it to the basin below the cornice, which can be by-passed on the right.

Gargoyle Wall, VI,6. Climbers Konrad Rawlik and Sam Loveday

32 Two-Step Corner 150m V,5 ***

D.Kirtley, D.Montgomery Mar 1975

Another good ice climb which is fairly often in condition. Start 20m right of the snow bay at the foot of Number Three Gully Buttress below an icy groove. Climb the groove to the prominent ledge on which Number Three Gully Buttress crosses rightwards, and continue up the very steep corner to the top. There is often a large cornice which can be avoided by a traverse to the right.

33 Thompson's Route 110m IV,4 **

R.Marshall, J.R.Marshall, J.Stenhouse Dec 1963

The steepest section of the buttress is bounded on the right by a line of icy chimneys which are effectively on the left wall of Number Three Gully. These provide a good and sustained route which has a well deserved reputation for quality amongst Nevis regulars. Climb the chimneys to a headwall, then move left to the large platform above the very steep lower buttress. Finish as for Number Three Gully Buttress original line, which it meets coming from the other direction.

34 Gargoyle Wall 120m VI,6 ***

R.Carrington, I.Nicolson Dec 1977; Complete Ascent, as described: S.M.Richardson, C.Cartwright 22 Feb 1998

One of the finest mixed routes on the mountain with a memorable crux. The route traverses past the Gargoyle – a prominent head shaped feature that can be seen on the right skyline when descending Number Three Gully. Icing can ease the difficulty of the first two pitches, but the route has become popular in recent years as a snowed up rock climb, with good protection when not iced. Lying high on the mountain it hoars up fast and comes into condition quickly. Start on a ledge 20m up and right of the chimney of Thompson's Route below a right-facing chimney-flake.

1. 10m   Climb the flake to a well defined ledge.

2. 30m   From the left end of the ledge, descend slightly and enter the chimney on the left. Climb this, surmount a chockstone and gain a snow bay with the Gargoyle now visible on the right. In icy conditions it is possible to climb the chimney directly from below and eliminate the first stance.

3. 30m   Cross a groove and follow a short gangway to reach the top of the Gargoyle. Climb the ridge above, passing a perched block, to gain a ledge. Traverse right into a shattered corner, and climb this to a stance and block belay below a steep cracked wall.

4. 15m   Climb the Gargoyle Wall Cracks (crux) on the left side of the wall to a platform.

5. 25m   Traverse 6m left to a chimney-crack, and climb this to where it steepens. Move left along a ledge to reach a right-trending ramp.

6. 10m   Finish easily along the ramp to the top of the buttress.

5 Babylon   100m   VII,7 *
S.M.Richardson, C.Cartwright   8 Apr 2001

A very steep mixed line up the right edge of Number Three Gully Buttress finishing up the prominent hanging chimney slot overlooking Winter Chimney. Challenging and sustained with each pitch harder than the last. Start at the foot of Winter Chimney.

1. 40m   Step left onto the buttress edge and climb it using a flake-crack. Continue up an open groove to a rectangular rib. Climb the corner on the right side of the rib to reach the platform below the Gargoyle Wall Cracks.

2. 15m   Climb the Gargoyle Wall Cracks to a good ledge.

3. 15m   Step up and right around the edge and traverse right (tenuous) to gain a small ledge below the roof guarding entry to the hanging chimney.

4. 30m   Pull over the roof (crux) and climb the off-width above to gain the chimney which leads to a good platform at the top of the buttress.

Winter Chimney   70m   IV,5 *
D.Haston, D.Gray   Mar 1963

The deeply recessed icy chimney lying in the back of the bay to the right of the buttress is a late season gem and graded for good thick ice. It is a sustained route with three or four short steep ice sections. The crux is an overhang at two-thirds height that is turned on the right.

Number Three Gully   90m   I **
J.N.Collie, M.W.Travers   Apr 1895

This is the large gully situated at the back of Coire na Ciste, separating Number Three Gully Buttress from Creag Coire na Ciste. Walking directly up the Tourist Path leads to the top of this gully. It can be easily identified from above by a pinnacle standing as a flat topped blade of rock at the head of the gully. This is a useful landmark when trying to locate the gully when the plateau is shrouded in mist. The gully is a straightforward snow slope, although the final 10m may be quite icy. If using the gully for descent, start to the right of the pinnacle.

Creag Coire na Ciste

Alt 1100m   North-East facing   Map p149   Diagram p135, 152

The buttresses between Number Three and Number Four Gullies are known as Creag Coire na Ciste. The left end of the cliff is set at a high angle, and is seamed by a number of steep gullies. The cornices may present a formidable problem.

38 Cornucopia   90m   VII,8 *
C.Cartwright, S.M.Richardson   14 Apr 1996 (1 rest point); FFA: U.Stoeker, D.MacLeod 20 Feb 2001
The smooth steep corner on the right wall of Number Three Gully. A sought after test piece which heralded modern mixed climbing on The Ben. Pitch 2 is well protected but is sustained and technical with a puzzling crux. It was originally climbed under powder and graded technical 9, but several recent ascents have found it easier in more icy conditions. Start by climbing Number Three Gully until opposite the foot of Winter Chimney.
1. 10m Climb easily up and right across steep snow to a small stance at the foot of the main corner-line.
2. 25m Follow the crack-line on the right wall of the corner for 5m, then step left into the corner (thread runner). Climb the impending corner with increasing difficulty (crux) to a welcome alcove. Traverse right along a narrow ledge, and move up to a good, but small and exposed stance on the edge of the buttress. In icy conditions it is easier to avoid the section on the right wall at the start and follow the corner throughout.
3. 20m Climb the booming flake above the stance to its top (3m), then step down and left into the corner which is now a narrow chimney. Climb this, past two chockstones, to gain the large platform above. Another difficult pitch.
4. 35m Move up over blocks and snow to the top right corner of the platform. Pull up an overhanging wall just left of an arete with a large spike, and continue up easier ground to the top.

39 Darth Vader   100m   VII,7 ***
S.M.Richardson, C.Cartwright   30 Mar 1997
This outstanding mixed climb takes the striking chimney-crack which slices through the blank vertical wall at the left end of Creag Coire na Ciste. Another well known line, but hard enough to discourage or repel previous attempts. It has now become popular. Start directly below the chimney, just right of the foot of Number Three Gully.
1. 25m Climb an open icy groove to a ledge running beneath the vertical wall. Move right to belay on blocks just right of the chimney-crack.
2. 20m Entry to the chimney is barred by a 3m wall. Climb this (awkward) and continue up the chimney to a surprise cave stance.
3. 25m Pull over the roof of the cave and enter a bottomless groove. Continue up the chimney above to belay on a large platform (as for Cornucopia).
4. 30m Continue in the same line of the main chimney-crack by climbing the chimney at the back of the platform, before moving up and right to finish.

40 South Gully   120m   III *
G.G.Macphee   10 Apr 1936
A bold solo by Macphee. Start from the foot of the narrow section of Number Three Gully, level with the lowest rocks of Number Three Gully Buttress. Climb an obvious slanting ledge leading right to the foot of a steep gully which turns back left. Normally there will be a couple of ice pitches, although they can bank out under heavy snow.

41 Lost the Place   140m   V,5 **
C.Cartwright, R.Clothier   17 Dec 1988
This neglected gem takes a superb natural line through one of the steeper features on the cliff. The buttress between South and Central Gullies is cut by a hidden left-trending groove system. Follow this trending left to a platform overlooking South Gully. Continue moving up and left along an awkward narrow left-trending break to reach a deep icy chimney that leads straight up to the cornice.

42 Une Journee Ordinaire dans un Enfer Quotidien   110m   V,6 **
G.Perroux, F.Bossier, J.Douay   15 Apr 1993
A good steep ice climb that is often good late in the season. The cornice can be very large and is best turned on the left. Start just right of the left-trending groove

BEN NEVIS

Darth Vadar, VII,7. Climber Kenny Grant

system of Lost the Place.

1. 20m Climb an ice groove to a small cave stance with a thin icefall just to its right.

2. 45m **Cloudwalker** (110m VI,6) moves into a steep shallow slot on the left. For this route, climb the icefall, exit left, then continue up a further short steep section to belay on the left.

3. 45m Continue up easy snow and climb a steep 8m ice wall to reach the cornice.

Central Gully   120m   III,4 **

I.S.Clough, J.M.Alexander   28 Jan 1959

A popular gully climb. Start by climbing snow left of a rib to reach the foot of two parallel ice gullies. Climb the left-hand gully on steep ice (strenuous but with good protection) and continue up snow to the plateau.

Central Gully Right-Hand   120m   IV,4 ***

I.A.MacEacharan, J.Knight   Date unknown

An excellent and sustained ice pitch with good belays. Start as for Central Gully and climb the right-hand chimney throughout.

152

BEN NEVIS – Creag Coire na Ciste

37. Number Three Gully — I **
38. Cornucopia — VII,8 *
39. Darth Vader — VII,7 ***
40. South Gully — III *
41. Lost the Place — V,5 **
42. Une Journee Ordinaire — V,6 **
43. Central Gully — III,4 **
44. Central Gully Right-Hand — IV,4 ***
45. Wendigo — IV,4 *
46. North Gully — II **

5 Wendigo   120m   IV,4 *
T.W.Patey, J.Brown   24 Feb 1963

This was Patey's last new route on Ben Nevis and takes a right-trending line into a big snow funnel above steep walls. According to native American folklore, a wendigo is a man-eating monster who haunts the desolate forests and icy wastelands of the northern USA and Canada. Those surviving the route uneaten will have found an enjoyable climb, consisting of ice in its lower section, and interesting mixed ground in its upper half. Start in a bay right of Central Gully. Climb moderate ice then snow to the terrace below the steep part of the cliff. Continue by trending right up mixed ground to a large platform. Move up and right to enter the snow funnel which leads to the cornice. This can be huge, but is often avoidable on the left.

6 North Gully   110m   II **
J.Y.MacDonald, H.W.Turnbull   24 Mar 1934

The obvious narrow gully close to the entrance of Number Four Gully gives a good little climb. The first section is often full of ice, and the route is reliably in condition early in the season (it tends to bank out later to become much easier but less good). Climb the initial gully, then traverse up and right to a large snow fan leading to the plateau. Beware of avalanche danger on the final slopes. A scoop and steep ice groove on the left gives an alternative Grade III last pitch.

7 Number Four Gully   100m   I *
A.E.Maylard, W.W.Naismith, F.C.Squance   Apr 1895

The most straightforward of the Nevis gullies, and the best descent route from the plateau. There is a marker post at the top. The gully is a simple snow slope, and the cornice can always be turned on the right towards the upper slopes of Number Four Gully Buttress. About halfway up the gully, a chimney splits the left wall. This can be climbed at Grade III.

Trident Buttresses

Alt 950 to 1050m   East facing   Map p108   Diagram p135, 157

The triple buttresses right of Number Four Gully and forming the right wall of Coire na Ciste, are the South, Central and North Trident Buttresses. The most southerly (topmost) and best defined of the three is composed of three tiers and is bounded on the left by Number Four Gully, and on the right by Central Gully. The following three routes climb the middle tier, which is reached by traversing the middle ledge from below the narrows of Number Four Gully. An obvious feature at the right end of the tier is the huge corner of The Clanger. The next route climbs the slab left of it. Both routes can either finish up the upper ridge of the buttress (Pinnacle Arete), or descend leftwards to the base of Number Four Gully – both about Grade II.

The Slab Climb   100m   VI,7 **
A.Nisbet, J.Preston   9 Nov 2001

The slab left of The Clanger is somewhat hidden from many angles but gives a superb and unexpectedly helpful direct line through some impressive ground. Generally well protected and a good early season choice under powder. The first ice pitch of The Clanger would make a good start if well formed. Start right of a corner which is 20m left of the huge corner of The Clanger.

1. 20m Climb up towards this corner, then traverse right (or go further up and descend right) to a short wall below the main slab. Climb the wall to the base of the slab which has two thin cracks.

2. 40m Climb the slab near the right crack (or the crack itself) towards an overlap. Traverse left into the left crack and climb near it to a ledge (possible belay). Continue up to a prominent overhanging chimney slot.

3. 15m Climb the chimney (strenuous).

4. 25m Follow the continuation of the chimney to the top of the tier.

49 The Clanger 90m IV,5 **
J.R.Marshall, R.Marshall, R.N.Campbell Mar 1967
The chimney-groove at the back of the large corner near the right end of the middle tier gives a sustained and difficult mixed climb. Be warned – it is not a route for the broader climber! Start at the foot of the groove, and climb mixed rock and ice to a steep cave pitch (35m). Escape from the cave by the right wall, where a narrow through route leads behind a large flake onto the crest of the buttress. Easier climbing leads to the top.

50 Pinnacle Arete 200m IV,4 *
R.H.Sellars, J.Smith 1 Feb 1959
The grade assumes some consolidated snow, as it is quite hard under powder. Start from the right end of the middle terrace at a point overlooking the steep north wall of the buttress. Climb a series of snow and ice grooves immediately right of the crest to the easier upper section of the buttress.

51 Joyful Chimneys 250m IV,4
R.N.Campbell, J.R.Marshall Feb 1971
This worthwhile mid season route follows a series of four icy chimneys on the right flank of the buttress about 50m down and left of Central Gully. Start just right of a distinctive long thin rib and climb the first chimney. The second chimney is bottomless and entered from a flake on the left, and the third is avoided by grooves immediately to its left. These lead to a further series of grooves and the crest of South Trident Buttress.

52 Central Gully 240m III *
H.Raeburn, C.Inglis Clark, J.Inglis Clark Apr 1904
A fine climb with an alpine feel. It lies almost directly above Lochan na Ciste, separating the right-hand end of South Trident Buttress from several subsidiary buttresses to the right. The lower gully is well defined, and the upper half consists of large snowfields which can be avalanche prone after heavy snowfall. Follow the lower gully to a steep ice column. Turn this on the left, and return right to the original line as soon as possible. Climb the snowfields, with some short difficult steps, to reach the plateau. The ice column can be climbed direct (30m III,4).

53 Nasturtium 250m IV,4 *
D.Cuthbertson, J.Wells, R.Murray 26 Mar 2002
A good and varied expedition based on the attractive right-curling icy groove just right of Central Gully.
1. 20m Start by following Central Gully to the foot of the right-curling groove.
2. 40m Continue up the groove and belay below a right-facing corner.
3. 50m Climb the corner to its top. Belay on a rocky plinth.
4. 40m Move up snow to an icefall. Climb this (15m) to reach a wide snowfield.
5. and 6. 100m Move up to the left-bounding ridge and follow this to the top.

54 Jubilee Climb 240m II
G.G.Macphee, G.C.Williams, D.Henderson 5 May 1935
An interesting climb on snow with some short ice pitches. From near the foot of Central Gully, trend right up a ramp to reach a wide snow terrace, where a choice of lines leads to the top. Care should be taken in avalanche conditions.

To the right of Jubilee Climb is Central Trident Buttress, easily picked out on the approach as an extremely steep, rounded wall hopefully with a prominent icefall.

55 Mega Route X 70m V,6 ***
J.Murphy, A.Cain 18 Dec 1982
This very steep icefall has a substantial reputation, but it was made to look almost ridiculously straightforward by Dave 'Cubby' Cuthbertson during a filmed ascent for the BBC series *The Edge*. The lowest 5m takes a long time to form, and the

icefall sometimes crashes to the ground at about the point it becomes climbable.

North Trident Buttress is smaller and right of the steep wall. It is split by the S shaped **Neptune Gully** (150m III). The crest right of this is the line of **North Trident Buttress** (200m III), a good mixed climb up the buttress which overlooks Moonlight Gully.

6 Moonlight Gully   150m   II *
W.Inglis Clark, T.Gibson   3 Jan 1898
This pleasant snow gully, the next gully left of Number Five, separates North Trident Buttress from Moonlight Gully Buttress. It is narrow and straight and ends in the wide upper funnel of Number Five Gully.

Moonlight Gully Buttress

Alt 900m   East facing   Map p155   Diagram p135, 157

The two-tiered buttress between Moonlight Gully and Number Five Gully offers a number of options for poorer conditions. It is split at two-thirds height by a broad shelf. On a wild winter's day it may be preferable to descend by following the shelf to the left (looking in) and descending a snowslope to Lochan na Ciste.

7 Diagonal Route   150m   III
D.Hawthorn, C.MacLean, A.Paul   17 Dec 1983
Start at the foot of Moonlight Gully and climb up then right to a broad ledge. Continue by the left-hand of two chimneys to the top of the first tier. Climb the upper tier by the continuation chimney.

8 Right-Hand Chimney   150m   IV,4 *
D.Hawthorn, C.MacLean, A.Paul   17 Dec 1983
A good sustained mixed climb. Start mid-way between Moonlight Gully and Number Five Gully, at the foot of the rightmost and better defined of the chimneys splitting the buttress. The route follows the chimney throughout, and is steep and sustained in its lower half. Thereafter, easier climbing leads to the top of the first tier. Climb the upper tier by the continuation of the chimney with little difficulty.

Number Five Gully   450m   I **
J.N.Collie and party   Apr 1895
The gully immediately left of Càrn Dearg Buttress is wide and shallow in its lower reaches, and higher up it opens out into a small corrie. The cornices can be massive, but the rim is extensive and an exit should always be possible. There is often a large cone of debris at the foot of the gully which testifies to its tendency to avalanche.

Ledge Route   450m   II ****
SMC party   Easter 1897
This is probably the best route of its grade on the mountain, with sustained interest and magnificent situations. Start up Number Five Gully, but leave it by a right-slanting ramp soon after it becomes a gully proper. Follow the ramp over the top of The Curtain to a broad almost horizontal ledge which fades out on the right. Before the ledge narrows, leave it by a left-slanting gully which comes out on a broad snow shelf. Pass a large pinnacle block before rounding the corner to reach a platform. Continue up the ridge, narrow in places, to the north-west summit of Càrn Dearg. In good visibility, Ledge Route can be used for descent. From the top, follow the narrow ridge down to the top of Càrn Dearg buttress, then take the broad highest shelf (marked by the pinnacle block) to reach Number Five Gully. Instead of descending the gully (which may contain a short ice pitch), continue to the far side where another broad shelf leads gradually down from the large ledge at the top of Moonlight Gully Buttress towards Lochan na Ciste.

CÀRN DEARG BUTTRESS

Alt 800m   North-East facing   Map p156   Diagrams p157, 158

The Great Buttress of Càrn Dearg lies to the right of Number Five Gully. The rock architecture of its magnificent front face, consisting of overlapping slabs, huge corners, and sweeping overhangs, is unequalled anywhere else in the British Isles. The right-hand end of the buttress is defined by an impressive vertical wall, with a long gully to its right (Waterfall Gully). The best descent is to follow Ledge Route into Number Five Gully (on the left looking up).

Càrn Dearg is an awe inspiring place in winter and the routes tend to be hard mixed climbs with sections of ice. Most of the climbs are of high quality, but they are not often in condition. Optimum conditions occur usually in mid-season, after a heavy snowfall, followed by a sustained freeze. Much of the ice here is stripped quickly by thaw. However, The Curtain (the huge icefall down the left-hand side of the buttress) is more often in condition, although it gets too much sun later in the season.

61 The Curtain Rail   80m   IV,4 *
D.F.Lang, R.T.Richardson, C.Stead   31 Jan 1988
The groove and icefall left of and parallel to The Curtain. A good alternative when the queues on The Curtain are too long. Beware of falling ice and other debris!
1. 30m Follow the groove to the foot of the icefall.
2. 50m Climb the icefall on the right to reach Ledge Route. An easier alternative is to continue up the groove on steep snow (50m II).

62 The Curtain   90m   IV,5 ***
J.Knight, D.Bathgate   Feb 1965
This magnificent exercise in ice climbing is an excellent introduction to the steeper routes. It probably receives more ascents than any other route of its grade on the mountain. Start at the foot of the huge iced slab at the left end of the buttress. For confident parties, the last two pitches can be combined and the top belay reached on the rope stretch.
1. 40m Climb the slab to a cave belay at its top.
2. 20m Move left and climb the bulging wall above to reach an exposed stance under a rock wall, immediately left of a steep iced wall.
3. 30m Climb the wall trending right to gain an icy groove which leads to Ledge Route. Belay well back.

63 Route I   175m   VI,6 **
D.Knowles, D.Wilson   1972
A challenging mixed route, climbed several years ahead of it time. Near the left-hand side of the cliff (but right of The Curtain), above a curving subsidiary buttress, is a long deep chimney which runs up to join Ledge Route. This is the line of Route I. From the foot of The Curtain, follow the obvious ledge right over the top of the subsidiary buttress for 60m to the foot of the chimney. The first pitch is difficult, and the final chimney may call for some cunning. If it proves too tight a squeeze, it is possible to avoid it by steep moves on the right wall.

64 Route II Direct   265m   VI,6 ***
M.G.Geddes, A.Rouse   12 Feb 1978 (3PA); Direct: G.Smith, I.Sykes   15 Feb 1978
A superb outing traversing from right to left across the central slabs of Càrn Dearg Buttress. It is graded for good conditions, with ice on the slabs, otherwise the grade might be higher and tension used, as on the first ascent. Immediately right of the subsidiary buttress taken by the Direct Start to Route I is a right-facing corner. Start below the deep corner next to the right. Climb the corner, traverse left below an overhang, move up to a large block and continue up the groove above. Traverse right round an arete and climb the bulge above to reach the traverse ledge. Climb the first chimney pitch of Route I (20m), then take a diagonal line across the slabs close under the overhangs, to reach a groove on the far edge of the buttress. Follow this up the crest to easy ground. It is possible to avoid the lower section of the

BEN NEVIS – Trident Buttresses & Moonlight Gully Buttress

Q. South Trident Buttress
R. Central Trident Buttress
S. North Trident Buttress
T. Moonlight Gully Buttress
U. Càrn Dearg Buttress

47. Number Four Gully	I *
50. Pinnacle Arete	IV,4 *
51. Joyful Chimneys	IV,4
52. Central Gully	III *
53. Nasturtium	IV,4 *
54. Jubilee Climb	II
55. Mega Route X	V,6 ***
56. Moonlight Gully	II *
57. Diagonal Route	III
58. Right-Hand Chimney	IV,4 *
59. Number Five Gully	I **
60. Ledge Route	II ****
62. The Curtain	IV,5 ***

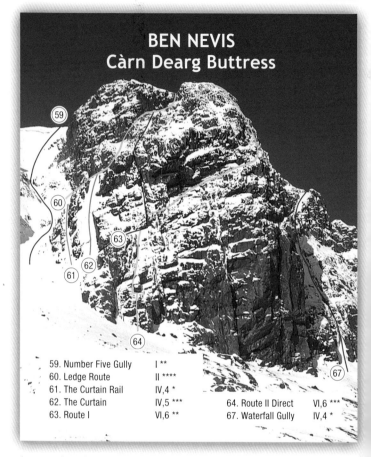

BEN NEVIS
Càrn Dearg Buttress

59. Number Five Gully	I **	
60. Ledge Route	II ****	
61. The Curtain Rail	IV,4 *	
62. The Curtain	IV,5 ***	
63. Route I	VI,6 **	64. Route II Direct VI,6 ***
		67. Waterfall Gully IV,4 *

buttress altogether and reach the top of the Direct Start by traversing in from the foot of The Curtain, but this is definitely inferior.

65 Shield Direct   285m   VII,7 ****

M.Fowler, A.Saunders   15 Mar 1979

The Shield is the line of chimneys formed by the junction of Titan's Wall (the big vertical wall on the right side of the buttress) and the huge flake on its right. This outstanding route combines very steep ice with sustained and technical mixed climbing. Although it is rarely in condition, and the initial groove is often bare, its reputation for quality has attracted many repeat ascents. This was another route talked up by everyone, but Mick Fowler and Victor Saunders plucked up courage first. Start at an ice groove directly below the line of chimneys.

1. 50m Climb the ice groove and continue over two bulges to gain a large ledge on the right, at the foot of the chimney section.
2. 30m Climb the ice chimney and continue up steep ice to a cave stance on the left.
3. 35m Follow the line of icy grooves to easier climbing in the now wider chimney.
4. 40m Continue in the same line to the top of the chimney-flake.
5. 45m Move up left onto a flake, cross the bulge above trending right, and

continue by the easiest line to ledges.

6. 35m Climb up and right to a left-slanting ledge line. Follow this to the crest of the buttress.

7. 50m Follow the arete to its top and a junction with Ledge Route.

56 Gemini   300m   VI,6 **

A.Paul, D.Sanderson   23 Mar 1979; Direct Start, as described: A.Kimber, A.McIntyre 1 Apr 1979

One of the most interesting and atmospheric ice climbs on the mountain. The steep ice smear, if in condition, is prominent from the Allt a' Mhuilinn. Climb a steep ice groove just left of the first pitch of Waterfall Gully to join a right-trending groove after 70m. Follow this to an enormous detached flake. Climb the very steep ice smear on the left wall of the flake to reach a ledge below some right-sloping grooves. Follow these for 60m to the foot of obvious twin grooves. Climb either groove to a broad ledge. Traverse right along the ledge for 15m and climb iced slabs for 45m to easier ground.

Variation: **Direct Finish   45m   VI,6 ***

M.Garthwaite, A.Wainwright   21 Mar 1995; Complete Route, as described: B.Poll, A.Teasdale   13 Mar 1999

A stunning finish to a stunning route. Climb the thin tongue of ice above and then move left on to the main icefall and climb it direct to join Ledge Route.

Gemini, VI,6. Climber Chad Harrison

BEN NEVIS

67 Waterfall Gully   300m   IV,4 *

D.Pipes, I.S.Clough, J.M.Alexander, R.Shaw, A.Flegg   8 Jan 1959

The prominent gully which defines the right flank of Càrn Dearg Buttress provides a good and varied winter climb, but unfortunately it becomes much easier after the initial icefall. Climb the 40m icefall to its top where the angle eases. Follow the bed of the gully for 150m to a cave or possible through route on the right. Exit right (sometimes difficult) onto mixed ground and follow this up left for three pitches to join Ledge Route. Care should be taken on the slabby rocks in the exit area which may present a hazard in avalanche conditions.

Variation: **True Finish   VI,6 ****

D.Cuthbertson, C.Fraser   3 Mar 1984

Although the difficulties are short lived, this is a very worthwhile finish. At the point where Waterfall Gully swings right, climb the steep crack on the left wall and continue up the narrow chimney above to a small snow basin (40m). Either finish by the line of the crack or exit left onto easier ground to join Ledge Route.

North Wall of Càrn Dearg

Alt 850m   North facing   Diagram p162

The North Wall of Càrn Dearg is the name given to the northern flank of Càrn Dearg Buttress, right of Waterfall Gully. Above and to its right is a hanging corrie, from the base of which dangle some impressive icicles. The wall left of the icicles is traversed by several large ledges, but the intervening walls are impressively steep and provide some challenging climbing. Just right of the toe of the buttress, a grassy rake leads up left to the first of the large ledges. The rake is **Easy Way**, and the ledge it gains is **Broad Terrace**, which slants up gradually from left to right. The next ledge is **Flake Terrace**, which runs across the face from the lower reaches of Harrison's Climb. It is gained via a series of easy chimneys. The ledge above Flake Terrace is **Diagonal Terrace**, and the final ledge below the top of the buttress is **Green Terrace**.

68 Macphee's Route   165m   V,6 *

C.Cartwright, S.M.Richardson   12 Feb 2000

An interesting and unusual mixed route taking a logical rising traverse across the North Wall of Càrn Dearg. Since the route does not lead to the top of the mountain, it is recommended in wild weather or conditions of deep snow. About 50m right of Waterfall Gully is a crest. Another 50m right is a bay, beyond which is the main North Wall. Start on the right side of the bay by following a shelf to reach a vegetated groove on the left edge of the North Wall.

1. 40m   Climb the groove and ensuing chimney to a belay on Broad Terrace.

2. 25m   From the left end of the terrace climb a narrow vegetated groove and exit right on a slab to reach the left end of Flake Terrace.

3. 40m   Traverse the terrace rightwards to a stance at the top of a downward step.

4. 20m   Slither down a chimney, then negotiate the Crevasse by climbing down into it and moving along its base. Belay on a huge block at its end above a narrow chimney.

5. 40m   Climb down the chimney and traverse right to a prominent block to the left of The Shroud. From here a 25m abseil leads to easy ground.

69 Kellett's North Wall Route   200m   VII,7 ***

M.Charlton, M.Burrows-Smith   1 Feb 1991

A sustained and technical mixed climb. Pitch 3 is hard and serious, but has good belays. Start right of the grassy rake of Easy Way, below a large flake with a deep chimney on the right.

1. 30m   **Flake Chimney**: Climb the chimney to exit by a window in the flake, then scramble up to Broad Terrace.

2. 20m   Climb a corner to the left of a conspicuous crack to reach Flake Terrace.

3. 30m   Traverse 6m right along the terrace and move up to a recess. Move right to a steep groove and climb this to join Diagonal Terrace.

4. 30m   Move up left along Diagonal Terrace and continue up a steep turfy groove line.

5 and 6. 95m Exit left into Waterfall Gully and follow this to the top.

70 The Shroud   275m   VI,6 ***
A.Clarke, J.Main   2 Feb 1993
The spectacular free hanging icefall to the left of Cousin's Buttress gives an exceptionally steep ice route and a highly prized climb. It was nowhere near forming during the cold winters of the late '70s but has seen several recent ascents, although on the first, the ice fang was one metre short of connecting with the belay ledge, requiring a forceful but delicate touch. Start up an ice gully and continue up the slope above to belay on the right side of the icefall (50m). Climb the centre of the icefall for 25m, and continue up a free standing icicle to join the upper ice wall (optional belay on a small ice ledge to the right of the icicle) 50m. Continue up short ice walls to easier ground and the hanging snow corrie, where various routes lead to the top (175m).

Cousin's Buttress is next right and has the appearance of a huge flake or pinnacle some 60m high, butting against the North Wall of Càrn Dearg, and separated from it by a deep chimney. This chimney, close on the right of the Shroud icicles, provides the following route:

1 Harrison's Climb Direct   275m   IV,4 ***
K.V.Crocket, C.Gilmore   7 Feb 1976
This superb climb gives some of the best ice climbing of its grade on the mountain. Start below the deep chimney-gully. Climb a steep ice pitch (The Chimney Start), then continue up the icy corner to reach the saddle behind the top of Cousin's Buttress. Traverse left to a 30m icefall, then take a rising line up the buttress on the right, to gain the edge overlooking Raeburn's Buttress. Follow this for two pitches to the upper corrie, from where a selection of routes lead to the top.

CASTLE AREA

Alt 900m   North-facing   Map p108   Diagram p162

The Castle is a wedge shaped buttress between the two straight Castle Gullies. Right of the gullies is Castle Ridge and to its right is its North Face, the final face of the Ben Nevis cliffs.
Descent: An easy descent can be made down the extensive boulder field on the north side of Càrn Dearg to reach Lochan Meall an t-Suidhe. From the top of Castle Ridge it is important to first head due west for 300m before descending, to avoid the North Wall of Castle Ridge.

Raeburn's Buttress

Between Càrn Dearg and The Castle lies a tall slender buttress of generally good rock which appears as a pinnacle from some angles. This is Raeburn's Buttress. The left side of the buttress is defined by a gully system which splits into two chimneys after 60m, and is bordered on the right by South Castle Gully.

2 Boomer's Requiem   250m   V,5 **
C.Higgins, D.MacArthur   Feb 1973
This route starts up the left branch of the gully system to the left of Raeburn's Buttress to reach the icefall which plunges from the hanging corrie to meet the lower section of the buttress. It has a daunting crux on very steep ice, and was originally graded IV and regarded as the test piece for the grade! Follow the initial gully of Raeburn's Buttress to the bifurcation, where the left-hand fork is barred by an impressively steep icefall. Climb this in two pitches and continue up snow slopes into the hanging corrie. Either descend Ledge Route or finish up one of the routes on Càrn Dearg Summit Buttress. Of these, the left-hand and right-hand gullies are Grade II and the central gully is Grade I. The buttress on the right of the right-hand gully is **Baird's Buttress** (150m IV,4).

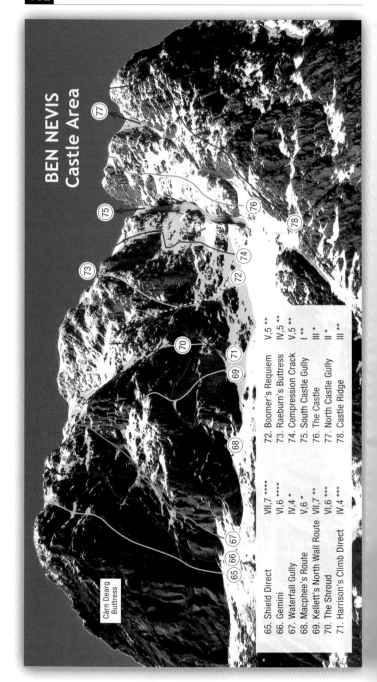

BEN NEVIS
Castle Area

Càrn Dearg Buttress

65. Shield Direct	VII,7 ****	72. Boomer's Requiem	V,5 **
66. Gemini	VI,6 ****	73. Raeburn's Buttress	IV,5 **
67. Waterfall Gully	IV,4 *	74. Compression Crack	V,5 **
68. Macphee's Route	V,6 *	75. South Castle Gully	I **
69. Kellett's North Wall Route	VII,7 **	76. The Castle	III *
70. The Shroud	VI,6 ***	77. North Castle Gully	II *
71. Harrison's Climb Direct	IV,4 ***	78. Castle Ridge	III **

3 Raeburn's Buttress 250m IV,5 **
R.Ashley, G.G.I.S.Clough, C.H.Oakes 14 Apr 1938
An excellent and sustained mixed climb. The natural winter line does not follow
the crest but takes **Intermediate Gully** which separates Raeburn's Buttress from
Baird's Buttress to the left. Start as for Boomer's Requiem by climbing the
introductory gully to the bifurcation at 60m, and follow the right branch to the
cave. Climb the short right wall of the cave (very hard if insufficiently iced),
traverse 5m right, and continue up Intermediate Gully passing a cave exit at its top
to reach the buttress crest. Continue up grooves left of the final arete to the top.

Castle Gullies

4 Compression Crack 230m V,5 **
M.Hind, C.Rice 9 Feb 1985
A good route following the prominent series of ice smears left of South Castle Gully.
It is often in condition mid to late season, and the lower icefall is sometimes climbed
for its own sake with an exit into South Castle Gully. Climb the icefall below the north
face of Raeburn's Buttress and make a long traverse right to gain the left-hand of two
icy chimneys. These lie 30m apart halfway along the steep wall to the right of the
final section of Raeburn's Buttress. Climb the icy chimney-corner for 50m, and
continue up steep ice for 25m to gain the snowslopes above. Follow these up and
left to enter the fan shaped corrie which leads to the Càrn Dearg summit slopes.

South Castle Gully 210m I **
W.Brunskill, W.W.King, W.W.Naismith 1 Apr 1896
This gully divides Raeburn's Buttress from the recessed buttress of The Castle on
the right. Extreme care should be taken after a heavy snowfall, as the outward
sloping rock stratum makes the gully avalanche prone. The gully is normally an
uncomplicated snow ascent. However in very lean conditions at the start of the
season it can give a fun climb (Grade III).

5 The Castle 210m III *
W.Brown, J.MacLay, W.W.Naismith, G.Thomson Apr 1896
An atmospheric route, largely because of its reputation for huge avalanches (be
warned!). A steep pitch at the toe of the buttress between the two gullies, often
well banked, leads to a central snowfield. Go up the centre, then trend left and
climb a steep groove until beneath the final steep wall. Exit right on slabs.

7 North Castle Gully 230m II *
J.H.Bell, R.G.Napier 4 Apr 1896
The gully to the right of The Castle contains several short chockstone pitches which
are sometimes completely covered, giving an uncomplicated snow ascent. The
cornice is seldom large.

Castle Ridge

Castle Ridge is the final great ridge on the north face of Ben Nevis. It is the easiest
of the four ridges, and while not in the same class as the others, it does have a
distinct quality of its own, mainly derived from the tremendous views out over
Lochaber.

Castle Ridge 275m III **
J.N.Collie, W.W.Naismith, G.Thomson, M.W.Travers 12 Apr 1895
A good climb which is possible in most conditions, although it should be avoided
after heavy snowfall as the approach slopes can be swept by huge avalanches from
above. Gain the ridge from below the Castle gullies, and follow the easiest line until
the crest is blocked by a steep wall. Traverse up and right, and climb an awkward
flaky chimney to a good ledge. Climb another difficult pitch to gain the upper part
of the ridge, which leads to the top with no further difficulty.

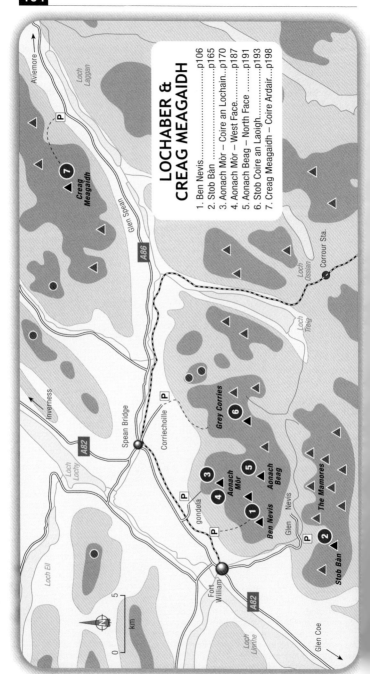

LOCHABER

There is a wide choice of venues in this area around Fort William, including of course Ben Nevis which is so extensive it is given a chapter of its own. It is easy to see why the Fort William area has become so popular, too popular for some, but information about conditions is more easily available, particularly from the Internet. South of Ben Nevis are the Mamores (with Stob Bàn) while to the east are the Aonachs (Aonach Mòr and Aonach Beag) and the Grey Corries (with Stob Coire an Laoigh). Glen Coe and Creag Meagaidh offer alternative options of a middle height range and about an hour's drive.

Maps: OS L41, E392; Harvey Superwalker Ben Nevis; Harvey Mountain Map Ben Nevis.

SMC Climbers' Guide: *Ben Nevis* (2002) covers Lochaber and Ben Nevis.

Public Transport: Contact Traveline at 0870 608 2608 or <www.traveline.org.uk>. Train and bus from Glasgow to Fort William; bus from Inverness to Fort William.

Tourist Information Centres: The Fort William centre (01397 703781) is closed Nov to March; try Aviemore (01479 810363) or Strathpeffer (01997 421160).

Mountaineering Huts: Several - see <www.mountaineering-scotland.org.uk/huts>.
SYHA Youth Hostels: <www.syha.org.uk> Glen Nevis (NN 127716), (0870 004 1120).
Independent Hostels: <www.hostel-scotland.co.uk>. There are six in Fort William and several others nearby.

Amenities: Fort William is a substantial town catering for winter sports and has all the necessary facilities including 24hr petrol.
Climbing Walls: The Ice Factor at Kinlochleven has an ice wall as well as a rock wall and other facilities (01855 831100), <www.ice-factor.co.uk>. There is a wall at Lochaber Leisure Centre, Belford Road, Fort William (01397 704359).

LOCHABER

The Mamores

A long ridge of generally sharp peaks situated south of Ben Nevis. Stob Bàn, near its west end, has the best climbing.

STOB BÀN

(NN 148 654)   Alt 999m   Map p164

The attractive profile of Stob Bàn, with its distinctive summit cone, can be seen from many points in Glen Nevis. The main peak is comprised of quartzite, but the two northern tops are mica schist. The rock is too broken for good rock climbing, but in cold and snowy conditions the north-east face provides an interesting selection of medium grade winter routes.

Weather and Conditions: Similar to Glen Coe, being of middle altitude and a definite west coast climate. The buttress climbs are mixed and only require the turf to be frozen. But this is essential, as the rock is unhelpful and loose blocks are used for moves and protection. The gullies and grooves have not had many ascents and it is not known how quickly ice forms or whether it is essential.

Approach: From Glen Nevis follow a good path on the east bank of Allt Coire a' Mhusgain until opposite the cliffs, then descend to cross the stream and strike up snowslopes to the foot of North or Central Buttresses (1hr 30mins). For South Buttress, an option is to continue up the path to the main ridge. Follow the ridge to where it is met by the left end of the buttress. Descend steeply leftwards to the base (2hrs). This is better under powder when there should be a trail up the path. The direct option is better under good snow and certainly for South Gully, where the descent from the ridge is as hard as the gully.

Descent: The shortest descent is by the exposed north ridge which drops steeply over two subsidiary summits to reach more open slopes after 2km. It is best to head north-west from here to avoid a series of rocky outcrops. Once on the summit,

STOB BAN

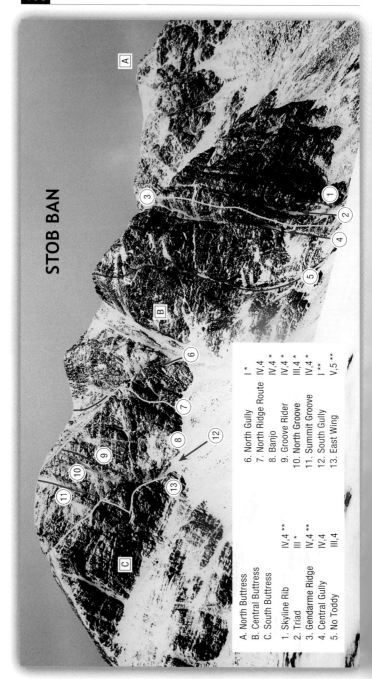

A. North Buttress
B. Central Buttress
C. South Buttress

1. Skyline Rib	IV,4 **
2. Triad	III *
3. Gendarme Ridge	IV,4 **
4. Central Gully	IV,4
5. No Toddy	III,4

6. North Gully	I *
7. North Ridge Route	IV,4
8. Banjo	IV,4 *
9. Groove Rider	IV,4 *
10. North Groove	III,4 *
11. Summit Groove	IV,4 *
12. South Gully	I **
13. East Wing	V,5 **

it is as quick to descend the main ridge eastwards to reach the ascent path. Down South Gully and the slopes below is quicket if the snow is extensive and friendly.

Layout: The cliffs can be divided into three principal buttresses. North Buttress is the lowest and nearest to Glen Nevis. It is comprised of mica schist and lies approximately 600m north of the summit directly below a small top at NN 146 659. Central Buttress lies north-east of the summit and is set forward from, and at a lower level than South Buttress. It is distinguished by a large triangular front face, and a slanting shelf and gully which separates it from South Buttress. South Buttress is the large mass of quartzite directly below the main summit which is split by two wide snow gullies. The routes are described from right to left.

NORTH BUTTRESS

(NN 149 661)   Alt 750m   North-East facing

East Ridge   200m   II/III **
W.Brown, W.Tough, L.Hinxman, W.Douglas   Apr 1895
A fine mountaineering route with an excellent finish along the fine arete at the top. It is best approached as for the routes on Central Buttress, followed by a traverse right across the corrie floor.

CENTRAL BUTTRESS

(NN 149 657)   Alt 750m   North-East facing

A huge triangular north or front face of the buttress dominates the view on the approach. But once level with the buttress, the hidden gems of the two deep gully lines and their attendant steep narrow buttresses on the left flank of the buttress are seen. A short arete links the top of Central Buttress to the main ridge some 200m north of the summit. Although all the routes are relatively short, they are followed by about 150m of easy climbing to reach the summit ridge.

Skyline Rib   120m   IV,4 **
R.G.Webb, B.A.Mattock   13 Feb 1987
The right-hand and deepest gully is bordered on the right by the prominent line of Skyline Rib, which forms the left edge of the broad triangular front face of the buttress. Follow the crest of the narrow buttress, taking care with several loose blocks, and continue to the top via the ramp of Triad.

Triad   150m   IV,4 *
D.Hawthorn, R.Lee, D.N.Williams   10 Apr 1986
The right-hand gully is defined by a narrow rock buttress on the left and Skyline Rib on the right. The gully gradually steepens and narrows to a chimney which leads to the final stance of Skyline Rib. Follow a snow ramp on the right, then traverse left along a narrow ledge to the crest of the buttress. Join and move left along an easy ramp to the crest of the ridge, which leads easily to the top.

Gendarme Ridge   150m   IV,4 **
J.Maclay, Parr   4 Jan 1904
A remarkable route for the time. The slender buttress right of Central Gully has what appears to be a gendarme near its foot, but this is actually part of the buttress. Climb up to the supposed gendarme, and continue steeply for 60m to where the angle eases. The upper part of the buttress is straightforward. Finish along the left-slanting ramp as for Triad.

Central Gully   150m   IV,4
J.Grieve, C.MacNaughton   1969
An uneven climb. Most of the gully is straightforward, except for a steep 25m section at the start. At the top of the gully, finish along the left-slanting ramp as for Triad.

South Gully, I, Stob Bàn

5 No Toddy   150m   III,4
M.Creasey and party   Feb 1986; Final pitch, as described: D.Hawthorn, R.Lee, D.N.Williams   10 Apr 1986
A third gully which lies further left between wider buttresses. Start at a small snowfield some distance up the left flank of the buttress. Climb a steep ice pitch (crux) to easier ground and a stance on the right. Move back left and ascend the gully easily to where a possible escape slants right. Instead, traverse left and bridge up the continuation of the lower line. Continue up mixed ground to the top of the buttress.

SOUTH BUTTRESS

(NN 148 654)   Alt 850m   North-East facing   Diagram p166)

This, the highest buttress, has a deep central gully (South Gully) set between a very steep buttress to its left (East Wing) and to its right, a large ridge which finishes near the summit. Right of the ridge is North Gully, then a smaller buttress with a pointed base.

6 North Gully   150m   I *
A straightforward snow gully, narrow at the start, then fanning out.

The next five routes start by climbing the left side of the large ridge, which provides a steep face overlooking South Gully. They finish up the ridge from various arrival points. The grooves fill with ice, but the first two routes are mixed.

7 North Ridge Route   200m   IV,4
S.Kennedy, A.Nelson   29 Jan 1995
The toe of the ridge is formed just left of North Gully. Start in a bay left of this where there are two corner-lines. Climb the left-hand corner for 30m, then move out right to belay just short of the ridge (50m). The right corner might be easier under powder. Continue to the ridge which leads easily to finish very close to the summit.

8 Banjo   200m   IV,4 *
V.Chelton, D.McGimpsey, A.Nisbet, J.Preston   20 Nov 2004
Start just right of the base of South Gully below a long fault which starts above a barrier wall. Start up the fault but soon move right to reach steeper ground (35m). Go right and back left to break through a steep wall by a short V-groove about 6m right of the fault (30m). There is now a long smooth V-groove on the right. Climb mixed ground on its right, finishing up the groove or its right rib to reach the North Ridge (45m). Finish easily up this.

Groove Rider   160m   IV,4 *
A.Nisbet, C.Wells   18 Mar 2008
Start about 30m up from the foot of South Gully at a prominent rocky recess on the right. Traverse out right below a steep wall to gain and climb a well defined groove (50m, 35m). Gain and climb the ridge to the summit (75m). A direct start will be possible given enough ice.

North Groove   160m   III,4 *
S.Kennedy, A.Paul   30 Dec 1996
Start as for Groove Rider and traverse out right below the steep wall, then move up and back left into a groove which runs up from the initial recess (45m). Continue directly up the groove over a steep step to more broken ground (45m). Gain and climb the ridge to the summit (70m). A steep direct start will be possible given enough ice.

Summit Groove   140m   IV,4 *
A.Nisbet, C.Wells   18 Mar 2008
Start about halfway up South Gully and climb a big groove, almost a gully, which leads close to the summit. Graded for soft ice, would be Grade III in better conditions.

South Gully   200m   I **
A straightforward ascent through impressive scenery

East Wing   180m   V,5 **
D.McGimpsey, A.Nisbet   26 Feb 2006
A devious but spectacular line near the crest of the very steep East Wing of the buttress. Start about 15m up South Gully at the highest ramp leading out left.
1. 35m Work out leftwards to the crest, always keeping above steep lower walls.
2. 25m Gain the highest ledge up thick moss, then traverse it leftwards to a vertical column of wedged blocks.
3. 10m Climb the column to a ramp leading up right.
4. 30m Climb the ramp to easy ground.
5. 80m Climb the easy crest to the top of the buttress.

LOCHABER

The Aonachs

The broad ridge of The Aonachs (Aonach Mòr and Aonach Beag), runs north to south and is sandwiched between Càrn Mòr Dearg (Ben Nevis) to the west and the Grey Corries to the east. The altitude of the hills, second only to Ben Nevis in this guide, means that they offer some of the most reliable winter climbing in the area. Two days walking up The Ben taxes the legs, so most folk will seek a more accessible venue for one of the days. The obvious choice is Aonach Mòr, with easy access via the Nevis Range Gondola cable car.

AONACH MÒR

(NN 193 730)   Alt 1221m

At first glance, the great rounded bulk of Aonach Mòr would seem to be an unlikely climbing ground, but it has cliffs on both its east and west flanks. The opposite aspects mean that at least one should be in good condition. Lying close to Ben Nevis, development of these crags has been slow, and it was only in the late 1980s that they were systematically explored. The east facing cliffs of Coire an Lochain can be seen from Spean Bridge, but they are dwarfed by the vast scale of the mountain's eastern aspect. The West Face is more remote and provides very long easier routes.

COIRE AN LOCHAIN

(NN 192 737)   Alt 1100m   East facing   Map p164

Coire an Lochain, on the east face of Aonach Mòr, presents a long line of granite cliffs. Their base is very high, and the rock is generally well vegetated which means the routes come into condition rapidly and provide good climbing with the first snows of winter. A convenient descent allows two or more climbs to be done in a day. The fine grained granite has been fractured along a vertical plane, resulting in many cracks, chimneys and gullies. The buttress routes are sometimes well protected, but the rock on the sidewalls of the gullies is compact and protection can be hard to find.

Weather and Conditions: The high cliff base and the vegetated rock means that the routes come into condition rapidly and provide good climbing when other crags in the west are too low to be properly frozen. Facing east, they receive a lot of drifting snow which can build to a great depth and shorten the routes later in the season. As a result, snow will survive even a big thaw and subsequent cold weather can produce a lot of ice, even if the wind blown approach slopes look bare. This drift can produce large cornices. Late in the season these can reach monstrous proportions to make direct exits from some of the routes impossible. It is often possible to traverse to a place with a smaller cornice but this may still be the crux, particularly for those with modern bent shaft axes.

The other consequence of drifting snow is a large number of avalanches on the cliff so conditions should be carefully assessed, particularly if there is a high category avalanche warning report. All the routes either finish on steep snow or require a steep snow traverse to approach, so there may be no safe options if conditions are dangerous. However the popularity of the venue means that there are often reports about conditions on the Internet; these are very useful but like the avalanche reports, they can change overnight or may have been written with over enthusiasm after a good day out. So treat with caution unless there is confirmation.

Approach: The easiest way to reach the cliffs is take the Nevis Range Gondola to the top station at 650m. There is often an early climbers' lift at 8.00am but then the Gondola runs continuously from 9.00am (sometimes 8.30am). The Gondola is normally closed for just over a month for maintenance from mid-November to mid-December. Current arrangements can be checked via: <www.nevisrange.co.uk> or Nevis Range (01397 705825).

From the top station, a walk west for about 300m gains a chairlift which provides

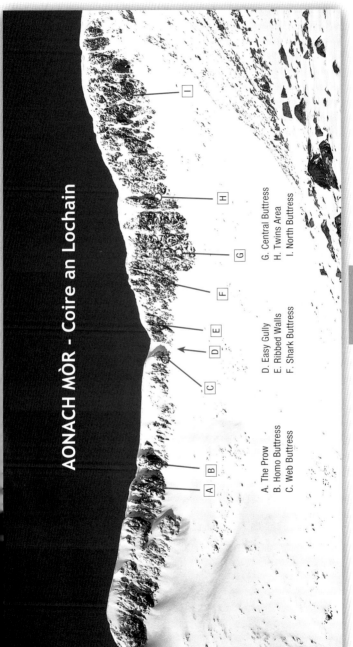

AONACH MÒR - Coire an Lochain

A. The Prow
B. Homo Buttress
C. Web Buttress
D. Easy Gully
E. Ribbed Walls
F. Shark Buttress
G. Central Buttress
H. Twins Area
I. North Buttress

LOCHABER

further uplift to 910m (for an extra £1 paid at the base station), then continue alongside the upper ski tows to their end (about 45mins walk). This point is marked by a small shack and a large cairn. From here it is 150m to the rim of Easy Gully (grid bearing 185 degrees). In poor visibility it may be difficult to locate the top of the gully, and extreme caution should be exercised as the cornices can be very large. The bearing is away from the cliff edge and since Easy Gully cuts in a long way, the bearing is safe in white-out until the gully is reached (perhaps rope up and belay after 120m). It is normally possible to enter the gully by its northern edge, which appears to escape much of the cornicing, but this edge is steeper than the back of the gully. The alternative is to abseil, although the popularity of the cliff sometimes maintains a slot in the cornice through which it is possible to down climb.

For the climbs on North Buttress, it is quicker but less easy to find a descent just to the north of the north bounding ridge of the corrie. From the shack, walk for 280m on a grid bearing of 20 degrees to the point where the cornice needs to be breached. This line almost touches the cornice after 50m (top of Forgotten Twin, but there are posts here) then heads just left of a slight knoll on the cliff-top where rocks are often visible. The end of the bearing is at the cornice (in white-out, an original bearing of 30 degrees, then roping up and heading direct for the cliff edge might be better). Sometimes there is a post which acts as a marker for the correct place. In white-out without footsteps, this navigation will be worrying even for the experienced. The descent is steep snow initially but eases. A right traverse over the bounding ridge leads to further steep slopes under North Buttress.

Descent: Easy Gully is the most commonly used descent back into the corrie. The best way off the mountain after finishing climbing is to walk north along the summit plateau and descend the ski slopes to the top Gondola station. Missing the last Gondola (often around 5pm) means an hour's walk down the line of the mountain bike track.

Layout: The corrie forms part of an almost perfect spherical bowl, centred around a lochan at NN 198 739. The apex of the corrie rim is cut by a broad snow gully which lies almost due east of the lochan. This is Easy Gully, which is a convenient reference point for describing the climbs. Left of Easy Gully, the south side of the corrie contains a series of shorter north-east facing buttresses. Right of Easy Gully the climbs can be divided into five main sections. First are the Ribbed Walls, which are divided into a series of grooves and ribs. This joins into the larger Shark Buttress, often with well defined icefalls, and separated from Central Buttress by the deep gully of Tunnel Vision. Further right are two narrow buttresses separated by three deep gullies. This is the Twins Area. The left-hand buttress can be recognised by the deep cleft of The Split, which is a useful landmark in poor visibility. Further right is North Buttress, which terminates with a wide gully left of the ridge bounding the north end of the corrie.

The Prow

The following climbs are located on The Prow, which lies approximately 100m south of Easy Gully. This distinctive buttress, which lies left of a deep gully (suitable descent late in the season but an abseil is possibly required), is characterised by a rock prow high in the centre. The obvious line of Stirling Bridge takes the right-angled corner near the right edge, and the twin parallel grooves on the front face are taken by The Betrayal and The Guardian. The first two routes are some 50m left of The Prow and stay in condition late in the season because they are sheltered from the sun. They often have a huge cornice but sometimes with a break or through route on the left.

1 Streamline 70m III
R.Hamilton, S.Kennedy   16 Feb 2004
This climbs the left side of a wide fault-line which is overlooked by a high bounding wall on its left. The lines of ramps at the top of the bounding wall is **Three Kings** (70m IV,5).

AONACH MÒR
Coire an Lochain,
The Prow & Homo Buttress

1. Streamline	III	7. Pro Libertate	V,6 **
2. Sideline	III	8. Stirling Bridge	VI,7 ***
3. Back Street Boogie	VI,6 *	9. Ribbon Groove	IV,4 *
4. The Betrayal	IV,5 *	9a. Ribbon Development	IV,4 **
5. The Wave	V,5 *	10. Gowan Hill	VI,7 *
6. The Guardian	IV,5 **	11. Homo Robusticus	VI,7 **

Sideline 80m III
S.Kennedy, A.Nelson, D.Hood 25 Jan 1998
This climbs the right side of the wide fault-line. Climb a narrow groove to reach the upper fault (45m) and continue up a groove on its right side to below the large cornice.

The gully right of Sideline and immediately left of Back Street Boogie is **Whitecap Gully** (80m IV,5), very icy but prone to a huge cornice.

Back Street Boogie 70m VI,6 *
M.Pescod, F.MacCallum 20 Dec 1999
A steep mixed climb up the front face of the narrow buttress up and left of The Prow. Start by climbing a short gully left of The Prow to reach the base of the buttress.
1. 30m Climb ice slightly leftwards to a bulge that leads to an icy slab. Gain a right-facing corner and climb it to the top of a pillar.
2. 40m Climb the steep wall above on turfy cracks (strenuous), continue to a snow crest that leads to the summit.

The Betrayal 90m IV,5 *
S.Kennedy, D.Ritchie 28 Mar 1990
The left-hand of the two parallel grooves on the front of the buttress. Climb the groove over a series of bulges to a small snow bay immediately under the prow. Steep awkward moves out left lead to easier ground and the cornice.

Stirling Bridge, VI,7. Climber Graeme Ettle

5 The Wave   70m   V,5 *
A.Clarke, M.Thomson   11 Jan 1995
A direct line up the front of the buttress between The Betrayal and The Guardian.
1. 40m Climb an icy groove over steps to a slabby left-slanting turf groove, followed to a ledge.
2. 30m Continue up leftwards below a steep rock wall to reach the right-hand side of the small bay of The Betrayal. Gain the wide V-groove in the prow directly below a large cornice. Finish by a bulging rock wall right of the cornice.

6 The Guardian   90m   IV,5 **
S.Kennedy, D.Ritchie   28 Mar 1990
The right-hand of the two parallel grooves leads to a prominent flake-chimney. Climb the chimney and exit by steep but easier ground.

7 Pro Libertate   90m   V,6 **
S.Kennedy, R.Hamilton   6 Mar 2004
A fairly sustained mixed route on the buttress between The Guardian and Stirling Bridge following a prominent chimney come corner in the upper reaches. Quite close to The Guardian in the lower section. Start at the foot of The Guardian and climb the buttress just to the right (banks out later in the season) to reach a short wall. Step right under the wall into a slabby corner. Follow the corner then move up rightwards over a jammed block to below a steep corner. Steep moves across

the wall on the left lead to a ledge. Move back up rightwards into another corner containing a large booming flake. Make exposed moves out left from the top of the flake to easier ground close to the chimney of The Guardian. Belay at the foot of the prominent chimney on the right (45m). The right wall of the chimney was climbed to a wide ledge below the steep upper corner. Climb the corner to a large block belay on the crest overlooking Stirling Bridge (20m). Finish up the easy upper slopes as per Stirling Bridge (25m).

8 Stirling Bridge   70m   VI,7 * * *
S.Kennedy, D.Ritchie   4 Apr 1990
The route is all about the first pitch, which is truly memorable. Climb the prominent right-angled corner (steep and strenuous) close to the right edge of the buttress, and pull out right near the top. Continue up a short groove to a large block belay on the left. Easier ground leads to the cornice.

Homo Buttress

Diagram p173

The impressive barrel shaped buttress to the right of The Prow contains the greatest concentration of difficult mixed routes on the mountain. A key identifying feature is a pillar on the right side of the buttress. Homo Robusticus takes the triangle shaped groove on the left side of the pillar and Piranha climbs the right-facing corner on the right side of the pillar.

9 Ribbon Groove   60m   IV,4 *
A.Forsyth, J.Turner   Jan 1995
A natural line of weakness up the left side of the buttress. Start just left of the toe of the buttress and climb into a large recess. Pull steeply out left to gain a groove splitting the left side of the upper buttress. Climb the groove (50m). Easier mixed ground leads to the cornice, which can sometimes be very large (10m).
Variation: **Ribbon Development   60m   IV,4 * ***
A.MacDonald, K.Grant   13 Feb 2003
A direct variation on Ribbon Groove, starting as for that route. After pulling out steeply left as per Ribbon Groove, move up right into a narrowing chimney with a chockstone at the top. Climb the chimney (well protected) and pull over the chockstone on to easier ground. Move left to belay at the top of Ribbon Groove (50m). Easier ground leads to the top (10m).

Gowan Hill   70m   VI,7 *
M.Robson, D.Jarvis, T.Ward   25 Jan 1998 (with rests); FFA: M.Pescod, T.Barton   6 Feb 1999
The obvious hanging off-width crack high on the front of the buttress. Start below a crack on the left side of the buttress, a few metres up and left of the buttress toe.
1. 35m Climb to a ledge at the base of the crack and climb it steeply to a large ledge.
2. 35m Step right and climb the crest of the buttress to an easy finish.

Homo Robusticus   75m   VI,7 * *
M.Garthwaite, A.Clarke   31 Dec 1994
This difficult test piece climbs the obvious triangle shaped groove on the right side of the front face of the buttress.
1. 45m Start at the lowest point of the buttress and climb cracked slabs trending rightwards to a large ledge (15m, possible belay). Continue trending right and gain the base of the triangle shaped groove. Climb this, step left (crux) at its top, and continue up the obvious groove above.
2. 30m Continue in the same groove to easy ground and the plateau.

The corner on the right is **Piranha** (70m VII,8), a technical test piece for adze torques.

LOCHABER

Homo Robusticus, VI,7, Homo Buttress. Climber John McKenzie

Web Buttress

This is the buttress just south of Easy Gully. It offers a number of good possibilities in lean icy conditions, often early in the season, but it banks out after heavy snow. Three routes have been recorded but more have been done. The first two routes can be Grade IV or Grade II depending on the build-up of snow and ice screws are required for protection.

12 Nausea   90m   III *
J.Naismith, C.Watkins   25 Nov 1989
An icefall about 50m left of Easy Gully.

13 The Web   100m   III *
S.Kennedy, C.Grindley   25 Nov 1989
Climb the icy chimney about 30m left of Easy Gully

14 Spider Rib   90m   II
S.M.Richardson, C.Cartwright   16 Nov 1996
The buttress at the base of Easy Gully on the left (south).

15 Easy Gully   100m   I

This broad snow gully cuts deep into the plateau, and gives the best descent route back to the corrie. The cornice can normally be avoided on the right.

Ribbed Walls

Diagram p178

The cliff to the right of Easy Gully is characterised by a series of vertical ribs seamed by grooves. The most obvious feature in the centre of the face is the deep cleft of Temperance Union Blues.

6 Muddy Waters   90m   III *
C.Jones, S.Kennedy, D.Ritchie   17 Nov 1990
About 10m right of Easy Gully is an obvious chimney high on the buttress. Climb easy mixed ground to the foot of the chimney, and follow it trending right to the cornice. Good early in the season but the lower section banks out later.

7 Barrel Buttress   90m   IV,4
S.Kennedy, S.Thirgood   7 Feb 1993
Between Muddy Waters and the Temperance Union Blues is a small recess defined on the right by a sharp narrow arete, and on the left by a broad buttress. This climb follows the buttress. Start just right of the foot of the buttress and climb it directly, avoiding the steep wall at the top on the left.

8 Nid Arete   90m   IV,5 *
S.Kennedy, S.Thirgood   7 Feb 1993
This good and well protected mixed route starts up a groove line on the left side of the narrow arete to the right of Barrel Buttress. Climb the groove to gain the arete, then follow the furthest corner on the right (overlooking the final section of Temperance Union Blues) to the top. Starting up the arete makes the route V,5.

9 Temperance Union Blues   90m   III *
S.Richards, G.Armstrong, C.Millar, J.Owens   18 Feb 1989
The cliff is split by a deep cleft at half-height about 50m right of Easy Gully. The bulge at the top of the cleft needs a big build-up to be iced, otherwise it is harder.
1. 45m Take either of two converging lines to the bottom of the cleft.
2. 45m Climb the cleft to where it steepens, then exit by a ramp to reach the cornice.

10 Pernille   80m   III
C.Jones, A.Taylor   27 Mar 1990
The buttress immediately right of the deep cleft of Temperance Union Blues. Climb into an obvious scoop just right of the cleft, and continue up right to a steep left-trending ramp which leads to a snow bay. Exit right to reach the cornice.

Right of Pernille is a snowy section often topped by a huge cornice. But in lean conditions or after a big thaw, this can provide several icy lines of Grade II or III.

Shark Buttress

Diagram p178

Right of Pernille and the snowy section is this more massive buttress. Left of centre is an ice filled gully which gives the fine White Shark. Right of centre is a wide gully taken by Maneater. At the right end, just left of the broad gully of Tunnel Vision is a prominent tower taken by Hammerhead Pillar.

Aquafresh   100m   IV,4 *
N.Marshall, D.Ritchie   26 Mar 1990
Start 40m left of Tunnel Vision. Climb the left-hand icefall, trending left up mixed ground at the top.

LOCHABER

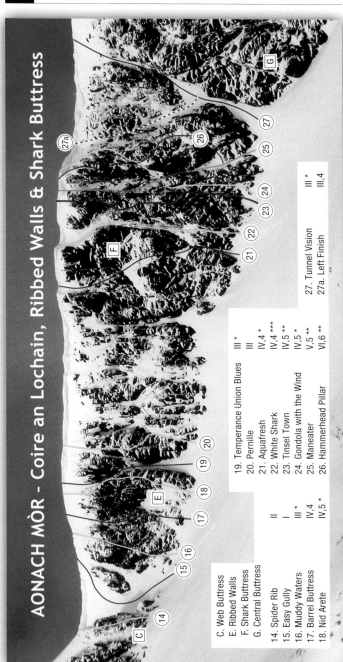

AONACH MÒR - Coire an Lochain, Ribbed Walls & Shark Buttress

C. Web Buttress
E. Ribbed Walls
F. Shark Buttress
G. Central Buttress

14. Spider Rib	II
15. Easy Gully	I
16. Muddy Waters	III *
17. Barrel Buttress	IV,4
18. Nid Arete	IV,5 *

19. Temperance Union Blues	III *
20. Pernille	III
21. Aquafresh	IV,4 *
22. White Shark	IV,4 ***
23. Tinsel Town	IV,5 **
24. Gondola with the Wind	IV,5 *
25. Maneater	V,5 **
26. Hammerhead Pillar	VI,6 **

27. Tunnel Vision	III *
27a. Left Finish	III,4

White Shark, IV,4. Shark Buttress. Climber Rab Anderson

White Shark   110m   IV,4 ***
C.Millar, R.G.Webb   27 Jan 1990

The right-hand icefall gives an excellent route. Climb the shallow gully, characterised by a steep slabby corner at half-height, to a ledge. Continue up the steep icefall which forms down the corner, to an exit onto easier ground.

Tinsel Town   110m   IV,5 **
S.Kennedy, P.Mills   3 Feb 1991

An elegant climb up the groove line left of Gondola with the Wind. Start 10m right of White Shark.

1. 40m Climb a system of grooves just right of the buttress crest, then continue up a chimney to a stance on the left.
2. 50m Move back right into the main groove and climb steep mixed ground to a belay below the cornice.

3. 20m The cornice can be huge and if so, the grade may be higher. On the first ascent it was outflanked by a long traverse to the right.

24 Gondola with the Wind   125m   IV,5 *
S.Kennedy, S.Thirgood   30 Dec 1989
An interesting mixed climb trending left to right across the buttress taken by Hammerhead Pillar.
1. 45m Start up a short groove 10m left of the prominent gully of Maneater. Climb to a small amphitheatre, then exit on the right.
2. 35m Follow a system of shallow grooves close to the edge of the buttress, and spiral right, around the side of the tower, to reach a steep corner.
3. 45m Climb the corner (an exciting crux) and continue up the snowslopes above.

25 Maneater   90m   V,5 **
S.M.Richardson, R.G.Webb   14 Jan 1995
An ice line up the prominent wide gully between the buttress taken by White Shark and Hammerhead Pillar.
1. 50m Climb the gully past a small amphitheatre, and continue up the gully to where it steepens at an overhung cave. Thin ice on the left wall (crux) leads to a groove and belay.
2. 40m Climb steep ice directly above the belay to reach the final groove of Tinsel Town and the plateau.

26 Hammerhead Pillar   100m   VI,6 **
C.Cartwright, S.M.Richardson   9 Feb 1997
A good direct mixed route up the prominent buttress to the left of the wide gully of Tunnel Vision. Start as for Maneater.
1. 40m Move up into the base of the amphitheatre, then follow a ramp up and right for 10m. Continue up a short open groove on the left edge of the buttress to a stance below a steep headwall.
2. 30m Climb the wall and continue up the groove above to a stance below the headwall.
3. 30m Climb the steep groove in the centre of the wall (difficult to start), then step left at the top to gain a hanging V-groove. Climb this and finish up a short snowslope to the cornice.

27 Tunnel Vision   120m   III *
S.M.Richardson, R.D.Everett   22 Jan 1989; Left Branch: S.Kennedy, S.Thirgood   Winter 1990
The wide gully between the Ribbed Walls and Central Buttress. An initial narrows leads to a snow bay with three possible exits. The normal finish is the right branch which reaches the upper easy section of Morwind.

Central Buttress

This buttress lies between the gullies of Tunnel Vision and Left Twin. It is the highest section of crag in the corrie, and it provides some of the finest mixed routes on the mountain. The two most prominent lines are Morwind, which takes the fault-line up the left crest of the buttress, and Typhoon, which climbs the left-facing corner system on the right side of the front face. The cornices on this buttress are sometimes large, but a vague snow arete on the final snowslopes can normally be relied on to provide a safe way through. If the cornice is impassable, it is possible to traverse right for 50m and descend the gully of Forgotten Twin.

28 Morwind   150m   IV,4 ***
R.D.Everett, S.M.Richardson   10 Jan 1988
This classic mixed route was the first climb to be recorded in the corrie. Start at the toe of the buttress and climb a short gully to enter a shallow chimney-line. Follow this for two pitches to a small bay beneath a cave. Exit right up mixed ground to reach snowslopes and the summit cornice, often small or absent.

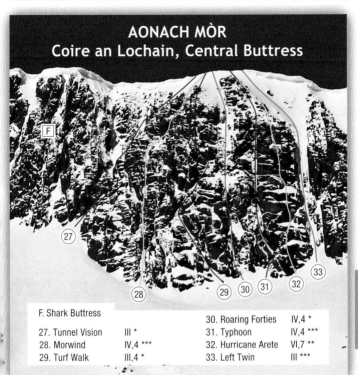

AONACH MÒR
Coire an Lochain, Central Buttress

LOCHABER

F. Shark Buttress			
27. Tunnel Vision	III *	30. Roaring Forties	IV,4 *
28. Morwind	IV,4 ***	31. Typhoon	IV,4 ***
29. Turf Walk	III,4 *	32. Hurricane Arete	VI,7 **
		33. Left Twin	III ***

Turf Walk   150m   III,4 *

C.Grant, R.D.Everett   25 Nov 1989

An interesting mixed climb taking the right-slanting fault-line that crosses the left side of the front face of the buttress. Start 15m right of Morwind and follow a left-slanting gully to belay in a bay below the fault. Follow the fault up and right to ledges leading rightwards. Step right, then climb up and back left to belay below steep grooves left of the central depression. Climb the groove on the left, step left onto the exposed prow, and continue to easier ground and the top.

Roaring Forties   140m   IV,4 *

S.M.Richardson, R.D.Everett, J.C.Wilkinson   2 Mar 1991

This fine route takes the icefall which forms in the depression in the centre of the face. Good and varied, but not in condition as often as other routes on the buttress. Start 5m left of the corner-line of Typhoon.
1. 45m Follow icy grooves into a recess.
2. 25m Climb the steep back wall by a groove on the right.
3. 50m Climb the icefall above to reach the final snowslopes.
4. 20m Easy climbing leads to the cornice.

Typhoon   130m   IV,4 **

R.D.Everett, S.M.Richardson   14 Jan 1989

An excellent climb, taking a direct line up the left-facing chimney-groove on the right side of the front face. Wind speeds of 220kph were recorded that day! Start 15m left of the deep gully of Left Twin.

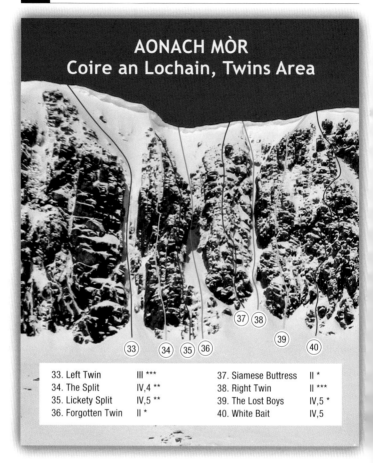

AONACH MÒR
Coire an Lochain, Twins Area

33. Left Twin	III ***	37. Siamese Buttress	II *
34. The Split	IV,4 **	38. Right Twin	II ***
35. Lickety Split	IV,5 **	39. The Lost Boys	IV,5 *
36. Forgotten Twin	II *	40. White Bait	IV,5

1. 40m Climb the lower slabby grooves to belay at the base of a chimney.
2. 30m Climb the chimney and groove past an overhang.
3. 40m Continue straight up on steep ice to exit onto the final snowslopes.
4. 20m Easy climbing leads to the cornice.

32 Hurricane Arete   140m   VI,7 **
S.M.Richardson, R.D.Everett   4 Mar 1989
This technical mixed climb weaves an intricate and unlikely line through the
overhangs just left of the right arete of Central Buttress. Start mid-way between
Typhoon and Left Twin.
1. 50m Take icy slabs for 30m to reach a short left-slanting gully. Climb this, then
move up right along a narrow ramp to a small ledge. Belay beneath a prominent
overhang, just left of a right-facing corner that is capped by yet another overhang.
2. 20m Pull over the roof directly above the belay onto a steep snow slab, then follow
a left-slanting crack to a prominent spike. Move right below an overhanging wall,
then climb very steeply into a small snow bay. A difficult and sustained pitch.
3. 50m Climb the groove on the left to the final overhangs. Bridge up and exit on
the left and continue up easier ground.
4. 20m Snowslopes lead to the cornice.

Twins Area

To the right of Central Buttress are two steep and narrow buttresses, Split Buttress and Siamese Buttress, which are bordered by three deep gullies. The gullies are rather confusingly known as 'The Twins'. The left side of Split Buttress is cut by the deep chimney of The Split. This is a useful point of reference in poor visibility which can be easily recognised by its large jammed blocks.

3 Left Twin   120m   III ***
R.D.Everett, S.M.Richardson   22 Jan 1989
The deep gully immediately right of Central Buttress is the most popular climb on the mountain. It is a superb traditional gully climb and is similar in difficulty and quality to SC Gully in Stob Coire nan Lochan (Glen Coe). Graded for a good build-up, otherwise IV,4.

4 The Split   120m   IV,4 **
S.M.Richardson, R.D.Everett   19 Feb 1989
The prominent chimney, which almost slices Split Buttress in two, provides a climb of character and interest.
1. 25m Start at the foot of the buttress and climb the introductory gully to enter the chimney.
2. 45m Climb the chimney passing beneath several large jammed blocks until it is possible to exit left, 4m below the capping roof. Continue up the arete to belay.
3. 50m Easy snow leads to finish. The cornice may force a finish left as for Left Twin.

5 Lickety Split   120m   IV,5 **
G.Mulhemann, S.M.Richardson   2 Dec 1989
This fine varied mixed climb takes the clean right-facing corner on the right side the lower half of Split Buttress.
1. 30m Climb the icefall of Forgotten Twin and belay below the corner.
2. 20m Follow the corner to a good stance.
3. 20m Continue up the steep wall above, passing two overhangs, to reach a rock ridge overlooking the gully of Left Twin.
4. 50m Follow the ridge to the final snowslopes. The cornice may force a finish left as for Left Twin.

6 Forgotten Twin   120m   II *
R.D.Everett, S.M.Richardson   22 Jan 1989
The gully between Split Buttress and Siamese Buttress provides the easiest climb on the face. Start by climbing an icefall to gain the start of the gully. In lean conditions this can be avoided by following the short snow ramp leading up left from the foot of Right Twin.

7 Siamese Buttress   120m   II *
S.M.Richardson, R.D.Everett   19 Feb 1989
The well defined buttress left of Right Twin gives an enjoyable scramble. It is easiest if started from the right, but Grade III if started up the steep corners on the left.

8 Right Twin   120m   II ***
S.M.Richardson, R.D.Everett   22 Jan 1989
A good traditional gully, narrow and well defined, with steep sections at the bottom and at mid-height. Exit left at the top.

The Lost Boys   120m   IV,5 *
K.Howett, A.Todd   17 Feb 2001
A line of icy grooves on the buttress about 8m to the right of Right Twin. Start at the left edge of the buttress and climb slabby ice direct to a barrier of steep rock. Either climb direct through this or pass it by mixed ground just on the right. Continue up a left-facing corner, then another better defined corner to reach a snow arete which leads to easy slopes.

LOCHABER

40 White Bait   110m   IV,5 *

M.Edwards, D.McGimpsey   5 Feb 2007

Climbs the right-hand side of the icy buttress containing The Lost Boys. Start just left of the lowest rocks, approximately 20m right of Right Twin.

1. 50m Climb a short ice groove, then move up and right into an icy bay. Follow this up and left to its top, then gain a narrow ledge on the right and break out through steep walls to a ledge.

2. 30m Continue up then move right into a large snowy bay. Climb up the left side to the top of the bay.

3. 30m Exit the bay and continue out left, then straight up to the cornice.

The following route starts in a large bay about 50m right of Right Twin.

41 Golden Promise   100m   VI,7 *

B.Davison, S.Kennedy, S.Venables   23 Feb 1992

A difficult mixed route taking the steep right-slanting groove line situated at the top right-hand side of the bay.

1. 45m The lower part of the groove is a straightforward snow gully which leads to a large block belay on the right below the main difficulties.

2. 45m Climb the steep groove above, and pull over a large bulge at 20m to reach a small cul-de-sac. Exit by a groove on the left and follow easier grooves above to belay just short of the upper gully of Molar Canal.

3. 10m Follow the gully to the top.

42 Molar Canal   100m   III *

C.Jones, S.Kennedy, B.Williamson   25 Jan 1990

This gully, which deepens and bends left in its upper reaches, forms the right end of the Twins Area. It lies 35m left of Grooved Arete. Start up a short icefall and continue up grooves into the gully. It may be necessary to outflank the cornice off to the left.

North Buttress

North Buttress is the last continuous section of crag at the northern end of the corrie and comprises of three distinct buttresses, divided by the deep Icicle Gully on the left and the clean-cut ice groove of Jet Stream on the right. The left end of North Buttress is formed by two narrow ribs, the right of which is Grooved Arete. Between this and the left rib is a wide easy angled slot with a distinctive overhanging top. The following route is based on this but avoids the overhanging section well to the right.

43 Slipstream   140m   IV,5

A.Nisbet, J.Preston   23 Dec 2007

A devious line, but impressive ground for the grade.

1. 50m Climb the easy angled section of the slot until immediately under the overhanging section.

2. 20m Gain a ledge on the right and follow it to the end of a vertical wall above.

3. 20m Climb two short vertical walls rightwards, then move up left to a ledge with a big spike.

4. 45m Climb a short chimney to easier grooves. Move left to the continuation above the overhanging section and follow it to a blocky arete under the cornice.

5. 5m Finish over this.

44 Grooved Arete   130m   V,6 **

S.M.Richardson, R.D.Everett   26 Nov 1988

A good well protected mixed route up the narrow buttress immediately left of Icicle Gully.

1. 45m Start at the foot of the gully and gain the arete to the left. Follow this, easily at first, then with increasing difficulty up grooves on its left side. Move back right to below a steep tower.

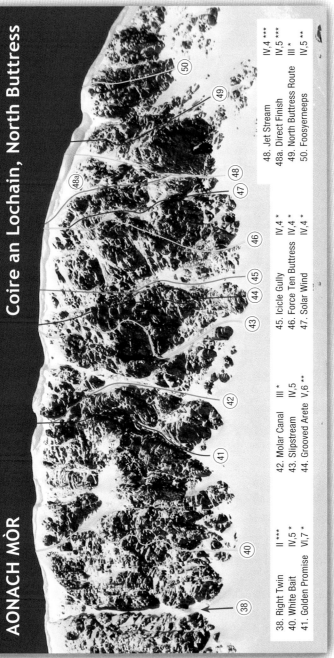

Coire an Lochain, North Buttress

AONACH MÒR

38. Right Twin   II ***
40. White Bait   IV,5 *
41. Golden Promise   VI,7 *

42. Molar Canal   III *
43. Slipstream   IV,5
44. Grooved Arete   V,6 **

45. Icicle Gully   IV,4 *
46. Force Ten Buttress IV,4 *
47. Solar Wind   IV,4 *

48. Jet Stream   IV,4 ***
48a. Direct Finish   IV,5 ***
49. North Buttress Route   III *
50. Foosyerneeps   IV,5 **

Jet Stream, IV,4, North Buttress. Climber Dave Cuthbertson

2. 35m Climb a series of grooves on the crest of the tower, step left to a ledge and continue up a vertical corner. An excellent pitch.
3. 50m Easy climbing on the crest leads to the plateau.

45 Icicle Gully 130m IV,4 *
R.D.Everett, S.M.Richardson 26 Nov 1988
The gully between Grooved Arete and Force Ten Buttress has a section of steep ice at mid-height. Grade III in its best condition.

46 Force Ten Buttress 140m IV,4 *
R.D.Everett, S.M.Richardson 3 Dec 1988
A good mixed route up the buttress between Icicle Gully and Jet Stream. It tackles some surprisingly steep ground, but is well protected.

1. 45m Start up mixed ground just left of the crest, then move right to a belay at the foot of a steep chimney where the buttress steepens.
2. 30m Climb the chimney, then step right and climb a short difficult crack.
3. 40m Continue up interesting mixed ground to the right of the crest to join a gully. Follow the gully to a col where the buttress merges into the final snowslopes.
4. 25m Easy snow leads to the cornice.

Between Force Ten Buttress and North Buttress route is a small bay which contains two prominent gully lines. They form ice readily, lie in the shade until late in the season, and are often in condition throughout the winter.

47 Solar Wind   110m   IV,4 *
S.M.Richardson, R.D.Everett   8 Mar 1992
1. 45m Start hard under Force Ten Buttress, and climb the well defined left-hand chimney to a snow patch.
2. 40m Above is a steep square-cut groove. Climb this, exiting left near the top to reach the continuation gully. Follow this to belay where Force Ten Buttress merges into the final snowslopes.
3. 25m Easy snow leads to the cornice.

48 Jet Stream   100m   IV,4 **
R.D.Everett, S.M.Richardson   3 Dec 1988; Direct Finish: C.Grant and C.Rice   27 Jan 1990
The striking right-hand chimney immediately left of North Buttress Route is one of the finest ice routes on the mountain. It is especially good early in the season before the first pitch banks up.
1. 45m Climb the chimney over several steep sections to a snow ledge.
2. 45m Either exit right up a steep wall to reach easier ground, or better, take the Direct Finish (IV,5) directly up the headwall above.
3. 10m Easy climbing leads to the cornice.

49 North Buttress Route   85m   III *
S.Kennedy, B.Williamson   25 Jan 1990
The shorter buttress at the north end of the corrie provides a quick route for the end of the day. This is left of two small buttresses which end the cliff. Its lower section is a steep smooth wall which is characterised by a prominent icefall. Avoid this by starting in a bay about 20m up and right from the base of the buttress. Follow grooves up left to the crest, then follow this to the top, where there may be a large cornice.

50 Foosyerneeps   50m   IV,5 ***
A.Clark, J.Davis   13 Apr 1998
The attractive clean pillar on the far right of the corrie is another possible second route. Climb the pillar via cracks and corners for two pitches slightly right of the prow to finish directly through a V-notch at the top (crux). Excellent protection and clean cracks throughout.

WEST FACE

(NN 189 729)   Alt 900m   West facing   Map p164   Diagram p188

The 2km long West Face of Aonach Mòr is a wonderful mountaineering playground of long gullies and granite ridges. The finest routes are the Summit Ribs which are over 500m long and finish by the summit cairn. The routes are open to considerable variation and good route finding will determine the most rewarding line for the conditions of the day. The relatively short approach followed by 500m of good climbing leading directly to the summit has proved a popular formula for an enjoyable, yet not too exacting winter expedition. Less sustained and committing than Tower Ridge on Ben Nevis or the North-East Ridge of Aonach Beag, these climbs provide worthwhile adventure in a wild and remote setting well away from the bustle of Coire an Lochain and the ski development.

LOCHABER

AONACH MÒR - West Face

1. Downhill Gully   I   ***
2. Golden Oldy   II   ***
3. Western Rib   III   ***
4. Easter Gully   II
5. Daim Buttress   III **
6. Solitaire   II *
7. The Red Eye Routine   III

Golden Oldy, II, Summit Ribs, West Face

Approach: From the Nevis Range Gondola station, follow a good path west and slightly descending to a small top overlooking the Allt Daim. Head straight down initially, then bend left on a slight terrace until traversing to the Allt Daim. Follow the stream to the Summit Ribs. They lie in a slightly recessed bay and are not visible until just past the prominent east ridge of Càrn Dearg Meadhonach (1hr 30mins to 2hrs).

Descent: From the summit walk north for 1km along the summit plateau to reach the summit ski tow and descend the ski slopes to the Gondola station.

Summit Ribs

A wide buttress with four defined ribs lies below the summit and is formed between two big gullies. A fifth rib lies right of the right gully and there are less distinct ribs and gullies either side of this area. The summit rib, Daim Buttress, is third from the left and perhaps the most distinctive particularly at half-height where it contains a prominent slab. Detailed descriptions are not necessary, for although the routes follow well defined features, they are open to considerable variation.

Downhill Gully   500m   I
The furthest left of the defined gullies often fills well with snow and has seen a number of ski descents.

Golden Oldy   500m   II ***
A.Kimber   21 Dec 1979
The established classic of the crag. Follow a groove in the centre of the leftmost rib, to reach the better defined ridge line higher up. A direct start is possible at Grade III.

Western Rib   500m   III ***
S.M.Richardson   17 Dec 1988
From below, the third rib from the left appears as a flying buttress to Daim Buttress

on its right. It is in fact distinct and gives the best route on the face. It has an easier but less good alternative start, up a rib bounding the gully on its left.

4 Easter Gully   500m   II
M.Tighe and party   Easter 1992
Climb the gully between Western Rib and Daim Buttress in three pitches to easier ground (100m). Either continue up the gully, or move right onto the upper part of Daim Buttress and follow this to the top.

5 Daim Buttress   500m   III **
R.D.Everett, N.Barrett, S.M.Richardson   25 Feb 1989
The third rib. Follow snow and rocky corners for 200m to the base of the prominent slab. Move left and climb cracks on the left edge of the slab to a platform (50m), and continue up the cracks and corners above (50m). A further 200m of scrambling leads to the summit cairn.

6 Solitaire   500m   II *
R.D.Everett, S.M.Richardson   1 Jan 1990
The fourth rib, which starts just left of a deep gully, is slightly easier than its neighbours to the left, but is an enjoyable excursion nonetheless.

7 The Red Eye Routine   500m   III
O.Metherell, J.Marsham   13 Dec 1996
The furthest right rib. Start 30m right of Solitaire at a small snow bay just right of a large pink block. Climb up the snow bay and move left up the short gully, serious (30m). For the next seven pitches continue up by the line of least resistance (mainly on turf). There is a short chimney on the sixth pitch. Easy ground leads to the plateau.

SGÙRR FINNISG-AIG

(NN 196 765)   Alt 300m   North-East facing

The broken north-east face of Sgùrr Finnisg-aig is cut by the Allt na h-Aire Waterfall. During a sustained period of cold weather it freezes to give a good ice climb and a worthwhile addition to other low level ice in the area such as the Steall Waterfall in Glen Nevis.

Approach: From the Nevis Range base station following the forestry track to its crossing of the Allt na h-Aire and continuing up the right bank of the burn to NN 196 765 where the fence crosses the burn. It is possible to avoid the first pitch, and walk up to the foot of pitch 2 at the start of the main difficulties.

Descent: It is best to follow the well marked path to the Gondola top station.

Smoking the White Owl   450m   III,4 **
F.Kincaid, S.Powell   1984
A long water ice climb consisting of short walls separated by large stances with a final steep headwall pitch. Take a good selection of ice screws for protection and belays. The crux is the last pitch, up the centre of a steep headwall (50m), although a slightly easier line on the left is also possible.

AONACH BEAG

(NN 197 714)   Alt 1234m

Nestling deep between Aonach Mòr and Càrn Mòr Dearg, this secluded and rather secretive mountain is the second highest in the Central Highlands. It boasts several crags which retain an air of remoteness despite the nearby ski development on Aonach Mòr. In contrast to the granite of Aonach Mòr, the rock on Aonach Beag is schist and the routes are generally more serious. This is particularly true of the north face which has a number of superb, but poorly protected, ice routes.

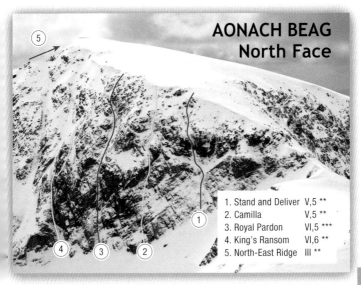

1. Stand and Deliver V,5 **
2. Camilla V,5 **
3. Royal Pardon VI,5 ***
4. King's Ransom VI,6 **
5. North-East Ridge III **

LOCHABER

NORTH FACE

(NN 196 718)   Alt 950m   North facing   Map p164

The large triangular face between the Aonach Mòr-Aonach Beag col and the North-East Ridge provides a good selection of excellent ice routes in a remote setting. The rock is difficult to protect, so a good selection of pegs and ice screws should be carried on the harder routes.

Weather and Conditions: Good conditions on the ice routes are likely to be found when the routes of similar altitude on Ben Nevis are well iced, although it is rare for good ice to remain here after the end of March. These are magnificent routes but good conditions are not common. The North-East Ridge is possible in any conditions. Despite the gondola, this is a serious venue with a high approach and especially descent, so good weather is recommended.

Approach: The Aonach Mòr – Aonach Beag col (NN 194 719) is the key to the approach. The Aonach Mòr Gondola provides the easiest access to the plateau area (see Aonach Mòr approach section for details). Descend to the base of the North Face (and beyond for the North-East Ridge) from the col, taking care with a potential cornice and avalanche prone slopes which occasionally form on the east side. If the cornice is large, it can often be negotiated by descending at the south end of the col.

Descent: The summit plateau, ringed by giant cornices on the east and north faces, is a serious place in winter. The small summit cairn lies perilously close to the summit rim and is normally buried by snow. After finishing a route, it is best to locate the sharp north ridge of the mountain (not easy), and descend this to the safety of the Aonach Mòr-Aonach Beag col.

Layout: The face has a rock wall and steep buttress nearest the col, a gully area in the centre, and the lower rocky part of the North-East Ridge on the left. All the described routes except the North-East Ridge are on the rock wall and buttress near the col. Described from right (near the col) to left.

Stand and Deliver   150m   V,5 **
C.Cartwright, R.Clothier   16 Apr 1989

A high rock band forms from the north ridge of Aonach Beag across the top of the right section of the face. A steep and often fat icefall forms down its left end. This is more often in condition than the thinner icefalls further left. Climb a wide low angled icefall which leads to the steep section. This provides a long and sustained ice pitch, high in the grade, which leads to the final snowslopes.

About 100m down and left of Stand and Deliver the rocks steepen into an impressive buttress of compact schist, which provides the finest ice routes on the mountain.

2 Camilla   230m   V,5 **
S.M.Richardson, R.D.Everett   31 Jan 1993
A good sustained ice route with some fine ice scenery. It is based on the twin icicles which hang down the overhanging wall at mid-height on the right side of the face. Start at the toe of the buttress, about 50m right of the prominent icefall taken by Royal Pardon.
1. 40m   Climb snow trending left to beneath steeper rocks. Work back right, then climb steep ice to reach the crest of the buttress.
2. 50m   Continue up the snowslope above and follow a shallow icy gully to below the twin icicles. Move past or behind these to rock belays high on the right.
3. 50m   Step down to climb the upper part of the right-hand icicle, then continue up easier angled ice to the crest of the buttress.
4. 50m   Continue up ice on the left to reach a snowfield.
5. 40m   Climb snow to the top.

3 Royal Pardon   220m   VI,5 ***
R.G.Webb, S.M.Richardson   18 Feb 1987
The ice smear which hangs down from the shallow depression in the centre of the buttress is a compelling line and has become a modern classic. In good conditions it is possible to belay on ice screws throughout.
1. 50m   Start directly below the ice smear and climb a series of icefalls to a flake belay at the bottom right side of the smear.
2. 40m   Climb the smear, passing two vertical sections, to a poor peg belay on the right.
3. 20m   A short pitch up the final ice wall leads to a broad snow couloir.
4. to 6. 110m   Follow the couloir for 50m to where it steepens into an icy gully which trends up and left. Two good ice pitches up this lead to the top.

4 King's Ransom   250m   VI,6 **
S.M.Richardson, R.G.Webb   14 February 1987 (1PA); FFA: A.Clarke, T.Ralphs   Feb 1995
An exciting and varied route that combines steep ice with a difficult mixed section. It remains in condition longer than Royal Pardon because the ice is deeply hidden. It starts up the narrow gully which cuts deep into the left flank of the buttress, before breaking out right across steep mixed ground to reach the crest.
1. 20m   Start about 40m left of Royal Pardon, beneath the gully, and climb easy angled ice to its start.
2. 50m   Climb the gully, passing behind a large chockstone, and climb the vertical free standing ice pillar above. An excellent pitch.
3. 40m   Continue up the gully to its end. Belay on a spike below the impending wall on the left edge of the buttress.
4. 20m   It is possible to escape left from here onto easier ground, but this avoids the challenge of the upper pillar. Instead, follow the ramp-line on the right to where it fades, and pull over the steep wall above to reach a second ramp. Climb this for 10m (delicate) to reach the crest of the buttress.
5. to 7. 120m   A fine snow arete and easier mixed ground lead to the plateau.

5 North-East Ridge   500m   III **
J.Maclay, W.Naismith, G.Thomson   Apr 1985
This classic mountaineering expedition finishes virtually on the summit of the mountain. Although not quite in the same class as the great Nevis ridges, this route is in a wild and remote setting. The traditional approach is from Glen Nevis but it is more often climbed from the Gondola. Descend from the col, initially steep then levelling out. Reach large boulders at the lip of a steeper section. Despite thinking

you must be there, continue descending, then make a descending traverse right until a short shallow snow gully leads up right to the base of the ridge. This gully starts at about 750 to 800m altitude. The lower section of the ridge is broad, broken and open to much variation, but after 100m the climbing becomes steeper. Turn the pinnacles at half-height on their right side, regain the crest of the ridge, and pass an overhung nose on its left. The knife edge snow ridge above leads to the easier and broader upper section and the summit.

GREY CORRIES - STOB COIRE AN LAOIGH

(NN 240 725)   Alt 1115m

Stob Coire an Laoigh is the central of three Munros on the main ridge of the Grey Corries.

STOB COIRE AN LAOIGH

(NN 242 728)   Alt 1000m   North facing   Map p164   Diagram p195)

This long quartzite cliff lies north-east of the summit of Stob Coire an Laoigh, the central of three Munros on the main ridge of the Grey Corries, and is clearly visible from Inverroy near Roy Bridge. The rock is very steep with good holds and cracks interspersed by occasional smooth sections and the protection is generally good. The cliff is vegetated but the turf is thin in places. The shortness of the routes is balanced by their fine lines and the sustained nature of the climbing.

Approach: From the end of the public road at Corriechoille (NN 252 807), it is tolerated to drive up a track to a right branch after 1.5km. It used to be possible to drive to a dam at NN 239 766 but in 2007 a gate at NN 251 792 was usually locked. Cycling is best although only strong cyclists will make the last 200m to the dam. Walk to the dam and over a stile, then head steeply uphill to reach a high river terrace. Make a rising traverse along the terraces and descend slightly to a major fork in the burn (NN 242 756). Cross the eastern branch just above the fork (slippery rocks) and continue to the cliff on a line generally on the hillside above the western branch, 3hrs including the cycle. The going is generally good apart from the river crossing which is impossible in spate.

Descent: At either end of the crag. The east end is often more convenient but can be corniced. The west end is longer due to broken ground and a lower cliff base. An abseil down Pentagon is another possibility, especially from routes near there; there is sometimes a sling in place. If a sudden thaw has made the river crossing difficult, it is better to stay west of the west branch, traverse out on to the spur running north from Beinn na Socaich and cross the river at a bridge well below the dam.

Weather and Conditions: This is a high venue so holds conditions well. But it does need to be frozen, as many of the placements are around loose blocks and the rock under the turf is very smooth, so the axes skid without an icy surface. The cliff is sheltered on a southerly wind but very bleak on a northerly. The altitude and aspect of the cliff coupled with the high precipitation of the area, means the crag can sometimes form large amounts of ice in the grooves. But this is intended as a mixed climbing venue. The many steep blank walls can make the crag look bare from a distance but conditions are often much wintrier than they appear.

Easter Sunday Gully   80m   I
S.M.Richardson, J.Ashbridge   Mar 1993
This is the snow gully at the right end of the leftmost section of cliff. The party wasn't sufficiently impressed to return to the cliff, much to the surprise of the later teams.

Loopy Louie   60m   IV,5 ✶✶
D.McGimpsey, A.Nisbet   8 Feb 2002
This is the best of the easier routes. The arete right of Easter Sunday Gully has a small pinnacle and col low down. Start right of the base of the arete and climb an

awkward wall before going up left to the col. Climb the short wall above the col and follow the crest (30m). Continue up the crest to a steep wall, move left into a corner, go up this and regain the crest. Move left again and climb grooves just left of the crest to the top (30m). A more direct line on the upper crest, passing the steep wall on the right, is possible at technical 6.
Variation Start: Without a build-up at the cliff base, an overhanging wall of technical 6 appears. It is then easier to start on the opposite side of the crest and climb a groove which leads into a through route behind the pinnacle to regain the route.

3 Slim Jim   80m   V,6 *
B.Davison, D.McGimpsey, A.Nisbet   17 Feb 2001
The narrow pillar left of the prominent central buttress taken by Centrepoint. It finishes in a distinct pinnacle which is not obvious from below. Start by traversing in from the gully between the pillar and Centrepoint (10m). Climb a line of weakness just right of the steep crest until the angle of the crest eases. Traverse left across the crest and up its left side to a short chimney (30m). Climb the chimney and steep ground above to reach a col behind the pinnacle. Go up a short awkward wall to reach the top (40m).

4 Tat Gully   70m   IV,4 *
V.Chelton, D.McGimpsey   13 Feb 2002
The gully to the right of the narrow pillar of Slim Jim is better with some ice. Climb the gully to a steep section. At its top transfer into a groove on the right and climb this to an awkward belay (30m). Traverses left and short steep grooves lead to the upper right-hand groove near the gully top (40m). Continue easily to the top.

5 New Labour   70m   V,6 *
D.McGimpsey, A.Nisbet   16 Feb 2002
Climbs the outside edge of the left face of Centrepoint buttress. Start round the corner from the front face and go diagonally right to a ledge just left of the edge (15m). Take a line of walls and shallow grooves keeping just left of the edge (35m). Move round on to the front face and climb easily up to the summit crest (20m).

6 Centrepoint   90m   VI,7 ***
D.McGimpsey, A.Nisbet   24 Dec 2000
A superb mixed route up the front face of the central buttress. This is the most prominent feature of the crag, and is vaguely shaped like a tower block. The unexpected success on such a steep line showed how helpful the rock was and inspired the team for many future visits.
1. 40m Start at the left end of the lowest rocks of the buttress. Climb diagonally right across a low ledge, then continue straight up over blocks and up a steep short wall. Move left on turf and climb up to finish parallel to a huge corner which is the dominant feature of the lower tier. Walk about 10m right along a ledge to below the groove furthest left on the upper front face.
2. 25m Climb the groove, then traverse left to a ledge. Climb a short wall and groove, then step left and climb up to a wider crack with chockstones. Traverse right and make a long exposed step to reach a turf ledge in the middle of the face. Climb up to a bigger ledge. The wider crack can also be climbed throughout instead of the right traverse, leading to a finish up New Labour.
3. 25m Trend rightwards up a wall, and continue up a wide crack passing the right end of a roof to an easier finish.

7 Blue Rinse   80m   VI,7 ***
D.McGimpsey, A.Nisbet   18 Feb 2002
The big roofed corner on the right side of Centrepoint Buttress. A sensational and very good line, although with a big build-up, you can walk off after pitch 1. The turf should be thoroughly frozen. Start right of the buttress base and climb a big corner, not the smaller one further right (25m). This leads directly to the base of the corner in the upper buttress. Climb this through an initial roof, quite big but responds to brain as well as brawn, then continue to swing out left below a second

STOB COIRE AN LAOIGH

1. Easter Sunday Gully   I
2. Loopy Louie   IV,5 **
3. Slim Jim   V,6 *
4. Tat Gully   IV,4 *
5. New Labour   V,6 *
6. Centrepoint   VI,7 ***
7. Blue Rinse   VI,7 ***

8. Central Gully   II
9. Cobra Corner   VI,6 **
10. Jammy Dodger   VI,6 **
11. Some Like it Hot   VII,7 ***
12. Serve Chilled   VII,6 **
13. Pentagon   VI,7 *
14. Taliballan   V,6 ***

Some Like It Hot, VII,7. Climber Dave McGimpsey

roof (30m). Climb blocks and trend slightly left to finish as for Centrepoint (25m).

8 Central Gully   120m   II
B.Davison, D.McGimpsey, A.Nisbet   17 Feb 2001
The biggest gully on the crag, forming the right side of Centrepoint buttress. It contains a short vertical ice step which can vary in grade from I to IV.

9 Cobra Corner   80m   VI,6 **
B.Davison, A.Nisbet   13 Dec 2002
Another 'impossible' line. The next buttress has a long left wall leading out from Central Gully, then a rounded crest with a huge roofed gully immediately to its right. Climb the gully over two steps (20m). Continue up the very steep corner (the moss is slow to freeze), move right and up turf to a ledge. Traverse right into a groove and climb this to below a steep corner (30m). Climb the corner and its continuation (or move left and climb steep turf) to reach a ledge leading left to easier ground. Go up over steps to the top (30m).

10 Jammy Dodger   85m   VI,6 **
D.McGimpsey, A.Nisbet   3 Feb 2000
The slabby right wall of the huge roofed gully (Cobra Corner). On the first ascent it was climbed largely on ice, but it should also be possible as a mixed route. Start up the gully until level with the base of a large slab which forms the right wall of the gully (20m). Traverse horizontally right on icy turf to near the arete and make steep moves up to a ledge 5m from the arete. A serious pitch with only ice hooks for protection (20m). Climb a short crack and move right to the arete. Move round the arete and climb a steep groove until an easier traverse left reaches a roofed alcove just below the top (40m). A final bulge on the right gains the top (5m).

1 Some Like it Hot   70m   VII,7 * * *
M. Edwards, D.McGimpsey, A.Nisbet   13 Feb 2007
Climbs a right-facing corner in the steep wall between Jammy Dodger and Serve Chilled. A fine line, steep and sustained, but not obvious on the approach as it faces away. Start about halfway along the wall, below and just right of the corner, which starts 20m up.
1. 25m Climb over a short wall into a roofed V-groove. Pull out left from the groove and step back right on to a 'diving board' above its roof. Climb a steep wall above to turf. An earlier attempt climbed direct to the base of the corner, but this ascent stepped right, moved up and returned left to below the corner.
2. 45m Climb the corner!

2 Serve Chilled   70m   VII,6 * *
D.McGimpsey, A.Nisbet   6 Feb 2002
To the right of the huge roofed gully (and the vague rib of Jammy Dodger) is a slightly recessed section divided by another rib from a more obvious bottomless chimney-line blocked by a large horizontal roof taken by Taliballan. This route climbs a steep groove just left of the rib. On the first ascent the groove was filled with ice of variable quality providing a precarious and poorly protected route. Start up a short chimney, then traverse right along a ledge to the start of the groove. Climb the groove trending slightly left to a short vertical screen of ice. Above the screen is a niche with an excellent belay (40m). Continue up the groove through a slot, then traverse left to another groove which leads up and right to the top (30m).

3 Pentagon   50m   VI,7 *
S.Allan, A.Nisbet   16 Apr 2005
A steep line up the wall which forms the left side of the rib left of Taliballan. Start as for Serve Chilled.
1. 15m The short chimney and right traverse, as for Serve Chilled.
2. 20m The wall above is overhanging so climb up left for 6m, as for Serve Chilled, before a short traverse right gains a ledge. Gain a second ledge. Steep moves slightly right, then back left over a bulge gain a shallow corner which leads to the base of a big left-facing flake-line, an obvious feature on the upper half of the wall.
3. 15m Climb the flake-line, then a corner on the right to pass a smooth wall and finish back in the original line. Abseil descent.

Taliballan   70m   V,6 * * *
D.McGimpsey, A.Nisbet   27 Dec 2001
A superb mixed route up the bottomless chimney-line blocked by a large horizontal roof. Despite its improbable appearance, the chimney provides amenable and well protected climbing, provided the turf is fully frozen. High in the grade.
1. 20m Climb a couple of steps towards the chimney and leading to a vertical wall. Traverse 5m left and climb a cracked ramp (crux) before returning to the line.
2. 10m Pull through a bulge on turf and continue up a groove to a cave at the base of the chimney.
3. 10m Climb the chimney to a ledge below the big roof.
4. 10m Move out right and climb cracks leading to the outside end of the roof and a comfortable stance on top.
5. 20m Continue up the line, now a steep groove to a chockstone below a steeper groove. Traverse left, go up and return right over blocks into the less steep finishing groove.

The next continuous ice line to the right of Taliballan and left of the more obvious line of The White Streak is **Yee Ha** (70m IV,5). Some of the ice is in chimneys and is not obvious from a distance. **The White Streak** (50m IV,5) is the icy groove towards the right end of the cliff that goes directly up from a point where a right-slanting ramp leads up to a terrace. When icy it can be easily recognised from a distance as a thin straight white line.

CENTRAL HIGHLANDS

There are a number of remote cliffs in the central area of the Highlands. Many like Ben Alder have long approaches and are not described here. Creag Meagaidh is less remote and situated north of Loch Laggan, roughly halfway between Fort William and the Cairngorms.

Maps: OS L42, E401.

SMC Climbers' Guide: *Ben Nevis* (2002)

Accommodation and Amenities: See Cairngorms p208 if approaching from the east or Lochaber p164 if approaching from the west. The nearest accommodation is the SMC Raeburn Hut (NN 639 909), on the A889 Dalwhinnie to Laggan road.

CREAG MEAGAIDH

(NN 418 875)   Alt 1130m   Map p164

A large and sprawling mountain, with an extensive summit plateau and several ridges that enclose a number of deep corries. The finest of these is the north-east facing Coire Ardair, which lies 1km east of the summit. Over 3km long, and nearly 500m high, its mica schist cliffs are among the highest in Britain. The quality and scale of its winter climbing puts many of the climbs in Coire Ardair into the same class as the Ben Nevis classics. Creag Meagaidh is a great ice climbing venue; the turfy buttresses are much inferior.

COIRE ARDAIR

Diagram p202

The rock strata lie horizontally and slope inwards, which results in a large number of snow holding ledges. Some of the rock is compact with few cracks; in other places it is shattered and both pegs and nuts are required for runners and belays. Ice screws are essential for the steeper ice routes, but normally only as runners.

Weather and Conditions: The cliff is very wet in summer and in winter collects plenty of snow, so the majority of the routes come into condition most winters, requiring only cold weather. Because of the length of the routes, the cliff base is relatively low, so colder weather is needed than the highest venues. With the exception of Pinnacle Buttress, where suitable conditions are less common, the main gullies are very reliable.

These attributes combine to make Creag Meagaidh a classic gully venue. Although the gullies can also provide good climbing on water ice during a period of cold weather early in the season, the best conditions are likely to be found during a cold and settled spell in February or March following heavy snow fall earlier in the winter. However, it should be noted that, as with any cliff in Scotland with a big and high plateau to its west, the corrie is particularly prone to severe avalanche conditions. Also the cliff has less steep areas on all buttresses where windslab is able to collect. The wind also builds up big cornices, so the corrie should be avoided during thaws.

Approach: Start from the A86 road, at the track to Aberarder Farm, where there is an expansive car park. Take the track to the farm, passing through a gate just east of the buildings and continue by a path on the north side of the Allt Coire Ardair. The path stays well above and parallel to the burn as the glen takes a great curve to the west, at which point the cliffs come into view. The path eventually descends to the floor of the glen, about 500m before the Lochan a' Choire Ardair, then it continues to the north-east corner of the lochan. This takes about 2hrs 30mins under normal conditions. In heavy snow, the path may be obliterated and progress becomes very laborious and time consuming.

Descent: The summit plateau of Creag Meagaidh is very flat and featureless, and great care is necessary when navigating in poor visibility. Many climbers, who are notoriously reluctant to get the map and compass out, have been benighted or have inadvertently descended to Glen Roy. In good conditions, descend by Raeburn's

Gully from Pinnacle Buttress or Easy Gully from the Post Face. The ridge of Sròn a' Ghoire, which leads back to Aberarder, may also be used and this is the easiest descent from the Bellevue Buttress or Pinnacle Buttress areas when conditions are poor. Otherwise, descent is best made by the Window, which leads to the Inner Corrie and so to the lochan. There is a line of old fence posts running down to the Window, and a little rock buttress which has to be avoided on the left. These are useful identity features in poor visibility.

Layout: From the Lochan a' Choire Ardair, there is an excellent panoramic view of the cliffs. High on the left is Bellevue Buttress, which is separated from the magnificent, towering Pinnacle Buttress by the left-trending line of Raeburn's Gully. To the right of Pinnacle Buttress are the gentler slopes of Easy Gully, above which rises the Post Face with its four great gullies, or Posts. A prominent feature of Bellevue Buttress, Pinnacle Buttress and the Post Face is a virtually continuous ledge line which crosses their upper half. This gives the line of the unique Creag Meagaidh Girdle Traverse, **The Crab Crawl** (2400m IV,4), one of Tom Patey's enduring monuments. Right of the Post Face, the crags turn in to form the Inner Corrie, whose features are not clearly distinguished when viewed from the lochan. The Inner Corrie terminates at the Window, the name given to the very prominent bealach between Creag Meagaidh on the left and Stob Poite Coire Ardair to the right.

1 Eastern Corner   300m   III *
C.G.M.Slesser, K.Bryan   28 Jan 1961
A deep corner which is the first ice line left of Raeburn's Gully and separated from it by a narrow buttress. This is the most accessible route in the corrie and passes through some fine rock scenery. The first 150m provides some potentially steep ice climbing, followed by 150m of steep snow which leads to the plateau and possible cornice difficulties.

2 Raeburn's Gully   360m   I ***
H.Raeburn, C.Walker, H.Walker   31 Oct 1903
The gully which slants up left beneath the impressive left side of Pinnacle Buttress gives a straightforward snow ascent. The gully is long, continuously steep and the Pinnacle Buttress face provides exciting scenery. The cornice is not normally a problem. If the snow is deep but still safe, the upper section of Raeburn's Gully Buttress can be taken after the first 150m. The gully is sometimes used in descent and it also gives access to Ritchie's and Smith's Gullies.

Pinnacle Buttress

(NN 434 877)   Alt 850m   East facing

The great buttress between Raeburn's Gully and Easy Gully is nearly 500m high and at least as far across. The broad, triangular frontal face, which tapers towards Easy Gully on the right, is bounded on the left by a steep wall which towers above Raeburn's Gully. This is one of the highest continuously steep cliffs in the British Isles, and exposure on the upper part of the face is both bewildering and Dolomitic. The routes do not come into condition as quickly as the Post Face.

The summit tower of the buttress is bounded on its right by the prominent exit gully of 1959 Face Route which rises from the central snow patches. The Raeburn's Gully wall has three parallel slits rising from the middle section of the gully. From left to right these are the lines of Ritchie's Gully, Smith's Gully and The Fly. There are three ledge lines which cross this section of the face. The upper ledge is unnamed and unclimbed. The middle line is taken by the exposed **Appolyon Ledge** (500m II), and the lower line, which is gained by a difficult 30m traverse from 15m up Smith's Gully, is **Vanishing Ledge** (360m IV,5). Lower down, starting from the foot of Raeburn's Gully, is the diagonal line of Raeburn's Ledge which is taken by the initial pitches of **Nordwander** (300m IV,4).

Ritchie's Gully   165m   IV,4 **
J.R.Marshall, G.J.Ritchie   Feb 1957; Direct, as described: G.N.Hunter, N.Quinn   March 1969
The shortest and furthest left of the three parallel slits on the Raeburn's Gully face

gives a fine and varied route, although snow build-up can affect the length of the lower part of the climb. Climb a steep icefall, turning an overhang by a right traverse, and continue up to Appolyon Ledge. The initial icefall can be avoided by traversing right along Appolyon Ledge. Continue up the gully to the cornice which can sometimes be difficult.

4 Smith's Gully   180m   VI,5 ****
J.R.Marshall, G.Tiso   8 Feb 1959
The central gully on the Raeburn's Gully face gives a tremendous climb of great character, continuously steep and sustained. The route takes a while to come into condition and the crux fourth pitch can be particularly difficult if unconsolidated. This was a step cutting tour-de-force by Marshall and the name was a jibe at Robin Smith who had failed on the route two years earlier. Despite the passage of time, it is still considered to be one of the hardest traditional Scottish gullies. Climb the gully and exit left at the top chockstone to belay on the left above a snow bay (35m). Continue up the gully to where Appolyon Ledge crosses. Climb the vertical ice wall above (crux) to easier ground. Snow slopes lead to the cornice, which can normally be avoided on the right.

5 The Fly Direct   240m   VII,6 ****
M.Fowler, A.Saunders   19 Feb 1983
The narrow gully to the right of Smith's Gully is one of Scotland's most sought after ice climbs. The route is serious and very sustained, and although it is not often in condition, there have been a number of repeats. The third pitch is probably the crux and can be very intimidating if thinly iced.
1. 20m Start about 7m left of the gully line and climb steep mixed ground trending up and right to reach the base of the gully proper, which is guarded by a bulge split by a wide crack. This point can also be reached by starting in a niche 10m right of the gully line, climbing up, then left under a roof to gain the foot of the gully.
2. 30m Bridge the wide crack for 5m, then continue up the depression above to a good block belay.
3. 50m Climb the steep icefall for 20m to where it eases. Continue straight up and step right into a niche (good peg belay); there is also a belay on the left wall.
4. 40m Move easily up to Appolyon Ledge. Belay on the right.
5. 30m Climb the open continuation chimney above and exit right under a big roof to belay below a steep icefall.
6. 50m Climb the icefall (optional but awkward belay on the left at half-height).
7. 30m Move left to reach the easy exit snow groove.

6 The Midge   400m   VI,5 **
G.Harper, A.Nisbet   19 Feb 1983
This route tackles the huge wall to the right of The Fly. It is long and impressive, but lacks technical interest and is probably climbable quite often, the only critical factors being ice in the initial corner and the presence of the icefall in the upper section of The Fly Direct. Start at the snow fan near the foot of Raeburn's Gully, where Raeburn's Ledge slants up to the right.
1. and 2. 80m Straight up a steep icy corner to reach the left end of a big snow patch.
3. and 4. 60m Continue up the short groove above, then move left and climb iced slabs to the right of a big right-facing corner (which holds little ice) to reach Vanishing Ledge.
5. 40m Traverse left and belay below a second right-facing corner which initially leans to the right.
6. 50m Climb the corner, passing an old peg, and exit left at the top. Move up to belay under a roof.
7. 40m Pass the roof on its immediate right, then move briefly left before trending right to Appolyon Ledge.
8. to 11. 130m Traverse left for 30m to join pitch 5 of The Fly Direct, which offers the easiest way through the upper rocks.

7 1959 Face Route   450m   V,4 **
J.R.Marshall, J.Stenhouse, D.Haston   9 Feb 1959
A largely mixed route with exciting situations which takes an intricate line up the front face of Pinnacle Buttress leading to the prominent gully to the right of the

Ritchie's Gully, IV,4. Climber Jules Cartwright

summit tower. Start at a small bay about 80m right of Raeburn's Gully. From the bay, a depression leads up to a shallow gully, which develops into a series of icy chimneys higher up. Climb the depression for 60m, then continue up the shallow gully for another 60m to a point 50m below the base of the first chimney. Traverse left for 60m to the foot of a left-slanting chimney-groove with an obvious chockstone. Climb the groove for 90m to the large snow patches in the centre of the face. Go up left to the foot of the prominent exit gully with its 30m barrier icefall, then climb this to the buttress crest. Easy climbing leads to the top.

Post Face

(NN 432 880)   Alt 900m   East facing

This stretches from Easy Gully on the left to Staghorn Gully on the right where the cliffs turn in to the Inner Corrie. Its most prominent features are the four parallel slits of the Posts, separated by well defined buttresses, known as the Pillars. As Easy Gully rises, the Post Face diminishes in height. Last Post is the leftmost and North Post the furthest right of the four gullies. To the right of North Post is Great Buttress. From its base two parallel shelves slant up right to the foot of two smaller gullies, known as the Pipes. Due to the big slopes below the plateau the face is very prone to avalanche and it should be avoided when collecting snow or after heavy snow fall.

Easy Gully   450m   I *
W.Tough, W.Douglas, H.Raeburn   Apr 1896
This is the easiest route in the corrie. It lies right of Pinnacle Buttress and slants up left under the Post Face. The lower part of the gully is narrow, but it widens in its upper section. For the easiest line, move out left from the lower part below its

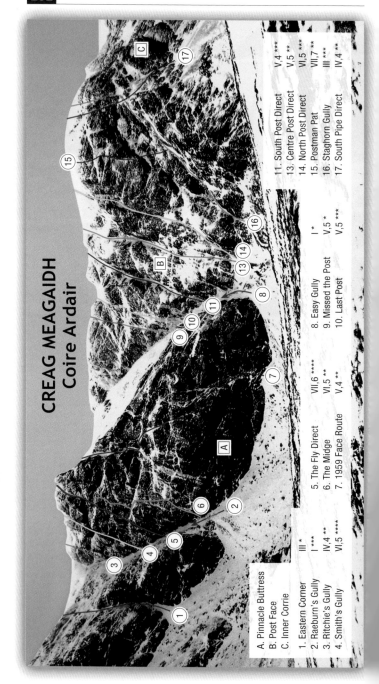

CREAG MEAGAIDH
Coire Ardair

A. Pinnacle Buttress
B. Post Face
C. Inner Corrie

1. Eastern Corner	III *	
2. Raeburn's Gully	I ***	
3. Ritchie's Gully	IV,4 **	
4. Smith's Gully	VI,5 ****	
5. The Fly Direct	VII,6 ****	
6. The Midge	VI,5 **	
7. 1959 Face Route	V,4 **	
8. Easy Gully	I *	
9. Missed the Post	V,5 *	
10. Last Post	V,5 ***	
11. South Post Direct	V,4 ***	
13. Centre Post Direct	V,5 ***	
14. North Post Direct	VI,5 ***	
15. Postman Pat	VII,7 **	
16. Staghorn Gully	III ***	
17. South Pipe Direct	IV,4 **	

Last Post, V,5. Climber Kevin Callaghan

steepest section. In descent, the reverse; keep well out from the Post Face initially, then cut back in below it at mid-height.

Missed the Post 220m V,5 *
P.Brownsort, P.Smith 9 Feb 1985
The narrower and almost parallel ice line to the left of Last Post. This is the highest of the main ice lines out of Easy Gully, so less prone to thaw, but probably less thick originally. Start in Easy Gully at an obvious icefall about 20m up from Last Post. Climb the icefall in two 50m pitches to a snowfield. Continue in the same line through two shallow icy chimneys, the second being the crux.

Last Post 240m V,5 ***
T.W.Patey, R.F.Brooke 5 Mar 1962
This excellent ice climb, the leftmost of the Posts, starts as an impressive icefall (crux) halfway up Easy Gully. Above, a snowfield steepens to a second icefall, which is climbed in two pitches. Easy snow then leads to another 30m icefall, which is followed by easy ground to the plateau. For maximum value, all the icefalls should be climbed direct. The route is Grade IV if the left side of the first icefall and the right side of the second are climbed. The third icefall can also be avoided on the left.

South Post Direct 400m V,4 ***
N.S.Tennent, C.G.M.Slesser 10 Feb 1956; T.W.Patey, R.F.Brooke 5 Mar 1962 (pitch 1 direct); A.MacEacharan, J.Knight Mar 1964 (pitch 3 direct)
An excellent climb, often in condition and low in the grade. This is the second Post from the left, and has two steep and exposed ice pitches linked by an easier section. The first pitch is a steep tapering icefall, although it can bank out

South Pipe Direct, IV,4. Climber Ian Jones

substantially in a year of heavy snow. Continue up the couloir above to the foot of the long second ice pitch. Climb this from left to right (crux) and follow the gully, with one more ice pitch, to the plateau. The route is Grade III if the initial steep icefall is avoided by traversing up and left from the foot of Centre Post and the crux pitch avoided on the left.

12 Centre Post   400m   III ***
C.M.Allan, J.H.B.Bell   21 Mar 1937
The third Post from the left provides a magnificent climb of alpine proportions. The lower 250m is a steep snowfield which leads, perhaps with one ice pitch, to the foot of the impressive icefall taken by Centre Post Direct. Turn this on the right, by making a steep and airy traverse up and across the right wall to gain a snowfield, then move back left around a rock outcrop to rejoin the main gully. Much variation is possible after the traverse. The ordinary route continues up the gully without further difficulty; the **Skidrowe Finish** (150m III) climbs the narrow gully after the traverse.

13 Centre Post Direct   400m   V,5 **
B.W.Robertson, F.Harper, E.Cairns   22 Feb 1964
The impressive icefall at just over half-height in Centre Post is a spectacular feature which was recognised as a 'last great problem' for many years. Depending on the build up of snow, the pitch may vary from 45m to 60m, with the first half being the steepest. It eases only slightly in the upper half. The start and finish, by the Centre Post normal route, are easy.

14 North Post   400m   V,5 ***
T.W.Patey, J.H.Deacon, G.R.Mcleod, P.Danelet   6 Feb 1960
This is the rightmost and narrowest of the Posts. It is an excellent climb, but variable, and rarely in good condition. When conditions are good the direct finish is formed, not so common, the normal route is probably Grade IV. Steep snow leads to a narrow chute and a chockstone pitch (crux). Where the gully above widens, a vertical chimney in the left corner gives access to an easy ledge leading to a large platform on the right. Cross back left across the terminal face overlooking the gully by an exposed 25m traverse. A further 30m, first right, then back left, leads to an easy open couloir and the top.
Variation: **Direct Finish   60m   VI,5 ***

Avoid the vertical chimney by climbing a short steep ice pillar directly above the snow gully to reach a terrace. An impressive ice sheet on the upper wall leads to the top.

15 Postman Pat 300m VII,7 **
A.Perkins, M.Duff 10 Feb 1991 (1 axe rest); FFA: A.Clarke, T.Ralphs 21 Mar 1995
A demanding route combining steep ice with technical mixed climbing. To the right of the upper mixed section of Great Buttress is a shallow wide gully undercut by a steep wall. Below this are a sloping shelf and an overhanging wall. Two icicles hang down the overhanging wall from the shelf.
1. 45m Climb the left-hand icicle to the shelf. Go up this to belay just below a narrow turf ledge on the steep retaining wall.
2. 45m Traverse left along the ledge for 5m, then climb steeply through the wall (crux) to reach the shallow wide gully.
3. and 4. 100m Continue up the gully for two pitches to the terrace.
5. to 7. 110m Finish up an icy runnel that leads to the upper snowfields.
Variation: **Icicle Variation 40m VI,6 ***
P.Thorburn, D.McGimpsey 25 Jan 2000
In good conditions it is possible to avoid the left traverse on pitch 2 and climb the wall direct via an icicle.

16 Staghorn Gully 400m III ***
C.M.Allan, J.H.B.Bell, H.M.Kelly, H.Cooper 29 Apr 1934
This excellent and popular climb is often in condition. As the cliff bends round from the Post Face into the Upper Corrie, there are two parallel gullies on the upper part of the crag. These are the South and North Pipes which can be approached by the long partially hidden shelf which slants up right from near North Post. The North Pipe, which is better known as Staghorn Gully, is the right-hand and easier of the two gullies, and leads by a series of short ice pitches to a snow bowl below the plateau.

7 South Pipe Direct 250m IV,4 **
J.H.B.Bell, V.Roy Jan 1935; Direct: J.H.Deacon, T.W.Patey 7 Feb 1960
A fine sustained climb but less often in condition than Staghorn Gully. Start well up and right of the shelf of Staghorn Gully and climb the shallow gully to the foot of the Pipes. Cross Staghorn and climb the South Pipe.

Inner Corrie

(NN 430 883) Alt 900m North-East facing Diagram p207
The Inner Corrie stretches from Staghorn Gully to the Window. The climbs here are mostly shorter and less serious than those on the other faces, but their higher altitude and more northerly aspect means they stay in condition until late in the season. The main features from left to right are: the well defined Trespasser Buttress; the deep ice corner of The Pumpkin; then a narrow gully leading to the twin icefalls of The Wand and Diadem. Right of this lie broken rocks with a central snowfield, bounding the left side of the gully taken by Cinderella. Two further gullies cut the rocks between Cinderella and the Window.

Trespasser Buttress 300m IV,5 **
G.N.Hunter, H.MacInnes, D.F.Lang, N.Quinn Mar 1969
One of the best mixed climbs on the mountain. The buttress to the right of South Pipe Direct has a well defined narrow chimney system which slants up from left to right. Start from a shelf below the left corner of the buttress and climb up steeply to gain the chimney, which leads to a snow bay. Go right to a short chimney and climb this to an overhung bay. Make a long step right to reach an exposed ledge known as the Diving Board, then continue more easily to the top of the first buttress. Follow easy snow to the foot of the obvious chimney on the right side of the upper buttress. Climb this to where it steepens, then take a ledge leading out left to the crest of the upper buttress. Finish by a small chimney to reach easier ground and the top.

19 The Pumpkin   300m   V,4 ****
R.McMillan, G.S.Peet, N.Quinn   14 Apr 1968
A classic – the longest and most popular of the Inner Corrie ice routes. It climbs the long ice corner right of Trespasser Buttress and comes into condition for long periods most winters. The belays are good but the ice pitches are long and sustained, although never too steep. Ice screw runners are required, perhaps placed in awkward positions. Confident parties may find the route easy, but continuous ice becomes tiring. Climb the corner in two long pitches to easier ground. Snow leads to a steep left-slanting chimney, usually ice filled and with an awkward bulge at 20m. An easier mix of snow, ice and turf leads to a sometimes difficult cornice. An easier finish (really an escape) traverses left from below the foot of the left-slanting chimney and climbs the deep gully to the right of the final tower of Trespasser Buttress.

20 The Sash   240m   II *
T.W.Patey, R.W.Barclay, M.Laverty, E.Attfield   Mar 1963
A pleasant but uninspiring route which is often in condition. Start in the narrow ice gully which leads up to the two parallel icefalls of The Wand and Diadem. From below the icefalls, follow a line of shelves up and left to reach the plateau.

21 The Wand   210m   V,5 **
Q.T.Crichton, D.F.Lang, G.N.Hunter, N.Quinn   2 Feb 1969
The left-hand of the prominent twin icefalls provides a sustained ice route that is often in condition. Climb the snow gully of The Sash to the foot of the icefall. The next section varies in height between 45m and 60m, depending on conditions, and is best climbed by keeping close to the right wall. A good cave belay is available early season when the icefall is more than one pitch. Above, the angle eases and the line of least resistance is followed to the plateau.

22 Diadem   210m   IV,4 *
J.Brown, T.W.Patey   19 Feb 1964
Another good ice climb which follows the right-hand icefall. It is easier than its twin to the left, but is less often in good condition as it forms a funnel which collects fresh snow. Approach as for The Wand and climb the icefall and easy ground above to the foot of a long ice corner. Follow this to easy snow and the top.

23 Fairy Godmother   210m   III **
M.G.Geddes, N.G.Rayner   27 Dec 1970
A good varied route – probably the best on this section of the cliff. Start mid-way between The Sash and the narrow chimney of Glass Slipper, at a right-sloping ramp. Follow the ramp for one pitch, then trend up and left by a series of ramps and walls to reach the central snowfield. Climb the obvious short gully someway left of the three exit gullies above the snowfield, then go left up a ramp to an airy perch overlooking Diadem. Finish by the steep tower above.

24 Glass Slipper   210m   III *
I.A.MacEacharan, J.Knight   Mar 1964
The steep narrow chimney just left of Cinderella leads to the central snowfield in two pitches. Above, climb the central break to the top.

25 Cinderella   210m   II **
W.Tout, T.W.Patey   Feb 1963
The prominent snow gully in the centre of the corrie gives a pleasant climb, often straightforward to a big cornice. There may be one or two short ice pitches early in the season. There have been a number of avalanche accidents in this gully over the years.

26 Crescent Gully   210m   III *
J.Clarkson, R.J.Tanton   17 Feb 1958
The curving gully mid-way between Cinderella and the Window. It is characterised by a steep and imposing right wall. Climb up left on snow to an ice pitch, which leads to a snow bowl and the cornice.

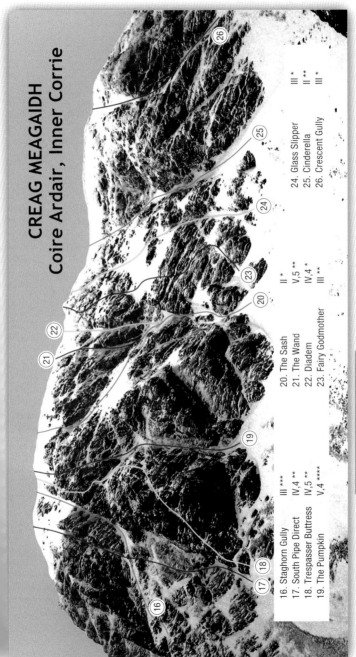

207

CREAG MEAGAIDH
Coire Ardair, Inner Corrie

16. Staghorn Gully   III ***
17. South Pipe Direct   IV,4 **
18. Trespasser Buttress   IV,5 **
19. The Pumpkin   V,4 ****

20. The Sash   II *
21. The Wand   V,5 **
22. Diadem   IV,4 *
23. Fairy Godmother   III **

24. Glass Slipper   III *
25. Cinderella   II **
26. Crescent Gully   III *

CENTRAL HIGHLANDS

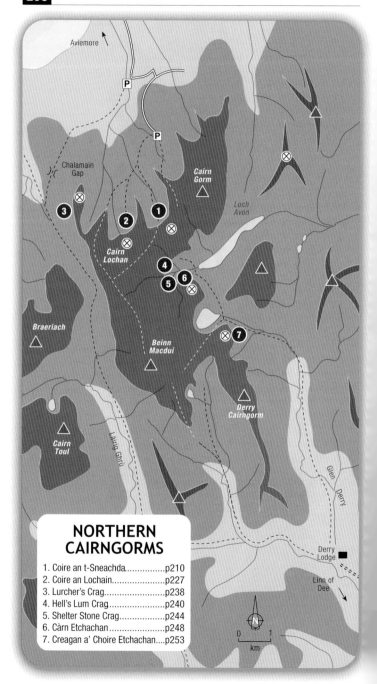

NORTHERN CAIRNGORMS

THE CAIRNGORMS

Being a high plateau area and far from the prevailing Atlantic westerlies, the Cairngorms offer a different style of climbing to the other areas. The reward is to climb in a remote mountain setting, the colder climate providing reliable conditions and the turfy granite offering a unique style of climbing. The challenge is sometimes to cope with wind and spindrift, producing the navigational difficulties of white-out on the plateau. There are reliable ice climbing venues, like Hell's Lum Crag, but it is for turf and rock mixed climbing that the Cairngorms have become famous. Many of the easier routes follow gullies whereas the harder ones often climb the turfier rock climbs under hoar frost and verglas. The challenge is the technical move with axes on rock, in cracks or embedded securely (you hope) in the turf of the next ledge.

The more remote cliffs have not been included, because a day visit is difficult without local knowledge and good walking fitness, and as a result they are less often visited. The exceptions are the icy Creagan a' Choire Etchachan with its grand central setting, and a small selection of climbs in Garbh Choire of Beinn a' Bhùird, because their quality defied omission. The corries of Braeriach are the snowiest in the Cairngorms and with the climate warming, it was a close decision to leave then out.

A word of warning. While the Cairngorms are a good option when the weather is too warm further west, the same does not apply to escape wind. The high plateau forms even stronger winds, and coupled with the colder temperatures, produces excruciating spindrift leading often to huge windslab avalanches in sheltered locations (Lochnagar being a common example). If the snow is deep and soft in the west, conditions may be better in the Cairngorms because there was less snowfall, or they may be worse because the last thaw was longer ago!

The selection has been divided into two areas; Northern Cairngorms and Southern Cairngorms. The cliffs in the former are generally, but not exclusively, approached from Aviemore. Those in the latter are usually approached from Ballater or Braemar, or in the case of Glen Clova, from Dundee.

Maps: OS Central & Northern Cairngorms – L36 (L43), E403, Harvey Superwalker Cairngorm (but Beinn a' Bhùird on E404); OS Lochnagar, Creag an Dubh Loch & Glen Clova – L44, E388, Harvey Superwalker Lochnagar & Glen Shee; complete area – Harvey Mountain Map Cairngorms & Lochnagar

SMC Climbers' Guide: *The Cairngorms* (2007)

Public Transport: Contact Traveline at 0870 608 2608 or www.traveline.org.uk. Regular bus and train to Aviemore en route to Inverness. Several buses per day run from Aviemore to the Coire Cas (Cairn Gorm) car park. There are several buses from Aberdeen to Ballater, but this leaves the problem of a long approach to the road end in Glen Muick.

Tourist Information Centres: There are all year Tourist Offices in Aviemore (01479 810363, Ballater (013397 55306) and Braemar (013397 41600).

Accommodation: Many B&Bs and hotels. Several mountaineering huts <www.mcofs.org.uk/huts>. SYHA Youth Hostels, <www.syha.org.uk>, Aviemore (NH 893 118), (0870 004 1104). Cairngorm Lodge is at Glenmore (NH 976 099), (0870 004 1137).

Independent Hostels: There are 18 independent hostels in the area, costing £10 to £15 per night, but many offer B&B or full board. See <www.hostel-scotland.co.uk> or list from SIH secretary, PO Box 7024, Fort William PH33 6RE.

Amenities: As a winter sports area, most facilities are open. There is 24hr petrol in Aviemore. Petrol in Ballater is 7.30am until 6.00pm Mon to Fri, 5.30pm on Saturday but only for a few hours in the middle of the day on Sunday. The Coilacriech Hotel (5km west of Ballater, NO 323 969) has petrol and diesel normally provided during bar hours.

Climbing Walls: In Aviemore is Extreme Dream in Dalfaber Industrial Estate (01479 812466, www.extreme-dream.com) including dry tooling and winter training facilities and also a bunkhouse. Climb Caledonia is at the Inverness Sports Centre and Aquadome, Bught Park in Inverness (01463 667505), with 9m leading and bouldering walls.

Northern Cairngorms

Map p208

The northern Cairngorms are very popular, probably because of the excellent road links to Aviemore and the convenience of the ski road to the Cairn Gorm car park at 620m. They even offer a retreat from mild conditions in the Northern Highlands, perhaps in the direction of home.

NORTHERN CORRIES OF CAIRN GORM

COIRE AN T-SNEACHDA

(NH 994 033) Map p208

Coire an t-Sneachda is the central of the three north facing corries of Cairn Gorm. It is separated from Coire Cas, the main ski area, by the Fiacaill a' Choire Chais and from Coire an Lochain on its west by the Fiacaill Coire an t-Sneachda (unnamed on the 1:50000 map). The latter, usually known as the Fiacaill Ridge, is a hump-backed ridge which steepens after a shallow col to form a narrow rocky ridge leading to the plateau near Cairn Lochan, the westerly top of Cairn Gorm.

The corrie itself is deceptive in size as it has a recess which extends westwards. This cannot be seen from the Glenmore area and it contains a large mass of rock buttressing the Fiacaill Ridge. Due to the wealth of good easy and middle grade routes, combined with the ease of access, this is a very popular corrie.

Weather and Conditions: The corrie is high and north facing and therefore it has a very long season. It is a good choice in poor weather and conditions (within reason) as a route safe from avalanche should be available, the Fiacaill Ridge being the ultimate resort (although not approached direct from the corrie). However, the corrie is a very windy place, never sheltered. South-westerly winds, which one might expect to provide shelter, funnel down the Goat Track to a vortex in the corrie. In general, hard snow and ice are more likely in the second half of the season.

Approach: From Aviemore, follow the ski road to the Coire Cas car park. From the top of the car park, take a traversing path south-westwards and after 400m branch left and uphill on an equally good path, heading for the corrie. The path ends just before a boulder field which surrounds the corrie lochans. Move left and find the easiest route through the boulders (with difficulty) to reach a first aid box just beyond the lochans, 1hr.

Descent: The normal descent is to follow the corrie rim round to spot height 1141m and descend Fiacaill a' Choire Chais to the car park. This is usually easiest on the right, down a strip of snow overlooking Coire Cas (beware of cornices). There are several options to return to the corrie floor, but the simplest is to descend the Goat Track. This is the snow slope down from the col between the top of the corrie rim and Cairn Lochain, i.e. the back right of the corrie from the approach. From Fiacaill Buttress, it may be quicker to descend the Fiacaill Ridge and drop down into the corrie.

Layout: There are four main rock masses in the corrie. High on the left is a rectangular buttress, the Mess of Pottage, which is bounded on its right by Jacob's Ladder, an obvious straight gully. Next comes a wide area of broken ground, followed by the large dog-leg gully of Aladdin's Couloir. This bounds Aladdin's Buttress, which lies in the centre of the corrie and has the lowest cliff base; its lower section is characterised by some obvious corner-lines. Right of Aladdin's Buttress is the more complex Fluted Buttress. This is cut by many gullies particularly on its left, where Central Gully, the leftmost of the Trident Gullies, forms the boundary between these two buttresses. On the right, Fluted Buttress fades out near the lowest point of the skyline where the Goat Track, usually a snow slope around 40 degrees, leads onto the plateau at the head of Coire Domhain. The fourth buttress, Fiacaill Buttress, lies at the head of a westerly recess below the summit of the Fiacaill Ridge.

Honeypot, IV,6, Mess of Pottage. Climber John Bracey

Mess of Pottage

(NH 998 032)   Alt 1060m   North-West facing   Diagram p212

This small, fairly slabby buttress lies high on the left of the corrie. The climbs are short, accessible and with a less serious atmosphere than the rest of the corrie, although not all the routes are well protected. The climbing comes into condition very quickly, only needing a decent covering of snow. Its left side consists of a dome shaped mass of rock with some defined corner and crack-lines. The right side is more broken and cut by a couple of diagonal faults and some areas of easier ground. The right edge of the buttress is defined by the straight gully of Jacob's Ladder. The cliff base has an obvious bay right of centre. From its top right a diagonal fault system leads up and left to peter out below a big roof near the top of the dome. The Message starts here and No Blue Skies is a parallel slabby fault further left. On many of the routes it is possible to interchange pitches and to escape fairly easily. The slopes round the base of the crag are prone to avalanche. The slopes left of the crag are easy (35 degrees) and can be used for descent.

The Opening Break   100m   IV,5
A.Cunningham, A.Fyffe   Nov 1990
A pleasant early season route but the start can bank out under heavy snow; it then becomes Grade III. Start near the left edge of the buttress, below and just left of a big left-facing corner which starts 10m up. Climb rightwards, then up cracks leading to the corner, turning the biggest bulge on the right. Climb the corner to easy ground on the terrace, then go up right. Follow the continuing fault, going left below a steeper wall, and break back right up twin cracks to an easy finish. An alternative and technically easier start in lean conditions is to start further left and traverse right to the corner; protection is limited.

Honeypot   90m   IV,6 **
J.Lyall, M.Sclater   25 Mar 1989
This route climbs near the left side, finishing by a roofed parallel sided shallow slot near the left boundary of the upper slabs. Start at a triangular recess at the bottom

Mess of Pottage

COIRE AN T-SNEACHDA

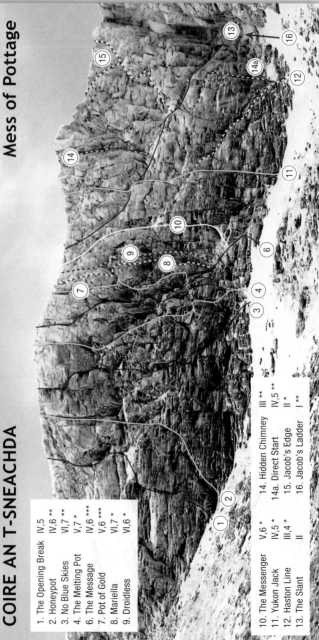

1. The Opening Break IV,5
2. Honeypot IV,6 **
3. No Blue Skies VI,7 **
4. The Melting Pot V,7 *
6. The Message IV,6 ***
7. Pot of Gold V,6 ***
8. Mariella VI,7 *
9. Droidless VI,6 *

10. The Messenger V,6 *
11. Yukon Jack IV,5 *
12. Haston Line III,4 *
13. The Slant II

14. Hidden Chimney III **
14a. Direct Start IV,5 **
15. Jacob's Edge II *
16. Jacob's Ladder I **

The Message, IV,6, Mess of Pottage. Climber Graeme Ettle

left corner of the face. Go right up the obvious slanting line, hard to start but it soon banks up, then go straight up a gully. Climb the wide but shallow chimney, passing the capping roof on the right wall (distinct crux). It is easier when icy but, this only occurs in prime conditions. The start of the climb is V,6 with no build-up; move up left on hooks, then make a long step right and either climb through the apex of the recess, or step right again on to slabs.

**3 No Blue Skies   110m   VI,7 ** *
A.Fyffe, L.Healey   20 Dec 1990
The first pitch is very thin, but ice will ease it considerably. Start at the top left of the bay where an obvious diagonal line leads left above slabby ground to a shallow horizontal cave. Climb the diagonal corner to near the apex, traverse left, then go up the left side of the apex to exit onto a ledge by the horizontal cave. Continue up the crack and corner (or a left-facing one further right) to easier ground and belay by a squat pillar. Climb broken ground, then gain a fine flake-crack below and left of the big roof and follow it to its end. Traverse left to a crack which goes through a short bulging wall and finish up this.

The Melting Pot   90m   V,7 *
A.Cunningham, A.Nisbet   Feb 1987
This route follows the main diagonal fault in its middle section, then takes a continuation crack which passes the right end of the big central roof system. If icy, VI,6 may be a better grade. The start is made left of the main diagonal fault and is hard (but optional) without ice or a good build-up. Start close on the right of No Blue Skies, aiming for a big right-facing corner 10m up. Either climb direct, or come in from the right across slabs to gain the corner. Exit from the corner over a bulge and traverse left round an arete onto broken ground leading to the main diagonal fault. Take the obvious line leading left to the top right corner of a large bay. Climb the overhanging groove above, then continue up a crack-line passing a roof to the top.

5 The Hybrid 100m IV,4 **

This easier combination takes the diagonal fault all the way, that is the start of the Message, then the middle of The Melting Pot. Below the final corner of The Melting Pot climb up and right onto a ledge below the final corner of The Message. Move out right to finish, or climb the last pitch of The Message (technical 5).

6 The Message 90m IV,6 ***

A.Cunningham, W.Todd 23 Jan 1986

A natural system of grooves gives short well protected pitches. Very popular, so some of the turf has been lost. It can now be V,6 if the cracks are iced up. It starts up the diagonal fault but then takes the deepest groove running straight up the cliff on the right. Start at the right side of the main bay right of the lowest rocks.

1. 40m Climb as much as 20m of icy ground leftwards to reach the top of the bay. Climb a blocky chimney and two short corners trending left to the foot of the main groove.
2. 10m Climb a fault on the right (the left is harder), break left, then go right to the foot of the deepest section of groove.
3. 20m Climb the groove and continue leftwards up the fault to the foot of a square, right-facing corner.
4. 20m Climb the corner to a bulge at the top, swing left onto the edge and climb cracked slabs to finish.

7 Pot of Gold 90m V,6 ***

J.Lyall, S.Spalding 26 Nov 1988

The crack-line in the buttress just right of The Message is sustained, helpful and very well protected.

1. 30m Start as for The Message with up to 20m of icy ground, then climb the blocky chimney of The Message.
2. 20m Traverse a narrow ledge right to the crack-line. Follow this past a short chimney until near The Message.
3. 20m Climb up right to a large ledge, then move back left to climb steep cracks slightly rightwards through a bulge (crux). Continue to below an easier chimney.
4. 20m Follow the chimney to finish.

8 Mariella 80m VI,7 *

C.Forrest, G.Ettle, A.Nisbet 6 Jan 1991

A deep roofed groove which looks like a narrow slot from a distance and lies 5m right of the blocky chimney of The Message. Recent ascents have found the crack-line on the firt pitch hard and VII,7 suggested. Start as for The Message and climb up icy slabs to below the groove.

1. 30m Climb the groove, swing left below the roof, and continue up a crack-line with thin moves to a ledge common with Droidless.
2. 15m Continue up the crack-line.
3. 35m Move left and climb walls and slabs to the top (good but very artificial).

9 Droidless 85m VI,6 *

C.Forrest, G.Ettle 21 Dec 1990

The parallel crack-line 3m right of Mariella gives a good sustained lower section. Start just right of Mariella.

1. 30m Gain the main crack-line by a slanting corner just on its left. Some parties have failed to start this way and have started up Mariella for a short distance before moving right. Follow the crack-line over a bulge to a ledge below parallel cracks.
2. 20m Continue up the cracks with a difficult start to an easing in angle in a bay below an obvious right-facing corner.
3. 35m Climb the corner then easier ground.

10 The Messenger 80m V,6 *

G.Ettle, C.Campbell 15 Nov 1991

Hidden Chimney, III, Mess of Pottage. Climber Roy Taylor

An obvious left-facing corner about 10m right of Mariella and Droidless. It looks improbable but has excellent cracks. Perhaps worth V,7.
1. 30m Climb the corner, pulling left past an obvious roof with difficulty.
2. 30m Trend right into and climb an open fault, then take a steep right-facing corner on the left.
3. 20m Easy climbing leads to the top.

A corner right of The Messenger, **The Three Decrees** (45m V,5), looks easier but the cracks are blind and very hard without ice. The right side of Mess of Pottage is more broken. The lower slabs are cut by two diagonal faults which lead to a large snowfield shaped like an inverted triangle.

Yukon Jack   90m   IV,5 *
M.Sinclair, C.Schiller   30 Dec 1993
A fine line, graded for ice, but can often be a grade easier or harder. Gain a big right-facing corner via a crack. Above, climb its continuation, crossing the Haston Line and finish up a chimney in the upper rocks in the same line.

Haston Line   120m   III,4 *
D.Haston and party   1965
The lower slanting fault starting from the corner of the buttress has two short awkward corners before an easy direct ascent can be made to a choice of finishes in the region of the upper snowfield. Going too far up the slanting fault leads into a corner of The Messenger, which is good but harder. There is a third line up, reached just before The Messenger corner, which is also technical 4. The route is III,5 in lean conditions, the crux being the second awkward corner.

The Slant   110m   II
Start a pitch up Jacob's Ladder at a bay where a diagonal fault goes left. Follow this, only Grade I if banked out with snow, and continue diagonally to the easy big upper snowfield.

Hidden Chimney   100m   III **
Start as for The Slant and follow it to reach a wide chimney defining the right side of the steeper upper buttress. Climb this over a chokestone and so to the top.

Variation: **Direct Start   40m   IV,5 ** **

The right-facing corner just left of Jacob's Ladder is well protected but strenuous at the start and quite thin higher up without ice. Often climbed as a single pitch, abseiling from a spike at the top of the corner (the normal belay is after pulling out left).

15 Jacob's Edge   110m   II *

Follow The Slant until it is possible to break back right over short steps to overlook Jacob's Ladder. Continue up to finish right or left. It is slightly harder to go to the base of Hidden Chimney and trend back right through a steeper wall. Low in the grade if the easiest line is chosen, but the harder variations are more fun.

16 Jacob's Ladder   110m   I **

A.Henderson, F.Mitchell   Easter 1939

The gully bounding the right side of the buttress is the hardest at its grade in the corrie. The finish is the crux; in lean conditions a small cave blocks the way, and a large build up can produce a big cornice. The answer to either problem is usually to finish on the right, often Grade II.

Aladdin's Buttress

(NH 995 031)   Alt 1000m   North facing   Diagram p220

This is the obvious buttress in the centre of the corrie right of Aladdin's Couloir. Its lower section is a steep dome shaped mass of rock at the top left of which is a 10m pinnacle, Aladdin's Seat. Above and right of the lower buttress and separated from it by a diagonal break of easier ground are several triangular rock buttresses. The right-hand and best defined is Pygmy Ridge; the ground below this is easy angled and much of it banks out in winter. The lower rocks of Aladdin's Buttress give some of the most interesting climbing in the corrie. The two main features to aid route location are the big left-facing corner of Doctor's Choice in the centre of the buttress and the wide chimney of Patey's Route near the right side. Routes on this part of the cliff finish on easy ground just below the level of Aladdin's Seat where the plateau can be gained via the top of Aladdin's Couloir or Aladdin's Mirror, or these routes can be used to return to the corrie floor.

17 Aladdin's Couloir   180m   I **

A.Henderson, E.M.Davidson   24 Mar 1935

The obvious large dog-leg gully bounding the left of the main buttress. In lean conditions, an easy ice pitch may form at the narrows before the bend. This is the steepest section even when banked out; this happens readily and the gully becomes the easiest Grade I in the corrie. Above, the gully widens and leads to a col above the pinnacle of Aladdin's Seat. A long pitch then leads to the top, any cornice normally petering out on the right. It is sometimes skied when in prime condition.

18 Original Route   100m   IV,5 **

W.March, B.Manson   13 Feb 1972

This line on the left of the buttress overlooking the couloir is a good choice under powder and sometimes a little sheltered from the wind. One abseil to the left gains Aladdin's Couloir from the route and there is an in situ sling at the top. Start about 10m up and right from the foot of the narrow rib which forms the left end of the buttress. Climb a shallow corner to gain a flake on the crest and continue up to an obvious fault. From the top of the fault, move steeply out left. Cross a sensational ledge overlooking Aladdin's Couloir to gain a groove. Follow this if icy, or just to its left if not, to easier ground. Move left to the abseil point, or continue up.

Variation: **V,6**

It is more satisfying to start at the toe of the buttress, but harder. Take the line just on the left of the toe to gain the crest.

The Lamp, V,6, Aladdin's Buttress. Climber Finlay Wild

The Lamp   100m   V,6 *
A.Liddell and party   Jan 1988
An interesting line up the linked diagonal breaks just right of Original Route. Start below an open groove at the top left corner of the bay right of the narrow rib. Climb the groove to a steepening which forces you out on to steep but helpful ground on the right (unless the groove is iced). Climb this sustained section (needs to be frozen!) to an easing, then follow a smooth but low angled ramp right to its end in the central bay. Go diagonally right to below an obvious break leading back left (or continue right to the final corner of Doctor's Choice, which may be temptingly icy). Follow this break, then climb the buttress crest. The abseil descent into Aladdin's Couloir is an option.

Doctor's Choice   105m   IV,4 **
W.March, N.Dilley   12 Feb 1972
An interesting climb taking the prominent large left-facing corner in the centre of the buttress. It is only recommended when the top corner is iced; this is visible from below. Start below the corner and climb to a cave below an overhang. From the foot of the cave go diagonally left to a snow bay, exit this on the right and return on easy ground to below the main corner. Climb this to the top. A more direct start can be taken when it is very icy (5).

The left of the three main corners is **Doctor Janis** (130m V,7), which requires a good build-up for its start.

The Genie   110m   V,7 ***
D.Sanderson, J-C.Tomasi   14 Mar 1982
A fine climb taking the central of the three main corners. It is graded for powder but it can ice and be a little easier. Start down and left from the narrowing at the foot of Patey's Route.
1. 25m Gain the lower and left of two ramp lines. Follow it over a bulge and continue left.
2. 25m Follow two corners which curve up leftwards to the foot of the main corner.

CAIRNGORMS

3. 40m Climb this to the top.
4. 20m Finish easily.

22 Magic Crack   90m   VII,7 ***
A.Cunningham, A.Nisbet   7 Dec 1985; A.Huber, A.Mullin   10 Mar 1999 (pitch 4)
A sustained but well protected test piece. The highlight is the unique torquing crack right of Genie main corner; it is strenuous to climb and even more strenuous to place the excellent protection. Descent is a 50m, then a 40m abseil.
1. and 2. 50m Follow Genie to its stance below the main corner. Make a thin move right to gain a ledge at the base of the right-slanting crack.
3. 20m Follow the crack to a ledge on the left.
4. 20m Go up a continuation crack to an overlap. Above is a difficult right-slanting crack but this leads to an easier left-slanting one and a tricky move to reach easier ground and the abseil point.
Variation: **Original Finish**
From the ledge after pitch 3, step down and traverse right under an overlap (inventive torquing but overhead protection) to the top of a corner (Damnation). Gain the ledge above. Finish above via a narrow chimney.

23 Damnation   90m   VI,6 **
J.Grosset, M.Sclater   20 Nov 1985
The rightmost corner gives a sustained pitch with thin cracks but too little for the feet. It drops a grade if the corner is well iced, but this is rare nowadays. Start at the foot of Patey's Route.
1. 40m Climb a slabby ramp leading left. This is a parallel but higher ramp to the start of Genie. Work up right to a huge spike at the foot of a corner.
2. 25m Climb a crack in the slab left of the corner, then the corner itself which leads into the main corner. Gain a ledge at the top.
3. 25m Finish above via a narrow chimney.

24 Salvation   100m   VI,7 *
J.Lyall, A.Nisbet   27 Dec 1989
This route is on the cracked slabs left of Patey's Route. Start at the foot of Patey's Route.
1. 35m Climb about 10m up a slabby ramp going left (the higher and right of the two ramps). Leave the ramp via a short chimney groove, then pass left of a short wall to reach a broad ramp.
2. 40m Break through the overlap above at some flakes and reach right, or go straight up about 2m right of the flakes, and climb cracks up the slab.
3. 25m Move up right to a block, then follow the continuation crack to the top, finishing close to Patey's Route.

25 Patey's Route   120m   IV,5 **
T.W.Patey   Feb 1959
This follows the obvious wide chimney-line on the left side of the buttress. The more ice, the easier the climb; it is graded for icy conditions. There are two main pitches, both of which have a difficult bulge where they narrow. The top one is usually climbed by going up left at the top, then making a long move back right above the bulge. It can also be climbed by continuing leftwards.

26 Aladdin's Mirror   180m   I *
E.U.M.C. Party   Easter 1946
An exposed snow route taking the easy ground right of the lower part of the buttress. Climb the diagonal snow shelf on the right-hand side to reach open slopes. Trend back left under the upper rocks to reach Aladdin's Seat and finish up Aladdin's Couloir.

27 Aladdin's Mirror Direct   25m   IV,4 **
A popular ice problem, sometimes underestimated. It varies in length and steepness

Magic Crack, VII,7, Aladdin's Buttress. Climbers Graeme Ettle & Rab Anderson

according to build up. It has even been descended on a snow board, but that will be no consolation if you try it when lean. Climb the steep ice pitch on the right of the buttress up from the start of Aladdin's Mirror. An easy chimney leads to the main route.

Pygmy Ridge   100m   IV,5 ***
The right-hand ridge in the upper tier above Aladdin's Mirror gives an excellent little climb following the well defined rib. Normally reached via Aladdin's Mirror, it also makes a good combination with Aladdin's Mirror Direct, offering the contrast of snowed up rock (no turf) with pure ice. The start, up a groove to the right of the toe of the ridge, has a hard move low down but the rest is easier (35m). The summer start, just left of the toe, is harder. The second pitch crosses a horizontal arete (35m) and the third pitch takes an upper tower (30m), although it is easy to escape to the right.

Fluted Buttress

(NH 994 030)   Alt 1020m   North facing   Diagram p220

This area stretches west from Aladdin's Buttress to the lowest point of the corrie rim. A recessed section on the left is split by the Trident Gullies which spring from a prominent snow bay which extends high up into the cliffs. Central Gully, which slants left and is the left-hand of the three, forms the boundary between Aladdin's and Fluted Buttresses. The Runnel is the prominent direct line while the rightmost of the Trident Gullies is Crotched Gully; this uses the wide fault in the upper cliffs. Right of this the rocks are less broken and are cut high up by the right-slanting upper section of Spiral Gully. This lies above a fairly unbroken section of cliff which from below appears as a tapering wedge of rock bounded by Broken Gully on the right. After Broken Gully is Fingers Ridge, with its distinctive pinnacles high up near the plateau. Right again are Red Gully and Goat Track Gully, before the buttress fades out into the easier ground of the Goat Track.

The area of the Trident Gullies is quite low angled and the ribs between the gullies give routes only slightly harder than the gullies themselves. Further right at

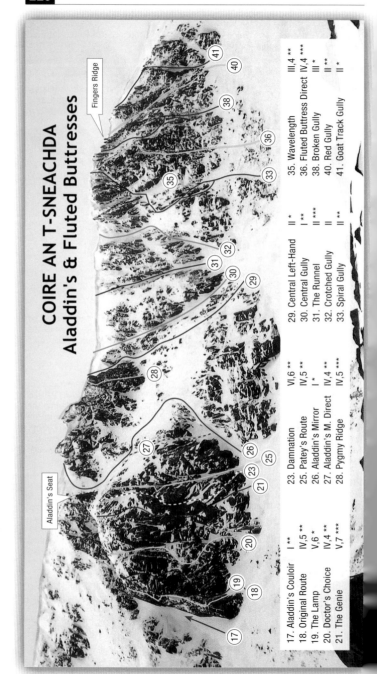

COIRE AN T-SNEACHDA
Aladdin's & Fluted Buttresses

Fingers Ridge

Aladdin's Seat

17. Aladdin's Couloir	I **	
18. Original Route	IV,5 **	
19. The Lamp	V,6 *	
20. Doctor's Choice	IV,4 **	
21. The Genie	V,7 ***	

23. Damnation	VI,6 **	
25. Patey's Route	IV,5 **	
26. Aladdin's Mirror	I *	
27. Aladdin's M. Direct	IV,4 **	
28. Pygmy Ridge	IV,5 ***	

29. Central Left-Hand	II *	
30. Central Gully	I **	
31. The Runnel	II ***	
32. Crotched Gully	II	
33. Spiral Gully	II **	

35. Wavelength	III,4 **	
36. Fluted Buttress Direct	IV,4 ***	
38. Broken Gully	III *	
40. Red Gully	II **	
41. Goat Track Gully	II *	

the highest part of the cliff the buttress has a slabby lower section which can bank out. If this is not the case, Spiral Gully and routes in the area of Fluted Buttress Direct may have an extra easy pitch to start.

9 Central Left-Hand   135m   II ***
Climb the broad easy rib below Pygmy Ridge, overlooking Central Gully, by a choice of lines then finish up the well defined funnel shaped gully immediately right of Pygmy Ridge. There is often a good ice pitch in the upper section; the route is Grade I when it is banked out.

**0 Central Gully   135m   I ** **
T.E.Goodeve, A.W.Russell, A.E.Robertson   1 Apr 1904
The leftmost of the Trident Gullies slants leftwards and separates Aladdin's and Fluted Buttresses. It is straightforward with no pitches and an easily outflanked cornice. It can contain much ice in lean conditions, when it becomes a very good easy Grade II.

1 The Runnel   135m   II * **
E.U.M.C. Party   Easter 1946
The central and best defined of the three gullies rises from the top of the snow bay. Straightforward climbing leads a fine icy chimney (well protected) near the top. It is arguably better in lean conditions, but the final chimney will be Grade III without ice, although it only needs a little.

2 Crotched Gully   135m   II
E.U.M.C. Party   Easter 1946
The right-hand of the Trident gullies leads out from the snow bay, steepens and finishes by an easier gully on the right. It reduces to Grade I in peak conditions when there is often a big cornice. But the steepening is nearer Grade III in very lean conditions.

**3 Spiral Gully   200m   II ** **
T.W.Patey   Feb 1959
The longest of the gullies is quite easy under heavy snow but rock belays are not obvious and the line is not simple. There are many short tricky moves in lean conditions but the grade remains the same. Start right of the Trident Gully bay and climb steep broken ground which readily banks out. Aim for twin gullies. If icy the left is better, but the right is easier. Above these, climb snow and bend right (not straight up, which leads into Crotched Gully) into a well defined right-slanting fault which leads to a small col just below the plateau. It is rarely corniced. A direct finish from the base of the diagonal fault is Grade III.

Vortex   60m   IV,5 *
G.Ettle, J.Lyall   10 Jan 1992
The rib between the top sections of Crotched and Spiral Gullies gives a short interesting climb. Reach it by climbing Spiral Gully above the twin gullies, then move right. Follow the shallow groove line up the rib and turn the capping roof on the left or on the right (slightly easier). An easy crest leads to the top.

**Wavelength   130m   III,4 ** **
A.Fyffe, D.Bowen   13 Feb 1985
An interesting and varied route which takes the left branch of the fault of Fluted Buttress Direct. High in the grade. Climb Spiral Gully, or just right of it, to the base of the twin gullies, then slant up right to a shelf. Move right round a steep wall and go up to gain a right-slanting shallow chimney which leads up to a short traverse right into the main fault just above where it splits. Go up this fault. A steep corner (crux) with a helpful spike then leads to the rib overlooking Spiral Gully. Follow the rib to finish. The slightly harder original start was near Fluted Buttress Direct, heading more directly to the steep wall.

CAIRNGORMS

Fingers Ridge, IV,4/5, Fluted Buttress

36 Fluted Buttress Direct   140m   IV,4 ***
A.Fyffe, S.Crymble   18 Mar 1978
An excellent climb which follows the narrow but defined groove system on the left of the most continuous section of slabby rocks. It is graded and starred for continuous ice in the grooves. Under powder it is thin and quite serious (V,5), although still worth doing. Go up easily for up to 50m to below the groove (not included in length). Climb it to where it forks and increases in size (50m). Continue up the right fork to the crest of the buttress (40m). Climb this to the col between Spiral and Broken Gullies and hence the top (50m).

37 Cruising   140m   V,5 *
K.Spence, R.Anderson   8 Nov 1980
A line up the right side of the steeper rocks. Some good climbing but escape into Broken Gully is easy at one point. Climb easily up the lower slabs to start at a left-facing corner (50m up the cliff when the build-up is small). Climb the corner, or initially just left of it, and continuation fault to a niche in a steeper section. Climb this and follow the fault curving rightwards to a ledge, almost into Broken Gully (50m). Take a crack-line on the crest to a ledge. Traverse left, then go up and back right to another ledge (or climb direct, technical 6) – 30m. Continue up the crest and finish up Fluted Buttress Direct (40m, 20m).

38 Broken Gully   130m   III *
T.W.Patey, J.McArtney, J.Cleare   Feb 1967
The fault between the highest part of the buttress and Fingers Ridge has a good start but is disappointingly discontinuous thereafter. The upper section of the gully is large and funnel shaped. Start in the first bay right of the lowest rocks. Climb the gully up and right until a left traverse (crux) can be made onto the top of a slabby pillar and thus into the main gully (this is not very obvious but is at the top of a fairly long pitch). Follow the upper gully to finish up the right or the left of the upper funnel.
Variation: A Left-Hand Start takes a smaller gully left of the ordinary start and leads directly into the upper fault. This forms ice readily but is slightly harder.

39 Fingers Ridge   140m   IV,4/5 *
J.R.Dempster, J.I.Wallace   19 Jan 1969
The slabby rib which culminates in two obvious pinnacles (the 'fingers', which are visible on the skyline from the corrie floor) gives a fine climb with sustained mixed climbing but never too hard. Start at the foot of Red Gully. When very lean, a start further left avoids a smooth slab which becomes exposed. Go up and left over slabs and ledges to a bay near the left edge of the buttress (close to Broken Gully). Climb a rib overlooking Broken Gully, then a short wall on the right via a flake to gain a large right-facing open groove left of some slabs. Climb this groove to a narrow ridge (there is an easy escape left from here into Broken Gully) and follow this past the 'fingers' to a col. A short hard wall (5), but avoidable on the right or left, leads to the top.

Broken Fingers (130m IV,4) is a good combination, more sustained than Broken Gully and offering both ice and mixed climbing. Start up Broken Gully when icy but continue up, past the left traverse, to join and follow Fingers Ridge.

**40 Red Gully   120m   II **
The fault right of Fingers Ridge gives a fine climb, graded for good conditions when it has a lot of ice in the chimney and excellent rock runners. Unfortunately its popularity thins the ice, so it is often Grade III, but it is easy after the first pitch which leads into the easier funnel shaped upper gully.

**41 Goat Track Gully   120m   II *
Starting at the same point as Red Gully, the gully on the extreme right of the buttress has a short sharp but well protected section. It cuts up deeply rightwards to a short pitch which is usually taken on the right, initially on ice. Continue up a shallow gully for 25m from where it is easy to the top or for those who don't want to go to the plateau, a 40m traverse leads to the Goat Track.

Fiacaill Buttress

(NH 989 029)   Alt 1060m   North-East facing   Diagram p224

This is the fine mass of rock high up in the western sector of the corrie, forming the corrie face of the Fiacaill Ridge. It is split in two by the large diagonal gully of Fiacaill Couloir, but this is hidden from most angles. Left of the gully the face is wedge shaped and the upper section above a ledge which cuts the face from the left is scored by several right-slanting ramps. The face above and right of the gully has more large scale vertical features. Conditions here can sometimes be better than elsewhere in the corrie because it is higher in altitude and sheltered from west winds.

Men in Black   50m   VI,8
G.Ettle, M.Garthwaite   31 Jan 1998
This route climbs a wide corner-crack left of Houdini. The route has become popular as a technical test piece, which is sometimes claimed to be straightforward. Large Cams and no verglas are recommended.
1. 15m Start up a fault 8m left of Houdini. Climb it for 10m, then move right to a left-facing corner-crack.
2. 15m Ascend the wide crack past two essential chokestones to an easier finish and good ledge.
3. 20m Move right into Houdini. A wide crack splits the wall on the right. Climb the thinner crack on its left to the Terrace.

Houdini   160m   VI,7 *
A.Cunningham, A.Fyffe   Feb 1990
A fine climb which works its way up the front face of the buttress. Start in the middle of the lower tier and climb the main left-slanting groove to its top, then trend left to the mid-way ledge. Climb the open right-slanting groove to a ledge

CAIRNGORMS

COIRE AN T-SNEACHDA

Fiacaill Buttress

Mid-Way Ledge

43. Houdini   VI,7 **
44. The Stirling Bomber   V,7 **

45. Fiacaill Couloir   II ***
46. Rampant   IV,5 *
47. Burning and Looting   V,6 *
48. Belhaven   V,6 **
49. Invernookie   III,4 **
50. Short Circuit   IV,5 *
51. The Seam   IV,5 **
52. Fiacaill Ridge   II *

with big flakes below a steep wall and traverse delicately right until ramps lead upwards. Go up a short way, step left and climb to the left side of a huge block and belay. Go right, climb a big groove and either thread or pass on the outside of the chokestone. Continue up by some thin climbing to below the upper wall. Climb this diagonally left, starting in a vague niche to gain the top by the step in the wall.

44 The Stirling Bomber   55m   V,7 **

A.Cunningham, A.Fyffe   4 Jan 1990

This great little climb takes the obvious right-facing chimney right of centre on the lower part of the buttress. Gain the chimney by flakes and cracks leading leftwards into it, and climb it by an inch by inch struggle to a diagonal fault. The chimney is rather too wide for comfort, more back and neck than back and foot, but it is well protected. Finish up the fault to the halfway ledge which leads easily off left, back to the corrie floor.

45 Fiacaill Couloir   150m   II ***

T.W.Patey   17 Jan 1958

The diagonal gully which cuts deeply through the buttress gives a sustained climb with limited protection and sometimes continuous snow ice. Start in the snow bay in the centre of the buttress and follow the gully up and left. Near the top a chokestone may be difficult if there is a poor build up (Grade III). Above the col descend slightly to the left to a smaller col, then continue up to finish.

The next route climbs the wall overlooking Fiacaill Couloir and starts some way up that fault.

46 Rampant   75m   IV,5 *

A.Fyffe, T.Walker   1 Mar 1979

This route takes a line of narrow ramps then a big corner in the upper buttress. Start 75m up Fiacaill Couloir where a big ledge is 5m up on the right wall. From its left side, climb an upper set of ramps up left into a corner, go up this, then back right at its top. Move right into a big corner and follow this, exiting through a hole onto the ridge.

47 Burning and Looting   75m   V,6 *

G.Reid, J.Hepburn   Jan 1988 (pitch 1); As described: A.Cunningham, A.Fyffe   13 Feb 1991

The rib between the corners of Rampant and Belhaven. Start on the big ledge 75m up Fiacaill Couloir, as for Rampant, where a ledge leads right into Belhaven. From near a huge block on the ledge, go up steeply to a ledge going right, then move into a hanging groove capped by a block. Surmount this into a short slot (strenuous) or turn it on the right then go up to a ledge (this can be climbed as a direct start to Rampant). Climb the sharp rib above by cracks and blocks on the right of the crest.

48 Belhaven   75m   V,6 **

A.Fyffe, K.Geddes   19 Feb 1979

A good climb up the prominent corner immediately above the start of Fiacaill Couloir. It sometimes ices up when it will be easier but less well protected. Climb Fiacaill Couloir for a pitch to below the corner. Either climb directly into the corner (good build-up or good torquing technique required), or continue up the gully to use the big ledges going right. Climb the main corner in one long pitch; protection is strenuous to place at the start and the climbing is sustained throughout.

49 Invernookie   120m   III,4 **

K.Spence, J.Porteous   4 Jan 1969

An interesting and popular climb which takes a line of ramps on the wall above and right of Fiacaill Couloir. Loss of turf means there are some tricky moves (IV,5 under powder) but these become much easier with consolidated snow or a little ice. Start just right of Fiacaill Couloir. Slant right, then go back left to a short wall

CAIRNGORMS

Invernookie, III,4, Fiacaill Buttress. Climber Susan Jensen

which leads to the ramps. Follow these to below an overhanging wall. The right-hand corner leads into a chimney-cave from which a right traverse arrives at a groove and the ridge.

50 Short Circuit 110m IV,5 *
S.Monks, G.Reid, A.Fyffe 9 Feb 1987
This climb takes the snow ramp above and right of Invernookie. Start as for Invernookie, then go right and up to gain this higher ramp. Go to its end and climb the corner. If there is no ice in the corner, go left round the arete and climb a wide crack to the same snow patch. Climb a short wide crack into the right-hand of two grooves and finish by a crack in the slab on its right.

51 The Seam 100m IV,5 **
J.Grosset, J.Lyall 2 Jan 1986
A good route, low in the grade, which follows the obvious chimney immediately left of the steep triangular wall on the buttress edge. Start as for Invernookie but continue the initial right slant until underneath the triangular wall. Pull up left round the edge of this wall and continue up to the base of the chimney. Climb the chimney-fault directly to the top; tricky and sustained but well protected. An easier start is to follow Invernookie further and gain the base of the chimney from the ramps.

The Hurting (35m XI,11) was climbed by Dave MacLeod in 2005, up the triangular wall right of The Seam. It was suggested as the hardest single pitch traditional mixed climb in the world?

52 Fiacaill Ridge 130m II *
This is a good option under powder, when other routes are deeply covered and possibly avalanche prone. Stick to the crest as closely as is sensible. It offers some short technical sections but an escape right to much easier ground is slightly too convenient.

COIRE AN LOCHAIN

(NH 984 026)   Alt 1150m   North facing   Map p208

The corrie lying below Cairn Lochan, the most westerly top of Cairn Gorm, is compact and well defined. Its crags are short but steep, the home of technical mixed climbing. Some easier mixed routes and a limited selection of easier gullies are also available, but they have a more serious feel than the neighbouring Coire an t-Sneachda, largely because of the steeper approach (effectively Grade I) and consequent exposure caused by The Great Slab which lies below.

Weather and Conditions: The corrie is very high, with a base at 1100m, and it is amongst the first places in Scotland to come into good winter condition, with a potential season from October to May. This is also because the majority of routes are mixed. Ice does not usually form until later in the season. Hoar frost builds up to great depth and the steeper routes are best avoided in these conditions, although it is difficult to know the thickness from a distance. There is slightly better shelter from the wind than in Coire an t-Sneachda, but this is counterbalanced by the longer approach and greater avalanche risk. This shelter allows windslab to accumulate, particularly in The Vent, along the top of the Great Slab and around No.4 Buttress. Great care should be taken to assess avalanche risk when approaching routes.

Layout: There are four main buttresses separated by obvious gullies. These form an arc overlooking the corrie's most outstanding feature, The Great Slab. This is a huge, easy angled slab of pink granite which is also a notoriously avalanche prone slope, both for windslab and for the huge full depth avalanche which sometimes occurs in Spring. The four buttresses are numbered from left to right. The Vent separates No.1 and No.2 Buttresses while the obvious diagonal fault of The Couloir in the centre of the corrie lies between No.2 and No.3. Between No.3 and No.4 is a large recess tucked in the corner of the corrie, which houses the two branches of Y-Gully.

Approach: Leave the Coire Cas car park as for Coire an t-Sneachda but continue traversing round Fiacaill a' Choire Chais and cross the burn which comes out of Sneachda. Take either of two paths which ultimately lead to the lochans at the back of the corrie. There is not much difference in time and the choice may be more to do with snow conditions and previous parties. The path which breaks off uphill (south) immediately after the burn is marginally better for Nos. 1 and 2 Buttresses; don't go to the lochans but head up a vague ridge towards No.1 Buttress and go diagonally right for No.2. The alternative is a diagonal path towards Lurcher's Crag, leaving it soon after crossing a stream and heading up to the lochans, and is better for Nos.3 and 4 Buttresses. From the inner lochan, go right and back left to the foot of No.4, the rightmost buttress. Despite the short distance, the target is quite small and navigation is not easy in mist and snow; it is quite easy to land up in Lurcher's Gully! 1hr 30mins.

Descent: It is common to climb with sacks and walk off. The easiest descent is to the west, but care is necessary to keep away from the cornice, but note that later on the convex slope can divert you too far left (west). In white-out, a dog-leg away from the cornice is best. The east side of the corrie is steeper (close to Grade I). The top of the Goat Track and a descent into Coire an t-Sneachda is also nearby. For the harder routes, sacks are often left at the base of the route followed by a descent down The Couloir – take care and probably face in, as the run-out is very long. There are abseiling options for some of the shorter routes.

No.1 Buttress

Diagram p228

The buttress on the left side of the corrie has a steep right wall rising out of The Vent and a front face which merges into more broken ground on the left. The front and side walls are cut by some large corners which offer hard and distinctive routes. Auricle climbs the prominent overhanging groove at 40m on the front face while Ventricle and Big Daddy take the corners in the vertical wall left of The Vent.

1 Auricle 90m VI,7 **
C.MacLean, A.Nisbet 29 Nov 1984

A steep climb up the front face of the buttress taking the big right-facing corner. Start 10m up right from the base of the steep right wall of the buttress, below a broken corner-crack leading left to a short chimney.

1. 35m Climb the crack, chimney and a short wall before moving easily left and back right to a rock slab below an obvious wide crack in an overhanging groove which is the start of the main corner system.

2. 15m Climb the strenuous groove with several chokestones (crux).

3. 40m Continue up the corner above, ignoring an apparent escape left, to a large fin like flake. From the top of the flake, climb an overhanging recess to the top of the buttress which is separated by a crevasse from the main face. Step over this and continue to easy ground.

COIRE AN LOCHAIN - No. 1 Buttress

1. Auricle	VI,7 **	4. Daddy Longlegs	VIII,9 ***
2. Ventriloquist	VII,7 *	5. Inventive	IV,5 *
3. Ventricle	VII,8 **	6. The Vent	II/IV *

Ventriloquist, VII,7, No. 1 Buttress. Climber Nick Carter

2 Ventriloquist 80m VII,7 *
J.Lyall, A.Nisbet 21 Dec 1990
A strenuous route climbing cracks in the wall just right of Auricle. The crux is well protected (but a bold start) if the wide crack is not verglassed. Start as for Auricle.
1. 30m Climb the crack and chimney, then move right to climb a bulging crack-line into a recess. Pull even more steeply out of this to below a wide crack 3m right of Auricle's crux groove.
2. 10m Climb the crack (crux), Friend 3.5 and 4 useful.
3. 10m Move up right by two short corners to a ledge.
4. 15m Climb a thin crack 2m right of the belay.
5. 15m Cross the crevasse and finish up a deep crack.

Ventricle 95m VII,8 **
C.MacLean, A.Nisbet 27 Dec 1984 (1PA, 1 rest); FFA: B.Davison, A.Nisbet 8 Mar 1997
This route takes the cracks and grooves on the left wall of The Vent, providing a series of desperate technical but well protected problems separated by ledges. Start 5m right of Auricle's initial crack and chimney.
1. 15m Climb an overhanging crack, move right along a ledge and climb a wall near the right edge to a small mossy recess.
2. 20m Move up a thin crack on the right and swing left into the top of a short overhanging groove. Move up to a larger overhanging groove and climb this to below a corner.
3. 15m Climb the corner to a ledge.
4. 15m Climb just right of a prominent wide corner crack, then step left into it and climb it.
5. 30m Traverse left to finish up Ventriloquist.

Daddy Longlegs 70m VIII,9 ***
B.Davison, A.Nisbet 25 Feb 1991 (pitch 1); Pitch 2,3: P.Benson, G.Robertson 7 Dec 2002
Two excellent hard pitches, the first quite bold (but safe) and the second very strenuous, with escape possible after pitch 1 into Inventive. Start up a steep groove

Chute Route, V,5, No. 2 Buttress

on the left wall of The Vent about 15m below the chokestone.
1. 35m Climb the groove, step right into a second groove and follow this past an overhang to ledges.
2. 10m Scramble up left.
3. 25m Climb two consecutive vertical cracks in the wall right of the wide corner-crack of Ventricle.

5 Inventive   70m   IV,5 *
A.Fyffe, J.Hepburn   20 Apr 1994
This route takes the largest corner on the left wall of The Vent. Follow The Vent to above the chokestone (or if the chokestone is not built up, go up Ventilator and descend The Vent easily to the lip of the steep section of the gully), then traverse left and go up to the main corner. Climb this big corner, steep but very helpful, to the top.

6 The Vent   110m   II/IV *
E.M.Davidson, R.F.Stobart, Miss Macbain, J.Geddes   13 Apr 1935
A pleasant but short lived route up the obvious gully between No.1 and No.2 Buttresses. It is narrow and defined at the bottom but it opens out into an easy angled funnel above. The difficulties depend on the build-up and the amount of ice on the lower chokestone section. It is a bad choice in early season when the chokestone will be at least Grade IV. It requires a large build-up to be Grade II.

No.2 Buttress

Diagram p232

This is the widest buttress in the corrie, extending between The Vent and The Couloir. Its left-hand side consists of several vertical ribs which do not continue all the way to the plateau. The central and right-hand sections are characterised by steep walls and horizontal breaks and there is a conspicuous square-cut wall at the top. There are several worthwhile middle grade mixed routes here.

7 Ventilator   100m   III *
D.S.B.Wright and party   1969
Start below a big snow bay about 30m right of The Vent. Gain the bay (as much as 30m early season but not included in the length), then go left to blocks below a slab. Climb the slab to a headwall, then traverse left to a shallow gully. Move left again to a corner on the right of The Vent's rib. Climb the corner to an arete overlooking The Vent. Finish up The Vent. Grade II if there is consolidated snow on the slabby sections, which is quite common.

8 Chute Route   70m   V,5 *
M.Harris, D.Scott, R.Shaw   24 Dec 1968
A fine ice pitch up the groove at the left corner of the big bay right of The Vent. It is usually in condition only in late season. Protection is limited, so V,4 if good ice. Climb the iced groove with a smooth left wall for a pitch and finish up the top of The Milky Way.

9 The Milky Way   100m   III **
T.W.Patey, V.N.Stevenson, I.W.Armitage   Feb 1959
This is a pleasant route, low in its grade, which takes an obvious diagonal line overlooking the bay and on the left of the more massive section of the buttress. Climb over an initial wall (often banked out late season) just right of the bay, then up a shallow trough before trending left to the top of the rib right of The Vent. Finish up a shallow groove leading rightwards (possible big cornice), or finish up The Vent. In early season, start as for Ventilator and gain the big bay. Make an awkward pull out right on to a ledge and traverse right into the trough above its initial wall.

0 Andromeda   120m   IV,4 **
R.D.Barton, J.C.Higham   30 Dec 1971
This route takes the shallow trough as for Milky Way, then follows a groove line which slants up right. Start up the trough to near its top, then trend right and follow the groove which abuts a steep wall. This is excellent when icy and leads to the buttress crest. Another groove just on its right is technically harder (IV,5 or IV,6) but better protected, a better choice under powder. Finish as for Central Crack Route on the left of the conspicuous upper wall. The cornice may be large.

Astroturfer   120m   III,4 *
J.MacKeever, I.Dawson   31 Dec 1985
A good middle grade mixed line. Start as for Milky Way but take the lowest fault line leading right onto a ledge on the crest. The subsequent wall, usually climbed on the right, is the crux without a good build-up to reduce its height. Early season, it may have to be climbed on the left (technical 5). Finish up the front of the buttress to join Central Crack Route.

Central Crack Route   120m   IV,5 **
T.W.Patey   2 Feb 1958
A fine climb taking the fault right of the centre of the buttress. Start just right of the lowest rocks. The start is technical but a lot easier with a big build-up. The continuation is also hard in early season without a build-up. Climb a slanting right-facing corner-crack and continuation fault for about 75m, then zigzag up to below

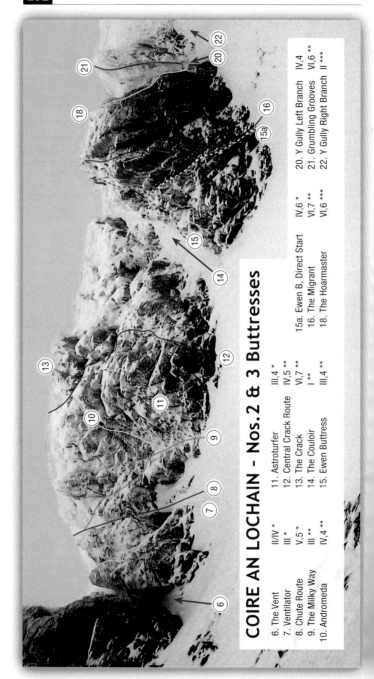

232

COIRE AN LOCHAIN - Nos.2 & 3 Buttresses

6. The Vent	II/IV *	11. Astroturfer	III,4 *
7. Ventilator	III *	12. Central Crack Route	IV,5 **
8. Chute Route	V,5 *	13. The Crack	VI,7 **
9. The Milky Way	III **	14. The Couloir	I **
10. Andromeda	IV,4 **	15. Ewen Buttress	III,4 **

15a. Ewen B, Direct Start	IV,6 *
16. The Migrant	VI,7 **
18. The Hoarmaster	VI,6 ***

20. Y Gully Left Branch	IV,4
21. Grumbling Grooves	VI,6 **
22. Y Gully Right Branch	II ***

a great square wall and exit on its left. The cornice can be huge and necessitate a long traverse.

**13 The Crack   20m   VI,7 ** **
R.Anderson, R.Milne   12 Jan 1992
The obvious wide crack in the great square wall which sits under the plateau above Central Crack Route. Its exposed position means it can be snowy when the starts of the full height routes are bare. To reach it, either start up Central Crack Route or traverse left from a recess about halfway up the left wall of The Couloir.

**14 The Couloir   150m   I ** **
E.M.Davidson, A.Henderson   24 Mar 1935
The slanting gully in the centre of the cliff, above the top of the Great Slab, is serious for the grade because the approach is as hard as the route. It is slightly hidden from a distance so is often in condition even when there appears to be a break in the snow. The easiest approach is from the left. The gully leads to a small col (Y-Gully Left Branch is the other side) and there is rarely a cornice. In early season it is a good Grade II climb. The best approach is from the right (under No.3 Buttress) by icy steps and there is usually an easy pitch in the gully itself.

No.3 Buttress

This well defined buttress lies between the diagonal of The Couloir and the Left Branch of Y-Gully. Its left flank forms an easier angled rib, Ewen Buttress, overlooking The Couloir. To its right is a huge overhanging recess topped by a groove, right of which is a steep and more massive frontal face. Where this turns into the Left Branch of Y-Gully, there is a set of well defined vertical features, mostly corners.

**15 Ewen Buttress   90m   III,4 ** **
T.W.Patey, V.N.Stevenson   Feb 1959
This route follows the left edge of the buttress overlooking The Couloir. Start just inside the narrow part of The Couloir. Climb steep broken ground to a saddle. The face above and right is cut by an open gully; reaching this provides a short but sharp crux which is technical 5 under powder. Above the climbing becomes straightforward and leads to the top at the same point as The Couloir.
Direct Start: **45m   IV,6**
The obvious fault right of the toe of No.3 Buttress leads steeply up and left to join the normal route above the first pitch, near the saddle. It has two starts; a deeper left-hand groove has a tricky pull out right to gain the upper fault. A shallow right-hand groove is thin but technically easier.

**16 The Migrant   100m   VI,7 ** **
A.Cunningham, A.Nisbet   13 Mar 1986
A devious but spectacular line to the left of the huge groove on No.3 Buttress. Start just right of Ewen Buttress Direct Start. A more direct start is easier with a good build-up, but this misses the good first pitch.
1. 20m Climb the deceptively steep right-hand groove and make a delicate step right to a belay.
2. 20m Work up right under the overhanging wall and go through it at the first possible place to the base of the huge groove.
3. 40m Return a short way and break out onto a ledge on the arete (exciting). Follow the ledge left, then go up over a chokestone to the top of a pinnacle. Move left to gain the rib above and follow it to easier ground.
4. 20m Go easily right to the finish of Ewen Buttress.
Variation Start: Climb the shallow groove leading directly to the short overhanging wall and the huge groove.

The huge corner-groove at the back of the recess and avoided by Migrant is **Migrant Direct** (95m VII,8), although VIII,7 when icy . The corner and huge flakes

Climbers on The Hoarmaster, VI,6 (left) and Hooker's Corner, VI,6, No. 3 Buttress

on the right wall of the recess is **Nocando Crack** (70m VII,8) while cracks in the wall to its right are **The Vicar** (70m VII,8). Two modern routes take overhanging crack-lines on the overhanging wall right of and outside the recess, **Demon Direct** (60m IX,9) takes the left line and **Happy Tyroleans** (60m IX,10) takes the right.

17 The Overseer Direct   70m   V,6 **

A.Nisbet, E.Clark   10 Dec 1983; As described: N.Main, A.Nisbet   28 Nov 1992
A steep interesting line towards the right edge of the buttress. Start at the foot of the Left Branch of Y-Gully. Pull onto a ledge and climb two consecutive steep corners (bold) to reach slabs. Climb direct to the base of a capped chimney. Pull out left and climb a vertical corner (technical) to emerge on easier ground.

18 The Hoarmaster   60m   VI,6 ***

R.Anderson, G.Nicoll, R.Milne   19 Nov 1988
This exciting route takes a line of chimneys on the right edge of the main face of the buttress. It is strenuous but well protected, and just scrapes into the grade. Pulling into the chimney is hard, but staying there and placing protection is even harder if the cracks are iced. It drops a grade if Cams can be placed quickly. Pull onto the same ledge as the start of The Overseer but climb the square-cut chimney on the right for the first pitch and continue in the same line up a chimney with bulges for the second. Instead of climbing the last bulge, it is slightly easier to exit left on to a pinnacle and go up the corner-crack above (the original line of Overseer).

19 Hooker's Corner   60m   VI,6 **

R.Anderson, C.Greaves   26 Nov 1988
This route takes the obvious open corner right of the buttress edge. Graded for icy conditions, which are common, but the protection is less good. From the toe of the buttress, climb easily up just right of the corner. Step across and climb the corner to its top. Finish as for The Hoarmaster up the chimney-fault.

The bottomless groove system to the right of Hooker's Corner is **Conundrum** (50m V,7) and a bulging chimney right again is **The Deviant** (50m V,6).

20 Y-Gully Left Branch   100m   IV,4
T.W.Patey, A.G.Nicol, A.Wedderburn   16 Nov 1952
This is the wide gully between No.3 Buttress and the steep pillar at the head of the bay between No.3 and No.4 Buttresses. Start at the top left of the bay and climb up rightwards to an impasse. Move left to climb ice through a bulge, then follow easier ground to the top. The ice through the bulge is slow to form and requires a good build-up followed by a substantial thaw and freeze, so late season is more likely (it was climbed on 1st June 1994).

**21 Grumbling Grooves   60m   VI,6 ** **
S.Allan, A.Nisbet   17 Dec 1983
A steep narrow pillar lies between the two branches of Y-Gully. Climb the big groove on the left side of the pillar direct.

22 Y-Gully Right Branch   100m   II ***
R.F.Stobart, T.Stobart, Miss Harbinson   14 Apr 1934
This branch starts from the top right-hand end of the bay. In mid to late season it is a wide high angled gully generally without pitches, although the cornice can be large and difficult to pass. It is also a good climb in freezing but lean conditions when it can contain continuous ice. After a big early season thaw and refreeze, it may be the only climb in condition in the Northern Corries. Note that despite being snow, it is steep and poorly protected and never a soft touch for its grade, harder than many of the Grade IIs in Coire an t-Sneachda.

No.4 Buttress

Diagram p236

The largest and most important buttress. From its left side, starting by the Right Branch of Y-Gully it presents a fine, steep wall cut by a series of compelling vertical lines of which the large central corner of Savage Slit is unmistakeable. On the right side the wall swings round to form a longer but less steep face looking north. This degenerates into easier ground on its right flank. Right of the main buttress are several small buttresses and gullies just below the plateau rim.

**3 Oesophagus   70m   III ** **
W.March and party   9 Apr 1971
About 10m right of the Y-Gully Right Branch is a groove which often holds good ice. Climb the groove into the upper snow amphitheatre, then follow this to the top.

**4 Deep Throat   70m   V,6 ** **
R.Anderson, T.Prentice, R.Milne   2 Dec 1989
This unusual route takes an unlikely line up a wide crack through the stepped overhangs up the left side of a pillar.
1. 30m Climb a wide groove and move up to gain the crack. Follow this over or round three roofs, then make a delicate traverse across the left wall below a large roof to a ledge left of a large chockstone.
2. 15m Regain the crack and follow it to the top of the pillar.
3. 25m Climb a groove onto the crest on the right (or escape easily up left).

5 Gaffer's Groove   80m   V,5 *
J.Cunningham, A.Fyffe   Feb 1975
Occasionally, and almost always late in the season, a fine icefall flows out of a wide chimney right of the pillar and down a groove. It is often necessary to start on the right and gain the icefall by a traverse left above a triangular roof. Without ice it is VI,7 and best finished by a corner leading up right towards the finish of Bulgy.

COIRE AN LOCHAIN
No.4 Buttress

22. Y-Gully Right Branch	II ***	
23. Oesophagus	III **	
24. Deep Throat	V,6 **	
25. Gaffer's Groove	V,5 *	
25a. Summer Finish	VI,7 *	
26. Bulgy	VII,7 *	
27. Savage Slit	V,6 ****	
28. Fallout Corner	VI,7 ***	
29. The Third Man	IV,6 **	
30. Sidewinder	III,4 *	
31. Western Route	IV,6 ***	

Fallout Corner, VI,7, No. 4 Buttress. Climber Brian Duthie.

6 Bulgy 80m VII,7 *

A.Nisbet, J.Preston 27 Nov 1988

Climb a groove just left of the left arete of Savage Slit, and finish up a wide crack through the obvious twin roofs. Traversing out under the first roof is the crux and worrying if you don't have large Cams or if the crack is verglassed. So sometimes it is a soft touch for the grade.

7 Savage Slit 90m V,6 ****

G.Adams, J.White, F.Henderson 21 Apr 1957 (1PA)

A very fine climb up an impeccable line, technical but well protected. It takes the wide chimney-crack in the big right-angled corner in the centre of the buttress. There is no turf so it comes into condition with the first snows. Climb a tricky little introductory pitch to belay at the foot of the slit. The main chimney can be climbed inside or out depending on girth, conditions or fear factor. Occasionally the lower section of the crack (crux) fills with ice and the route becomes a little easier. It is normal to belay on large chokestones at half-height. Because of the inconvenience of rucksacks in the narrow chimney, it is possible to leave them at the foot of the climb and one abseil from the top of the chimney regains the base (take care the abseil rope is down the wall right of the chimney; it may get stuck if down the chimney). The more aesthetic finish is up an easy left-slanting gully and awkward short wall.

28 Fallout Corner   80m   VI,7 ***
A.Cunningham, A.Nisbet   9 Dec 1985
An excellent climb, sustained, technical and very well protected, which goes up the impressive corner right of Savage Slit. Start below the corner. Go up to below the roof blocking the corner (10m). Cross the roof and climb the corner to a ledge on the right (30m). There is an optional belay at half-height on the left. Continue in the same line (15m). Finish as for Savage Slit; abseil or climb its last pitch.

29 The Third Man   100m   IV,6 **
S.Allan, A.Nisbet   18 Dec 1983
A more direct line than the nearby Sidewinder offers interesting climbing. Fallout Corner is the leftmost of three big corners. **War and Peace** (70m VII,8) is the central and this route climbs the third. Climb a lower angled ramp running up right (Sidewinder), move left to gain the third corner, then climb it and the subsequent short wall to easier ground. Go up to cross Sidewinder and climb a shallow corner 5m right of Sidewinder chimney. Finish up the short wall of Savage Slit.

30 Sidewinder   120m   III,4 *
A.Nisbet, E.Clark   11 Dec 1983
This route finds a way up the buttress by a big zigzag around Savage Slit; an easier route threading the hard classics. Start below Savage Slit and the three corners, where a big ramp leads up to the frontal face. Traverse right to gain and climb the ramp on to the edge of the front face. The original route went up blocks here, then diagonally right up a hard little wall to easier ground (better but at the top end of the grade). It is easier but less direct to traverse right and go up a short wall on to the easier ground. Now go left to climb a blocky chimney (the opposite side of Savage Slit) and squeeze through a gap to gain and finish up the top of Savage Slit.

31 Western Route   120m   IV,6 ***
T.W.Patey   Feb 1959
Starting from the left corner of the buttress, this route slants out right to finish up the front face. A very technical wall on the second pitch becomes much easier when banked up with snow; the grade assumes some snow, but not as much as found by Patey, who soloed the first ascent and graded it III. Start near the lower left corner of the buttress. Climb a diagonal crack slanting right to a platform, then move up to a snowy recess. Next is the crux; climb the crack on its right wall. An awkward chimney on the right follows, then easier climbing up the prominent final gully leads to a finish up flakes on the right wall. The gully can be finished direct in good conditions.

32 Torquing Heads   125m   VI,8 *
W.Todd, A.Cunningham   20 Jan 1986
The prominent chimney-fault on the front face of No.4 Buttress. Being such an obvious line makes it popular but many don't get past the crux. This is easier with some ice but you would always like it to be thicker! VII,7 has been suggested too. Climb the fault over a chokestone and a leaning wall (crux) to belay below a wide flake-crack. Climb the crack and the bulging chimney above to easy ground and finish up the right of the steep upper buttress.

LURCHER'S CRAG

(NH 966 033)   Alt 780m   West-South-West facing   Map p208
Also known as Creag an Leth-choin, this broken rambling cliff lies on the flank of

the Làirig Ghrù below the summit of the same name. The main northern section lies directly below the summit of Creag an Leth-choin. Because of the cliff's westerly aspect, conditions here can be very different from other crags in the area and may give the best and iciest climbing around. This is particularly so after early season cold weather and strong westerly winds, which strip the crag of snow and leave great quantities of ice.

Approach: Follow the path from the Sugar Bowl car park (NH 986 073) through the Chalamain Gap, then contour the slopes to the crag. Alternatively, from the Coire Cas car park follow the approach to Coire an Lochain but continue up the ridge on its west towards spot height 1083 to about 980m altitude before traversing right to the top of South Gully. Its top is at NH 969 031, a minor col between Creag an Leth-choin and a very slight rise to its south (shown as a flat area on the 1:50000 map). It is shown on the map as a significant break in the cliffs but actually is a fan shape closing to a narrow gully. Descend by it (easy Grade I). Once out of the narrow section, descend further to below the slabby base of the main cliff and traverse south. The former is shorter for North Gully and the latter for Window Gully; Central Gully depends on walking conditions at the different altitudes and is your choice.

Descent: The main ridge of Creag an Leth-choin can be followed north towards the Chalamain Gap where it is possible to return to the Sugar Bowl car park. Or reverse the approach to the Coire Cas car park.

North Gully 240m III *
R.Campbell, F.Harper, M.A.Thompson 23 Dec 1965
The big sprawling gully towards the north end of the cliff usually has two big but not too difficult ice pitches. Higher up it forks; either fork can be good depending on conditions. The left fork often contains an excellent ice pitch. The right fork has a short steep iced corner with fine bridging moves. Low in the grade.

There are many mixed routes on the ridges of the crag, particularly either side of South Gully. They come into condition quickly early in the season but also catch the sun. The following route is a good option if the ice in the gullies is poorly formed.

Arctic Monkey 300m III,4 *
S.Allan, A.Nisbet 6 Jan 2008
The ridge on the left of Central Gully. Start left of Central Gully's lower icefall and climb easily to where the ground steepens. A line on the right of this steep section was taken, climbing up a line of weakness, passing a smooth groove which heads left to reach a recess below a prominent jutting block. Pull out left through a small cave (crux) and go left up a less well defined groove to reach the crest (50m). Follow the crest which becomes progressively easier until just scrambling to the top.

Central Gully 300m IV,4 **
B.Taplin, O.Ludlow 4 Mar 1970
The most obvious gully in the middle of the cliff, but finishing north of the summit of Creag an Leth-choin, has several ice pitches in the bottom half. Either the left or right branches can be followed to the top. The grade and stars are for lean icy conditions when the route can be excellent; Grade III with a good build-up of snow (North Gully will be Grade II on that day).

Window Gully 220m IV,4
W.March, J.Cleare, J.Bradshaw 9 Mar 1972
Mid-way between Central and South Gullies is a large icefall halfway up the face. Climb ice up the lower slabs for 75m to an overhanging wall, from which the icefalls in a screen. Go left between the ice and the rock, cut a window and follow steep ice to easier ground. If the front face is climbed on the outside the climb is slightly harder. Continue up the much easier gully to the top.

CAIRNGORMS

LOCH AVON BASIN

Loch Avon lies at 730m in the heart of the Northern Cairngorms entrenched between Cairn Gorm, Ben Macdui and Beinn Mheadhoin. At its head, a superb arc of cliffs cluster round its main feeder streams, the Garbh Uisge, Feith Buidhe and Allt a' Choire Domhain. Dominating this scene is the spectacular square topped Shelter Stone Crag. On its left is the triangular Càrn Etchachan while high at the back right of the cirque are the glaciated and often ice covered slabs of Hell's Lum Crag. Although still fairly accessible from the Cairn Gorm ski road, dropping out of sight from ski development and Aviemore produces a better mountain atmosphere coupled with the knowledge that return to civilisation is more than just a plod downhill. Each of the cliffs offers a different aspect and consequently differing rock formations, each with its characteristic style of winter climbing.

HELL'S LUM CRAG

(NH 995 017)   Alt 920m   South-East facing   Map p208   Diagram p243

This slabby cliff is frequently wet in summer but it provides fine icefalls in winter. Although it lies close to Shelter Stone Crag, it is far more accessible and popular, since descent to the loch is unnecessary. The Hell's Lum itself is the huge gully on the left-hand side of the cliff.

Approach: From the Coire Cas car park, follow the path into Coire an t-Sneachda (see that section) and up the Goat Track to the head of Coire Domhain. Descend the corrie until the ground steepens sharply then cross the stream and find a way down through rocks to cut diagonally under the cliff. This can be avalanche prone; a sensible line may help but there is always the option of retreat to Coire an t-Sneachda, 2hrs.

Descent: Reverse the approach.

Weather and Conditions: Because of its south-easterly aspect, conditions are susceptible to sun. Sunny days in December or January are generally alright, but not thereafter. Partially cloudy days in mid-season are also acceptable, but the ice has usually been stripped by mid March. The ice forms reliably, the longer the cold spell the better. It is a bad choice with north-westerly winds and spindrift, as it will be avalanche prone. Beware of avalanches both on the approach and at the top of the routes.

Layout: Hell's Lum, the huge chimney towards the left, splits the crag into a smaller left-hand section and a large right-hand section. The buttress just right of the Lum contains the prominent narrow chimney of Deep Cut Chimney. Further right are the main slabs and icefalls.

1 The Gullet   130m   III *
J.Bower, B.S.Findlay   28 Dec 1969
The central and best of three ice filled faults on the slabby face left of The Lum. Start about 20m left of The Lum and climb the fault, slabby and shallow at first, to reach the deeper central section. Continue up this with occasional diversions to the left. The cornice can be large and difficult, potentially impossible.

2 The Chancer   90m   V,6 **
J.Cunningham, W.March   Jan 1970
First climbed using Cunningham's daggering technique, a transitional step in the development of front pointing, this route remained as Scotland's hardest icefall for only two years until Labyrinth Direct was front pointed. The historical significance adds to the atmosphere provided by the scenery. The icefall is slow to form and the difficulty varies with the amount of ice. In prime conditions there are three icefalls, about Grades IV,5, V,6 and VI,6 (left to right), but the central icefall is the traditional route. The crux is the middle pitch, which may be a free standing icicle or a short vertical ice wall. There is a good belay below it and behind the ice.

Hell's Lum, II/IV. Climber Jonny Baird

Hell's Lum 150m II/IV ****
G.McLeod and party Mar 1956
This classic route up the major fault which splits the crag gives interesting climbing through superb scenery but with a noticeable lack of good protection. It can vary from high angle snow to having up to four ice pitches. In early season conditions it is just as good a route but IV,5 may apply. The cornice, which can be huge, can normally be turned on the right. It is a dangerous route on a sunny day, both from cornice collapse and icicle fall.

Deep Cut Chimney 150m IV,4 ****
T.W.Patey, D.Holroyd 19 Jan 1958
A narrow chimney forming the right side of the rock buttress right of Hell's Lum. This intriguingly deep fault is the same grade in lean conditions. The normal approach is via a left-slanting diagonal fault, but this lower part can be banked out. The chimney becomes increasingly deep and is normally finished by back and foot up to a pile of wedged boulders in the outer jaws. Great fun!

Nobody's Fault 150m IV,6 **
G.Smith and party 1979
The shallower fault parallel to and right of Deep Cut Chimney gives a good climb but the difficulties are disappointingly short. The hanging chimney at mid-height is tricky (eased by ice) but well protected.

6 Brimstone Groove   170m   IV,4 ***
S.Docherty, K.Spence   27 Dec 1970
A fine sheet of ice regularly forms right of Grey Buttress (the buttress with Deep Cut Chimney and Nobody's Fault). It is technically straightforward but serious, and graded for good conditions. Follow the left edge of this ice to break through a steeper section, which may be thin in poor conditions, into the largest and widest fault on the left. This is the route perhaps most affected by the sun, deteriorating as the season progresses, but runners appear as the ice thins and it becomes IV,5.

7 Salamander   160m   V,4 **
J.Cunningham, W.March, R.o'Donovan   Feb 1973
Another good ice route with a significantly more technical section than Brimstone Groove. Climb the right side of the ice sheet to belay below a chimney slot in the overlap above, then pull through this to an easier finish. The difficulty will vary unpredictably with the amount and shape of the ice (IV,5 may apply).

8 Devil's Delight   160m   V,5 ***
J.Cunningham, W.March, R.o'Donovan   Feb 1973
A superb ice route but slow to come into condition. The icefall forms on the right side of a steeper section, left of the big left-facing corner of Wee Devil and characterised by a large triangular niche. A cascade of ice leads into the triangular niche, then continues to the Haven. Above, narrow ice runnels hopefully exist in grooves and corners; these constitute the crux.

9 Wee Devil   150m   IV,4 **
D.Dinwoodie, J.Mothersele   17 Nov 1971
This route follows the prominent left-facing corner system halfway up the face, hopefully thick with ice (add a grade if not) and leading up to an overhang. Climb a discontinuous gully into the corner, climb this then exit left below the overhang (or just trend left on thick ice). Go right about 10m above the overhang by a large flake onto a slab, perhaps thinly iced, until a right-facing corner line can be followed to a bigger right-facing corner right of a steep tower. This leads to easier ground.

10 Kiwi Gully   150m   III,4 **
W.March, I.Nicholson   2 Jan 1972
A line of ice following a shallow left-slanting gully forms regularly, deepest at about two-thirds height. Exiting from this is the steepest section, but it often has good ice. The gully now fades out so trend left to finish up the top right-facing corner of Wee Devil. The line is slightly sheltered from the sun so it may last longer into the season.

11 Kiwi Slabs   150m   IV,3 *
T.W.Patey, V.N.Stevenson   Feb 1959
Open climbing on ice smears, serious but quite easy in ideal conditions. Either start up Kiwi Gully to its deep section, then break up and right on easy angled ice smears to a slanting left-facing corner (Grade III) or gain this corner more directly up iced slabs if conditions allow (for which the route is graded). The corner normally has thicker ice and leads to the snow apron at the top.

12 Auld Nick   150m   III *
M.Freeman, G.S.Strange   20 Nov 1971
Another very variable route but graded for good ice which forms on the right side of the main slabs. It can bank out substantially.

13 Escalator   150m   II **
J.Y.L.Hay, A.Thom   Jan 1960
This route can form every possibility from continuous ice to a snow slope, but often there is much low angled and reliable ice. Climb the obvious line of ice which forms in a shallow fault at the right edge of the cliff.

HELL'S LUM
CRAG

1. The Gullet   III *
2. The Chancer   V,6 ***
3. Hell's Lum   II/IV ****
4. Deep Cut Chimney   IV,5 ****
5. Nobody's Fault   IV,6 **

6. Brimstone Groove   IV,4 ***
7. Salamander   V,4 **
8. Devil's Delight   V,5 ***
9. The Wee Devil   IV,4 **

10. Kiwi Gully   III,4 **
11. Kiwi Slabs   IV,3 *
12. Auld Nick   III *
13. The Escalator   II **
14. Sneer   III *

14 Sneer   120m   III *
D.Haston, B.Robertson, J.Heron   23 Jan 1966
A big sheet of ice right of Escalator. It is good during early season (for which it is graded), when it forms readily, but later banks out. Start up Escalator or more direct if possible.

About 200m east of the stream which flows out of Coire Domhain is a large outcrop which holds a steep icefall at NH 999 020, alt 900m. It is seriously affected by the sun, so it is unlikely to be in condition after mid February.

Cascade   45m   V,6 *
W.March, D.Alcock   Feb 1977
The obvious steep icefall which develops on the largest outcrop mid-way between Coire Domhain and the left section of Stag Rocks. Normally two icefalls form, the left-hand being considerably steeper (and central on the outcrop) while the right-hand fall is less than vertical (Grade IV,5). Ice screws provide the only protection.

SHELTER STONE CRAG

(NJ 001 013)   Alt 850m   North-East facing   Map p208   Diagram p246

This big and impressive cliff is perhaps better known for its hard rock climbs, but it offers a few chinks in its armour which provide magnificent winter routes. Although Càrn Etchachan dominates on the approach, the true stature of the crag is clearly seen from the loch.

Weather and Conditions: The remote location and the potential hazards of a return across the Cairngorm plateau mean that it is a bad choice in poor weather. It is somewhat fickle in the amount of snow it holds, particularly on the steeper routes. A westerly wind and spindrift will plaster the cliff with powder, but this is stripped quickly in a thaw. Sticil Face requires ice, which is commonly present in good conditions. Raeburn's Buttress and Castle Wall are climbable in any conditions.

Approach: From the Coire Cas car park, follow the path into Coire an t-Sneachda (see that section) and up the Goat Track to the head of Coire Domhain. Descend the corrie and traverse across snowy boulders to reach the crag. 2hrs 30mins.

Descent: A high level return to the top of the Goat Track is the most likely option, as snow conditions on the plateau are often better than under Hell's Lum Crag. Castlegates Gully is the best descent to the cliff base.

Layout: A slabby lower half rears up to a steep prow right of centre. In the centre of the left face are the Central Slabs, with Sticil Face taking an ice line at their left edge and defining the right side of a tapering buttress. The left side is Breach Gully before the left-bounding buttress of Castle Wall. Right of the steep prow are the lines of Postern and Clach Dhian Chimney. The cliff is bounded by the snow gullies of Castlegates Gully on the left and Pinnacle Gully on the right.

1 Castle Wall   210m   III *
B.S.Findlay, G.S.Strange   31 Jan 1970
This is the initially well defined arete which starts near the foot of Castlegates Gully. Follow the ridge throughout, the lower 90m being the most difficult. Above, the ridge merges into the upper rocks but still gives interesting climbing with fine situations.

2 Raeburn's Buttress   240m   IV,5 *
W.March, J.Hart   Feb 1971
A good line, but with little technical interest and perhaps best treated as an option for poor conditions. The big feature of Breach Gully towards the left edge of the cliff marks the start. Start at the bottom right side of the bay below the gully. Follow a line of right-trending grooves to a stance on the right. Go diagonally left to a line of weakness splitting the buttress. Climb this to a deep narrow chimney and exit right to reach a large shoulder on the buttress. The normal route finishes

Sticil Face, V,6. Climber Andy Munro

more easily up the left side of the upper buttress but the crest can be climbed via a cracked wall, right-slanting groove and short wall (45m IV,4) to easier ground.

Sticil Face   240m   V,6 ****
K.A.Grassick, A.G.Nicol   27 Dec 1957

An excellent long route with varied climbing, following the angle between Raeburn's Buttress and the Central Slabs. It requires good but not exceptional conditions for the ice to form. Basically, the more ice there is, the easier and better the route becomes. The grade is for good conditions (sometimes it is VI,6); a steep ice corner at about 100m is the guide to conditions. Although the route is technically hard, it is not sustained and therefore can be climbed quite quickly by a competent party.

Start below and left of the ice corner. Climb diagonally out right onto the face, then gain the depression leading up to the ice corner. In good conditions this is mostly on snow and ice and quite easy. Climb the steep ice corner and continue to

SHELTER STONE CRAG

1. Castle Wall — III *
2. Raeburn's Buttress — IV,5 *
3. Sticil Face — V,6 ****
4. The Citadel — VII,8 *****
4a. Variation
5. Postern — VI,6 **
6. Western Union — IV,5 **
7. Western Grooves — IV,5 *
8. Pinnacle Gully — I *

A. Castlegates Gully
B. Forefinger Pinnacle — I **

Càrn Etchachan

below a narrow chimney. Climb this awkward chimney (mixed) to easy ledges. Go diagonally right above the Central Slabs (easy but exposed) to a wide finishing fault. This can be straightforward with ice but it is hard under powder or verglas.

4 The Citadel   270m   VII,8 ****
M.Hamilton, K.Spence   23 Feb 1980; Variation: A.Rouse, B.Hall   1975 (to Sticil Face); R.Anderson, G.Nicoll   21 Mar 1987 (variation as described)
A magnificent route, hard, sustained and sensational. The first ascent was long sought after, and it was the scene of many epic failures, like Cunningham and March's bivouac in the early 1970s. The lower section takes the line of shallow chimneys bounding the right side of the Central Slabs, the upper is on the slabby left side of the prow. Good conditions are rarely found; it requires ice on the slabs below the lower crux, and enough snow to justify a winter ascent on the lower section, but the top slabs have to be not too deep in powder.

Climb the shallow chimney-line to a ledge system (Low Ledge). Continue up the chimney until steep ground forces an exit to ledges on the left. Trend rightwards on slabs (hopefully ice) to a corner with a crack in the right wall. The next pitch is the lower crux. Climb the strenuous corner with a hard move right (two peg runners in situ have recently made it easier to free), then move right and climb a grassy fault. Traverse right into an open corner which leads out right; climb this and the corner into which it develops to gain a ridge. Follow this, then go left to a spectacular stance by a huge flake. Next is the upper crux. Flake traverse left, then climb the crack and chimney system above to a good stance. Continue up the crack above, then traverse right with a step down to ledges (not easy to find under deep powder, but it can be tensioned). Climb the ensuing right-slanting fault until the left of two short chimneys leads to the plateau.
Variation: A worthwhile easier route, particularly if energy has run out or the upper section has been stripped by the sun. After the lower crux, go up and left on easier mixed ground to reach the right-rising fault of Sticil Face. Go up this for 10m, then take an obvious thin ramp trending slightly left up the headwall.

5 Postern   240m   VI,6 **
M.Hamilton, K.Spence, A.Taylor   5/6 Jan 1980 (original line)
This is another impressive route which takes a largely diagonal line right of the prow to reach the prominent Second Step on the skyline. It is a good natural line and it is possible in most conditions with harder direct finishes for those with energy to spare. Two earlier starts down on the left, the corners of Steeple and the summer line, are very good but a grade harder even with ice. Start up a big left-facing corner just left of Clach Dhian Chimney. Climb this past a prominent wedged block, then go up a ramp slanting left to the terrace. Go right to the Slanting Crack and climb this slanting rightwards to where it develops into a deep chimney. Climb the chimney and traverse left to a long wall and groove which ends at a narrow ledge. Move left on a short catwalk, then climb an obvious right-trending line to the Second Step. Finish out right overlooking Pinnacle Gully.

6 Western Union   220m   IV,5 **
A.Cave, G.Ettle, J.Jeglic, A.Stemfelj   14 Feb 1997
The start of **Clach Dhian Chimney**, a big chimney left of Pinnacle Gully, is obvious but harder (220m V,5). Start mid-way between this and the right edge of the face and follow a gully system for 100m to a point where it is possible to move right into a shallow groove. Climb this direct into and up a large chimney fault which has an awkward entry and at its top exit right onto the First Step. Go up left to the Second Step below the final wall and finish up right overlooking Pinnacle Gully (as for Postern). The original finish was more direct above the Second Step, technical 6.

Western Grooves   220m   IV,5 *
A.Fyffe, R.D.Barton   Mar 1978
Start near the right edge of the face at a snow bay. Climb wide shallow grooves into a short deep red chimney. Climb this to an awkward exit, and continue up and

right until a ramp goes left into the large chimney fault, joining Western Union (as described above). Finish up this route via the First and Second Steps.

8 Pinnacle Gully   200m   I *
Another straightforward gully with no nasty surprises. The Forefinger Pinnacle near the top provides scenic interest.

CÀRN ETCHACHAN

(NJ 003 012)   Alt 850m   North facing   Map p208   Diagram p250

This is a crag for the connoisseur of mixed climbing, and it has some of the best cracks and chimneys in the Cairngorms. It is composed of the Main Face, split into Upper and Lower Tiers at its left end, and the Gully Face, which rises above Castlegates Gully.

Weather and Conditions: The Main Face offers fine mixed climbing with much turf and often good cracks for protection and torquing moves. As such, no special conditions are required; indeed the Main Face is climbable in almost all conditions and at any time of the winter season when the turf is frozen. Route Major has been climbed in October and in May! The cliff can be sheltered from a strong southerly wind. The Gully Face has gullies and ramps which are best with ice; ice forms slowly here so the second half of the season is generally better.

Approach: From the Coire Cas car park, follow the path into Coire an t-Sneachda and up the Goat Track to the head of Coire Domhain. Descend the corrie and traverse across snowy boulders to pass under the Shelter Stone Crag, 2hrs 30mins to 3hrs with some soft snow.

Descent: A high level return to the top of the Goat Track is the most likely option, as snow conditions on the plateau are often better than under Hell's Lum Crag. Castlegates Gully is the best descent to the cliff base.

Layout: The left side of the Main Face is split into two tiers at half-height by The Great Terrace. The lower tier routes are easier, less interesting and less often in condition than those on the upper tier, but a continuous ascent is more satisfying to some. Others will climb the more technical upper routes alone. Right of the end of The Terrace is a vague buttress with many turfy ledges and ramps (Route Major and Red Guard weave up here) before the gully of Scorpion. This starts just inside Castlegates Gully but its upper half is more obvious.

Lower Tier

1 Eastern Approach Route   100m   IV,5
A.Fyffe, A.Liddell   4 Feb 1979
This is the right-slanting fault-line near the left end of the crag which leads to The Great Terrace. It leads to Crevasse Route or Equinox on the Upper Tier. The grade assumes an average build-up, but it can vary from III in exceptionally icy conditions to 7 at the start under early season powder.

2 Western Approach Route   110m   III *
A.Nisbet, D.McCutcheon   19 Dec 1989
This is a fine natural line which can be icy in good conditions. Start left of the lowest point of the buttress (which is next to Castlegates Gully), just left of a mound of huge blocks. Climb a series of three narrow left-slanting ramps (parallel to the Diagonal Shelf) and a short chimney to the Great Terrace below Equinox.

Upper Tier

Approach: Unless doing a route on the Lower Tier, the simple approach is from the left via The Great Terrace, particularly suitable as far as Equinox. To save a little time and gain a little more interest from the exposure, approach by the Diagonal Shelf. It can be followed direct in the best conditions, but it is normal to meet rocks where Route Major leaves on the right. Go left off the shelf by a short chimney and ramp. Traverse left into a gully and follow it up; it leads directly to Guillotine. A higher traverse back right leads to the routes to its right.

3 Crevasse Route   100m   V,6 **
S.Kennedy, A.Nisbet   13 Jan 1981
This has four short, technical but very different pitches. Go up to the leftmost main buttress in the Upper Tier which lies between a large diagonal ramp; **Inside Edge** (75m V,6) and the obvious gully fault of Equinox. Start right of centre and take the turfiest line leading to a corner on the right (40m). Climb a large leaning block, then the overhanging curving crack above (technical crux). Step left and climb huge flakes to a crevasse. A queer contorted chimney exits through a hole to a fine eyrie. Climb the first crack above for 25m, veering right at the top, and go up a nose to the true finish of the buttress.

4 Time Traveller   90m   VII,7 **
A.Cunningham, A.Nisbet   3 Jan 1987
A sustained and strenuous route following the crack system high on the right wall of the leftmost main buttress. Start at the foot of the Equinox gully. Climb Equinox to just above the first chimney. Chimney up to gain a ramp on the left wall which leads to a fine flake-crack above a roof. Climb this, then continue up the wall above and go over a final bulge to small a ledge. Continue up the crack and a gradual easing in difficulties, finishing up a short corner.

5 Equinox   110m   VI,6 **
S.Kennedy, A.Nisbet, N.Morrison   14 Feb 1981
The gully line of Equinox is best distinguished by an overhanging square-cut tower high on its right. Climb the left side of the fault for two pitches, then move steeply right to an obvious chimney with a constricted top which is tucked under the square-cut tower on the right. Finish straight up or out left if the cornice is large.

6 Guillotine   110m   V,6 ***
A.Fyffe, A.Liddell   4 Feb 1979
Guillotine takes the deepest part of the next recessed section right of Equinox and immediately left of a pink spur (not to be confused with a pink rockfall scar on a less distinct spur further right). The highlight is the cavernous but not difficult chimney of pitch 3. Start below its chimney-line.
1. 30m Climb direct up a groove and shallow chimney into a wide chimney. In lean conditions it is easier to zigzag on either side to avoid the first groove.
2. 20m Climb this, steep but helpful, and continue to a vertical headwall.
3. 25m Take a unique chimney on the right which cuts deeply into the spur and passes below a huge blade of rock. Exit by a tunnel roofed with blocks to a platform on the spur.
4. 35m Pull into and climb the chimney above with an overhang at the top (crux). Easy steps to finish.

7 Python   115m   V,6 **
A.Nisbet, P.Langhorne   9 Dec 1981
This climbs a great flake up the front face of the pink spur, giving sustained technical climbing in an exposed position. Start at the base of the Guillotine fault.
1. 15m Move right and climb a crack-line and ledges to a big ledge.
2. 15m Walk to its right end, step round the corner overlooking the Nom-de-Plume fault and return left up two big steps to a ledge. Make exciting moves up right to another big ledge. For an easier start, this ledge can be gained from the right by a wide crack.
3. 20m 4c Climb a corner forming the right side of the great flake, then curve up and left to a ledge on top of the flake.
4. 30m Step down left and walk round the left side of the spur to climb the first chimney to the platform.
5. 35m Finish as for Guillotine up the chimney above.

CÀRN ETCHACHAN

1. Eastern Approach Route IV,5
2. Western Approach Route III *
3. Crevasse Route V,6 **
5. Equinox VI,6 **
6. The Guillotine V,6 ***
7. Python V,6 **
8. Nom de Plume VI,6 **
9. Pagan Slit V,6 *
10. Route Major IV,5 ****
11. Red Guard VI,6 **
12. Scorpion V,5 ***
13. The Sword V,5 **
14. False Scorpion V,5 *
15. Sideslip III **
16. Castlegates Gully I **

A. Approach to Great Terrace

Shelter Stone Crag

Great Terrace

**8 Nom de Plume   90m   VI,6 ** **

A.Nisbet, P.Langhorne   23 Dec 1982

The chimney-crack in the corner formed by the right side of the pink spur is steep and strenuous. Follow the chimney line until near the top to reach a huge diamond-shaped block. Pass this on the left wall to a platform and finish up the final pitch of Guillotine. Or move out right just before the platform and climb icy mixed ground, but this is not as good.

9 Pagan Slit   100m   V,6 *

M.Fowler, A.Strapcans   27 Feb 1980

Between the pink spur and the next rocks with their pink rockfall scar is a prominent right-slanting chimney which gives the line of the route. Climb the initial section on the right, then follow the chimney. Andy Nisbet thought he had made the first ascent a few days later but found footsteps leading out of the top.

Main Face

**10 Route Major   285m   IV,5 ** ** **

T.W.Patey, M.Smith   10 Feb 1957

A classic winter route, but more notable for finding a relatively easy route up the centre of the huge face than for the quality of the climbing itself. It is possible in any conditions although it is better when the Battlements Groove is iced. The most obvious feature towards the right side of the lower tier is the large left-slanting ramp of the Diagonal Shelf, usually snow covered. It starts from the wide initial section of Castlegates Gully before it narrows. Follow the Shelf to about half-height, then take a ramp (second ramp on the right) leading right to a snow basin. Exit from the basin by an obvious tapered chimney (technical crux, very well protected). Another ramp now leads to more broken ground. Go diagonally right for two pitches to The Battlements groove (this is difficult to see from below but lies to the right of the pink rockfall scar). Follow the groove over an overhang if iced, otherwise on the right followed by a traverse back in, to a fork. Continue up the V-groove (right fork) and move left up slabs (difficult under powder) to a bay and finishing chimney. The steep left fork ends in a recess with an awkward pull out right to gain easier ground and the bay, good but technical 6.

Variation: **Direct (Ramp) Start**

The initial snow basin can be reached by climbing the narrow ramp-lines on the right of the Diagonal Shelf. Start either from the base of the Diagonal Shelf and move right or move left from the foot of Red Guard. More interesting than the normal start.

Variation: **Alternative Finish**

This is easier under powder, but not as good. Climb a series of grooves right of The Battlements to join Red Guard, then move left high up to finish over its awkward bulge. In very lean conditions, the slab below the bulge is thin and the bulge can be bypassed on the right.

**1 Red Guard   250m   VI,6 ** **

N.D.Keir, M.Freeman   24 Mar 1978 (4PA); FFA, as described: G.S.Smith, R.D.Barton   1979

A fine lower tier, particularly the unusual chimney, with an easier but less interesting finish. Start below the huge block filled groove between the Diagonal Shelf and the start of the narrow section of Castlegates Gully. A pitch up the groove, hard if the ice is thin, gains a slightly left-slanting continuation chimney. The chimney is very deep, sometimes heavily verglassed and entertaining for troglodytes. Above the right side of a snowy bay is a continuation groove; reach this with difficulty (technical crux) and follow it to easier ground. Move 10m right and take a left-slanting ramp and open corner to a small bay. Traverse left to a line of weakness which leads right to an open groove above; follow this over a small but awkward bulge (or on its right) to the top. It is possible to escape at Grade II from below the crux, going up then down and left into the basin of Route Major (and down via the Diagonal Shelf).

Route Major, IV,5. Climber Adam Henley

12 Scorpion 240m V,5 ***

T.W.Patey, J.M.Taylor, A.G.Nicol, K.A.Grassick 6 Dec 1952

A route full of character and a notorious 'sting in the tail' which is either a hard ice pitch in lean conditions, but more commonly it is a problematical cornice. A subterranean chimney in the lower section is worthwhile but difficult to find and many parties have accidentally started by The Sword. The Sentinel is an apparent tower at the left base of Castlegates Gully. Just left of The Sentinel and leading to its top is a long open groove, The Sword, which continues logically but with less interest into the upper fault of Scorpion. Start immediately left of this. Climb a steep corner heading left towards Red Guard and, at about 20m, continue left for about 10m to below a steep wall (the right end of the steep smooth wall above Red Guard's initial block filled groove). Enter a subterranean slanting crack and above the exit, which may be a problem under hard snow, climb an overhung wall on the immediate right on good holds. Go round a corner to the right and go up in a left-trending line to cross left over a slab by a crack in its lower margin. The next pitch is obvious to below the upper fault. A long chimney below a leaning wall leads back right into the main fault which may hold one or several ice pitches. If the cornice is near impossible, it can be passed by a finish out left, ending up a short vertical wall which can be trickily freed or pegged.

13 The Sword   285m   V,5 **
J.C.Higham, D.Wright   5 Mar 1978
A good sustained route, initially climbing the buttress overlooking False Scorpion, then finishing by a ramp on the upper buttress. The start has often been climbed by those failing to find the start of the better known Scorpion. Start at an open groove on the left of the Sentinel. Climb the groove and continue up the buttress above the Sentinel, first by an open groove, then by short walls (50m). Go diagonally left on ramps and up short steps to reach an area of ledges (50m). Go a short way up the chimney of Scorpion, then gain and follow a big ramp leading up left (right of the ramp of Red Guard). At its top, climb the steps, the corner system and the awkward bulge (as for Red Guard) to the final slopes.

14 False Scorpion   240m   V,5 *
W.March, O.Ludlow   Mar 1970
A too logical option which follows the main fault throughout, with more ice but less variety. It is only worthwhile when icy; it is scrappy and serious under powder. Start just above The Sentinel and inside Castlegates Gully. A steeper and narrower section leads left to join the upper fault and Scorpion.

5 Sideslip   150m   III **
A.Fyffe, R.o'Donovan   14 Mar 1975
A committing outing into a land of snow sculptured aretes and gullies in heavy conditions, this route takes the line of a big slab leading left out of Castlegates Gully (a pink rockfall feature in summer). Follow the slab to its top (consolidated snow required), go round the corner and traverse left into a hanging gully. Follow this to the top.

6 Castlegates Gully   250m   I **
J.McCoss, W.B.Meff, R.Clarke   Easter 1914
A straightforward gully, rarely with any nasty surprises.

BEN MACDUI MASSIF

At the centre of the Cairngorms massif lie the cliffs of Creagan a' Choire Etchachan and Coire Sputan Dearg. Creagan a' Choire Etchachan is an icy venue but Coire Sputan Dearg (not described) is higher and has many mixed options if Etchachan is bare.

CREAGAN A' CHOIRE ETCHACHAN

(NO 016 997)   Alt 850m to 900m   East facing   Map p208   Diagram p255

This fine icy cliff lies in the remote heart of the central Cairngorms, so it is an understatement to say it is less crowded than the Northern Corries. Facing east and at a relatively low altitude, the cliff has more variable conditions than the higher venues. The routes are quite short considering the long approach, but they are of high quality when icy and a visit here can be highly recommended. The Hutchison Hut, the bothy in the corrie below the cliff, makes it ideal for a weekend visit.

Weather and Conditions: The cliff is of a middle altitude, receives the sun

CAIRNGORMS

particularly in the morning and therefore is generally in better condition in early or mid-season. Red Chimney, The Corridor and the easier gullies, however, are often still good in March. January may be the best month for the other routes, and a cold spell of weather after a wet autumn is ideal. The other consideration is the long approach, not recommended in poor weather, although the cliff has no unusual hazards.

Approach: Either from north or south.

1. From the south: From Braemar via Derry Lodge. From Braemar, take the public road to the Linn of Dee and go back towards Braemar on the north side of the Dee for 200m to a new car park in the woods. A signposted path leads from here to join a track from the Derry Gates (locked) to Derry Lodge, 5km. On bike, the track is best followed throughout. About 200m beyond Derry Lodge, turn right at a public telephone, cross a bridge and follow the forest and subsequent track up into Glen Derry. A path branches left from Glen Derry to the Hutchison Memorial Hut at NO 024 998, 3 to 4hrs. Approaching from the south, it is normal to stay in the hut.

2. From the north: Reach Loch Avon via Coire an t-Sneachda and Coire Domhain. Follow a path over the col between Beinn Mheadhoin and Càrn Etchachan to the outflow of Loch Etchachan and descend to the cliff, 3hrs in good walking conditions. Remember that there is a lot of Cairngorm plateau between you and your car should the weather turn nasty.

Accommodation: The Hutchison Memorial Hut (NO 024 998). This open shelter in Coire Etchachan, built in 1954, is ideally located amidst wonderful scenery.

Descent: Possible at either end of the cliff. At the left (Bastion) end, descend 45 degree snow, in or near the left-bounding gully (Forked Gully). At the right (Crimson Slabs) end, a line of small crags beyond the slabs must be passed before a descent down a short gully (Grade I) can be made.

Layout: The left end of the cliff is a large broad buttress, The Bastion, bounded on the right by the deepest gully, The Corridor. The central section of cliff is more broken with several shallow gullies leading up to a snow slope, often corniced. Next right are some big overhangs above half-height bounded on the right by the narrow Red Chimney. The right-hand end of the cliff features the Crimson Slabs with two left-facing corners, Djibangi and The Dagger.

1 Quartzvein Edge   120m   III *
J.Y.L.Hay, G.Adams, A.Thom   29 Dec 1956
The left edge of The Bastion is a good choice when snow or weather conditions are doubtful, as it should be possible in most conditions. Start well up left from the base of the buttress and just round the corner, where the wall of Forked Gully becomes defined. Climb a short wall onto the face. Follow the edge at first, then find a way up slabs which develop into a shelf leading round a false tower on the left. Climbing the tower direct is IV,5.

2 Original Route Direct   140m   V,6 **
J.Bower, G.Boyd   23 Dec 1969 (Original Route); Direct: J.Ashbridge, S.M.Richardson 29 Nov 1992
The route follows a line of grooves just right of centre of the Bastion. It is a direct and natural winter line although the Original Route, further left at the start and right in the middle, is easier (IV,5). Start to the right of the lowest rocks on the right of the buttress and go left up an easy depression which ends at a deep V-groove (the best means of locating the route, although it is better seen from below the centre of the buttress than from the route's start). Climb the groove (crux) to a snow patch in a depression. Exit from its right side and return left to follow a large V-groove. Alternatively, go further right to a ramp which joins the V-groove higher up (Original Route).

3 The Corridor   120m   IV,5 **
F.R.Malcolm, A.Thom   20 Mar 1954
An impressive route, both for the scenery and as an early step cutting achievement.

CREAGAN A' CHOIRE ETCHACHAN

Crimson Slabs

The Bastion

1. Quartzvein Edge — III *
2. Original Route Direct — V,6 **

3. The Corridor — IV,5 **
4. Architrave — IV,4 *
5. Central Chimney — III *

6. Square-Cut Gully — V,6 *
7. Winter Route — III
8. Carmine Groove — IV,5 **

9. Red Chimney — V,5 ***
10. Djibangi — V,4 ***
11. The Dagger — V,5 *

There are usually two major ice pitches, one leading over jammed blocks into a cave and one above the cave, usually the crux and often very steep. There is often a large cornice, best taken on the left.

4 Architrave   120m   IV,4 *
A.Fyffe, J.McArtney   29 Dec 1969
This is the prominent groove in the slabs close to the right wall of the Corridor recess. It can form an impressive ribbon of ice, more sustained than The Corridor but less steep.

5 Central Chimney   120m   III *
T.W.Patey, A.o'F.Will, G.Adams, M.Smith   27 Feb 1955
The route takes a shallow chimney between two ribs on the left of the central section of cliff (not far right of the Corridor recess). It is the best of the easier routes, and it can be reduced to Grade II in good conditions by starting up a fault leading leftwards from the base of Square-Cut Gully into the chimney proper. Climb an obvious V cleft which splits the lowest rocks and leads into the chimney. The chimney itself gives 60m of climbing over small ice pitches to the foot of a right-slanting snow ramp, which provides a beautiful finish. Beware of windslab on the final slopes.

6 Square-Cut Gully   150m   V,6 *
M.Forbes, M.Low   Mar 1966
The shallow slabby gully is dominated by a magnificent ice pillar. The start is easy but the finish may include a tricky slabby pitch if there is unconsolidated snow.

7 Winter Route   150m   III
W.D.Brooker, J.W.Morgan, D.A.Sutherland   2 Jan 1949
This is the easiest line on this section of cliff, only Grade II in good conditions. Start up Square-Cut Gully and take an obvious line of weakness leading up onto the buttress on the right (Pioneer Buttress). Mixed climbing leads to an ice pitch on the left near the top.

8 Carmine Groove   140m   IV,5 **
R.A.Smith, G.Stephen   Nov 1974
A barrier of overhangs rises diagonally rightwards from the foot of Pioneer Buttress to the upper reaches of Red Chimney. Two prominent snow scoops, The Meadows, are situated below the largest section of overhangs, just left of Red Chimney. Carmine Groove takes a steep ice filled groove which starts at the left edge of the upper Meadow and runs left of the big overhangs. It is not to be mistaken for an ice line even closer to the overhangs, partly flowing over their left edge, which is **The Red Snake** (90m V,4).

9 Red Chimney   150m   V,5 ***
J.Y.L.Hay, R.Ibbotson   Feb 1959 (Flanking Ribs finish); Direct Finish: I.A.Paterson, S.P.Hepburn   Jan 1967
This very fine ice climb may be relied on to give good conditions in all but the leanest winters. It is useful as a fall back if Djibangi and The Dagger have not formed. The lower section is usually filled with a cascade of clear ice overflowing the Crimson Slabs on the right. This is not steep but often thin. The upper chimney becomes choked by a series of very steep ice bosses, threaded up leftwards (ice screw runners) into the final corner. The cop out is to pull out onto the rib on the right and follow it to the top; **Flanking Ribs** (150m IV,4).

10 Djibangi   140m   V,4 ***
J.McArtney, W.J.Barclay   31 Jan 1965
The left-hand of two corners on the Crimson Slabs is well worth a gamble on conditions, and not to be missed if it is iced. It is quite easy in perfect snow ice conditions. Either start directly below the corner and climb ice directly, or more commonly climb a series of corners to the left. The main corner has an overlap which may be the crux. Above the corner, a snow ramp leads rightwards to join

Dagger but it is better and easier to finish up icy grooves trending left. Continuing directly up the slabs from the left start is **Djibooty** (140m V,4), a superb ice route on the rare occasions when it is thick enough.

11 The Dagger   130m   V,5 *
A.Nisbet, A.T.Robertson   29 Jan 1977
The right-hand corner provides an excellent climb, but it is rarely iced. Take a left-trending turfy line to the base of the corner. A thin ribbon of ice is sufficient in the corner. Pass the next bulge on the left (mixed) and continue to a large platform below the last slab. This may well be the crux. Climb the slab by a crack slanting right, then continue straight up to the top.

BEINN A' BHÙIRD

(NJ 092 005)   Alt 1196m

This is the remote mountain towards the east end of the main Cairngorm massif. There are many good climbs in three different corries, but with the long approach limiting its popularity, only a small number of routes on the best known cliff, Garbh Choire, have been selected. Coire na Ciche has good shorter routes, a possibility for a second day, but it is not described here.

GARBH CHOIRE

(NJ 107 015)   Alt 950m   North-East facing   Map p258   Diagram p258

A wild and beautiful corrie, one of Scotland's most remote, but worth the planning to deal with a long approach and long routes.

Weather and Conditions: Being high and east, good conditions occur at similar times to Lochnagar. The buttresses are possible at any time of a long season, November to April, but they are better without deep powder or rime so March is recommended. The gullies are definitely better in late season. Good conditions for the long approach are also important, including cycling to Glen Slugain, so a freeze after a good thaw is best. Good weather is also important as it is a long way to retreat or escape, and a mishap would be very serious.

Approach: From the A93 Braemar to Aberdeen road, starting from Invercauld Bridge. Leave the main road 100m east of the gates to Invercauld House (signposted Keiloch) and park in a Pay and Display car park on the right (£2.00 in 2008). If lower ground is clear of snow, then cycling is recommended and bikes can be taken as far as the top of Glen Slugain. Follow the road, initially tarmac, until just before a farm. Follow a track on the right (signs) and descend to rejoin the original road beyond the farm. Take the second track on the right (signposted Glen Slugain) and follow it through forest and a gate into the glen. A new track going through Glen Slugain becomes a good stalkers path at the ruined Slugain Lodge and arrives in Glen Quoich. Keep to the path leading to a huge boulder called Clach a' Chlèirich (NO 114 992). Follow the path past the stone and up to the sneck (col) between Ben Avon and Cnap a' Chlèirich, then contour left avoiding rock ribs by descending. About 4hrs (including the cycle), so many parties will choose to spend the night somewhere.

Descent: Head south to the summit of Cnap a' Chlèirich and follow the blunt ridge back to Clach a' Chlèirich (the edge of Coire nan Clach on the right is often corniced).

Layout: First reached and on the left of the corrie is the North Face with a large basin high up, The Crucible, usually capped by an enormous cornice. High on the right of this face is the west-facing Squareface. The central part of the cliff is more broken with several easy gullies, the exception being the waterfall of the Allt an Sluichd which freezes to form The Flume. Right of The Flume is Mandarin Buttress after which is the huge ridge of Mitre Ridge, the most impressive feature of the corrie. Between Mandarin and Mitre is the shallow South-East Gully.

BEINN A' BHÙIRD - Garbh Choire

Squareface Buttress

Mitre Ridge

1. Gold Coast Direct	V,5 ***	
2. Crucible Route	VI,5 **	
3. Comala's Ridge	II *	
4. Flume Left-Hand	IV,4 *	
6. Flume Direct	IV,4 **	
7. South-East Gully	V,4 *	
8. East Wall Direct	IV,5 **	
9. The Grail	V,5 **	
10. Mitre Ridge	V,6 ****	
12. North-West Gully	III *	

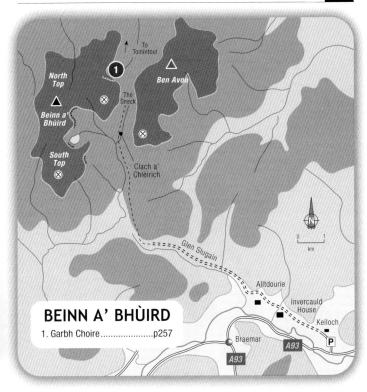

BEINN A' BHÙIRD

1. Garbh Choire p257

CAIRNGORMS

1 Gold Coast Direct   180m   V,5 ***

A.Nisbet, C.McLeod 11 Feb 1982 (1PA); Direct, as described: B.Davison, A.Nisbet 10 Mar 1997
Snowy conditions followed by substantial thawing produces icy conditions, when the face below the Crucible contains two icefalls separated by a snout of rock, with the left-hand usually containing more ice. This fine route climbs steeply into the Crucible by the left-hand icefall. Climb a short ice gully below the Crucible, then go up to the main icefall, which flows down a very steep wall to a slab. Climb the icefall direct in two pitches with a big block belay on the right below the steepest section. Climb into the Crucible and find a way past the cornice (out right is most likely).

2 Crucible Route   180m   VI,5 **

R.J.Archbold, D.Dinwoodie   Apr 1978 (1 peg for tension); Direct, as described: B.Davison, A.Nisbet 10 Mar 1997
Two consecutive iced grooves in the slabby ground right of the initial gully of Gold Coast lead to the right-hand Crucible icefall. Climb this direct. The route is steeper for longer than the Gold Coast icefall, but is low in the grade.

3 Comala's Ridge   200m   II *

The broad ridge left of The Flume is a good choice under powdery conditions or poor weather.

4 Flume Left-Hand   200m   IV,4 *

W.Moir   31 Jan 1987
Left of The Flume Direct a two-tiered icefall flows down from a snow bowl below the plateau into the easy lower couloir of The Flume; climb the icefall.

Mitre Ridge, V,6. Climber Chris Astill

5 The Flume 200m II **

J.M.Taylor, G.B.Leslie 31 Mar 1954

The easiest line, which can be very icy, starts up Flume Left-Hand, then makes a rising traverse rightwards to finish at the same place as Flume Direct. There is sometimes a big cornice, usually avoidable on the left.

6 Flume Direct 200m IV,4 **

D.F.Lang, N.W.Quinn 15 Dec 1974

This is the channel gouged in the cliff by the Allt an t-Sluichd, already a lusty stream on the plateau before it drops over the edge. The gully ends under the plateau in a huge waterfall which freezes in winter.

7 South-East Gully 200m V,4 *

R.H.Sellers, G.Annand Feb 1959

The shallow gully bounding the Mitre Ridge on the left gives a fine climb in good conditions but, with minimal rock protection, it becomes very serious when there is unconsolidated snow. Beware of avalanches when there is a south-westerly or westerly wind and spindrift. The crux is a steep narrows just above half-height. The cornice is seldom troublesome.

8 East Wall Direct 220m IV,5 **

T.W.Patey, A.G.Nicol 31 Mar 1954; Direct, as described: N.D.Keir, J.Mothersele, R.A.Smith 23 Feb 1974
A fine climb with sustained difficulties from start to finish. Start about 20m left of the lowest point of the slab apron on the east wall. After 30m, a short thin ice traverse left leads to a long chimney system. Above mid-height, a set of stepped ramps lead underneath an imposing vertical wall to reach an ice couloir. Climb the ice couloir to its top, then exit left of overhangs ringing the top and follow an easy gully to the final col of Mitre Ridge. It is possible to reach the ice couloir from just below the depression of South-East Gully.

9 The Grail 250m V,5 **
A.Nisbet, A.Clifford 15 Feb 1984
A direct and natural winter line up the centre of the east wall. The grade assumes the initial 10m wall is banked up, otherwise add a grade. Start just left of the lowest rocks and about 15m right of East Wall Direct. Climb very directly up a vegetated fault in three pitches to the terrace left of The Shoulder. Go up to the steep wall above and traverse left over a small rib to the base of a ramp overlooking the couloir of East Wall Direct. Climb the ramp to the col between the First and Second Towers (two pitches, crux).

◀10 Mitre Ridge 250m V,6 ****
W.D.Brooker, T.W.Patey 2 Apr 1953; Direct: J.Anderson, A.Nisbet Apr 1979
A great classic with short hard sections. With good snow, it is much easier and a fine finish over the towers is possible. With consolidated snow or ice, start up a big groove (the rightmost) at the base of the ridge near the right corner of the East Face. Climb the groove past a steep section to a rising shelf which leads into a deep chimney on the West Face. In less icy conditions, start up a line of weakness further up and right which leads to the shelf and chimney. Climb the chimney and shallow gully to a shoulder on the ridge. The short wall above is the crux; climb it by tricky torquing, moving up and right. Above and to the left is a platform, usually gained by moving left across a slab and climbing a splintered chimney (a second crux). Now climb the wall above and ascend rightwards to the col between the First and Second Towers. The tower is normally turned on the left to an impressive finish along the final arete. Bell's Variation is a possible finish for those with energy to spare (technical 7, see Cumming-Crofton Route).

A fine direct line up the crest of the ridge is taken by **The Cardinal** (250m VIII,8).

1 Cumming-Crofton Route 160m VI,6 ****
R.Renshaw, G.S.Strange 26 Feb 1977; Bell's Variation: R.Anderson, G.Nicoll 12 Apr 1986
This is a steep, sustained and exciting winter route in the modern style of snowy rock. One of the 'last great problems' of the '70s, there were at least two previous attempts, one very nearly successful in a storm, by Norman Keir. The route follows a right-slanting corner parallel to and on the right of the crest of Mitre Ridge, ending at the col behind the First Tower. Start directly below the corner and go straight up to climb a prominent chimney blocked by a flake. Pulling out right at the flake is hard (30m). Traverse right and continue rightwards up a smooth groove. When stopped by a vertical wall, return left into the main corner (optional belay). Climb the corner to a platform (40m). Continue in the same line to the col. Either finish by Mitre Ridge on the left or more directly by Bell's Variation (technical 7). Follow a shelf rightwards and climb a very exposed crack on the west face. Step back left from the crack and finish straight up.

2 North-West Gully 150m III *
R.H.Sellers, G.Adams Dec 1956
This corner gully, tucked hard against the west wall of Mitre Ridge, gives a good winter route which varies greatly in difficulty. After a period of freeze and thaw, a superb 30m ice pitch may form. Early in the season, under powder, it is much harder. The approach from the corrie floor is by a graceful arete of snow which swings up round the base of the ridge.

Southern Cairngorms

Save from Aberdeen, access to the cliffs of the southern Cairngorms, Lochnagar, Creag an Dubh Loch and Eagles Rocks is less convenient. The high cliff of Lochnagar has the most continental climate and provides the most reliable conditions, except that powder may lie deep for weeks and ice forms only reluctantly. The most southerly area, Glen Clova, is not extensive but it offers many lower grade routes in a charming setting and is therefore popular.

LOCHNAGAR

(NO 244 861)   Alt 1155m   Map p263

Lochnagar is understandably one of Scotland's most famous mountains. Its distinctive outline rises gracefully above Royal Deeside and provides a noble mountain landscape for residents, tourists and climbers. The climbing is situated in the magnificent North-East Corrie with its cliff front extending for 1.5 km, reaching a height of 230m and encircling the loch which has given its name to the mountain. It is split by great gullies into several well defined buttresses which give long natural winter routes.

Weather and Conditions: Conditions are generally reliable, but only for those who are flexible and willing to climb any style, ice or mixed. Good ice often appears only as late as March, after the powder has lain unchanged throughout January and February. The classic buttress climbs are traditionally climbed and graded for powder, progress being reliant on frozen vegetation. The deep enclosure of the corrie protects the snow from the effects of a thaw and shelters the climber from strong south-east through to west winds, so it is often possible to climb in reasonable comfort after battling up to the corrie in wind. The consequence of this shelter, combined with the colder eastern climate, is that windslab avalanches are common on days with spindrift (which are frequent).

The buttresses are generally well defined with ridges up to the plateau and some provide safe options in dubious conditions, as long as they can be reached safely. Even gullies on the opposite side of the corrie to the recent or current wind may be safe. After a long cold spell, the buttresses may be heavily rimed, but they should still be possible, although determination and about twice the normal time may be required. As a general rule, don't have fixed ideas about choice of route, but go for the best conditions on the day. If powdery, climb a buttress; if icy, climb a gully. The season is long, often lasting from November to April.

Approach: Approach from Glen Muick, which is reached from Ballater by 15km of single track road which ends at a large car park at the Spittal of Glen Muick (Pay and Display parking fee). From the car park, walk through the wood past the visitor centre, turn immediately right and follow a private unsurfaced road across the valley to a T-junction beside an out building of Allt-na-giubhsaich Lodge. Continue straight on by following a path alongside a fence that leads west from this out building. The path leads through pine trees to join a landrover track which is followed out of the pines and up the open hillside to the Muick-Gelder col. Here the path branches off the track to the left and is well marked to the summit plateau. Leave this main path and go over the col between Meikle Pap and Cuidhe Crom to descend into the corrie. Descend leftwards until not far above the left side of the loch, then climb slightly to the first aid box. Being very popular, there are often tracks in the snow and other parties to follow.

Descent: The normal winter descent is to follow the cliff edge back to near the Meikle Pap col (beware of cornices). In stormy weather, a foolproof but longer descent can be made via the Glas Allt and Loch Muick, by heading south from any point near the cliff-top. (If at the top of West Buttress, beware of The Black Spout which cuts into the plateau). Gentle slopes soon lead into the upper basin of the Glas Allt, which leads to Loch Muick. To return to the corrie floor, descend the main branch of The Black Spout. The cornice is almost always easily passed on the left (looking down).

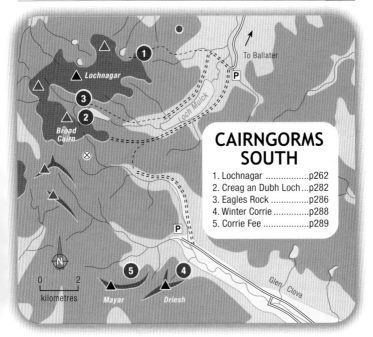

CAIRNGORMS SOUTH

Layout: The corrie has two different sectors. The Southern Sector, reached as soon as the Meikle Pap col is crossed, is a wide bay with a frieze of rock under the plateau. Further on is the first aid box on a small terrace above the loch, from where routes on the Main Cliff can be identified and conditions assessed. See that section for layout.

SOUTHERN SECTOR

The Cathedral

Alt 950m   North facing   Diagram p264

Between the lowest point of the plateau rim and the start of the main cliff are three distinct sections of cliff. On the left is a long wall with several ribs, Perseverance Wall. To its right is the triangular Sinister Buttress with The Cathedral suitably shaped in the centre. The short length of its routes and quicker approach means they are good options for a short day. They provide good early season options as the routes are generally turfy and come into condition quickly after a snowfall and short freeze.

Towards the left end of The Cathedral is an impressive mummy shaped tower (the cathedral spire). To its right are four slender ribs divided by chimneys and grooves (the cathedral body) which provide many of the routes. Above these ribs is a left-rising terrace ending at the deep chimney of Transept Route.

Transept Groove   80m   IV,5 *
R.J.Archbold, G.S.Strange   31 Dec 1982
A popular route and good for a short day. Climb the right-hand of twin fault-lines immediately left of the mummy shaped tower and finish by the left and deepest of two chimneys at the top of the terrace (as for Transept Route).

CAIRNGORMS

LOCHNAGAR - The Cathedral

1. Transept Groove   IV,5 *
2. Transept Route   V,6 **
3. Sepulchre   V,6 **
4. Spellbound   VI,7 **
5. Judas Priest   V,5 *
6. Cathedral Chimney   IV,4 **   7. Magic Pillar   IV,5 ***

2 Transept Route   100m V,6 **

S.M.Richardson, R.D.Everett 22 Jan 1994

A sustained turfy mixed climb, taking the prominent groove just right of the mummy shaped tower.

1. 40m Climb easy lower ground and step right into the foot of the groove. Climb this with increasing difficulty to a small triangular niche. Pull over the roof (crux) and continue more easily to a recess and large block belay.

2. 35m Continue in the same line up a narrow groove and climb to the top of a small hanging snowfield. Exit via the wall on the right to gain the left-rising terrace.

3. 25m Move left into the deep well defined chimney and climb this to the top.

3 Sepulchre   100m V,6 **

B.S.Findlay, G.S.Strange 13 Dec 1987

An absorbing route, taking the central groove of the crag. Start from the left side of a slight bay and climb a narrow groove twisting up right and continue up to ledges. Straight ahead are twin slabby grooves. Climb out right then move back left to follow the right-hand groove for 6m. Transfer to the left-hand groove and climb straight up to the left-rising terrace. Move left and finish by the chimney of Transept Route.

4 Spellbound   120m VI,7 **

C.Cartwright, S.M.Richardson 15 Nov 1998

The rib separating the grooves of Sepulchre and Judas Priest forms a fine tapering arete defended near its base by a large roof.

1. 20m Start directly beneath the roof and climb a short wall to a niche. Continue up the steep left-slanting corner and pull over the left end of the roof. Belay on the

ledge above.

2. 40m Continue up the arete, following the crack-line which splits the crest.

3. and 4. 60m Finish as for Judas Priest by moving right along the terrace and through a slot to reach the exit gully of Cathedral Chimney.

5 Judas Priest   100m   V,5 *
B.S.Findlay, G.S.Strange   14 Dec 1986

The larger right-hand groove rising from the bay is the easiest and most popular of the steep groove climbs on the front face of the buttress. Climb a corner on the right before moving left to enter the main groove, then follow it to easy ground. Work right through a slot to finish at the top of Cathedral Chimney.

6 Cathedral Chimney   70m   IV,4 **
M.Freeman, G.S.Strange   12 Dec 1977

The obvious deep narrow chimney left of the rightmost buttress. A good line that sees regular ascents. Start by climbing easy mixed ground to the foot of the chimney. Belay on the left.

1. 50m Climb the chimney, wriggle up the constriction (crux) and exit up and right.

2. 20m Finish up the easy wide gully to the cornice.

7 Magic Pillar   80m   IV,5 ***
C.Cartwright, S.M.Richardson   15 Nov 1998

The well defined pillar to the right of Cathedral Chimney. Delightful mixed climbing and considerably easier than it looks. A little gem! Start by climbing easy mixed ground to the base of the pillar.

1. 20m Follow the crack in the crest to a niche.

2. 40m Step round the roof to the right and continue up the crack-chimney to its top.

3. 20m Finish easily up the final gully of Cathedral Chimney.

MAIN SECTOR

Diagrams p267, 269, 273

Layout: For ready identification, a division of the buttresses into four natural groups has been made, the groups being divided by the three largest gullies. From left to right these are:

1. Central Buttress is the left edge with Shadow Buttresses A and B up and right, bounded by the obvious Douglas-Gibson Gully, a straight cut gash between high walls.

2. Eagle Ridge is immediately right of Douglas-Gibson Gully, then to its right are the Parallel Gullies and finally the large and smooth Tough-Brown Face. Raeburn's Gully bounds this group but it is hidden from the first aid box by its slanting course, although its snow fan is obvious

3. Black Spout Pinnacle is the slabby triangular face left of The Black Spout, unmistakeable as a wide Grade I snow gully

4. West Buttress forms the right-hand limit of the cliffs. The lower icefall of West Gully is often prominent near its right end.

The following are grid bearings from the first aid box to major routes. It should be noted that all the direct approaches cross regular avalanche paths:

Central Buttress (initial gully): **190** degrees

Shadow Buttress A: **214** degrees

Parallel Gully A: **258** degrees

Raeburn's Gully: **278** degrees

The Black Spout: **286** degrees

Central Buttress   300m   II **
S.R.Tewnion, J.Tewnion   Jan 1948

This is the easiest of the major buttresses and the first on the left; it gives a good introduction to Lochnagar style mixed climbing. The slopes above the arete can

CAIRNGORMS

avalanche and will funnel down Shallow Gully. Start up an introductory gully on the right which faces the first aid box. At its top traverse right as soon as possible and climb the crest to two gendarmes set on a level arete. From here take the easiest line to the plateau, usually via snow on the left. The route has ever present easier ground on the left which could be used as an escape.

9 Central Buttress Direct   90m   IV,6 *
M.Geddes, N.D.Keir   23 Mar 1975 (3PA); FFA: A.Nisbet, D.Wright   Dec 1979
The right wall of the introductory gully of Central Buttress is steep and smooth. Above and right of this is a parallel line of grooves, the furthest left of several lines on the corrie face.

10 Centrist   110m   V,5 **
M.Freeman, N.D.Keir   3 Feb 1974 (1PA); FFA: S.Kennedy, N.Morrison, A.Nisbet   20 Feb 1980
The established classic on Central Buttress. Start close to the groove line of Central Buttress Direct, just right of the lowest rocks. Climb a shallow groove slanting slightly right, go over a chockstone, then move up into a big groove with an overhang at its top. Avoid this on the left (crux) and continue curving left up ramps until an easier angled groove leads right to the crest just before the gendarmes.

11 The Finalist   110m   V,6 *
S.M.Richardson, C.Cartwright   8 Jan 2006
The prominent square-cut corner in the centre of the face.
1. 50m Start at the foot of Shallow Gully and climb straight up over turfy mixed ground towards the square-cut corner. Cross two diagonal faults and climb up right of a smooth undercut wall. Step left across the wall and move up to easier ground below the corner.
2. 30m Move up into the corner and make a difficult exit right at its top. Belay on blocks up and right.
3. 20m Continue up grooves in the line of the corner to join the crest of Central Buttress.

12 Shallow Gully   300m   IV,4 *
D.L.Macrae, F.G.Henderson   8 Feb 1959
The shallow depression between Central Buttress and Shadow Buttress A gives a good climb when in condition, but not being recessed, it fills up less readily than the major gullies. It rarely holds continuous ice, but would be easier as such (although poorly protected). Difficulties are confined to the lowest 60m, after which snow leads to the upper slopes of Central Buttress (but since these avalanche, it is not a safe choice in doubtful snow conditions).

13 Shadowlands   250m   VI,7 ***
A.D.Robertson, S.M.Richardson   19 Mar 1995
This intimidating direct route through the headwall of the lower buttress is one of the more popular modern mixed routes on the mountain. Start at the cave up and left from the introductory gully of Shadow Buttress A.
1. 30m Climb up and left to a good stance.
2. 25m Trend right over short steep walls until it is possible to make an awkward step down and right to the base of an imposing left-trending fault cutting through the headwall.
3. 20m Gain the fault from the right, and climb it for 15m until it is possible to break out right into an overhanging niche. Pull over this to reach a good ledge.
4. 25m Make a difficult step left and follow the fault to its end.
5. to 7. 150m Move up and right to the crest, soon joining the easier upper section of Shadow Buttress A.

14 Shadow Buttress A   300m   IV,5 ***
W.D.Brooker, J.W.Morgan   27 Dec 1949
A first class mountaineering route and a good choice for strong parties in poor

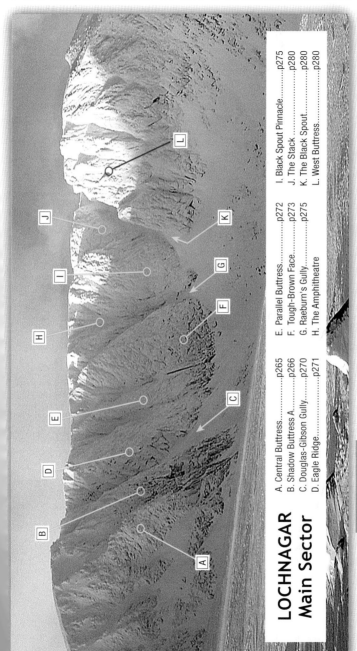

**LOCHNAGAR
Main Sector**

A. Central Buttress...............p265
B. Shadow Buttress A............p266
C. Douglas-Gibson Gully.......p270
D. Eagle Ridge.....................p271
E. Parallel Buttress...............p272
F. Tough-Brown Face............p273
G. Raeburn's Gully................p275
H. The Amphitheatre
I. Black Spout Pinnacle.........p275
J. The Stack p280
K. The Black Spout...............p280
L. West Buttress..................p280

Shadow Buttress A, IV,5. Climber Steve Stout

conditions. The route is low in the grade and not sustained, but it is long and has a notorious crux. The disappearance of a block at the base of the crux section has made the climb harder, but a peg for aid at this point reduces the climb back to its traditional Grade III. It is worth noting that a single abseil from below the crux down the chimney on the right, Shadow Chimney, gains the corrie floor. Start in a short introductory gully below the large overhangs. Climb up right towards the overhangs, then follow the Spiral Terrace round right underneath them to a balcony. From its end, climb a vague rib alongside Shadow Chimney, including a steep section (crux). It is possible to move right and climb Shadow Chimney as an alternative (less technical but more strenuous). Now trend left and regain the crest by a shallow gully. Follow the crest to a small tower, turn this by a short descent on the right (or climb it direct at Grade IV,5) and continue up easier ground to the plateau.

15 Moonshadow 225m V,5 **

S.M.Richardson, J.Ashbridge 21 Nov 1992

The well defined buttress between Shadow Chimney and Giant's Head Chimney Direct. Good sustained turfy mixed climbing at a reasonable standard.

1. 40m Start at the foot of Giant's Head Chimney and climb diagonally up and left for 15m to enter a steep, right-facing corner. Climb this and exit left on turf. Continue up behind a large boulder to belay in Shadow Chimney.

2. 25m Immediately leave the chimney by climbing an awkward wall on the right, which leads to a hidden ramp cutting back right to the crest of the buttress. Pull over the small roof above to reach a good ledge.

3. 40m Continue easily for 15m to reach a steep slabby wall cut by parallel cracks. Climb the right side of the wall via a left-facing corner, and finish up easier ground to a ledge.

4. 40m Climb the short steep corner behind the belay to gain a right-trending line

of weakness.
5. and 6. 80m Continue up mixed ground to reach Shadow Buttress A below the small final tower. Climb this to the top.

16 Giant's Head Chimney 220m IV,4 **
W.D.Brooker, J.W.Morgan 29 Jan 1950
A fine route, graded for good ice. It is a popular climb, and its recessed position hidden behind Shadow Buttress A allows it to stay in condition late in the season. Climb the initial chimney to the overhang and move right to belay. **Giant's Head Direct** (200m V,5) continues straight up but is not often in condition. Instead, follow a terrace round the corner on the right into a trough. The initial 30m of the trough is often very icy, and in these conditions it gives a superb exposed pitch. Higher up the trough becomes an easy snow scoop leading to the crest of Shadow Buttress A, but more difficult climbing may be found by moving right on to the right edge known as the Feathered Arete.

17 Polyphemus Gully 200m V,5 ***
K.Grassick, H.S.M.Bates 24 Jan 1953
The finest gully climb on the mountain. It has good rock belays, and in good conditions is considered a soft touch for the grade. The gully cuts deeply into the left side of Shadow Buttress B and is reached by traversing on steepening snow from the base of Giant's Head Chimney. There are two big pitches separated by

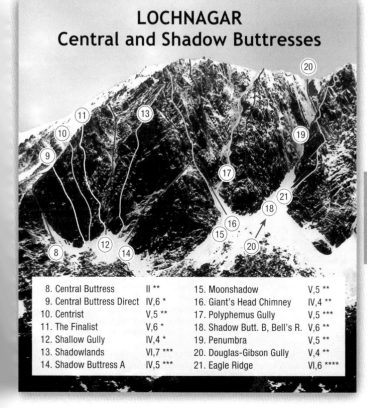

LOCHNAGAR
Central and Shadow Buttresses

8. Central Buttress	II **		15. Moonshadow	V,5 **
9. Central Buttress Direct	IV,6 *		16. Giant's Head Chimney	IV,4 **
10. Centrist	V,5 **		17. Polyphemus Gully	V,5 ***
11. The Finalist	V,6 *		18. Shadow Butt. B, Bell's R.	V,6 **
12. Shallow Gully	IV,4 *		19. Penumbra	V,5 **
13. Shadowlands	VI,7 ***		20. Douglas-Gibson Gully	V,4 **
14. Shadow Buttress A	IV,5 ***		21. Eagle Ridge	VI,6 ****

CAIRNGORMS

Douglas-Gibson Gully, V.4. Climber Alfie Robertson

60m of steep snow. The upper pitch can be climbed directly on ice above a cave. In thinner conditions, either take a little corner on the right, or more commonly, an obvious V-groove on the left. The cornice is often huge but can usually by outflanked by a traverse right on to Shadow Buttress B.

18 Shadow Buttress B, Bell's Route   200m   V,6 **
T.W.Patey, A.o'F. Will   23 Jan 1955
The narrow Shadow Buttress B is defined by steep walls dropping into Douglas-Gibson Gully on the right and Polyphemus Gully on the left. Its lies at a higher level than Shadow Buttress A, and presents a classical buttress form with a steep lower section that leads to easier angled ground before tapering to a narrow crest at the top. The classic route on Shadow Buttress B is a rewarding climb, and typical of the best winter buttresses on the mountain. It comes into condition early in the season. Start just inside the foot of Douglas-Gibson Gully where a turfy break leads left to the centre of the buttress. Go up a crack on the right until two teeth are encountered below a vertical wall. From a perch on the left tooth "flit quickly across a holdless wall to grasp a flake handrail". Beware – the flake is loose! Beyond this, ascend a groove to belay on a large platform at the top of the steep section. Continue by enjoyable climbing up the crest via snow aretes and short steps passing a tower on the left leading to a steep finish (occasionally a difficult cornice).

19 Penumbra   110m   V,5 **
C.Butterworth, P.Arnold   18 Mar 1972
The large prominent corner running from the narrows of Douglas-Gibson Gully to the top of Shadow Buttress B. A good line that becomes easier with more ice. From the point where Douglas-Gibson Gully suddenly narrows, climb the obvious discontinuous corner for three pitches to the cornice. Sometimes it is necessary to traverse left below this to exit on the true crest of Shadow Buttress B.

20 Douglas-Gibson Gully   200m   V,4 **
T.W.Patey, G.B.Leslie   28 Dec 1950

The great gully between Shadow Buttress B and Eagle Ridge was the first attempted winter route on Lochnagar, in March 1893. It was finally 'conquered' (to use tabloid speak) by a youthful and inexperienced Tom Patey. "When the ability to climb back down is lost, the only choice is to carry on." Although it has lost much of its original aura of impregnability, the gully still provides a fine and serious climb in impressive surroundings. It is perhaps unique among Lochnagar's major climbs in that it reserves all its defences for the final 60m, the last obstacle of which may be a huge unavoidable cornice. From the foot of the top wall, move left and climb grooves until it is possible to move left into an easier snow runnel leading to the cornice. In peak season the climbing will be easy but the cornice perhaps impossible. In early season it may provide continuous ice but an easier cornice.

21 Eagle Ridge   200m   VI,6 ****
T.W.Patey, J.M.Taylor, W.D.Brooker   25 Jan 1953
The Queen of Lochnagar's winter climbs, following the elegant ridge right of Douglas-Gibson Gully. Viewed from the corrie floor, the ridge sweeps up majestically in a series of alluring snow crests and intimidating walls. In calm weather and with good snow the climb is technically reasonable, but in powdery conditions the ridge becomes a big undertaking. The first ascent time of 4.5 hours shows how advanced Scottish mixed climbing had become by the early 1950s. The climbing is well protected but very sustained, and the grade assumes the route is climbed free in average conditions. A couple of points of aid or the presence of good ice will make it considerably easier.

Start just inside Douglas-Gibson Gully and climb an obvious V-groove (20m). Follow a shallow gully and an awkward short chimney (30m), then return left to the crest by a groove and climb a left-facing corner leading to the base of the Tower (50m). Pull into a recess on the right (hard), then continue up steep rock and trend slightly left to gain a sentry box (15m). Continue up the crest (approximately) until forced right to a short corner (30m). Climb this to an airy knife edge, and follow this to a short vertical wall. Occasionally this builds up with snow, without which it is very hard and a peg is often used (10m). Climb the crest to a projecting square-cut overhang. Traverse right across the wall and pull up to follow a corner slanting left to finish rightwards (45m). The Tower provides the winter crux, an exciting problem and one of the highlights of the climb.

22 Eagle Buttress   250m   IV,3 *
W.D.Brooker, J.M.Taylor   31 Mar 1956
The buttress to the right of Eagle Ridge holds snow well and is often in condition, but it is a serious route at the upper end of its grade, with poor protection and the crux near the top. Start mid-way between Eagle Ridge and Parallel Gully A. For about 120m, the climbing is straightforward up to the head of the central snow scoop. The line of least resistance then veers right to below the steep upper wall. Here a ledge leads right to three parallel V-grooves overlooking Parallel Gully A. Climb the central groove (crux), then bear left and follow the edge close to Parallel Gully A, joining it at the very top. The left and right grooves have also been climbed, but they are slightly harder than the central line.

23 Parallel Gully A   270m   III **
G.W.Ross, R.Still   28 Mar 1948
The left-hand of the two parallel gullies gives a variable but always enjoyable climb. It may have several long ice pitches or completely bank out into a snow chute. The first pitch can give as much as 30m of sustained ice, but this is avoidable by a traverse from the left. The shallow chimney in the gully bed above can be climbed direct, but it is better to go left on ice to a long stretch of snow leading past a narrow minor gully on the right to a bifurcation. A rising traverse left leads to the left fork which is straightforward, and the cornice can normally be bypassed on the left.
Variation: **Right Fork   60m   IV,4 ***
From the bifurcation, take the steeper and more direct right fork.

Simon Richardson

Parallel Buttress, VI,6. Climber John Ashbridge

24 Parallel Buttress   280m   VI,6 ***
T.W.Patey, J.Smith, W.D.Brooker   4 Mar 1956 (4PA)

The flat fronted buttress between the Parallel gullies tapers to a ridge near the plateau. An excellent climb with continuously interesting climbing. As with Eagle Ridge, consolidated snow will considerably ease the difficulties. Start up a wide groove just right of Parallel Gully A. Above is a big groove (the variation start, harder). Move right into a defined chimney. Climb this, then slant right up two recessed corners to a big flake, from where easy ground slants left to an easing in angle. Go diagonally right up easy ground to the edge of Parallel Gully B. Gain a shelf overlooking the gully and climb it to its end. Move left onto the face and ascend a succession of turfy grooves to the Tower. Gain a small ledge up on the left, then climb the shallow groove above for 3m to a large jammed spike (crux, particularly under powder). Move left onto a sloping snow shelf and follow this until it is possible to return to the crest behind the Tower. A graceful snow arete leads to the plateau.

25 Parallel Gully B   260m   IV,5
J.R.Marshall, G.Tiso   22 Feb 1958

Two huge rockfalls in 1995 and 2000 robbed Lochnagar of one of its most famous winter climbs, and the classic back and foot lower chimney is now a smooth right-facing corner. In exceptional conditions ice runs down the corner from the gully above, which would provide a difficult and serious start. More reasonably, the upper gully can be accessed via Tough-Brown Traverse to provide a worthwhile Grade IV,5 expedition. Once in the upper gully, entry to the top pitch is blocked by a bulge, that is sometimes easier on its left side. Alternatively, climb a groove on the right that leads to the top of Tough-Brown Ridge.

Tough-Brown Face

Alt 900m   North-East facing   Diagrams p267, 273

The massive buttress between Parallel Gully B and Raeburn's Gully presents a forbidding facade of steep boiler plate slabs, which taper gradually upwards to form a defined ridge. The true crest of the buttress commences near the foot of Raeburn's Gully and follows the extreme right end of the frontal slabs before merging with the upper ridge.

26 Tough-Brown Traverse   300m   IV,3 ＊＊
T.W.Patey, D.A.Aitken   20 Jan 1952
One of the great Lochnagar winter classics, this devious ascent of the Tough-Brown Ridge outflanks the lower slabs by starting on Eagle Buttress, and gains the front face of the ridge in its upper half. With successful route finding, the original summer line is technically straightforward, but it is easy to trend too far right at the end of the Great Terrace and encounter more difficult but good climbing near the crest of the buttress. The route should not be underestimated in poor weather or late in the day as it is a long climb and retreat is difficult.

Start on Eagle Buttress some distance left of the initial pitch of Parallel Gully A and traverse into the gully above its first pitch. Continue traversing right and up over the easy section on Parallel Buttress to the grassy scoop above the rockfall scar

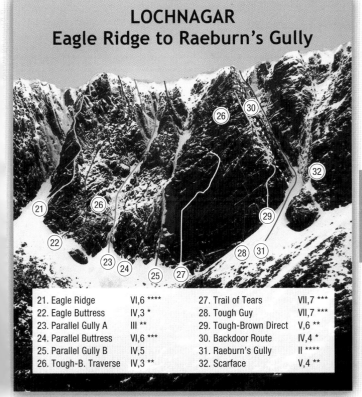

LOCHNAGAR
Eagle Ridge to Raeburn's Gully

21. Eagle Ridge	VI,6 ＊＊＊＊		27. Trail of Tears	VII,7 ＊＊＊
22. Eagle Buttress	IV,3 ＊		28. Tough Guy	VII,7 ＊＊＊
23. Parallel Gully A	III ＊＊		29. Tough-Brown Direct	V,6 ＊＊
24. Parallel Buttress	VI,6 ＊＊＊		30. Backdoor Route	IV,4 ＊
25. Parallel Gully B	IV,5		31. Raeburn's Gully	II ＊＊＊＊
26. Tough-B. Traverse	IV,3 ＊＊		32. Scarface	V,4 ＊＊

CAIRNGORMS

of Parallel Gully B. Use a short chimney to gain the Great Terrace, which runs across the buttress above the Tough-Brown Face. There is a network of possible lines above the Great Terrace. The original route leaves the Great Terrace about 10m before its upper end by climbing a wall to a ledge. Continue right up a slabby ramp for a short way and move onto a horizontal ledge to the left. Zigzag up to the crest and follow this to the top.

27 Trail of Tears 135m VII,7 ***
D.Dinwoodie, A.Nisbet 7 Mar 1986
A superb route, taking the easiest line up a futuristic piece of cliff. Fortunately it escaped the devastation of the rockfalls. Most recent ascents have used icy conditions, but under powder it is Grade VII,8 and it may be necessary to use a peg for aid on the big ramp on pitch 3. Start up the long corner just right of the rockfall scar.
1. 30m Climb the grassy corner and exit left to a ledge.
2. 10m Continue straight up the corner over a bulge and down the back of the great flakes for a very secure feeling.
3. 35m Climb the shallow groove above to a grass ledge, then go right up a big ramp to belay in a grassy niche.
4. 40m Follow the ramp to a break, descend right to a lower ramp, make an awkward move round a corner, then climb up to the continuation of the main ramp. Follow cracks in the ramp to its tip, then make a big step up round a block.
5. 20m The way to the upper terrace of Tough-Brown Traverse is now obvious as a line of flakes leading left.

28 Tough Guy 120m VII,7 ***
C.MacLean, A.Nisbet 18 Dec 1984 (by the escape rake); As described: A.Nisbet, B.Davison 26 Dec 1984
Another superb and sustained mixed climb taking a line based on a right-hand intermittent crack-line, at the right edge of the face before it curves round towards Tough-Brown Ridge Direct. It is often in condition and deserves more ascents. From the foot of Tough-Brown Ridge Direct climb a short wall (maybe banked out) and descend leftwards down a shelf onto the front face. Start at the base of this shelf.
1. 30m Go up, then left to gain and climb a crack-line which passes a roof on its right and leads up to a huge block belay.
2. 30m Behind the block is a corner. Make one move up the corner, then move round its left rib to a rockfall scar. Traverse under this and climb its left edge to reach the long ledge. Go right up this to its end.
3. 35m Swing left and move up on thin vegetation, then take a thin left-slanting crack (crux) to reach a rake which can be used as an escape out right. It is better to cross the rake to the left and continue diagonally left via a big flake and large cracked blocks to a ledge.
4. 25m Continue diagonally left into a trough and finish up this to the crest of Tough-Brown Ridge Direct.

29 Tough-Brown Ridge Direct 250m V,6 **
M.Rennie, N.D.Keir 23 Dec 1969 (4PA); FFA: D.F.Lang, N.W.Quinn 3 Feb 1974
A good mixed climb that sees regular ascents when the Tough-Brown Face is in condition. The steep initial 60m are difficult without a build-up of firm snow, but the difficulties soon ease after this. Start just inside the scree shoot of Raeburn's Gully. A short wall, then a slabby ledge passing right, leads to a long grassy groove sloping up left. At its top, make a sharp right traverse to a pile of huge blocks. Go left by a flake-crack, then by a short slab traverse that ends at a grass terrace. Walk up this rightwards to reach the edge of the wall above (45m). Instead of climbing slabs above, move round right and pass below a short vertical wall to a miniature arete poised above Raeburn's Gully. Climb the groove above the arete, or step down to the right beyond the arete, and climb a wall which leads to easier ground. Finish up grooves left of the prominent groove of Backdoor Route, or traverse right into Backdoor Route.

John Trudgill

Raeburn's Gully, II. Climber Pete Trudgill

30 Backdoor Route   220m   IV,4 *
T.W.Patey, A.o'F.Will, G.McLeod, A.Thom   20 Mar 1954
This fine natural line is relatively easy after the first pitch. Just right of the crest of Tough-Brown Ridge, a prominent groove system descends in a direct line to a point immediately below the bend in Raeburn's Gully. Start up a big corner but after 10m, traverse left, then go up and back right to gain its top (or climb it direct, harder). Follow the groove system above to reach the crest about 50m below the plateau.

31 Raeburn's Gully   200m   II ****
G.R.Symmers, A.W.Clark, W.A.Ewen   27 Dec 1932
This classic gully is often very good early in the season when it holds continuous ice and is Grade III, but it fills quickly to leave only one ice pitch at one-third height. There is often a very large cornice which may necessitate a steep traverse left to the top of Tough-Brown Ridge. The gully has a large catchment area, including the corniced rim of the Amphitheatre, and for this reason it is probably more prone to avalanches than any other gully in the corrie.

32 Scarface   170m   V,4 **
D.Stuart, G.S.Strange   12 Feb 1972
This route starts on the right wall of Raeburn's Gully, just above the bend and climbs a shallow depression into the big Amphitheatre. At times, particularly towards the end of the season, or after a long thaw, the depression becomes very icy. Above, the best winter line (with the most ice) is usually the leftmost of three faults above the Amphitheatre.

Black Spout Pinnacle

Alt 900m   North-East facing   Diagrams p267, 277

This region lies between Raeburn's Gully and The Black Spout. The Pinnacle itself, a massive wedge shaped structure, culminates in a true peak which is separated from the plateau by a narrow col. For routes finishing on the summit of the Pinnacle, descend to the col (often abseiled) and continue up the broad crest to the

CAIRNGORMS

plateau. The Pinnacle is demarcated by Pinnacle Gullies 1 and 2, which run up to the col from either side. Pinnacle Gully 1 starts from the Mound, a rock island at the foot of Raeburn's Gully. Around the back of the Pinnacle is Pinnacle Gully 2, an offshoot of the Left Branch of The Black Spout.

33 Pinnacle Gully 1   200m   III *
T.W.Patey, C.Morrison   27 Jan 1951
This gully leading from the Mound to the col behind the Pinnacle is an interesting expedition and a safe choice in powder snow. Only the final section up to the col shows true gully formation and lower down the climb follows a diagonal fault which leads towards the Amphitheatre. Start up the gully to the right of the Mound and continue up the left-slanting chimney below a prominent overhanging wall to a cave. Turn this on the left and return right by a rock crevasse above the cave. Continue more easily up the open upper gully to the col, a fine knife edge of snow. Easy mixed climbing up the ridge on the left leads to the plateau.

34 Grovel Wall   200m   V,6 *
M.Freeman, A.Nisbet   5 Feb 1977
A fairly direct line from the Mound to the summit of the Pinnacle. In lean conditions it gives a technical mixed climb, but it can become a grade easier with a big build-up. From the left edge of the Mound, climb diagonally right for 20m, then cut back left and go straight up to a short overhanging wall. Avoid this on the right, and climb a line of grooves and shallow chimneys parallel to Pinnacle Gully 1 to reach the top of the Pinnacle.

35 Pinnacle Face   250m   VI,7 ***
K.A.Grassick, J.Light, A.G.Nicol   16 Jan 1966 (3PA); FFA to plateau: D.Dinwoodie, A.McIvor   1974
A demanding climb of great quality and one of the most sought after winter routes on the mountain. It covers a fair area of The Pinnacle's lower slabs but only to take the easiest line, which is not always obvious. It is best when icy, but it will still have some short technical sections although the line will be open to more variation. Occasionally it is very icy and then much easier; in these conditions a direct line up the pinnacle should be possible. Start at the base of The Black Spout on the left wall where there is an obvious 10m V-groove.
1. 35m Climb the groove, then traverse left into a parallel line which leads past a shallow chimney and cracks (or climb the parallel line throughout).
2. 25m Continue for a few metres to a corner and pull onto the right-hand slab. Work left up a slabby fault to a large grass stance.
3. etc. Climb turfy corners to a steep wall, traverse right and pass the wall's right end into a groove which leads to Route 1. Follow this to the top.

36 Pinnacle Grooves   70m   VI,7 **
A.Nisbet, S.Kennedy, M.McLeod   17 Mar 1980 (1NA); FFA: S.M.Richardson, J.Ashbridge   23 Jan 1993
An excellent short route, following a direct line of grooves starting from the foot of Pinnacle Face and ending at easy ground on Route 1 just above and left of the Springboard. With more ice in the corner the climbing is easier, but the protection is poorer. Climb the right-hand starting groove of Pinnacle Face. At its top, move right then go left and up to a large down-pointing flake. Layback up its left side and step into a smooth groove on the left (crux). Climb the groove to a ledge on the right (45m). Step left, then go up for about 10m until a series of ledges leads right to easier ground above the Springboard. From here, either abseil off, or continue up Route 1 to the summit of the Pinnacle.

37 Route 1   200m   V,6 **
J.Smith, W.D.Brooker   11 Mar 1956 (1PA)
A classic mixed route with continuously interesting climbing and spectacular positions. The first pitch is the technical crux, but careful route finding is required to find the easiest way above. Start in The Black Spout just beyond the vertical

277

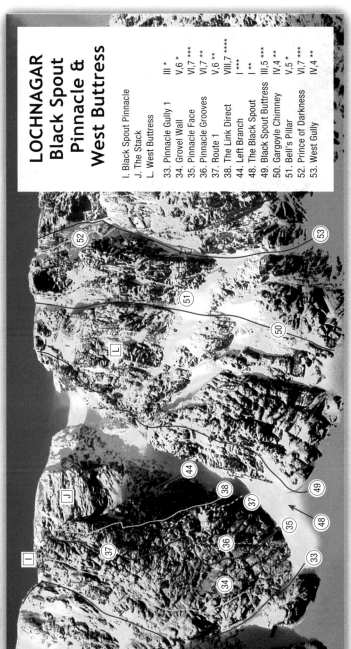

LOCHNAGAR
Black Spout Pinnacle & West Buttress

I. Black Spout Pinnacle
J. The Stack
L. West Buttress

33. Pinnacle Gully 1   III *
34. Grovel Wall   V,6 *
35. Pinnacle Face   VI,7 ***
36. Pinnacle Grooves   VI,7 **
37. Route 1   V,6 **
38. The Link Direct   VIII,7 ****
44. Left Branch   I ***
48. The Black Spout   I **
49. Black Spout Buttress   III,5 ***
50. Gargoyle Chimney   IV,4 **
51. Bell's Pillar   V,5 *
52. Prince of Darkness   VI,7 ***
53. West Gully   IV,4 **

CAIRNGORMS

The Link Direct, VIII,7. Climber Chris Cartwright

groove of Epitome that cuts through the steep smooth wall below the Springboard. Climb a prominent slabby ramp passing an overlap (hard when no ice is present), then traverse left soon above the overlap and gain the Springboard via a short difficult wall. Move up the ledges above (the central fault of Epitome), then traverse left into the left-hand fault and follow it to the front face. From here it is possible to continue left, but it is better to go up and right using a big flake to gain the crest at a point overlooking the fork in The Black Spout. Continue up a wall and the arete above to the summit of the Pinnacle.

38 The Link Direct   180m   VIII,7 ****
S.M.Richardson, C.Cartwright   1 Feb 1998
This outstanding mixed climb is one of the finest winter routes on the mountain. It follows a direct and natural line with continually varied climbing in a superb position. The first six pitches are very sustained and the route requires an efficient approach, but overall the route is low in the grade. Start in the snow bay just right of Route 1 below a steep vegetated groove.
1. 30m Start up steep parallel cracks and continue up and left over steep slabs to reach a stance on the rib 20m above the Springboard.
2. 20m Step left into a groove and climb it to below a prominent triangular overhang. Move up and right round a huge block to a small recess under an overhang.
3. 25m Climb the overhang to reach a big vegetated groove. Climb this for 15m to a good stance on the left.
4. 15m Continue up the groove for 5m to the junction with Route 2. Reverse the crux of Route 2 by stepping down and right, and move up to the groove running through the headwall.
5. 20m Climb the groove, past a rotating block, to a good stance.
6. 10m Pull over the roof (technical crux) directly above the stance.
7. and 8. 60m Move up to join Route 1, and follow this to the summit of the Pinnacle.

Above the fork in Black Spout, a broad sloping grass ledge cuts back left into the right side of the wall overlooking the Spout. Three routes start from this ledge, which all lead to the summit of the Pinnacle. Route 2 goes out left up the prominent chimney-crack from the bottom left end of the ledge. The huge corner of The Ice Ox runs up left from the top of the ledge to the crest of the Pinnacle. Left of this is the parallel corner of **Solstice** (100m VI,6) that ends in a short steep wall. Twin Chimneys Route takes the narrow deep chimney cutting into the well defined buttress on the right. Although short, these routes lie high on the mountain and come into condition early in the season.

39 Route 2   130m   VI,6 **

J.R.Marshall, J.Stenhouse   Feb 1962

A serious climb with magnificent situations. Start from the bottom left end of the broad sloping ledge. The chimney-crack often contains ice and may be quite straightforward, but the traverse will always be hard and sustained.

1. 35m Climb the prominent chimney-crack slanting left to finish at a little ridge projecting from the steep gable wall.

2. 25m Descend vegetated ledges left for 5m, then make a long traverse left into the middle of a big groove. Climb the groove to large ledges.

3. and 4. 70m Easy climbing leads to Route 1 and the summit of the Pinnacle.

40 The Ice Ox   100m   IV,5 *

G.Livingston, A.Mathieson   24 Dec 1984

A good early season route up the big corner starting from the fork in The Black Spout and leading to the summit of the Pinnacle.

41 Twin Chimneys Route   100m   IV,5 **

T.W.Patey, W.D.Brooker, C.M.Dixon   Apr 1961

An impressively steep line. Start as for The Ice Ox, but continue straight up via the obvious chimney system that bites into the rib on the right. Follow the rib more easily to the top of the Pinnacle.

42 Reiver's Buttress   80m   III,5 *

S.M.Richardson, R.G.Webb   18 Dec 1994

The prominent buttress just left of Pinnacle Gully 2 provides a worthwhile little climb that is often in condition.

1. 50m Follow turfy grooves on the right side of the buttress for 30m, then trend left up easier ground to a stance.

2. 30m Continue up the right edge of the buttress to a fine technical finish up the rounded arete overlooking the col at the top of Pinnacle Gully 2.

43 The Pinnacle via Pinnacle Gully 2   150m   II *

A.W.Clark, W.A.Ewen   28 Dec 1932

This good short route starts high up The Black Spout, Left Branch and leads to the col behind the Pinnacle, and provides an entertaining day out with some tricky manoeuvres. At peak conditions the gully is often a straight snow chute, but if conditions are lean, two chokestones will provide difficulties and the route can be Grade III,4. The chokestones are best taken on the left wall, although the second one has a through route. To gain the Pinnacle from the col, descend a little way on the other side then climb a crack trending right, go round a corner, and climb slabs to the top. Return to the col (possibly by abseil), and continue up the plateau by a long but easy pitch.

44 The Black Spout, Left Branch   250m   I ***

J.H.Gibson, W.Douglas   12 Mar 1893

This deep snow gully branches from The Black Spout at mid-height, and is hidden from the corrie floor. In summer, the only pitch, situated not far above the fork, is a huge chokestone with a small time honoured through route. The chokestone soon becomes buried, but at the start of the winter before the through route becomes blocked and the boulder remains uncovered, the pitch presents an interesting problem.

The Stack

Alt 1000m   North-East facing   Diagram p267

The bold steep sided buttress nestling between the two branches of The Black Spout. Its exposed position near the top of the mountain means it ices up early in the season, but later in the winter it can build-up huge quantities of unconsolidated snow and layers of deep hoar frost. The described routes tend to come into condition with first snows.

45 Crumbling Cranny   60m   II *
M.Inglis Clark, W.Hunter, H.Alexander   21 Dec 1913
The wide chimney cutting into the right wall of The Black Spout, Left Branch, almost opposite Pinnacle Gully 2, provides a short and surprisingly popular snow gully. The huge cornice often requires tunnelling, although it can be avoided by a harder variation to the right.

46 Sour Grapes   50m   V,7 *
S.M.Richardson, R.G.Webb   18 Dec 1994
The chimney and hanging corner on the right wall of Crumbling Cranny. A worthwhile mixed route, short but technical.
1. 25m Climb the right-slanting chimney to a good ledge of perched blocks.
2. 25m Step left into the corner. Pull over a bulge (crux), and continue directly to the top. An excellent pitch.

47 The Stack   150m   V,6 **
J.M.Taylor, G.B.Leslie, T.L.Fallowfield   29 Nov 1952 (1PA)
The line of chimneys high on the face overlooking The Black Spout, Left Branch gives an excellent route in a fine position. It is one of the first routes to come into condition in the corrie, but lying close to the plateau it rimes heavily and this can lead to considerable amounts of ice, producing very variable conditions. Start just below the chokestone in The Black Spout, Left Branch. Climb cracks in a slab leading to a steep wall 20m up on the right. Climb the wall by a strenuous corner, then step off a block and keep moving right to reach a large grass platform. An alternative start is by an icefall which forms to the left. Scramble left to the base of an obvious chimney blocked by jammed boulders. From a few metres up the chimney, move left and follow a narrow ledge provided with a continuous handrail downwards for 10m. Return to the right by two short cracks to an alcove above the jammed boulders. Follow the chimney directly ahead for a further 10m to a large bollard. Step boldly off this onto a sloping shelf on the right, then climb a short wall to a grass platform. Move left and climb slabs and walls leftwards to the plateau.

48 The Black Spout   250m   I **
The great corridor separating the main face from West Buttress provides a straightforward snow slope and the easiest way between the plateau and corrie floor. The cornice should always be possible on the right.

West Buttress

Alt 900m   East facing   Diagrams p267, 277

This is the buttress which lies to the right of The Black Spout. Its left edge is Black Spout Buttress and the deep West Gully is towards the right side. Between these features the lower face is indeterminate up to a Mid-way Terrace. Winter conditions on West Buttress are variable, as it catches the sun in the second half of the season and the buttress routes are often stripped of snow.

49 Black Spout Buttress   250m   III,5 ***
J.Tewnion, C.Hutcheon, D.A.Sutherland, K.Winram   9 Jan 1949

A good winter route which follows the buttress on the right of The Black Spout. It comes into condition early in the season, is a good choice under powder and has several technical but very short sections. Start at a chimney fault at the top of a grass slope about 10m right of The Black Spout. Climb this and continue to a level arete at half-height. Above the arete, a ridge of piled blocks leads to a deceptively difficult short chimney. Easy climbing leads to a 5m wall (crux), which is started in the centre and finished by an awkward corner on the right. Outflank a 10m wall by making a peculiar traverse right into the head of a flanking gully and return left to the crest as soon as practicable, usually just below the plateau.

50 Gargoyle Chimney   120m   IV,4 **
J.M.Taylor, W.D.Brooker   20 Jan 1952
The prominent thin chimney in the centre of the face is the best winter line on the upper tier above the Mid-way Terrace. Gain the Terrace by an easy shallow gully. The well defined lower chimney can provide an excellent pitch of up to 30m of ice. Above this, go up and left on snow to a steep finish and sometimes a difficult cornice.

51 Bell's Pillar   120m   V,5 *
G.S.Strange, B.S.Findlay   25 Oct 1992
The well defined rib right of Gargoyle Chimney. Start just right of Gargoyle Chimney and climb a shallow left-facing corner until it is possible to swing right to the crest. Follow this until under the smooth square Radar Wall, then skirt left and finish up the fault just right of the final pitch of Gargoyle Chimney.

52 Prince of Darkness   70m   VI,7 ***
S.M.Richardson, C.Cartwright   20 Dec 1998
This superb mixed climb takes the steep front face of the imposing tower that rises from the upper reaches of West Gully. Start by climbing West Gully to the foot of the tower.
1. 25m Climb a turf ramp up and left for 5m to a ledge. Move right along a flake to reach a niche, climb the wall above to reach a second niche, then step right around the arete to reach a hanging groove. Climb this to a good stance below the prominent right-facing corner which runs up the right side of the tower.
2. 25m The corner leads to a good platform. A superb pitch.
3. 20m Steep cracks lead through the headwall to the top of the tower. Another excellent pitch in an exposed situation.

53 West Gully   250m   IV,4 **
P.McIntyre, A.Nash   21 Mar 1948; Direct: A.F.Fyffe, M.D.Y.Mowat   4 Apr 1966
The prominent gully on the right side of the cliff. The lower section soon ices up and provides an excellent ice pitch. The upper gully, although impressive, is relatively straightforward. The final chimney to the plateau may be difficult if taken direct and the blocks are uncovered. The left branch is easier.

DUBH LOCH CLIFFS

The Dubh Loch is set in a high secluded valley between the extensive White Mounth plateau of Lochnagar to the north and the cone topped plateau of Broad Cairn to the south. Creag an Dubh Loch is the huge Broad Cairn precipice guarding the loch. The Dubh Loch is a lonely and intimidating place in winter, when the cliffs take on an impressive scale. But a visit will be memorable even if the easier option of a route on Eagles Rock is chosen.

BROAD CAIRN BLUFFS

The bluffs come into view on the left about 1km before the Dubh Loch on the approach from Loch Muick (see p282).

Funeral Fall   50m   IV,4 *
M.Freeman, N.D.Keir   3 Mar 1974

This is a very prominent icefall on the left wall of an easy angled snow gully, best seen when descending from the loch. It is a good climb for a short day, bad weather or change of plan, and also a good indicator of conditions on Creag an Dubh Loch. If it looks icy, hurry onward!

CREAG AN DUBH LOCH

(NO 235 825)   Alt 730m   North-East facing   Map p263   Diagram p284

At more than 1km in length and 300m in vertical height, this is the biggest cliff in the Cairngorms.

Weather and Conditions: In prime conditions Creag an Dubh Loch is one of the best and iciest in the Cairngorms, but it is less frequently in condition than the higher cliffs (like Lochnagar). Prediction of prime conditions has perplexed even the closest observers, but there are some reliable routes. Normally a long cold spell early in the season suggests good conditions. But a spell of very cold weather can freeze the springs at source while even a day's thaw can strip the cliffs bare. Deep powder in the valley is usually an indicator of poor conditions. An attempt has been made to choose the routes most liable to be icy, particularly the Hanging Garden area because ice also forms here later in the season, after heavy snow followed by thawing and freezing. The cliff is often a windy place, with less shelter than you might expect. The absence of big snow slopes means that avalanches are rarely a problem.

Approach: Drive to the Spittal of Glen Muick car park as for Lochnagar (Pay and Display parking fee). Walk past the visitor centre, ignore the Lochnagar turn off and continue on towards the south-east side of Loch Muick. Ignore the left fork to Glen Clova via the Capel Mount path. Just before the loch, a small path leaves the road on the right and follows the shore across the valley. Cross the bridge and gain the road which follows the north-west shore of Loch Muick to Glas Allt Shiel. From the head of the loch, continue up a good path to the Dubh Loch, which has a small path on either side. 2hrs 30mins in good conditions. Sometimes it is possible to cycle just past Glas Allt Shiel; this saves about 30mins.

Descent: There are easy descents at either end of the cliff, or more steeply by Central Gully.

Layout: The cliff is split into two main sections by Central Gully, a very easy Grade I which provides access up and down. At the left-hand end is South-East Gully. Above and right of it, under the plateau, is the very steep Broad Terrace Wall. In the centre of this left section is the Hanging Garden, with several ice lines leading out above it. Between here and Central Gully are the long and smooth Central Slabs. Beyond Central Gully is the big slab face of the Central Gully Wall, facing the top end of the loch. Its top right extension is the steep tilting False Gully Wall which forms the left flank of the broken North-West Buttress curving round to the right and out of sight. North-West Gully is tucked in here.

1 South-East Gully   200m   II **
W.A.Russell, M.Smith, W.Stephen   26 Jan 1947

The left-slanting gully near the left end of the cliff is overhung by steep walls on the right. A popular climb, and sometimes the only one in condition on the cliff. It is Grade I in full conditions, when an ice pitch near the bottom banks out in mid-season leaving a steeper section.

The area above the Hanging Garden provides reliable ice climbing, some of the best Grade V routes in the Cairngorms and a 'White Spider' atmosphere. Generally there is continuous ice, steep but less than vertical, but ice screws are required as rock cracks are limited. Start near the foot of South-East Gully and zigzag up to the left end of Broad Terrace, which is the snowy promenade under the steepest section

Vertigo Wall, VII,7. Climber Rob Goodyear

Guy Robertson

of wall. Traverse along the Terrace and enter the Hanging Garden. This is intricate Grade II so retreat would be difficult. A better and more direct approach in good conditions is the lower half of Labyrinth Direct (Grade III).

2 Bower Buttress   150m   V,5 **

J.Bower, G.R.Simpson   Mar 1970

The buttress which forms the border between the right edge of the vertical Broad Terrace Wall and the left wall of the Hanging Garden area is good when icy, but it also provides a mixed option if the ice routes further right are out of condition. Starting from the Hanging Garden, climb grooves slanting left to a big ledge, the Gallery. Follow ice choked cracks trending slightly right to enter a shallow gully which leads to snow slopes under the cornice (avoided on the left). A harder line further left can be taken in good conditions above the Gallery.

3 Yeti   140m   V,4 **

R.A.Smith, J.Moreland   Feb 1975

Between Bower Buttress and the prominent gully of Hanging Garden Route is an impressive set of slabby ramps. These can become sheathed in ice providing an exposed serious route, sustained but not steep for the grade. In the lower section the icefall may split in two; either branch can be climbed. It is hard to predict which of Yeti and Hanging Garden Route will be in better condition; they certainly vary, so choose the better looking line.

4 Hanging Garden Route (Left Fork)   150m   V,4 ***

A.Nisbet, A.Robertson   6 Jan 1977

This is usually the first of the steeper ice routes to come into condition. It has a steeper section than Yeti but is less sustained. Follow the gully at the top of the Hanging Garden to an imposing triangular buttress which splits the route into its two forks. Continue up the groove until a steep wall forces a left traverse across an exposed iced slab to a difficult cornice. Occasionally, the cornice will force a traverse to Bower Buttress to finish. The right fork is often easier but with cornice problems.

CAIRNGORMS

CREAG AN DUBH LOCH

1. South-East Gully   II **
2. Bower Buttress   V,5 **
3. Hanging Garden Route   V,4 ***
4. Labyrinth Direct   VII,6 ****
5. Labyrinth Edge   IV,5 *
6. The White Elephant   VII,6 **
7. Theseus Grooves   III *
8. Central Gully Buttress   II
9. Central Gully   I **
10. Sabre Cut   IV,5 *
11.
12. Vertigo Wall   VII,7 ****
13. False Gully   VI,7 *
14. North-West Gully   II **

A. Hanging Garden
a. approach to Hanging Garden

5 Labyrinth Direct   300m   VII,6 ****
A.J.Bolton, P.Arnold   11 Mar 1972
An amazingly steep climb for the early days of front pointing, before wrist loops!
It is one of the most sought after ice clinbs in the Cairngorms and probably in
condition most winters, but not for long. The lower couloir (easy snow after an
initial ice pitch) leads into the right edge of the Hanging Garden. The continuation
is all too obvious, following a steep and poorly protected groove to a good belay
on the right side of the cul de sac (if rock is visible). About 10m of near vertical
and perhaps thin ice (crux) leads up the left wall. A steep groove continues for
another 30m before the angle eases for the last 40m to the plateau. Perhaps not
too hard for the grade, but the route has a serious feel.

6 Labyrinth Edge   300m   IV,5 *
W.D.Brooker, D.Duncan   10 Feb 1959
This route takes the vegetated left edge of the Central Slabs, not far right of
Labyrinth Direct. It is a long route with increasing difficulty but it is possible in
most conditions, although the chosen line may vary. Start up the grassy right bank
of the Labyrinth Couloir (the Direct). Soon trend right, then climb grassy grooves
to emerge below the left side of the upper tier of slabs (Sea of Slabs). Climb
straight up these by a ribbon of grass choked cracks and move left towards the
'Lower Tower', bypassed on the right. Continue up to 'The Fang', a rock tooth
turned on the edge overlooking Labyrinth Direct. The 'Upper Tower' lies above,
and is passed on the right by a hidden chimney (crux). The finish is easier.

7 The White Elephant   300m   VII,6 **
*N.D.Keir, D.Wright   Feb 1975 (Lower Tier); J.Anderson, A.Nisbet   31 Mar 1979 (Upper
Tier); Complete Ascent: R.Anderson, R.Milne   12 Jan 1980*
A magnificent route taking a thin icefall emanating from the big left-curving groove
about 60m right of the upper section of Labyrinth Edge. Unfortunately the lower
tier is reluctant to form and will be thin at best. The upper tier can be gained by
Labyrinth Edge (Grade III to here) and climbed alone; this option is as good as the
Hanging Garden routes and at a similar grade (V.4). The lower tier is a continuation,
flowing down a shallow gully (Dinosaur Gully) and hopefully over big overlaps
near the base. In ideal conditions the grade is VI,5.

8 Theseus Grooves   300m   III *
J.T.Campbell, B.S.Findlay; G.R.Simpson, G.S.Strange   12 Jan 1969
Starting at the right end of the lowest rocks of the Central Slabs is a line of grassy
grooves and snow basins which trend right onto Central Gully Buttress. The first 10m
is slabby but in good conditions it ices up or banks out. The rest is a fine narrow ice
runnel or tedious wading in deep ferns (select one). There is minimal rock protection.

9 Central Gully Buttress   300m   II
T.W.Patey   Mar 1955
The easy angled ridge bordering the left side of Central Gully. The crest is
straightforward but the first pitch, starting at the base of Central Gully, will be
tricky unless there is a good build-up.

Central Gully   300m   I **
Miss McHardy, Miss Stewart   Feb 1933
This is the corridor running through the cliff, remarkable for its scale and
spectacular right wall. It is low angled for the grade and the cornice is usually
avoidable on the left.

Sabre Cut   80m   IV,5 *
T.W.Patey, F.R.Malcolm   13 Jan 1957
On the right wall at the top of Central Gully is a short but very steep section arrayed
with sharp hanging aretes. Below this and separating it from the main wall is a fault
which fills with ice. Short and sharp.

CAIRNGORMS

12 Vertigo Wall   160m   VII,7 ****

A.Nisbet, A.Robertson   3-4 Dec 1977 (8PA); FFA: A.Cunningham, A.Nisbet   Nov 1985

A candidate for Scotland's best winter route taking a stunningly exposed line out of Central Gully. With difficulties on ice, turf and rock, this is a genuine mixed climb, although only the third pitch requires ice and it usually holds enough. In the second half of the season the top wall receives sun and is stripped of snow. The route takes the huge recessed scoop below Sabre Cut. Start up from the true direct line where a grassy shelf leads right onto the face.

1. 30m Traverse right onto the face and climb a turfy corner, then go up to a platform.
2. 35m Move up right onto a big detached block, then go right and back left to gain a short hard section leading to stepped slabs leading up right to a belay beside a chimney icefall in the main corner-line.
3. 30m Climb the icefall until a line leads out right away from the steepest section. Return left above it and below a steep rock wall.
4. 25m Climb the slab on the left to the impending headwall. Traverse right beyond a creaking flake into a shallow corner. Climb this steeply, traverse right again and pull up to belay.
5. 40m The finish is easier but still steep.

13 False Gully   200m   VI,7 *

K.Grassick, W.James, J.M.Taylor   19 Dec 1964 (1 point tension); R.McHardy, A.Nisbet Mar 1978 (Ice Finish); Direct Finish, as described: S.M.Richardson, J.Ashbridge   4 Mar 1995

The dwindling ramp defining the bottom left edge of False Gully Wall provides an interesting and unusual winter route. The crux is spectacularly situated right at the top of the route, with the full height of Central Gully Wall dropping below. Follow the fault easily for several pitches until it peters out into a ledge. Continue by a prominent shallow chimney above, exiting left at the top (25m). Move left into a left-facing corner and climb its steep left wall to easier ground (35m). The original ascent tensioned to the chimney's left arete (V,5), and a later ascent continued left on ice from the ledge below the chimney but was forced to use tension (V,4).

14 North-West Gully   200m   II **

T.W.Patey, W.D.Brooker; J.M.Taylor, J.W.Morgan   29 Dec 1952

The obvious gully towards the right end of the cliff has a steep right wall, ice at the start and finish, but it is never steep. It is almost always climbable, but in lean conditions it is Grade III.

EAGLES ROCK

(NO 235 835)   Alt 770m   South facing   Map p263

These slabby rocks form a long discontinuous band of cliff on the White Mounth escarpment, opposite Creag an Dubh Loch.

Weather and Conditions: The summer drainage lines ice up readily, so no snow is required. The routes face south so they are at their best early in the season after hard frosts; later on they can bank out and by late season they have melted. They provide a good alternative to the big cliff on the other side of the loch, when ice or energy levels are low.

Layout: The most obvious feature is a big waterfall away to the left. Green Gully separates the Waterfall area from the rest of the crag. The Mid-West Buttress is the left-hand and largest of two zones of rock while the Mid-East Buttress is roughly triangular in shape and bounded by Diagonal Gully on the right. The smooth plaque of the Likely Story Slab is low down to the right of Diagonal Gully while the Plateau Buttress is high on the right and contains a prominent short icefall, **The Drool** (IV,4).

Approach and Descent: Approach as for Creag an Dubh Loch. Descent is either well left of the Waterfall (easy), down Green Gully (usually easy Grade II) or, particularly for the Mid-East Buttress, down Diagonal Gully (Grade I).

1 The Waterfall   150m   II *
N.D.Keir, J.Taylor   2 Jan 1974
Continuous low angled ice forms to the left of the flow of water (only occasionally does it freeze completely). Escapes are available to the left.

2 Spectrum   110m   III **
D.Dinwoodie, J.Mothersele   1 Dec 1971
Climb the obvious line of corners and grooves right of the Waterfall and immediately right of black overhanging walls. The route is distinguished by the big groove near the top which gives a fine finish to a sustained climb on continuous water ice (or finish more easily to the right).

3 Lethargy   120m   III *
J.Bower, G.R.Simpson   3 Jan 1970
This is the obvious corner on the left of Mid-West Buttress. It has been graded for when it forms a continuous ribbon of ice early in the season, but it tends to bank out later. The Green Gully descent is immediately on the left. The Direct Finish (IV,5) is the prominent steep icefall above the corner.

4 Indolence   140m   III *
A.Nisbet, A.Robertson   12 Dec 1976
The first groove line right of Lethargy forms a fine icefall, the best part of which does not bank out. Very early in the season, a good combination is the first pitch of Lethargy, an easy right traverse and the upper icefall of Indolence.

5 Sliver   150m   III *
R.J.Archbold, G.S.Strange   15 Dec 1974
A fairly continuous line of water ice forms reliably between the Mid-East and Mid-West Buttresses.

Three icefalls can form on Mid-East Buttress. **Gibber** (150m IV,3) forms in an L shaped corner, **Whisper** (150m IV,3) just to its right and **Shiver** (150m III) on the right edge of the buttress.

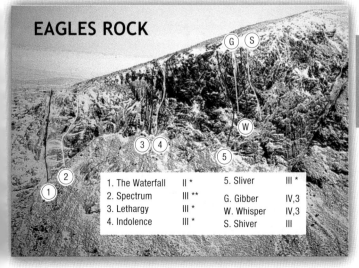

EAGLES ROCK

1. The Waterfall	II *	5. Sliver	III *
2. Spectrum	III **	G. Gibber	IV,3
3. Lethargy	III *	W. Whisper	IV,3
4. Indolence	III *	S. Shiver	III

CAIRNGORMS

GLEN CLOVA

Glen Clova provides easily accessible, good winter climbing, particularly in the lower grades. Although the drive from the north and the west is long, it is a good option when conditions are poor in the higher Cairngorms and mild or stormy in the west. The two main corries are the Winter Corrie of Driesh and Corrie Fee, on the north-east flank of Mayar.

WINTER CORRIE

(NO 277 745)   Alt 650m   North-East facing   Map p263

Winter Corrie is the high cupped corrie scooped out of the north-east flank of Driesh and lies on the left side of the glen opposite Braedownie. The conical outlying buttress bounding its right side is known as The Scorrie. The gullies are mainly watercourses, and ice may form here as early as November. The corrie is higher than Corrie Fee, and the routes tend to come into condition more quickly.

Approach: From the car park at Braedownie (Pay and Display parking fee) take the prominent track into Glendoll Forest. After 500m cross the White Water burn at a bridge (NO 279 763) and head back east out of the forest. Skirt the fields on the right and climb diagonally left below the steep rocks of The Scorrie to enter the corrie. As a more direct but less convenient alternative, a bridge still exists at NO 289 751.

Descent: In good conditions, Easy Gully is the simplest descent. Alternatively, contour around the corrie and descend the steep northerly slopes of The Scorrie to join a path that runs alongside Glendoll Forest.

1 The Waterfall   70m   II-III *
The frozen waterfall high up on the left side of the corrie. The easiest line is to climb the inset stepped corner left of the main stream. This forms quickly after a freeze and is one of the first routes in the corrie to come into condition. If the main fall is fully frozen, it is better to start up a V-groove down and right, and follow this up to the main fall.

2 Central Gully   150m   II
The obvious deep gully right of The Waterfall, in the centre of the corrie. The large icefall on the left, where the main gully bends right is Grade III.

3 Easy Gully   150m   I
The prominent straight gully in the centre of the corrie gives a straightforward snow climb and a good approach to the summit of Driesh.

To the right of Easy Gully is the highest section of cliff. The most prominent feature is Diagonal Gully, which cuts centrally through the steep lower section of the face (Main Buttress) and opens out at mid-height into a snow slope known as the Basin.

4 Backdoor Gully   200m   II *
H.G.Drummond, J.A.Parker   2 Jan 1910
This gully cuts deeply behind Main Buttress to emerge at the left side of the Basin. From here, either move left as soon as possible to reach easier ground, or (usually easier) cross the Basin to its top right corner and finish up a gully on the right (near the finish of Diagonal Gully).
Variation: **Direct Finish   80m   IV,4 ***
B.S.Findlay, G.S.Strange   31st January 1988
From the top left side of the Basin climb directly up steep ice to below a deep crack. Traverse right, then go back left to climb the wall right of the crack. Continue slightly right to finish at the apparent summit.

5 Diamond Slab   170m   IV,4 *

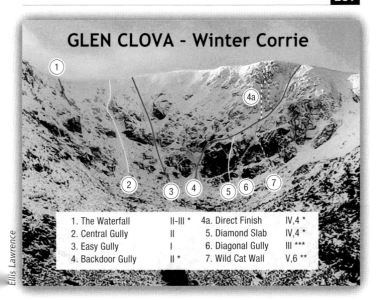

GLEN CLOVA - Winter Corrie

Ellis Lawrence

1. The Waterfall	II-III *	4a. Direct Finish	IV,4 *
2. Central Gully	II	5. Diamond Slab	IV,4 *
3. Easy Gully	I	6. Diagonal Gully	III ***
4. Backdoor Gully	II *	7. Wild Cat Wall	V,6 **

G.R.Simpson and party   1980
A good climb when icy. Climb the chimney and steep slab to the left of Diagonal Gully to the Basin (70m). Finish as for Backdoor Gully, preferably by the Direct Finish, which is most in keeping with the standard of the lower section.

6 Diagonal Gully   200m   III ***
The best climb in the corrie. In the centre of Main Buttress a 30m icefall originates from a right-sloping chimney. Climb the icefall and continue up the chimney to the Basin. From its top right-hand corner, climb an icefall and continue up until forced right to belay at a block. Continue more easily to the top.

7 Wild Cat Wall   180m   V,6 **
C.Cartwright, S.M.Richardson   27 Nov 2005
A direct mixed line up the centre of the cliff. Start 40m right of Diagonal Gully below a hidden left-slanting chimney-ramp.
1. and 2. 80m Climb the gully over a chokestone to the Basin. Move up to the foot of the headwall shaped like an inverted triangle.
3. 40m Gain the headwall steeply from the left, then climb easier ground to the foot of the vertical final wall. Belay below a prominent off-width crack.
4. 20m Climb the off-width and continue up the steep continuation crack to a good ledge below and right of a large sloping roof.
5. 40m Continue up the right of twin corners above and exit on to a left-trending ramp that leads to a long horizontal ledge. A superb pitch.
6. 20m Move right along the dwindling ledge to a break that leads to the top.

CAIRNGORMS

CORRIE FEE

(NO 248 748)   Alt 550m   North-East facing   Map p263   Diagram p290

The magnificent amphitheatre of Corrie Fee is the finest feature in the Glen Clova area for scenery and mountain atmosphere. In cold and snowy conditions, the South Wall gives the most rewarding winter routes in the glen.

Approach: From the car park at Braedownie (Pay and Display parking fee) take the forest track into Glen Doll. Cross the White Water burn at NO 267 758 and

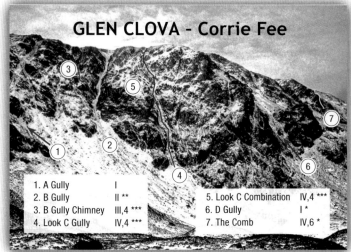

GLEN CLOVA - Corrie Fee

1. A Gully	I
2. B Gully	II **
3. B Gully Chimney	III,4 ***
4. Look C Gully	IV,4 ***

5. Look C Combination	IV,4 ***
6. D Gully	I *
7. The Comb	IV,6 *

Greg Strange

continue west along the track and continuation path to a stile at the edge of the forest at the mouth of the corrie (45mins).

Descent: A and D Gullies are often used for descent. In severe weather or white-out, follow the fence from the top of B Gully Chimney round to the Shank of Drumfollow, then go down the Kilbo path into Glendoll Forest.

Layout: From left to right there are five gullies named A, B, Look C, D and E. All except Look C are deep and well defined.

1 A Gully   200m   I
The gully in the left corner of the corrie provides straightforward snow climbing.

2 B Gully   200m   II **
H.Raeburn, W.Galbraith, W.A.Reid   May 1915
This deeply-cut feature is the best defined of the gullies, and is one of the first routes to come into condition. The gully generally contains at least one ice pitch, although it can be avoided by climbing up and right. The left branch, which takes the obvious deep chimney high up that contains several chokestones, is the recommended route.

3 B Gully Chimney   150m   III,4 ***
D.Crabb, D.F.Lang   29 Dec 1962
An excellent and recommended ice climb, following the chimney that breaks left out of B Gully after 60m. Some pitches bank out under heavy snow. It can be combined with Look C Gully, as described below.

4 Look C Gully   200m   IV,4 ***
C.L.Donaldson, J.R.Marshall   15 Feb 1953
The most sought after winter route in Glen Clova. It takes the steep shallow gully in the left section of Central Buttress. The route is low in the grade, but requires a good freeze to come into condition. Climb the left side up tiered ice to belay above a short chimney. Continue up the left-hand gully line to a basin, then follow the rib on the right to belay below the main icefall. Climb the icefall direct, a classic pitch (35m). Continue up short ice pitches to the gully bifurcation and take the right branch to the top.

5 Look C Combination   250m   IV,4 ***

The upper section of Look C Gully is easy angled and uninteresting. By climbing the left fork from the bifurcation and descending a small gully into B Gully, Look C Gully can be combined with B Gully Chimney to give 250m of excellent and continuous ice climbing.

6 D Gully   200m   I *

A straightforward and well defined snow climb running up the right side of the central buttress.

7 The Comb   60m   IV,6 *

A.Thomson, S.Cameron   January 1986

This attractive climb takes the crest of the small isolated buttress high up on the extreme right side of the face, some 300m left of the waterfall. It is good in lean conditions, with difficulties mainly on rock and being higher than the other climbs, is sometimes the only route in condition. Scramble up broken rocks to a platform at the foot of a short steep wall. Climb the wall to enter a smooth groove which leads to a belay. Go up the corner on the left to gain the crest of the ridge and follow this to a wide gap. Go along a ledge on the slabby eastern face and then climb straight up on good holds. Scramble to the top.

B Gully Chimney, III,4. Climber Pete Trudgill

NORTHERN HIGHLANDS

This huge area of mountains offers a lifetime of exploration, but many folk have yet to start! This guide can only offer a selection of the cliffs with good climbing, as we have preferred to include a range of routes at each described venue. Most of the routes have only been climbed recently and have had few repeats; in fact some are unrepeated. The visitor should savour the atmosphere of exploration, and not simply choose a route and follow it. Consider carefully the choice of venue, methods of approach and descent, and whether there are other routes in better condition.

All styles of climbing and grades are available in the Northern Highlands, although there is rarely a free choice. In terms of conditions, the area should be considered as an average of the rest of Scotland, its northerly position making it less susceptible to thaw than Glen Coe and the south, but due to lower altitude and the proximity of the sea it does not have the resilience of Ben Nevis or the Cairngorms. A January to March season is the average. It can be ideal if you get it right, but with the West Coast unpredictability, you can end up chasing conditions in circles round the area; part of the challenge! At present the chances of finding someone else on your route, apart from the classic mountain traverses, are close to nil.

The chosen cliffs are grouped into four areas, all 1 to 1hr 30mins drive from Inverness, and described proceeding in general from south to north. The many excellent but lower cliffs north of Ullapool have not been included, but they are fully described in the SMC Climbers' Guide to *Northern Highlands North*. The most southerly group is in Glen Shiel, which can be approached from Inverness or Fort William. The next group is based around Glen Carron, the next glen south of Torridon, and composed of Fuar Tholl and Sgòrr Ruadh, with the Applecross hills as another group to the west. Fuar Tholl and Beinn Bhàn (Applecross) form big ice routes but require cold weather; Sgòrr Ruadh is more varied and less fussy. The Torridon hills are to the north; Beinn Alligin, Liathach and Beinn Eighe are well known and the climbing here is gaining a reputation. The sandstone of Beinn Alligin and Liathach provides big icefalls and gullies while the quartzite of Beinn Eighe has the modern mixed style of torquing and hooking. A drive from Inverness towards Ullapool provides the Fannaichs, Beinn Dearg and An Teallach. These offer a wide range of routes, are further away from a mild sea but involve more committing approaches if the weather is doubtful.

Maps: Glen Shiel – OS L33, E414; Harvey Kintail & Glen Shiel; Glen Carron – OS L25, E429; Applecross – OS L24, E428; Torridon – OS L19, 24, 25, E433; Harvey Torridon; Beinn Dearg, The Fannaichs – OS L20, E436; An Teallach – OS L20, E435.

SMC Climbers' Guides: *Northern Highlands South* (2007) covers Torridon to Glen Shiel. *Northern Highlands Central* (2005) covers An Teallach & The Fannaichs. *Northern Highlands North* (2004) covers Beinn Dearg.

Public Transport: Limited and not recommended for this area, although access to Inverness and on to Ullapool is simple enough. See <www.traveline.org uk>.

Accommodation: Many B&Bs and some hotels in this area are closed in the winter, as are the SYHA Youth Hostels <www.syha.org.uk>. The best source of information is all year Tourist Office, either Strathpeffer (01997 421160) or Inverness (01463 234353).

Independent Hostels: <www.hostel-scotland.co.uk>. The following are open all year; Gerry's Achnasheallach Hostel (01520 766232); Kinlochewe Hotel bunkhouse (01445 760253); Sail Mhor Croft (Camusnagaul, NH 064 893, 01854 633224); Badrallach Bothy (01854 633281); Ullapool Tourist Hostel (01854 613126).

Climbing Hut: Ling Hut (Scottish Mountaineering Club) in Torridon, at NG 958 562.

Amenities: Most shops are open in the winter (often 9am to 5pm). Petrol is more expensive north of Inverness, so it is best to fill up there and there are at least three 24hr stations. Most stations beyond Inverness only operate 8am to 6pm Monday to Saturday at best (some 9am to 5pm), although Inverinate (Loch Duich) and Contin are open 7 days until 8pm, Ullapool also until 8pm but only 6pm on Sunday.

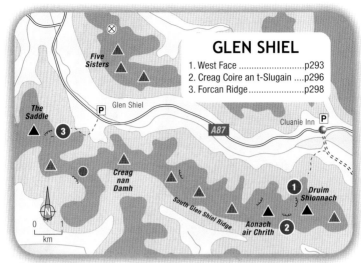

Glen Shiel

The South Glen Shiel Ridge links Creag a' Mhaim (NH 088 077) on the east to Creag nan Damh (NG 983 112) on the west. It includes seven Munros and is a classic hill walking expedition. The fine looking Coire an t-Slugain lies on the north side of the ridge between Druim Shionnach and Aonach air Chrith, towards the east end of the main ridge. The corrie has two main crags, the West Face of Druim Shionnach in the south-east corner of the corrie and Creag Coire an t-Slugain, facing the road from the back of the corrie. Beyond the seven Munros, the ridge continues past a Corbett, Sgùrr a' Bhac Chaolais to another Munro, Sgùrr na Sgine to finish on the complex mountain of The Saddle, with its renowned Forcan Ridge.

DRUIM SHIONNACH

(NH 074 085)   Alt 987m   Map p293

WEST FACE

(NH 069 084)   Alt 860m   West facing   Map p293   Diagram p294

This accessible crag is clearly seen from the road further down Glen Shiel but hidden on the approach. The routes are short but exciting as the helpful strata allows steep climbing. A winter venue offering turfy mixed climbing which varies unexpectedly between poorly protected slabs and the most helpful cracked ground.

Approach: Start just east of the Cluanie Inn and cross the loch by the old road. Take a stalking path on the right to reach the north ridge of Druim Shionnach. Follow the ridge, then move right along unusual small ridges before making a descending traverse in to the base of the cliff, 2hrs.

Descent: Descend easily northwards from cliff or summit (10mins away) to gain the north ridge of Druim Shionnach and reverse the approach.

The dominant feature of the crag is the large central and aptly named Cave Gully while the Silver Slab is the second buttress left. Routes are described right to left.

1 Poems   90m   III
A.Nisbet, J.Preston   17 Mar 2006
An ice line which crosses a diagonal ramp which runs up rightwards from neat the

DRUIM SHIONNACH - West Face

1. Poems — III
2. Bow Peep — V,6 **
3. Cave Gully — IV,4 **

4. Boxer's Buttress — IV,4 *
5. Capped Gully — II
6. Silver Corner — V,5 **

7. Silver Edge — IV,5 *
8. Silver Slab — VI,7 **
9. Deceptive Chimney — III *

base of Cave Gully. Start at a small bay 25m right of an icy groove which feeds from the base of the main ramp. Climb into the bay, out left on ice which forms left of a left-facing corner and up to the ramp. Follow the ramp up to an obvious chimney beyond steep walls. Climb this to the top.

2 Bow Peep   90m   V,6 **
J.Lyall, A.Nisbet   11 Jan 1995
On the face right of the obvious central gully (Cave Gully) is a left-slanting, slightly bow shaped fault finishing up a wide chimney. The fault was climbed throughout, the first pitch being the hardest.

3 Cave Gully   110m   IV,4 **
S.Kekus, A.Nisbet   16 Feb 1994
The prominent central gully, containing a cave. The route is the right corner of the gully, bypassing the cave by a narrow chimney with a steep entry (50m). Straightforward snow to finish.

4 Boxer's Buttress   100m   IV,4 *
A.Nisbet   25 Mar 1995
The snub nosed buttress left of Cave Gully. Two pitches of interesting and sustained mixed climbing up the right side of the buttress, starting from the same bay as Cave Gully but 5m left.
1. 30m Go up left into a shallow weakness and climb it to a huge detached block.
2. 30m Go up left then back right to surmount steep steps and bulges.
3. 40m Easy mixed ground then snow to the top.

5 Capped Gully   110m   II
A.Nisbet, G.Vaughn, M.Webb   20 Feb 1994
A shallow gully next left which tapers to an awkward chimney slot near the top.

Mid-way between Capped Gully and another cave to the left is a silvery slab high up and forming the next buttress, Silver Slab. At the cliff base are two chimneys.

6 Silver Corner   100m   V,5 **
B.Davison, A.Nisbet   24 Jan 1995
A serious first pitch, then a steep but well protected second. Climb the right-hand of the two short chimneys at the base of the buttress. Trend slightly right to flakes below a big right-facing corner (40m). Climb the corner (20m), and continue more easily to the top.

7 Silver Edge   90m   IV,5 *
A.Nisbet, G.Nisbet   24 Dec 1995
A slightly easier route on the Silver Slab, but high in its grade. Start as for Silver Corner up the right-hand chimney to a ledge, then trend left up an apparent line of weakness to finish up a wide and obvious easy trough left of the upper Silver Slab.

8 Silver Slab   100m   VI,7 **
B.Davison, A.Nisbet   14 Mar 1996
Start in the left-hand chimney but pull out steeply on to its right rib before moving back left to its top and joining Silver Edge. Follow this up left to belay (35m). The line is now a fault central to the slab but on the right of the belay. It has a prominent small flake low down and leads up to a crack through a steep smooth girdling wall. Gain the fault by following Silver Edge for a few metres, then traversing right (thin). Climb the fault and a short difficult crack through a bulge (1NA but possible to free) and continue up on flaky ground until a ledge leads out left (45m). Easy to the top (20m).

Deceptive Chimney   70m   III *
S.McKenna, A.Nisbet, I.Stewart   26 Mar 1995
A line of weakness left of Silver Slab buttress and just left of a left cave. Start left

of a lower cave in the fault leading to the main cave. Climb turfy ground up and then right to a narrow chimney hidden on the approach from below. This leads left to easier ground.

CREAG COIRE AN T-SLUGAIN

(NH 060 082)   Alt 850m   North facing   Map p293

The cliff offers largely turfy mixed climbing but collects more snow than Druim Shionnach West Face and later in the season, after thaws and freezes, can hold ice. The snow collection also means a potential avalanche risk, particularly from a snow bowl high up and just left of the crag.

Approach: Park opposite the Allt Coire an t-Slugain; a ruin on its right bank identifies the stream. Cross the main river, wide but shallow so often one can splash across with dry feet, and follow the left bank of the Allt until the angle eases. Go up left and climb the obvious gully in the lower crag band, the first half of Double Gully (easy Grade I); continue up steep snow to the crag base, 2hr.

Descent: It is normal to climb with sacks and make a high level descent. The quickest is to head towards Druim Shionnach, traverse above its West Face and descend easily northwards to gain the north ridge of Druim Shionnach. Return to the Allt Coire an t-Slugain; it is easy to return too early down steep slopes. To make a mountaineering day out, head west to Aonach air Chrith and descend its North Ridge (Grade I). Continue to the furthest point of the ridge and descend right on steep grass to rejoin the approach.

1 Tipperary   140m   III *
J.Ashby, M.Dennis, R.Jarvis, A.Nisbet   1 Feb 1995
Start about 30m right of the left-bounding ridge of the buttress where a ramp leads up left towards the ridge. Climb the ramp to a depression ahead of slabby ground before the ridge (35m). Go up the depression until forced by steep ground to go right, initially traversing, then rising, to reach a flake on a small ridge (35m). Pull over a bulge and move right again to climb the fault on the right (40m). Continue up to finish by the crest of the ridge.

2 Hong Kong   140m   IV,5 **
H.Chan, A.Nisbet   22 Feb 2005
Start right of Tipperary. Gain and climb a fine chimney set in a prominent left-slanting slab-corner. Move left to blocks (45m). Continue left up slabby corners to join Tipperary at its flake on a small ridge. Pull over the bulge but go straight up a groove to an overhung recess (30m). Pass the recess by the rib on the right, then go up left under a steep wall until it is crossed more easily (30m). Follow grooves until the crest of the ridge is joined.

3 Rowaling   135m   V,6 **
A.Clapperton, A.Nisbet   3 Jan 1997
Climbs the most prominent groove towards the left side of the crag, a regular ice forming line. A serious first pitch, which would be much easier with thick ice, followed by a technical second. The groove is right of the slab and wide crack of Hong Kong. Climb the groove to a ledge on the right (45m). Return to the groove, pull over a bulge and climb the next wall by a turfy pull up on the left. The final section of groove may be possible with more ice; otherwise follow a short overhanging chimney on the right to an easier turfy fault, climbed to easier ground (45m). Easier turfy climbing to the top (45m).

4 Rose Garden   120m   IV,4 **
J.Gillman, A.Nisbet, D.Roberts   20 Feb 1997
Climbs an ice line between the deeper grooves of Rowaling and The Furrow. Climbed on continuous ice; perhaps a grade harder if mixed. Start 5m right of Rowaling and climb direct to a barrier wall, taken at its top left corner. Move right

CREAG COIRE AN T-SLUGAIN

1. Tipperary	III *	
2. Hong Kong	IV,5 **	
3. Rowaling	V,6 **	
4. Rose Garden	IV,4 **	
5. The Furrow	IV,6 *	
6. The Ridge Direct	III *	
7. Pioneer Gully	III *	
8. Flaky Ridge	III,4 **	
9. Double Gully	I *	

on to a big inset and usually iced slab above The Furrow and obvious from below (45m). From the top of the slab a short iced rib led into a long groove, the source of the ice. The angle slowly eased (40m, 35m).

5 The Furrow   120m   IV,6 *
P.Foulkes, A.Nisbet   31 Mar 1994 (less direct); As described: A.Mullin, A.Nisbet, J.Preston 3rd December 1997

Another potential ice holding line on the cliff, just left of centre. A shallow trough with a overhung recess, almost a cave, at half-height and immediately left of a blunt ridge with many flakes. Climb directly up and into the recess and out of its back left corner, followed by an immediate traverse right across its lip to rejoin the line to finish. An easier (the original) version is to go right on to the ridge from below the recess and climb it until a ramp leads left to regain the trough immediately above the recess (Grade III overall).

6 The Ridge Direct   130m   III *
J.Ashby, J.Hubbard, A.Nisbet   2 Feb 1997

A fairly continuous line of shallow grooves on the crest of the blunt ridge in the centre of the crag. Start just right of The Furrow and climb a shallow groove trending right to below the more defined section of crest. Climb the flaky crest, then climb the ramp for 10m, common with the original line of The Furrow, after its easy traverse. Break off the ramp through a slot, then move right to a well defined groove in the crest which leads to an easier finish.

7 Pioneer Gully   110m   III *
A.Nisbet, G.Wallace   6 Apr 1993

The first route on the cliff. Andy Nisbet was looking for Aonach air Chrith and went up the wrong valley by mistake in the mist. It was a pleasant surprise to find an unclimbed crag. This is the narrow gully parallel to and 10m left of Double Gully. Low in the grade; Grade II in good conditions.

8 Flaky Ridge   110m   III,4 **
A.Nisbet   25 Mar 1995

The unusual arete of stacked flakes between Pioneer Gully and Double Gully. Start up a groove in its base, then follow the crest as directly as possible. Take many slings for runners and belays.

9 Double Gully   300m   I *

The lower gully and its continuation up the right end of the cliff. Steep at the top, often with a big cornice. Holds snow well in lean conditions.

THE SADDLE

(NG 935 131)   Alt 1010m   Map p293

The shapely mass of The Saddle is west of the main South Glen Shiel Ridge directly across the A87 road from the Five Sisters of Kintail. The best ascent of the mountain is undoubtedly by the east ridge of Sgùrr nan Forcan; the Forcan Ridge. The commonest approach is via an obvious stalker's path leaving the road at NG 968 143. In reasonable snow conditions, and certainly in descent, it is quicker to take a direct line south of Meallan Odhar to the ridge, avoiding the path's deviation to the north.

Forcan Ridge   I/II ***

A classic alpine style ridge. Climb close to the crest (Grade II) or take minor variations just below it if wished (Grade I). The crux is a steep descent, either abseiled down the crest or climbed down on either side. One should expect to use a rope here. The route is usually climbed with one axe, as there are excellent handholds on the steep sections. From the summit of The Saddle, descend to the south-east (beware of avalanches), traverse east under the Forcan Ridge and follow a traversing wall north-east back to the start of the ridge.

Rab Anderson

Forcan Ridge, I/II, The Saddle. Climber Chris Anderson

Glen Carron

This is the next valley system south of Torridon and a major geological fault, with older Torridonian sandstone and Cambrian quartzite to the north and largely Moine rocks to the south. The valley stretches from the sea loch, Loch Carron up towards the major junction of roads at Achnasheen.

SGÙRR NA FEARTAIG

(NH 030 454)   Alt 450-550m   North facing   Map p300   Diagram p301

A Corbett on the south side of Glen Carron, well seen from across the glen from the better known climbing venue of Fuar Tholl, has recently become recognised as a superb venue for waterfall ice in cold weather. The reclusive Coire na h-Eilde is the jewel. The head of the corrie has several waterfalls, even named as such on the OS map.

Weather and Conditions: Very cold weather is required for a full freeze. Below freezing for a few days is necessary.

Approach: There are two options with little difference in time (about 1hr 30mins).

From Lair: By the stalkers' path up the east side of Coire Leiridh. The bridge at NH 011 482 no longer exists. The crossing is wide and shallow when the river is low (dry in Yeti gaiters) but impossible in spate.

From Craig: Cycle upstream and downstream to the Allt Coire a' Bhainidh which is then followed via a stalkers path into the corrie. The path starts as a narrow

NORTHERN HIGHLANDS

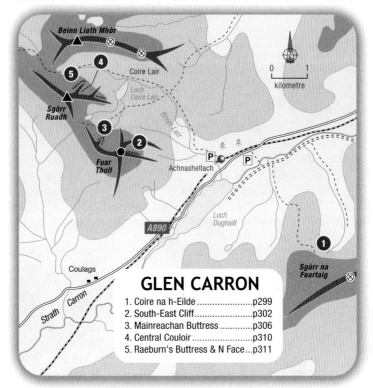

vehicle track which should be left at a wooden post when it heads away from the Allt (only 5mins extra if this turn is missed). The path is not in as good condition as the Coire Leiridh path but saves the descent into the corrie.

Descent: The Coire Leiridh path is easily found above the cliff. For a return to the cliff base and the Allt Coire a' Bhainidh path, there are two options.
1. Scramble down and abseil from a tree near the east end of the icefalls (just west of The Ice Channel).
2. Go to just east of the icefalls and walk steeply down, either just east of The Ice Channel or the next open gully to the east.

Layout: The biggest feature of the face is the main watercourse set in a gully (The Stonker), although a wide steeper icefall to the left is more obvious from the approach col. Either side of the wide fall are thinner falls and leftmost of the set is an ice filled gully. Routes are described right to left.

1 The Stonker   180m   IV,5 ***
J.Lyall, A.Nisbet, M.Welch   3 Feb 1996
The tremendous icefall that forms in the main stream bed right of the more visible icefalls. It drops into a small gorge so its full height is not immediately obvious. It gives four long ice pitches, continuous water ice between 50 and 70 degrees, finishing through some huge ice umbrellas (crux). The first pitch in the gorge may be reluctant to form, particularly after wetter weather, but one can traverse in.

2 The Topper   210m   V,5 **
A.Gorman, D.Williamson, H.Wyllie   4 Jan 1997
The icefall which forms on the left wall of The Stonker recess, gained by climbing

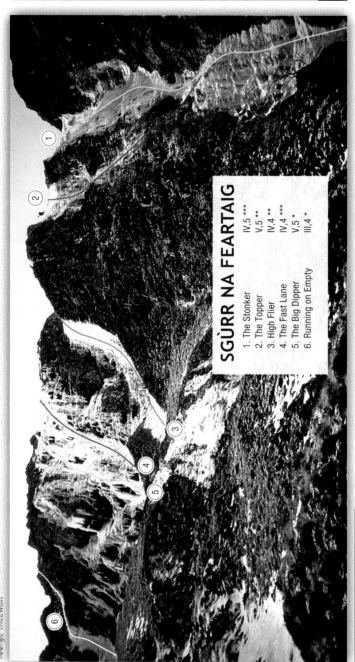

SGÙRR NA FEARTAIG

1. The Stonker	IV,5	***
2. The Topper	V,5	**
3. High Flier	IV,4	**
4. The Fast Lane	IV,4	***
5. The Big Dipper	V,5	*
6. Running on Empty	III,4	*

the first pitch of The Stonker. Steeper and more sustained than The Stonker, with the fourth of five pitches the crux. The amount of ice is variable according to the amount of drainage during freezing (very little ice in Feb 1996, but a lot in 1997). Ice screw belays used throughout.

3 High Flier 110m IV,4 **
M.E.Moran, A.Nisbet 2 Feb 1996
The thinner fall right of the wide fall (The Fast Lane). A low angled initial pitch may bank out (25m). The fall then steepened to below a crest (20m). This was climbed direct (technical 5), but the second ascent took its left side, less steep but more sustained (35m). Then an easier section, followed by a steep finish out left. Initially soloed, ice screw belays used throughout on the second ascent.

4 The Fast Lane 90m IV,4 ***
M.E.Moran, A.Nisbet, G.Nisbet 2 Feb 1996
Very sustained but never vertical up a vague groove towards the right side of the wide fall. Ice screw runners will have to be placed on steep ground.

5 The Big Dipper 90m V,5 *
M.E.Moran, A.Nisbet 2 Feb 1996
Two consecutive pillars on the left side of the wide fall lead to a relatively easier middle section and a capping bulge (led in a 60m pitch). Easy angled to finish.

6 Running on Empty 90m III,4 *
M.E.Moran, A.Nisbet 2 Feb 1996
The left-hand thinner fall has an impressively steep section low down which was passed by 70 degree ice on the left and a short bulge to gain a long easier angled finish.

7 The Ice Channel 80m III *
A.Bull, M.Kinsey, M.Welch 2 Feb 1996
This forms in a left-curving gully as the leftmost main ice line. A steep entry leads to a long runnel of ice.

FUAR THOLL

(NG 975 489) Alt 907m Map p300

This fine mountain on the north side of Glen Carron has two major cliffs with particularly good scope for winter climbing. The major cliffs are the South-East Cliff, which overlooks a small corrie just south-east of the summit, and Mainreachan Buttress, which rises from a north facing corrie and abuts the north-west ridge. The South-East Cliff, visible from the road at Achnashellach, should not be confused with a lower band of crags which line the east face of the mountain.

SOUTH-EAST CLIFF

(NG 978 488) Alt 750m North-East facing Map p300 Diagram p304

This is a typical Torridonian sandstone cliff, steep and hostile, providing tremendous winter climbing. Its steep icefalls have recently gained a good reputation, but there is also hard mixed climbing which is icy in good conditions and two good easier climbs.

Conditions and Weather: The cliff is lower than the Liathach corries so the season is shorter and more susceptible to thaw. It faces the road so conditions can be assessed (weather permitting) from the car, but January and February are most likely to provide good climbing. The corrie is sheltered from winds south-westerly through to northerly and can provide a venue when other cliffs are too stormy. The disadvantage of this is that the corrie collects huge amounts of snow and is prone both to unstable cornices and windslab avalanches. It is a good choice on windy showery days but assess snow conditions carefully.

Approach: The face is best approached from the south-east via the small plateau named Sgùrr a' Mhuilinn on the OS 1:50000 map. Obtaining this point from Achnashellach Station is problematical, as the River Lair is difficult and possibly dangerous to ford and the only bridge over the river carries the railway, along which there is no legal right of access. Once over the river climb the hillside to a doorway in a fence (NG 994 483) at about 200m altitude. Continue up steep rough slopes to the plateau at 420m. Reach the burn issuing from the corrie and climb its right side past a small lochan to gain the corrie, about 2hrs.

Descent:
1. In bad weather or complete snow cover (when the cornices cannot be seen), head away from the cliff southwards to the flat area near Càrn Eididh, descend a gully eastwards and traverse back to the plateau at altitude 420m (or continue from Càrn Eididh to Balnacra).
2. The more direct alternative is to descend south-eastwards along the top of the cliff (cornices). When the ground begins to steepen (after about 200m), turn right (west) and soon reach a snowy trough which leads south-east again. The slope is convex and briefly 45 degrees. Follow snow as long as possible, because the ground here is very rough, and trend left to the plateau at altitude 420m.
3. To return to the corrie, Access Gully is rarely used, as the cornice has to be abseiled. The usual choice is to descend the ridge on the north side of the corrie until it is possible to go down the short Right-Hand Gully, Grade I, to the floor of the corrie.

Layout: The left side of the corrie is the main face and the climbs are described from bottom left to right. The big corner of **Fuhrer** (190m VII,6) is to the left while the icefall of Tholl Gate in the centre is often the most obvious feature. At the top of the corrie there are two snowy gullies, the cul-de-sac of Cold Hole is the left one and Access Gully the right one, with Right End Buttress between them.

1 Fuar Folly Direct   190m   VI,8 **
R.J.Archbold, D.M.Nichols (original)   19 Feb 1978; As described: J.Lyall, A.Nisbet   12 Jan 1995
This was the original intention of Fuar Folly, climbing direct up 'the great rock bastion' right of Fuhrer. The original Fuar Folly climbed the first two pitches, then traversed into The Fuhrer along the ledge, tried this, then escaped left when darkness arrived. Start right of a line below the big corner of Fuhrer, at a big ramp leading right.
1. 30m Climb the big low angled ramp to the start of a snow shelf.
2. 40m Go up, then take a second right-trending ramp, until a short steep crack gains the ledge which is followed left to the crest just before the ledge curves round into Fuhrer.
3. 20m Climb a left-slanting ramp (groove) to a short overhanging corner. Climb this and pull left on to a smooth rock terrace with a big block at its right end.
4. 10m Fuar Feast crosses here and goes up a short overhanging groove on the left. Instead, pull up right on spikes to the base of a shallow right-facing corner with a perfect crack. Climb this (excellent protection) to a precarious finish on to the ledge above.
5. 45m A long pitch straight up leads to a right-slanting break.
6. 45m Finish by this.

2 Tholl Gate   170m   VI,6 ****
P.Butler, M.Fowler   31 Mar 1984
This takes the magnificent icy line in the centre of the cliff. Start slightly right of the line in a shallow bay.
1. 40m Climb a shallow icy groove (or mixed climbing trending left then right) to a ledge line. Traverse left for 10m to belay below the ice streak.
2. 35m The difficulty will depend on how far the icefall extends down an overhanging wall to the ledge below. Moving out right below the thick ice will probably be easiest. Once gained, follow the ice to a good ledge.
3. 50m The steep and fine icy corners on the right lead to a good ledge.
4. 45m Move left and continue straight up by corners and a final gully.

FUAR THOLL
South-East Cliff

1. Fuar Folly Direct   VI,8 **
2. Tholl Gate   VI,6 ****
3. The Ayatollah   VII,7 ***
4. Evasion Grooves   VI,6 ***
6. Pipped at the Post   V,5 **
7. Cold Hole   VI,5 ***
8. Right End Buttress   III,4

3 The Ayatollah   190m   VII,7 ***
I.Dring, M.E.Moran   23 Feb 1989
Takes an uncompromising line right of Tholl Gate, following an obvious steep slab corner in the second tier, and then a series of icy grooves directly above. The key to the route is reaching the ice on the slab (pitch 2). Start, as for Tholl Gate, at a shallow bay beneath the highest part of the cliff.
1. 50m Climb as for Tholl Gate, tricky icy grooves to a snow terrace, then a right traverse to a spike beneath the slab corner.
2. 30m Make some radical moves up the smooth corner until usable ice can be gained on the slab on the left. The second ascent climbed an ice smear which can form between the corner and Tholl Gate's icefall. Follow the ice smears to a narrow terrace, traverse right under an icicle, then up a rocky groove for 4m to belay at a cracked block.
3. 35m Bridge across left to gain the icicle, then climb up directly. If no icicle is present it can be mixed climbed. A short groove, an easier snow bay and a further iced groove lead to belays at a wedged block below a steeper icefall.
4. 45m Climb the icefall, then go left and back right in easier angled mixed grooves to gain a terrace below the final rock wall.
5. 30m Traverse 5m left, then go up steep snow and a runnel to the cornice.

4 Evasion Grooves   210m   VI,6 **
S.Jenkins, M.E.Moran   4 Mar 1988
This is a mixed alternative to Tholl Gate, up the big buttress to its right. It is more frequently in climbable condition than its neighbours. An excellent climb. Start, as for The Ayatollah and Tholl Gate, at a shallow bay below the highest part of the cliff.
1. 50m Climb tricky ice grooves, as for Tholl Gate, to a snowy terrace, and go right along this to the spike beneath the smooth corner of The Ayatollah.
2. 40m Traverse right for 4m to a very steep groove. Climb this direct to a hard exit, then continue to giant spikes.
3. 40m Go right on to a big easy snow ramp. Follow this for 25m to a left-sloping break in the tier above. Struggle up this to reach another terrace directly beneath a fine ramp.
4. 40m Climb the ramp to belay in an overhung corner.
5. 40m Traverse left for 15m, then trend left up snowfields and rocky grooves to a possibly large cornice.

A prominent gully, the Cold Hole, separates the right and higher side of the cliff from an easier buttress. The gully ends in a cul-de-sac. The first two routes climb the right side of the main cliff, starting just inside the gully.

5 Mixed Post   100m   IV,5 *
D.Jarvis, A.Nisbet   17 Dec 1993
In good conditions an icefall forms partly connected to Pipped at the Post but offering a slightly easier separate line. Without ice, a mixed route with a short hard section on pitch 1 (V,6). Start immediately left of Pipped at the Post. Gain a shallow chimney from the right. Climb it and the continuation fault slanting leftwards to the top.

6 Pipped at the Post   100m   V,5 **
M.Fowler, C.Watts   10 Jan 1987
About 30m down the gully from the cul-de-sac of Cold Hole is a continuous ice streak on the left wall. Often the best line of ice is the steep first pitch of this route, then moving left to finish up Mixed Post.
1. 40m Climb the ice to a thinly covered wall at 15m (crux) and continue to a big spike belay on the right.
2. 30m Continue in the same line to belay below an overhanging wall.
3. 30m If there is sufficient ice, climb the wall; otherwise traverse delicately left to easier ice or mixed ground leading to the cornice. Finish directly on mixed ground.

7 Cold Hole   50m   VI,5 ***
M.Fowler, C.Watts   10 Jan 1987
The gully is easy up to the cul-de-sac which forms a very steep 45m step. This climb takes the ice sheet forming the left corner of the step. Though short it is highly recommended and often in condition even when the other routes are too thin. This is a big and tiring pitch, but never vertical, and the crux is at the top. Finish either on steepening snow or traverse left and climb a long pitch on lower angled ice (Grade III).

8 Right End Buttress   180m   III *
W.S.McKerrow, D.M.Nichols   22 Feb 1976
The separate buttress at the top right of the cliff, between the Cold Hole cul-de-sac and Access Gully, can provide a fine icy climb or an easier option in bad conditions (if safe from avalanches). The belays are good but hard to find. Start at the bottom left corner and gain the centre. Climb a steep pitch, usually mixed, then a slabby pitch, quite low, to the left side of a big snow terrace. Regain the centre and climb rightwards, often on ice, then move back left to the upper snowfield.
Variation: **IV,4**
Climb the steep wall above the big snow terrace at its left side, going up cracks to a ledge on the left, then straight up to the upper snowfield.

9 Access Gully   130m   II
The obvious gully to the right of Right End Buttress has a steep exit, often dangerously corniced. A steeper right fork gives an alternative finish of 50m.

MAINREACHAN BUTTRESS

(NG 973 489)   Alt 700m   North-East to North-West facing   Map p300

This is one of Scotland's great winter cliffs, with several superb hard routes. The buttress presents a steep north face with a scree slope below it rising sharply from left to right. This upper right side of the buttress is an awesome place, particularly in winter, occasionally forming some ice between the overhangs!

Conditions and Weather: Being near the west coast and of middle altitude, the weather needs to be fairly cold for the turf to be frozen. Ice formation is less predictable, depending on how wet the buttress was before it froze; for Snoopy, very wet.

Approach: The best approach is on the good path from Achnashellach station to upper Coire Lair. There is a good parking place on the A890 near the sign to Achnasheallach Station. Walk up to the station and continue on the track which crosses the railway. Turn left at a junction (this is obvious) and through felled ground until a fence and kissing gate can be seen close on the left (small sign). Behind the fence is the stalking path which is followed into Coire Lair to a height of 360m where a second path branches left, crossing the River Lair (difficult in spate) and climbing up to the Bealach Mhor between Fuar Tholl and Sgòrr Ruadh. Just below the bealach branch off left to reach the base of the buttress, 2hrs 30mins. Alternatively, less scenic but perhaps slightly quicker, particularly useful if rucksacks are to be left at the top, start from Balnacra in Glen Carron (NG 983 463), climb to the summit of Fuar Tholl and descend either the west or east flank of the buttress to its base (depending on the intended route).

Descent: Descent back to the cliff base is easier on the west (left looking down), but both sides are possible.

Layout: The buttress has a small north-east face, a flat front face and a long steep north-west face.

1 Mainline Connection   200m   VI,6 **
R.Anderson, R.Milne   11 Mar 1989
This climbs the right-hand of two corner-lines on the north-east face. The left-hand

FUAR THOLL
Mainreachan
Buttress

1. Mainline Connection   VI,6 **
2. Enigma   VII,7 ***
3. Sleuth   VII,7 ***
4. Supersleuth   VII,8 ***
5. Snoopy   VII,7 ****

corner is **Nebula** (195m VI,6) which is a fine icy line but rarely in condition. Start below the right-hand corner, 15m right of the left one.
1. 50m   Climb the corner over several steps to a good ledge.
2. 45m   Ascend the fault directly above the belay and just left of the corner, then continue in the corner to the terrace.
3. 15m   Traverse left and belay below the first obvious groove (Nebula is further left).
4. 45m   Move up left and traverse right into the groove, which is climbed to smaller twin grooves, the right-hand of which leads to easy ground.

Enigma   230m   VII,7 *

S.M.Richardson, C.Cartwright   4 Jan 1997
A sustained mixed route up the front face of the buttress. Start up left from the toe of the buttress, below a short gully which is just right of a big corner.
1. 20m   Climb the gully to a terrace.
2. 15m   Continue up the prominent V-groove to a ledge.
3. 20m   Move up and right along a narrow slabby ramp to below a steep wall (junction with Sleuth, which traverses left to reach this point and then goes back

right along a horizontal ledge). Move left below a big square flake and continue up and left to a niche overlooking the big corner.

4. 15m Climb the groove just left of the niche to a bay.

5. 15m Don't follow the corner up and left, but instead, traverse horizontally right for 3m below an overlap, and move up to a small ledge. Climb the short groove above to a flat ledge.

6. 20m Climb the bulging groove just right of the left edge to reach the Great Terrace which girdles the cliff at two-thirds height. Move up to belay below a steep pillar.

7. 45m Traverse right along a dwindling ledge for 25m, then go up on mixed ground to reach a right to left diagonal line of weakness where the angle eases.

8. 30m Climb up diagonally left for 15m until about 10m below a big nose with a protruding flake. Traverse horizontally left along a ledge for 10m, then move up to the left edge of the buttress.

9. 50m Straightforward mixed ground leads to the top.

3 Sleuth 250m VII,7 ***
A.Fyffe, H.MacInnes, K.Spence 1970; With described start: D.McGimpsey, A.Nisbet 29 Feb 2000

A long hard route, probably the hardest in Scotland at the time, although the crux section is relatively short. A good start independent of Enigma was added later. Start about 25m up from the toe of the cliff at a short ramp which slants up leftwards into a steep groove of vertical flakes.

1. 20m Climb the ramp and groove to a ledge.

2. 40m A line of weakness now slants up left and continues to the First Terrace.

3. 40m Above is a smooth barrier wall. Continue rising leftwards, then go up a small corner to a higher ledge in the middle of the wall. Return right along this, despite heading for improbable ground, and include two short descents to reach a groove; go up this past a spike, then slightly right to near the edge and back left to belay.

4. 25m Go straight up a small wall to the Great Terrace.

5. 45m Traverse right along a dwindling ledge for 25m, then go up on mixed ground to reach a right to left diagonal line of weakness where the angle eases.

6. 30m Climb up diagonally left for 15m until about 10m below a big nose with a protruding flake. Traverse horizontally left along a ledge for 10m, then move up to the left edge of the buttress.

7. 50m Straightforward mixed ground leads to the top.

4 Supersleuth 240m VII,8 ***
G.Robertson, P.Benson, J.Currie 24 Feb 2002

A direct version of Sleuth.

1. and 2. 60m As for Sleuth.

3. 40m Above is a smooth barrier wall. Climb the very prominent thin torquing crack to a hard move below a steepening (crux). Step horizontally left and up into grooves which trend back right over an overhang to a good stance common to Sleuth.

4. 20m Step left into a short steep groove and climb this to easier ground which leads to the Great Terrace.

5. 40m Ten metres above is another steeper barrier wall, the only break in which is a groove just right of centre. Climb into and then up this with difficulty then with more ease to a ledge.

6. and 7. 80m Cross Sleuth by trending up rightwards, then back left to the top.

5 Snoopy 180m VII,7 ****
C.Dale, A.Nisbet 7 Mar 1998

Very spectacular, with bold pitches on thin ice leading to a strenuous but well protected section through roofs. The more ice, the easier it would become. The 'brown groove' is not visible from the ramp so ice conditions are difficult to assess until arrival (but the summer route on the right may be possible). Start at the obvious gangway near the middle of the north-west face, well up the sidewall from the lowest rocks.

1. 35m Follow the gangway to a bay beneath the ramp.
2. 30m Climb the corner of the ramp, generally on tufts and verglas (poorly protected), to a terrace on the left.
3. 15m Continue a short way up the ramp-corner, then traverse right along a foot ledge to climb the right side of the ramp to its top. Traverse right to belay.
4. 25m Climb steep rock trending right to gain an iced groove and follow it, probably on increasingly thick ice to a ledge below a prominent ice column.
5. 15m Climb the ice column into a recess. Make unlikely moves round the arete on the left to easier ground leading back right above the recess.
6. 30m Climb the chimney above and continue to a terrace.
7. 30m Move right and finish easily up grooves.

SGÒRR RUADH

(NG 959 505)   Alt 960m   Map p300)

Sgòrr Ruadh, the highest peak of the Coulin Forest, presents an impressive north-east and north face to the walker ascending Coire Lair from Achnashellach. In winter several of the gullies and faces provide good middle grade climbs in a fine situation.

Weather and Conditions: The climbs are mostly mixed, so the turf must be frozen. With the cliff base around 700m, the best conditions will be found from January to March on average. Deep snow on the longish but easy approach can be a problem.

Approach: As for Mainreachan Buttress but continue on the main path to upper Coire Lair, 2hrs 30mins.

Descent: The normal descent is down Central Couloir although North Gully is an alternative for those who have left rucksacks below the North Face. A pleasant and only slightly longer alternative is to descend south-east, crossing the stream below Loch a' Bhealaich Mhoir and join the stalking path which leads back to the Coire Lair path. Another option is to bag the Munro (about 15mins away).

Layout: Seen from Loch Coire Lair, the furthest skyline ridge marks Raeburn's Buttress, with the North Face behind it. Coming left from this is a broken face overlooking the broad Central Couloir, and then, in front of the Couloir and partially hiding it, the long line of Academy Ridge with an easy section in the middle and a steep upper part. Left of this is another large broken area, the South-East Face, with a number of rakes running up from left to right terminating in gullies. Robertson's Gully defines the left boundary of Academy Ridge and the next buttress left is Robertson's Buttress.

1 Robertson's Gully   180m   IV,4 *
A.Nisbet, N.Spinks   31 Jan 1976
A long snow approach climbing diagonally right leads to this steep gully on the left of Academy Ridge. There is a deep cave just over halfway up. Climb the gully by a series of chockstone filled chimneys to the cave (this section can largely bank out). Traverse right and re-enter the gully by the higher of two traverse lines above the cave.

2 Academy Ridge   350m   II *
A long mountaineering route, mostly easy. Move left at mid-height to regain the crest after a discontinuity. Avoid the steep upper section on the right by traversing into the top of Post Box Gully. Alternatively, a fine direct finish through the upper section is IV,5. Gain the grooves on the right of the top arete and follow them to a spike. From here gain and follow the arete.

SGÒRR RUADH - Central Couloir

2. Academy Ridge   II *
3. Post Box Gully   II ***
4. Croydon Chimney   IV,6

5. High Gully   IV,4 *
6. Central Couloir I *

CENTRAL COULOIR

(NG 966 506)   Alt 700m   North or South-East facing   Map p300

3 Post Box Gully   180m   II ***
A.Fyffe   Mar 1969
This is a narrow well defined gully low down on the left wall of Central Couloir, recognisable by a huge chockstone near its foot. Climb up to the chockstone and continue beneath it to emerge from a slot. Continue direct over small pitches to the top of Academy Ridge. Ice is not required so this route is climbable in most conditions, but Grade III when lean.

4 Croydon Chimney   160m   IV,5 *
H.MacInnes and party (1PA)   1969; FFA: M.E.Moran and party   1990
Just left of High Gully is a left-slanting chimney-line. Climb this direct with a hard slot (crux, mixed) at mid-height and a sustained upper groove. Escape left to easy ground below the final capstone. Again, ice is not required.

5 High Gully   120m   IV,4 *
M.Hillman, A.Nisbet   1 Feb 1976
High on the left wall of Central Couloir, just below and opposite Brown Gully, a large two-tiered icefall can form below a deep narrow gully. Climb the icefalls trending right and enter the gully from the right. Grade III in its best condition.

6 Central Couloir   300m   I *
The huge shallow gully with climbs leading out either side. Only just steep enough to be given Grade I and therefore a popular route to the summit of Sgòrr Ruadh.

7 Brown Gully   100m   III *
A.Fyffe   Mar 1969

This is the narrow gully on the right of and starting high up Central Couloir. Climb up right past a bend in the gully and go up an ice pitch. Climb straight up the gully to where it narrows and steepens. Follow a groove on the right and return to the gully as soon as possible. Continue easily to the top. A right branch is also Grade III.

8 Easy Gully   180m   II *
J.Cleare, P.Gillman   Mar 1969
Halfway along the right wall of Central Couloir is an obvious long gully starting just right of an isolated pinnacle. It may have several short ice pitches.

(NG 966 509)   Alt 630m   North-East to North facing   Map p300 Diagram p312

The ridge forming the right side of the Central Couloir formation, clearly seen in profile from the Coire Lair approach. Although it appears on the approach to have a well defined crest, in fact its upper part is much better defined than the lower, which has a broad frontal zone consisting of steep, slabby walls separated by discontinuous terraces. This lower face has two chimney-lines, a narrow one in the centre and a big obvious one (more of a gully) forming its right side. The crest arrives at a shoulder followed by the upper section, which is easier angled but a well defined crest. Routes on the north face of the buttress finish at differing heights on the upper crest.

Route lengths, apart from Raeburn's Buttress and its Direct, are given to the crest which is Grade II for its upper section. It is also possible to escape from the shoulder by descending diagonally left into the Central Couloir, finishing by the base of Easy Gully.

9 Raeburn's Buttress via Narrow Gully   350m   II **
H.Raeburn, E.B.Robertson   4 Apr 1904; Via Narrow Gully: G.Cohen, D.Rubens   Feb 1978
Start up the prominent narrow gully bounding Raeburn's Buttress on the left. The 1904 ascent gained the buttress after its first two pitches. The 1978 ascent climbed the gully throughout. Continue up the crest, with a couple of tricky sections but mostly easy, to the top.

0 The Jigsaw   200m   III **
H.Davies, G.Bardsley, A.Nisbet   6 Jan 1998
Provides a more difficult mixed start to Raeburn's Buttress, but not sustained. Start only a little right but much lower than Narrow Gully where a ramp leads rightwards up the face. Climb the ramp to its top (60m), traverse right along a ledge (50m) and reach a fault-line leading diagonally back left to the crest (70m). A short pitch on the crest leads to the upper section (20m).

1 Raeburn's Superdirect   190m   IV,6 **
M.E.Moran, P.Potter   17 Feb 1989
This big chimney-line is an obvious feature just before the buttress curves round to form the North Face. A fine line, climbed when icy and recommended as such, but this is not common. The length excludes the easier upper ridge.
1. 45m   Climb a short ice pitch, then a right-slanting iced groove passing a chockstone to a terrace.
2. 45m   Go up the groove above to a steeper iced exit.
3. 40m   Climb over short walls into an overhung cul-de-sac which is surmounted by tricky mixed climbing up the left wall, then bridging across to reach ice leading to easier ground. Belay on the right.
4. 40m   Climb a chimney and a short step. Belay on the left.
5. 20m   A final awkward step leads to easy ground and the upper crest of Raeburn's Buttress.

312

SGÒRR RUADH
Raeburn's Buttress &
North Face

10. The Jigsaw   III **
11. Raeburn's Superdirect   IV,6 **
12. Tophet Gully   IV,5 *

13. Fox's Face   IV,4 **
14. Gopher's Gully   IV,4 ***
15. North Gully   I **
16. Tango in the Night   VI,7 ****
A. Upper Buttress

(NG 963 508)   Alt 750m   North-North-West facing   Map p300

Raeburn's Buttress gradually bends round to form the 250m north face. This is bounded on the right by a deep scree or snow gully with an impressive vertical left wall (North Gully). The most obvious feature is the gully of the Superdirect which somewhat arbitrarily forms its left side. The route lengths apply to reaching the upper crest of Raeburn's Buttress. The best finish is to follow the crest to the top (Grade II at first) although there is an easier option to traverse left and finish up a shallow gully.

12 Tophet Gully   200m   IV,5 *
S.Duncan, A.Nisbet   20 Mar 1995
The obvious left-slanting fault in the centre of the North Face. It leads to the top of the steep lower section of Raeburn's Buttress. Access to the fault appears to be blocked by a big overhang. Attention is attracted by extensive smears of ice, but a thinly iced slab tucked in to the fault on the right is the key. A second barrier wall can be climbed on ice at its left side leading to an easier upper gully and in turn to the upper crest of Raeburn's Buttress.

13 Fox's Face   260m   IV,4 **
S.Jenkins, M.E.Moran   6 Dec 1987
A good mixed route up the highest part of the north face, finishing near the top of the Raeburn's Buttress. The lower part is the crux, originally graded III. Start 10m right of the obvious left-slanting fault-line of Tophet Gully. Take a right-slanting crack-line through the very steep lower tier (40m). Make a rightward deviation, then move back left into the big central depression of the face (40m). Go left at the top of the depression, then weave back right and take the final wall direct by grooves.

14 Gopher's Gully   200m   IV,4 **
M.E.Moran, A.Nisbet   28 Nov 1996
Takes a shallow gully starting just outside North Gully. It has the very obvious feature of a large chockstone on the first pitch underneath which one must chimney. The second pitch continues up the gully, also steep and leads to an easy broad rib and the upper crest of Raeburn's Buttress.

15 North Gully   200m   I **
The deep gully bounding the right side of the main face is scenically impressive because of its imposing left wall. Initially easy, it steepens and narrows in the upper half.

16 Tango in the Night   100m   VI,7 ****
S.Aisthorpe, N.Forwood, P.Yardley   1989
One of the best short routes in Scotland, taking a superb line up the huge imposing depression lying halfway up North Gully on the left. As suggested by the name, the first ascent of this intimidating line lasted well into the night. Start up a concealed left branch which ends in a formidable cul-de-sac but soon diverge right into the main corner. Follow this to a very steep succession of chimneys, which can be climbed in several short pitches. Despite the steepness, there are excellent cracks and many flakes (essential that it is well frozen). Almost at the top, the line is blocked by a final overhang. Move up right on blocks and finish on the left (the first ascent made a sensational but harder traverse right to finish).

Applecross

The Applecross peninsula has a group of three fine mountains, Meall Gorm to the west, the central Sgùrr a' Chaorachain and the larger Beinn Bhàn to the east. Britain's highest road outside the Cairngorms crosses a pass between Meall Gorm and Sgùrr a' Chaorachain and provides extraordinary access to Meall Gorm's winter routes. Beinn Bhàn is a magnificent winter cliff, arguably Scotland's best were it further from the coast and less affected by global warming. Coire an Fhamair is a truly awesome steep face while Coire na Poite's huge icefall of Silver Tear is the biggest steep icefall in Scotland.

BEINN BHÀN

(NG 804 451)   Alt 896m

This superb mountain offers some of the finest winter climbing in the Northern Highlands. There are six corries lining its north-east face. The first corrie, Coir' Each is somewhat open and less impressive than its neighbours. The second and third corries, Coire na Feòla and Coire na Poite, each rise from an outer corrie to a high inner corrie with a magnificent back wall. Coire na Poite is enclosed by two narrow ridges with precipitous sides whose outer ends form the great castellated buttresses of A' Chìoch on the left and A' Phoit on the right. Beyond A' Phoit the fourth corrie, Coire an Fhamair, contains on its south side one of the steepest cliffs on the Scottish mainland. There is a fifth corrie, Coire Toll a' Bhein, which is unnamed on the OS map and a smaller sixth, Coire Gorm.

Weather and Conditions: While there are a number of excellent gully climbs, the climbs on the buttresses tend to be open to traversing variations owing to the horizontal bedding of the sandstone. So, typical of sandstone, many of the best climbs here are gullies or icefalls.

The mountain is quite often in good winter condition, basically the colder the better, although the length of the cold spell coupled with the amount of drainage water makes conditions not completely predictable. January to mid March is the most likely but the low altitude of the cliff base allows damaging thaws. Applecross sometimes escapes a heavy snowfall, and it may be worth visiting when inland mountains are swamped with unconsolidated powder. On the other hand, being low and near the sea, there are inevitably times when the climbs have little snow and ice while the higher inland mountains are in good condition. Altogether, the magnificent mountain scenery of these corries, with their open views east to the Coulin Forest, makes them well worth a visit.

The corries can be very sheltered during strong westerly winds. But the presence of a 60m band of 50 degree snow around their rims makes them very prone to windslab avalanches. It is easy to underestimate the deposition of windslab because the cliffs are so big and the puffs of spindrift seem far away. The traverse of A' Chìoch is largely safe from avalanche and can be a bad weather option.

Approach: Coire na Feòla and Coire na Poite are approached from the road bridge at the head of Loch Kishorn, via a good path. The ground is heathery and takes longer than expected, especially with fresh snow. For Coire an Fhamair, see that section.

Descent: A straightforward descent to the road at Tornapress may be made by following the summit ridge and the south-east flank of the mountain. In white-out conditions, admittedly rare on the windswept plateau, there will be a serious problem with cornices, particularly where the plateau projects out towards A' Chìoch. Suspense Gully is a useful descent into Coire na Feòla, and can be used in an emergency if the plateau proves too windy.

COIRE NA FEÒLA

(NG 810 444)   Alt 600m   North-East facing   Map p315   Diagram p316

There are some interesting features on the walls of the enclosing arms of this corrie, but the best routes are on or near the back wall. This curves round to the left into the prominent Suspense Gully, which is split into parallel runnels by a narrow ridge with an apparent tower, and may be used as a descent route. To the left of this is Suspense Buttress. The steep lower rock band of Suspense Buttress is

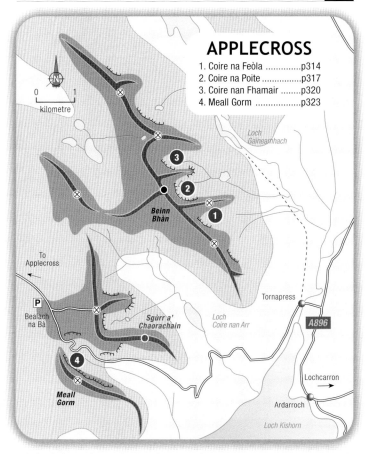

APPLECROSS

0 1
kilometre

Loch Gaineamhach

3

2

1

Beinn Bhàn

To Applecross

P
Bealach na Bà

Sgùrr a' Chaorachain

Loch Coire nan Arr

Tornapress

A896

Lochcarron →

Ardarroch

Loch Kishorn

4

Meall Gorm

sub-divided into three subsidiary buttresses by a steep wet or icy recess at each end, the central subsidiary buttress being much wider than the others.

1 Bounty Hunter   170m   IV,5 **

D.McGimpsey, A.Nisbet   28 Feb 2001

A sustained mixed route up a line on the central subsidiary buttress. The lower rock band is breached by a right-slanting line of weakness. Start on the left side of the central subsidiary buttress, down from the left recess which holds **The Acid Queen** (150m V,4). Climb turf to gain the base of the diagonal line and walk a few metres right (10m). Go up, then traverse left to reach the diagonal line above its initial steep section. Follow it to a ledge (30m). Continue up the line and finish on the right to reach the terrace above (40m). Suspense Buttress traverses this terrace. Move right and climb a long V-groove (40m). Two short walls and a steep flaky groove just left of the crest lead to the start of the final horizontal arete (50m).

2 Suspense Buttress   200m   III

Start at the base of the right recess of Suspense Buttress. Go diagonally right to reach the crest next to Suspense Gully and follow it to a terrace (50m). Make an exposed traverse left above the recess (45m). Pass the V-groove of Bounty Hunter

NORTHERN HIGHLANDS

BEINN BHÀN - Coire na Feòla

1. Bounty Hunter   IV,5 **
2. Suspense Buttress   III
3. Suspense Buttress Direct   IV,5 **

4. Suspense Gully   I **
5. Sheet Whitening   V,5
6. Sniper's Gully   IV,4

7. Y Gully   V,4 *
8. Man's Best Friend   IV,5 *

and either climb a second groove above, including a short chimney of technical 5, or traverse a little further towards the easier grooves of Acid Queen and climb a series of short walls broken by terraces to reach the top arete of the buttress.

3 Suspense Buttress Direct   175m   IV,5 **

J.Ashby, L.Sell-Blackaby, M.E.Moran   5 Feb 2001

A much better way of doing Suspense Buttress, keeping close to the crest, which runs parallel to Suspense Gully.

1. 50m As for Suspense Buttress.

2. 40m The original route now makes an exposed traverse left above the recess. Instead, go up the crest and climb a steep tier in the front face diagonally from right to left.

3. 45m Traverse 15m left on a steep terrace until a slim groove allows the next tier to be surmounted; belay at the next break 10m higher (more direct versions will be considerably harder).

4. 45m Climb an attractive corner-line in the final tier to the top (probably the same flaky groove as for Bounty Hunter; the crest is easier but less good).

4 Suspense Gully   150m   I **

A straightforward snow climb between Suspense Buttress and the main back wall. There are two parallel lines separated by an arete; the right one is more scenic but may be corniced or threatened by avalanche whereas the left one has a tricky finish. The right branch is the more likely descent.

5 Sheet Whitening   250m   V,5

M.Fowler, S.Fenwick, M.Lynden   30 Dec 1981

This is the leftmost of the obvious runnels on the back wall of the corrie. The crux is a hard ice pitch up a steep barrier rock band at 90m. The rest of the climb is straightforward.

6 Sniper's Gully   280m   IV,4

J.Mothersele, A.Nisbet   17 Feb 1986

The shallow gully just right of Sheet Whitening.

7 Y Gully   300m   V,4 *

At the right side of the back wall is a very prominent Y shaped feature. There is one big pitch but the rest is easy. The lowest band may be climbed slightly right of the steepest ice. After crossing some easier ground climb a long steep ice pitch in the 'stem' of the Y. Higher up either the left or the right branches of the Y may be taken, both giving pleasant climbing to the top.

8 Man's Best Friend   220m   IV,5 *

G.Ettle, J.Lyall   5 Jan 1994

Climbs a big corner-line to the right of Y Gully. Start from the bottom of Y Gully trending right to the foot of the corner. Climb the right-facing corner as directly as ice and turf allows, with a superb through route on the way. The final wall is easier than it looks from below.

COIRE NA POITE

(NG 808 451)   Alt 650m   North to East facing   Map p315   Diagram p319

Surely one of the most dramatic of Highland corries.

1 The Traverse of A' Chìoch   II ***

J.Brown, T.W.Patey   1968

This is the best mountaineering route on Beinn Bhàn, and also a good choice for those who wish to venture out on a wild westerly day. Climb easily up and along A' Chìoch, then with more difficulty down to the col; an easy line exists but requires good route finding. The crux is the ridge from this col to the summit

Silver Tear, V.5, Coire na Poite. Climber Pete Macpherson

Donnie Williamson

plateau, which has some tricky little walls. One in particular (after 50m) is losing its turf but there is an easier option further right. A direct line up the last of three long pitches is harder; the normal route deviates left to reach the easy finish. For a more sustained climb, start by the following route.

2 North Gully   120m   II ***
A.Fyffe, C.MacInnes, M.Alburger   2 Mar 1969
This is the prominent chockstone gully on the left side of the Coire na Poite face of A' Chìoch. It finishes halfway up the A' Chìoch spur. Start easily, then climb a couple of steeper pitches near the top. It is still good in lean icy conditions, but perhaps Grade III. It finishes on the ridge before the start of its difficulties (therefore misses nothing!).

3 March Hare's Gully   300m   IV,4 ***
C.J.S.Bonington, T.W.Patey   1 Mar 1969
This fine route was the first of the major winter climbs to be done on Beinn Bhàn. The hard sections are short, and it takes the obvious line on the left side of the upper corrie finishing at the point where the upper connecting ridge of A' Chìoch meets the summit plateau. There can be several ice pitches of which the first is often the hardest, particularly if unfrozen; sometimes it can be avoided on the left. In unusually heavy snow conditions much of this climb may bank out, but the grade will still be IV,3 because rock protection is limited. Equally, it is IV,5 when lean. It is a bad choice if there is spindrift as windslab avalanches are funnelled down the gully from near the plateau.

4 Mad Hatter's Gully   300m   V,5 **
M.Freeman, G.Stephen   1 Feb 1976
This is the large gully in the back left corner of the corrie. A huge feature with an

BEINN BHÀN
Coire na Poite

Coire nan Fhamair

1. Traverse of A' Chioch	II ***	
2. North Gully	II ***	
3. March Hare's Gully	IV,4 ***	
4. Mad Hatter's Gully	V,5 **	
5. Silver Tear	V,5 ****	
6. The Cooler	VI,6 ***	
7. Wall of the Early Morning Light	IV,5 ***	
7a. Moonshine	IV,5 **	
8. Upper Ridge of A' Phoit	V,6 *	

impressively big and steep ice pitch, but the rest is easy.

To the right of Mad Hatter's Gully is the huge back wall of Coire na Poite, the base of which often holds the biggest ice sheet in Scotland. The climbs here are long and impressive. In the upper part of the face, the obvious snow terraces allow numerous variations, though the routes will always be serious. Several routes have been recorded but it is not possible to be sure how much they have in common.

5 Silver Tear   350m   V,5 ★★★★
N.Muir, A.Paul   12 Feb 1977

In good conditions this gives a superb ice climb; four stars assumes the upper icefall is complete. The great icefall somewhat left of the centre of the wall is climbed directly for 120m to a terrace. Continue to a steep upper tier which ideally holds an ice pillar, but it may be necessary to pass the tier on the right. The easiest finish is up a right-slanting natural fault-line (Wall of the Early Morning Light).

6 The Cooler   150m   VI,6 ★★★
D.Dinwoodie, A.Paul   24 Feb 1983; Via even steeper finish: G.Ettle, M.Garthwaite   9 Jan 1997

This steep ice offers a direct start to Wall of the Early Morning Light or a steeper right-hand start to Silver Tear. Start at the right side of the Silver Tear icefall (well left of Wall of the Early Morning Light). Climb steep ice to a snow terrace, then even steeper ice to reach a terrace. Either traverse right to reach the right-slanting runnel taken by Wall of the Early Morning Light or traverse left to gain Silver Tear. The first ascent traversed right below the "even steeper ice".

7 Wall of the Early Morning Light   400m   IV,5 ★★★
K.Spence, J.Horsfield, B.Jones, P.Thomas   Feb 1971

A larger area of less steep ice usually forms in the centre of the back wall, to the right of Silver Tear and starting slightly lower. Climb this by a number of possible lines, the easiest involving a right-slanting ice runnel, to reach a barrier wall of very steep ice. The right end of this is an icy chimney which although steep, is the easiest way through this crux section. Make a long traverse left into a natural fault-line of chimneys and grooves which lead up slightly right through the upper bands of the face.

Variation: **Moonshine   300m   IV,5 ★★**
D.M.Jenkins, C.Stead   19 Feb 1978; As described: D.McGimpsey, A Nisbet   Jan 2003

This mixed variation on Wall of the Early Morning Light is good when ice conditions are not. Climb the central icefalls as for that route, but where it traverses left, make a long traverse right to bypass a big rock band. Trend back diagonally left by a series of traverses and short rock steps finishing by an easy left-slanting hidden chimney to finish just right of Wall of the Early Morning Light. The original line traversed immediately back left to join the right-slanting runnel of Wall of the Early Morning Light.

8 Upper Connecting Ridge of A' Phoit   180m   V,6 ★
B.Goodwin, J.Grieve, D.Tierney   Feb 1971

A short hard pitch with the rest much easier. The third tier is the crux. Climb a groove system with blobs of turf about 20m left of the true nose.

COIRE AN FHAMAIR

(NG 803 455)   Alt 600m   North-East facing   Map p315

A huge and very steep face on the left of the corrie provides some of the best routes in Scotland, but they are not for the faint hearted!

Approach: Follow the path to about NG 823 457. Go up the hillside on the left, make a slight descent and head direct to the cliff.

Descent: Either via the summit and as for the other corries, or return to the base

BEINN BHÀN - Coire an Fhamair

1. Genesis   VII,7 ****
2. Der Riesenwand   VII,6 ****
3. Gully of the Gods   VI,6 ****
4. Great Overhanging Gully   VI,7 ***

G. The Godfather   VIII,8

Andy Nisbet

of the cliff from the north and reverse the approach.

1 Genesis   305m VII,7 **

A.Cave, D.Heselden 20 Feb 2000

Climbs the stunning line formed by an overhanging chimney forming a chasm at the left side of the cliff. It is hard to believe how such an awesome overhanging feature could be breached at such a reasonable grade. The belays are excellent and situations are superbly intimidating. Comes into condition after a few cold days; if the icicle has formed at the base of the upper chimney the route will be climbable.

1. 30m Climb up to the base of the overhanging chimney and traverse out left along an obvious narrow turf ledge to belay up and left.

2. 35m Climb rightwards across a steep wall on to a small ledge and then climb a short left-facing corner. Move out right to a second corner and climb its right wall on thin ice to a terrace above. Belay out left on a natural thread.

3. 20m Move right across the gully under a large hanging icicle. Climb a steep left-facing corner on the right and mantel boldly up right to reach a huge monolithic block.

4. 45m Move up 3m and traverse left across the wall to reach the main line of ice. If the ice is too thin to climb at this point, struggle awkwardly up a mossy groove for 6m from the belay to gain an overhung ledge which offers an amusing leftward crawl to gain the ice a little higher. Follow the ice all the way to a giant chockstone. Climb on to the chockstone. Fantastic.

5. 25m Climb the steep finishing chimney with interest.

6. etc. 150m Go left up a snow gully for 50m to gain the upper part of the A' Phoit Ridge which is followed for 100m to the cornice.

Die Riesenwand, VII,6, Coire an Fhamair. Climber Martin Moran

Guy Robertson

2 Die Riesenwand 400m VII,6 ****
A.Nisbet, B.Sprunt 26 to 27 Jan 1980 (involving a bivouac)
This outstanding and exciting route takes the line of least resistance up the large face between the overhanging chimneys of Genesis and Gully of the Gods. A prominent zigzag of snow ledges marks the line through a very steep band at mid-height. Good conditions are advisable as a retreat from high up would be difficult. Repeats when very icy have thought it VI,5. Start towards the left of the face below a secondary corner. Climb steep ice for two or three pitches to a niche below a huge roof, 80m. (The second pitch climbs a short barrier wall which may be passed on the left if there is insufficient ice.) Traverse right from the niche across steep rocky ground to gain a large snow ledge, 30m. Continue traversing right for about 80m until another ledge leads back up left across the wall. Follow this for 60m passing some narrow sections and finishing with a memorable swing round a bulge in a very exposed position. The ground is now easier and a short traverse left leads to a shallow gully which gives a pleasant route to the plateau, 150m.

3 Gully of the Gods 180m VI,6 ****
M.Fowler, S.Fenwick 3 Apr 1983
The uniquely overhanging central gully splitting the cliff gives a tremendous climb. It is intimidating but surprisingly accommodating, providing unexpected runners and rests.
1. 25m A combination of back and foot with bridging on ice leads to an excellent ledge on the right.
2. 40m Climb the back of the gully for 5m, then back and foot out to the main ice streak and follow this into a very steep and difficult icy groove above the main overhangs. Pass the final capstone on the right.
3. 115m Climb more easily to the top.

The Godfather (230m VIII,8) is an awesome mixed route up the face between Gully of the Gods and Great Overhanging Gully, finishing up a big left-facing corner in the upper tiers.

4 Great Overhanging Gully   180m   VI,7 *
M.Fowler, P.Butler (2PA)   17 Mar 1984; FFA: C.Cartwright, D.Heselden   1994
This is the very steep line about 45m right of Gully of the Gods. Little ice is required, although it may be VI,6 if icy. Take some 4m slings for large chockstones.
1. 20m Climb turfy ground to below the overhangs.
2. 35m Climb the chimney to the overhangs; surmount these (crux unless on ice) and continue over an awkward bulge to a cave stance.
3. 35m Climb to beneath the chockstone and gain a traverse line. Continue up left to belay 5m left of the foot of a dry overhanging pitch.
4. 12m Move left and ascend to another ledge.
5. 12m Move up to reach deceptively hard turf climbing which leads back right to the gully bed.
6. 12m Surmount the overhang to belay below the final chimneys.
7. 50m Climb grooves and chimneys to the cornice finish.

MEALL GORM

(NG 779 409)   Alt 710m   Map p315   Diagram p324

The northern side of Meall Gorm presents a broken line of cliffs overlooking the Allt a' Chumhaing, the valley leading up to the Bealach na Ba. Scotland's most accessible winter cliff! It may not be as impressive as others in the area but 15mins from the road makes it an important option. The Bealach na Ba road is now often ploughed and even when not open over the pass, one can often get as far as the climbs.

Weather and Conditions: Meall Gorm is very near the sea and the most important factor for good conditions is that the turf be frozen (which happens more quickly on the steeper pitches than on the terraces which are often insulated by snow). The climbs near the top end of the cliff are much more likely to be frozen and are the ones described here.

Approach: Park just beyond the roadside cliff of South Face of Sgùrr a' Chaorachain (NG 787 412). This is opposite and slightly below the climbs. Walk across and up to the routes.

Descent: Descend to the first hairpin, having walked beyond the top end of the cliffs. To return to the cliff base, a diagonal snow gully right (facing up) of Blaeberry Corner is useful, or the broad snow gully right (facing up) of Cobalt and Wedge Buttresses. These gullies are also possible, but less pleasant, when lean, as they have no hidden pitches.

Layout: The largest buttress is also the lowest. Above this are many smaller buttresses leading to the second largest, Cobalt Buttress, which is at the upper end of the cliffs and prominent when driving up the road. There are smaller buttresses and gullies either side of this. Blue Pillar is a narrow buttress attached to the left side of Cobalt Buttress.

1 Gorm Gully   150m   II *
A.Fyffe and party   1970
This good wee route holds snow better than the other climbs on this face. Climb the deep narrow gully left of a three tiered buttress (the third gully left of Blue Pillar) via easy snow to a final ice pitch. There is an escape left below the ice pitch.

2 Blaeberry Corner   105m   V,6 *
K.Spence, J.Horsfield, B.Jones, P.Thomas   Feb 1971
Start at the foot of the first tier.
1. 30m Go left up a weakness for 10m, then move right up a steep flake on to the

MEALL GORM
d
1
2
3
4
5
6
7
8
8a
1. Gorm Gully II **
2. Blaeberry Corner V,6 *
3. Blue Pillar V,6 **
4. Lobster Gully IV,5 **
5. Rattlesnake V,7 **
6. Cobalt Buttress IV,5 ***
7. Turquoise Gully III *
8. Boulder Problem Buttress III
8a. Right Version III
d. descent

buttress crest and the belvedere above.

2. 25m Gain the black groove on the buttress crest by delicate moves up the wall on the left and climb it direct with continuous interest; an excellent pitch.

3. 20m Move 3m right to a chimney-ramp which leads to the top.

3 Blue Pillar   180m   V,6 **
J.Brown, T.W.Patey   Feb 1958

This is the conspicuous narrow pillar on the left of the massive Cobalt Buttress. Start at the foot and follow the crest. A vertical step at mid-height is the crux. Climb it either by a crack on the right with a precarious jammed flake at the top, or by cracks about 10m round on the left wall. Surmount the final tower by a deep chimney on the right.

4 Lobster Gully   200m   IV,5 **
M.Fowler, A.V.Saunders   15 Mar 1987

This is the prominent gully separating Blue Pillar from Cobalt Buttress. Several short steep steps lead to two fine well protected chimney pitches in the upper section. Some ice forms in the back, along with frozen vegetation, but requires cold conditions.

5 Rattlesnake   200m   V,7 **
G.Ettle, J.Lyall   13 Dec 1993

Sustained and varied climbing up the obvious line of corners running up the centre of the buttress, at the right edge of the long wall running across from Lobster Gully. Climb the first unavoidable tier by a groove line just right of a black patch. Climb the first and most impressive corner to half-height, then take the edge on the left. Follow the corner system to the top.

6 Cobalt Buttress   140m   IV,5 ***
I.Clough, G.Drayton, C.Young   10 Feb 1970

Short hard sections, but generally well protected. Start about 80m up to the right from the toe of the buttress, in Turquoise Gully, just above the toe of Wedge Buttress and below a short steep pitch in the gully bed. Follow a ledge to the left to a belay below a short corner.

1. 25m Climb the corner with difficulty and make an awkward traverse left to easier ground. Go up to the first terrace.

2. 25m Go up to a higher terrace and to its back below a steep wall.

3. 40m Climb an initial wall, then a slabby line of weakness leftwards to the crest and a barrier wall. Make the crux moves up this, then go rightwards to a terrace and continue to a higher terrace. Walk left for 10m up the terrace. Above is a wedged spike just left of the crest.

4. 25m Climb up and left to reach the spike, then pull carefully behind this and climb rightwards to a small terrace. Go up tricky short walls until a short overhanging block filled chimney leads back left to the crest.

5. 25m Climb a short difficult wall, then trend left to easier ground.

7 Turquoise Gully   200m   III *

Wedge Buttress is the triangular buttress immediately to the right of Cobalt Buttress. This is the narrow gully between the two. The first pitch is the steep crux and rarely forms good ice combined with a snow build-up, but if so, can be Grade II. Above are several short ice pitches. For a Grade II route, or if the first pitch is not formed and the rest looks good, traverse in from the right across Wedge Buttress immediately above this pitch.

To the right of Wedge Buttress is a broad easy gully (possible descent). The following route climbs the buttress to its right.

8 Boulder Problem Buttress   130m   III
R.Cooke, A.Nisbet   27 Feb 1997

There are two routes which join near the top. For the Left Version, start by a turf chimney about 50m up the easy gully and continue by turfy walls generally on the left side of the crest to finish by a 2m boulder problem wall (which banks out unless lean).

Variation: **Right Version**
Start at the base of the buttress and climb easily up its right side to a short ice pitch in a barrier wall (hard without ice). Continue by a turf chimney to the same boulder problem finish.

Torridon

Three of the most magnificent hills in Scotland lie north of Glen Torridon; Beinn Eighe to the east, Liathach central, and Beinn Alligin to the west. The quartzite of Beinn Eighe provides great rocky mixed climbing and is becoming increasingly popular as the warmer climate shortens the season when the famous icefalls form on Liathach.

BEINN EIGHE - RUADH-STAC MÒR

(NG 952 612)   Alt 1010m   Map p327

COIRE MHIC FHEARCHAIR

(NG 945 605)

Coire Mhic Fhearchair, on the north side of Beinn Eighe, is one of the classic corries in Scotland and is justly famous for its magnificent Triple Buttresses. Secluded from the road by a relatively long approach, they dominate the lonely corrie and offer routes of great length and character. Some of the climbs here compare with the best available anywhere in Scotland. This is a paradise for mixed climbing and pairs up well with Liathach and its ice.

Weather and Conditions: In winter, the corrie is a paradise for modern style mixed climbing. The steep blocky quartzite provides good axe placements, reliable protection and sensational lines. There is less reliance on frozen turf than, for example, in the Cairngorms so the corrie is a possibility in marginal conditions, especially early season. Also, the corrie usually holds more snow than one might imagine from the view of the south facing slopes from the car park. Good ice conditions are rarer, but the easier gullies of Sail Mhòr fill readily. When in condition, two of the most spectacular ice routes in Scotland are to be found in the corrie. The corrie is sheltered from southerly or south-westerly winds and deep snow does not alter the climbing, but it is too serious to be considered as an option for poor conditions. A problem for traditionally minded climbers is being discouraged by lack of snow on the crag. The harder routes are too steep to hold much of the white stuff, but they are often verglassed and feel more wintry than their appearance from below may suggest.

Approach: The best approach is to follow the well made Coire Dubh path between Liathach and Beinn Eighe starting from the Coire Dubh car park in Glen Torridon (NG 959 569). Fork right at a cairn about 2km beyond some stepping stones and follow a path contouring below Sail Mhòr and rising gradually to the lip of the corrie. If free of snow, this takes about 2hrs. Now meeting snow (one hopes), a further 40 to 60mins reaches the foot of the Triple Buttresses. Any depth of snow will increase the time significantly.

Descent: Head to the lowest point at the east end of a large grassy summit area (NG 953 598). Head over boulders and down a short gully. Go diagonally left (facing down) across the slope, the exact line depending on the snow conditions, to reach the right bank of a large stream valley. Follow this to the Coire Dubh path.

Layout: The Triple Buttresses are obvious! Seen from Loch Coire Mhic Fhearchair, the wall in the top left of the corrie is the Far East Wall. To its right is the steep left flank of the East Buttress, known as the Eastern Ramparts. Because the crests of the triple buttresses incline to the west, each buttress has an extensive left wall of steep

TORRIDON

Sundance, VIII,8. Climber Ian Parnell

quartzite facing north-east and a much narrower right wall tucked into the flanking gully. The left wall of Central Buttress is known as Central Wall, and the gullies have the obvious nomenclature East Central Gully and West Central Gully. The buttresses are composed mostly of quartzite standing on a plinth of sandstone. There is a big terrace above the sandstone tier, Broad Terrace. High on the quartzite is a smaller fault, the line of the **Upper Girdle** (VI,7), a sensational 700m climb across all three buttresses.

Far East Wall

(NG 949 602)   Alt 800m   North-West facing

It is remarkable that any winter routes climb this sometimes overhanging wall but those that do are memorable. Snowy conditions are required for enough to stick, although the wall does sometimes rime, but as always on quartzite, the routes feel more wintery than they look.

Sundance   95m   VIII,8 ****
G.Robertson, I.Parnell   10 Jan 2008

On the left side of the Far East Wall is an impressively compact, steep grey wall. Further left the Wall is less steep and decreases in height. To the right of the grey wall is an obvious steep and mossy corner-crack cutting through several overhangs in the upper part of the crag. A huge icicle hangs down from the top overhang and is a good locating feature, but the ground below is too steep for it ever to touch. The climbing is superb, generally well protected and exceptionally sustained, with spectacular exposure high up. The final short pitch is bold. Start at a depression directly beneath the corner, below a right-trending groove a short way up. .

1. 25m Climb up turfy walls to gain and follow the groove to a horizontal fault which traverses the whole cliff, and above which the main corner-line is formed.

2. 25m Climb the corner, following cracks in the left wall at first, then move back right to enter a hanging chimney which leads to a good ledge.

3. 30m Both the overhangs on this pitch had useful ice, the second sporting a 6m Damoclean ice fang. Climb cracks in the left wall to the first overhang which is taken directly. Turn the second overhang by a ledge on the right side, using the big ice fang to gain lodgement over its top.

4. 15m Continue up mossy grooves and walls to the top.

Vishnu   110m   VII,6 ****
A.Cunningham, A.Nisbet   14 Feb 1988

A fierce winter route up the major fault-line 20m left of the large protruding buttress which forms the right-hand section of the cliff. Although some of the climbing was on ice, much was mixed. Protection is poor on the icy sections but better on the mixed. It should be possible as a purely mixed route, but as yet it hasn't had a second ascent.

1. 15m Starting on the right an introductory pitch leads up left to below the initial groove.

2. 20m Climb the groove on deceptively steep ice to a belay in a deep recess below big icicles.

3. 20m An overhanging chimney leads out right to a small ledge from where a mixed line up an overhanging groove leads to another small ledge and good belay.

4. 50m Climb the vertical corner above until the ice can be regained above its steepest section. Now a deep gully leads over two steep sections to easier ground and the final snow slopes.

Kami-kaze   100m   VI,7 ***
A.Cunningham, A.Nisbet   6 Feb 1988

This follows the big chimney-line on the left of the large protruding buttress which forms the right-hand section of the cliff. Outrageous situations, but highly amenable rock, make this one of the best mixed climbs in the area. Chimneying features prominently, so sacks should not be carried. The climbing is sustained but largely well protected unless icy (the first pitch is the boldest). Start at an overhung recess about 30m left of a deep slit cave.

1. 25m Climb up the recess until it is possible to traverse right to a shallow groove. Go up this then right to belay below a chimney-crack in the obvious fault-line.

2. 25m Climb the chimney to belay in the base of a deeper wider chimney.

3. 25m Climb this overhanging chimney until it becomes a cave under the huge beak. Traverse sensationally out left and up a groove to easier ground.

4. 25m Finish up the groove above.

Eastern Ramparts

(NG 947 602)   Alt 800m   North-East facing

This wall is not as steep as the Far East Wall and therefore holds snow better. It is still very steep but the rock is more blocky, so offering more holds and protection. There are many good routes on the wall; this one has been repeated more than once and enjoyed.

NORTHERN HIGHLANDS

1 Shang-High   120m   VII,7 ***
B.Davison, A.Nisbet   18 Feb 1992
This climbs a prominent chimney which is formed above the main horizontal break (Upper Girdle), near the right end of the Ramparts, just before the top of the wall starts slope down East Buttress. The climbing is steep and strenuous, but a good winter line. There is a lower continuation to the cliff base but the route starts about 10m left of this below twin cracks.
1. 45m Climb the crack-line to a grassy ledge 10m below the Upper Girdle, then go diagonally right onto a huge flat topped block (a good locating feature) and up to the Upper Girdle.
2. and 3. 75m Follow the chimney-line direct, climbing through a large slotted roof before moving left into another chimney.

Triple Buttresses

(NG 945 603)   Alt 700m   North facing   Map p327

2 East Buttress   250m   IV,5 ***
This fine natural line has an imposing appearance, but it is the easiest of the buttresses. It is climbable in any conditions and can often be used to salvage a day for those originally intent on harder things. The normal start, and consistent in standard with the rest of the buttress, is to traverse all the way along Broad Terrace from the left. This has one very exposed icy section, about Grade II. Start the buttress proper about 10m left of the crest and climb the steep face on good ledges and some turf to an easier section (30m). Continue up an interesting and varied series of pitches to the top. A short vertical corner right of the crest is the technical crux and also the last difficulty before scrambling.

3 Icefall Start   50m   V,5
R.Arnott, E.Clark, A.Nisbet, S.Thirgood   12 Feb 1983
A substantial icefall forms in a wet depression left of the highest section of the sandstone tier and forming from a spring at the "bad step" on Broad Terrace. It provides two pitches of steep ice, with steeper options available.

4 East Central Gully   250m   III *
The normal start is to traverse all the way along Broad Terrace from the left (one very exposed section) and enter the gully easily from the base of East Buttress quartzite. The gully may provide several ice pitches, none too long or steep.
Variation: **Direct Start   V,4**
The sandstone section of the gully is the logical direct start but it is deceptively hard and serious. The ice is often hollow, covering a deep crack, and there is minimal protection.

Central Wall

Central Wall is the name given to the north-east facing left flank of the upper part of Central Buttress. It is bounded on the left by East Central Gully and on the right by the crest of Central Buttress. The lower part of the wall is formed by what appears from below to be a tower about 45m high rising from East Central Gully at the level of Broad Terrace.

In winter the easiest access is to traverse above the sandstone tier of East Buttress into East Central Gully and follow this until one can break out right onto the Tower (Grade II). A more satisfying approach is to climb the first pitch of East Central Gully, then take the right fork between the Tower and Central Buttress, finally breaking out left onto the Tower (Grade V,4). The right fork can also be reached by the traverse across East Buttress (Grade II) if the initial chimney of East Central Gully is insufficiently iced.

BEINN EIGHE
Coire Mhic Fhearchair
Triple Buttresses

1. Shang-High   VII,7 ***
2. Icefall Start   V,5
3. East Buttress   IV,5 ***
4. East Central Gully   III *
4a. Direct Start   V,4
5. The Cool Cleft   V,5 **
6. East Central Wall   V,4 **
7. Pelican   VI,6 *
8. Piggott's Route   VI,7 ****
9. Hamilton's Route (start)   VI,6 **
11. West Central Gully   VII,8 ***
13. Blood Sweat and Frozen Tears   VIII,8 ****
14. W.Buttress, West-Central Start   IV,4 ***
15. West Buttress Direttissima   VII,8 ***
18. Fuselage Gully   II **

A. Broad Terrace

5 The Cool Cleft   120m   V,5 **

R.Arnott, E.Clark, A.Nisbet, S.Thirgood   12 Feb 1983; Direct, as described: P.Thornhill, C.Watts, T.Saunders, M.Fowler   9 Apr 1983

This takes the shallow curving fault immediately right of the upper part of East Central Gully. It is often a continuous line of ice, particularly late in the season, and is best started by the icefall below East Buttress or by East Central Gully direct start (both of a similar grade), then climbing the gully until an easy traverse right leads to the foot of the fault. The second pitch in the fault is the crux.

6 East Central Wall   300m   IV,4 **

P.Barrass, A.Nisbet   22 Dec 1981

This is a good first excursion away from the buttresses with a fine mountaineering atmosphere. The route was originally started by climbing East Central Gully direct start through the sandstone (V,4 but rarely forms), but the normal start nowadays is via the normal start to East Central Gully, along the Broad Terrace. Cross the gully and take its steeper right fork, which is also quite hard if there is no ice. From the top of this gully, go up left on broken ground until about 10m below and right of a very prominent wide crack. Traverse 5m right along an overhung ledge to the base of a chimney. Climb this and a further right-slanting chimney to reach a triangular bay with ice in the overhanging corner at its top. The ice is very steep and may be avoided by climbing a shallow chimney to the right of the bay which leads to easy ground.

7 Pelican   180m   VI,6 ***

A.Cunningham, A.Nisbet   9 Jan 1987

A steep and sustained direct route formed by a chimney and groove line which leads from East Central Gully, just above its Direct Start, rightwards up the right fork and on up its continuation to slopes above the top of Central Buttress.

Central Buttress

8 Central Buttress (Pigott's Route)   270m   VI,7 ****

K.Spence, J.Rowayne, K.Urquhart   Feb 1971 (2 days); As described: A.McIntyre, A.Rouse   Feb 1978

One of the finest winter expeditions in Scotland, long and hard with the crux near the top. The awkward overhanging chimney-crack in the final tier is the crux by far. The shallow groove immediately to its left has also been climbed and is technically easier, although with several thin moves. Start about one-third of the way from the right-hand end of the sandstone tier at the base of a left-slanting diagonal line.

1. and 2. 70m Climb the prominent diagonal line, which has a difficult section past a cave at half-height.

3. 20m Continue quite close to the arrival point, from the highest point of the grass on Broad Terrace, in a bay just right of the crest. Climb up trending left to a stance in a corner.

4. 20m Traverse left to the crest, round it, and up an exposed chimney on good holds.

5. 70m Go up easy ground to the foot of the final tier. This top tier is the crux, taking a line just left of the crest, and strong parties have used a little aid, particularly when the chimney is heavily verglassed.

6. 20m Above is a left-facing corner and above this an obvious short bottleneck chimney with a crack just to its right. Gain the corner by first moving left into a groove, then go up and right to the base of the corner. This leads to a belay below the narrow chimney.

7. 30m Climb the bottleneck chimney with difficulty and continue up flakes on the right of an obvious cracked groove. Step up left onto the wall and move up to a flake overlooking the groove. Pull round into a continuation groove and follow this to ledges and a belay on the right.

8. 40m Above is a corner and on its right more broken stepped ground on the edge. Move up and right to gain a ledge, then pull up onto easier ground which leads to the top.

9 Hamilton's Route   270m   VI,6 **

D.McGimpsey, A.Nisbet   17 Nov 1998

The other traditional line, up the right side of the buttress. Not as good a line but the climbing is as good. A similar standard to Pigott's, perhaps a little more sustained but without the very awkward crux. Start at the right end of a grass terrace below the sandstone, about 10m left of West Central Gully. Climb slabby rock parallel to the gully, choosing the easiest line on good rock, for 70m to meet a barrier slab beneath Broad Terrace. Either climb this or if not iced, traverse right to a grassy groove near West Central Gully and climb this to Broad Terrace. Continue up a vegetated groove about 20m from West Central Gully. Follow this into a corner on the right which leads a ledge. Traverse a short way right along the ledge, then trend up right to the edge of the buttress, overlooking West Central Gully (20m). Go up a big groove slanting back left and continue to below a short bulging corner. Traverse back right round an edge to climb a short corner. Continue on easier ground to the base of the final tower. Start this about 10m right of the crest below a huge flange of rock curving up right. Go diagonally right on flakes to gain the right end of a ledge on top of a large detached flake below the flange. Climb slabs diagonally rightwards (crux) to reach and follow big open chimneys to the top, keeping always on the right side of the buttress.

10 Central Buttress, Grade IV Line   300m   IV,5 ***

D.Amos, E.Gillespie, A.Nisbet   15 Feb 2001 (first complete ascent)

A constructed winter line up Central Buttress at an easier grade to provide a magnificent (but devious) mountaineering route. Start up Hamilton's Route and climb this to Broad Terrace. Follow Hamilton's Route until the top of the big groove (which often ices). Traverse left along a terrace to join easy ground on the crest (Pigott's) and follow it to the final tier, described in detail:

1. 35m   From the crest of the buttress below the final tier (Pigott's), make a descending traverse rightwards along the Terrace for 25m to just past a rib which forces the terrace to narrow. Climb up turfy ledges in a stepped corner system to below a short steep corner.

2. 25m   Either go up left and traverse back right on to the top of the short corner or climb the corner direct (6) to a ledge. Move right up flakes to a steep wall, then round its right end to reach an easier line leading up left.

3. 50m   Follow this line up left to a short awkward corner and a short chimney which lead to the final crest.

11 West Central Gully   350m   VII,8 ***

M.Fowler, M.Morrison   5 Apr 1987

A very hard, serious but spectacular climb. The story goes that, pushed to the limit, Mick Fowler was forced to take a rest by hanging from his ice axe cords that he had tied to the top of his rucksac. Fortunately, this precarious arrangement held while he rested, grimly trying to avoid slipping from the shoulder straps! The gully is easy except for an impasse near the top, a very steep 60m step sporting an ice smeared overhanging chimney leading to steep, pure ice climbing. The grade is a guess; on the first ascent conditions were good, with some ice under the big overhang, but this may have made it poorly protected. A second ascent eliminated the rest point but declined to grade it. Late season, after freeze thaw from above, seems to provide the best chance for enough ice. From the base of the step, ascend the chimney forming the back of the gully and belay beneath a prominent overhang (25m). Climb into the groove-chimney below the overhang, move up to another overhang and follow an ice-choked crack to small ledges (20m). Take the mixed groove to the final overhang; step right onto icy smears (rest point) and follow these to good thick ice and easy ground 50m from the top (25m).

West Central Wall

The very steep wall forming the right side of West Central Gully is high, enclosed and very atmospheric. With some shelter from the wind, it holds snow and ice

Maelstrom Direct Start, VII,7. Climber Tim Marsh

better than the more exposed walls. Approach either up West Central Gully (Grade II) or by two abseils down the lines, which can be seen from the top of Central Buttress.

12 Maelstrom 100m VII,7 **
A.Nisbet, S.Roberts 29 Mar 1992

This takes a left-facing corner system in the left side of the upper part of West Central Wall, moving left to pass left of a big isolated roof near the top (the roof is perhaps the best locating feature). The corner defines the left side of a big inset slab which itself forms the corner of Blood, Sweat and Frozen Tears on the right. A very sustained route, protected with a large rack of rocks and thin pegs. Although often very icy, it requires good conditions for there to be sufficient ice to be helpful, but is climbable whatever. Start in West Central Gully where it steepens, at the height of the Upper Girdle Traverse, which consists of a lower and an upper ledge a few metres higher.

1. 30m Follow the lower Girdle ledge right for about 15m to an icy groove, very mossy in summer. Climb this to the upper ledge, then move right along this ledge past a break below another corner, to a chimney at the base of the main corner.
2. 30m Pull up left and enter the slightly overhanging chimney. Climb it and the subsequent corner for about 15m until a traverse leftwards leads to small ledges.
3. 40m Move up then left again into a parallel corner, often very icy, which passes left of the big roof. Follow this to the top.

Variation: **Direct Start   25m   VII,7**
P.Davies, T.Marsh   4 Mar 2008

A more direct start is recommended, although the original line is the easiest. About 15m left of the mossy groove of Blood, Sweat and Frozen Tears is another shallower groove. This, the summer line, might make a good start but the most recent ascent started at an ice filled groove higher up, the last groove below West Central Gully.

Climb the ice to the lower of the Girdle ledges. Traverse 3m right to a 10m vertical corner, climbed to the upper ledge and another traverse right past a corner (the lower continuation of the parallel corner of pitch 3; this is a harder alternative line) to beneath the main corner.

13 Blood, Sweat and Frozen Tears   100m   VIII,8 ****
M.E.Moran, A.Nisbet   26 Mar 1993

This is an outstanding and very sustained route up a big vegetated groove in the centre of the face (the left-hand of two big grooves). Above the Upper Girdle, the groove continues between an inset slab and a well defined arete. The line can be seen from the top of Central Buttress, although the groove is less obvious from here than from below. The first abseil is for 50m from a point 6m right of a big perched block. The second is from the belay at the end of pitch 2. Low in the grade: the first ascent thought VII,8 but they were used to the steep but positive style of climbing.

1. 30m Climb the groove, at times on the right wall, to belay on the lower Girdle ledge.

2. 20m Continue up the groove, then move left onto a steep slab to reach the upper Girdle ledge. Pull through the overhangs above the ledge, then immediately swing right into the continuation corner. Climb this and move left to a block belay.

3. 50m Go left and climb a big left-facing corner past a difficult overhang.

West Buttress

The lowest tier of the West Buttress is easily the most formidable of the sandstone tiers on the triple buttresses, and is largely bypassed by the ordinary winter route. The direct route climbs this and the quartzite more directly.

14 West Buttress   400m   IV,4 ***
R.MacGregor, A.Nisbet   13 Jan 1979

Another superb mountaineering route. The two options skirt the sandstone tier either on the left via West Central Gully or on the right via Fuselage Gully, the options joining to share a finish up the final tier.

Fuselage Gully Start

Climb some way up Fuselage Gully and go left at the first break in its steep left wall (this is high up but still sandstone). Follow the easiest practicable line to Broad Terrace. Alternatively (should be soloable), continue up the gully until above the sandstone and traverse easily left along Broad Terrace. Go along the Terrace to its apparent end where it goes round a bend. Climb shallow corners just right or on the crest to reach the final tier after about four pitches. A line up a large shallow scoop in the face right of the crest has also been climbed (as on the first ascent).

West Central Start

This provides wonderful scenery. Start up West Central Gully, easy slabby ground or banked out. Once into the wide part of the gully proper, keep to the right and climb a narrow right branch into a cave. Crawl out right on to the buttress, then go up into a bay exited by a chimney on the right. Go up to a steep band, the crux when climbed direct, but there may be an easier option. Now on easier ground, continue to the final tier and finish by the summer route going right, then back left.

Final Tier

Traverse right on snow or scree ledges for about 20m to the edge where the buttress turns towards Fuselage Gully. Climb a line of weakness and traverse back left along ledges. Climb a shallow chimney in a big corner to a ledge just below the top of the tier. A short narrow chimney leads to a walk along the final crest.

5 West Buttress Direttissima   310m   VII,8 ***
R.Anderson, R.Milne   5 Apr 1986: Lower corner direct: G.Robertson, E.Tressider   27 Feb 2005

This very direct winter line follows most of the large right-facing corner on the sandstone tier. On the top tier it takes a more direct left-hand finish. It is unusual, as it provides excellent climbing on both sandstone and quartzite. There was a fair amount of ice on the first ascent, although the crux, in the middle of the corner, was torquing up an overhanging crack. The second ascent was mostly under powder and is the line described. Start below and just right of the obvious corner-line in the sandstone tier.

1. 30m Climb an icefall, then go left across easy slopes to the base of the corner. Climb steepening ice to a tricky step left to belay.

2. 20m Step back right and climb the corner direct via a steep crack with a difficult exit.

3. 30m Follow the icy line just right of the corner with increasing difficulty to an awkward belay at a huge flake.

4. 25m Step back left into the corner, then climb this strenuously to reach the crest of the buttress.

5. 110m Continue up leftwards to the crest of the buttress, then take the easiest line to below the final tower.

6. 20m The line is now that of the Direct Finish. Climb a short wall, then another short wall with a thin crack in it; step left and continue to belay in a recess formed by a huge flake at the foot of the impressive final flake-line.

7. 30m Move up then left to gain the flake-line which leads to a fine finish over the obvious projecting block.

8. 35m Climb a short chimney and easy ground to the top.

Fuselage Wall

This is the west side of West Buttress's top tier and is bounded on the right by Fuselage Gully. At its base is a ledge which provides a walk from Fuselage Gully round on to the crest under the top tier of West Buttress. Being high and exposed to north-westerly winds, this is a good early winter season venue.

Approach: The direct approach is either up or down Fuselage Gully. In winter the descent of Fuselage Gully, using a 15m abseil from the aircraft wreckage, gives a quick access to these short steep routes.

16 Fuselage Wall   70m   V,7 *
R.Anderson, G.Nicoll   3 Jan 1987

In the centre of the wall about 20m up there is a 3m high pinnacle, more easily seen from the side than below.

1. 30m Climb steep cracks to reach the neck behind the pinnacle from the left.

2. 15m Climb straight up a shallow corner and crack to a good ledge on the left.

3. 25m Climb the flake beside the belay and continue up the fault over a small roof to follow a corner leading to the top.

17 Fight or Flight   70m   V,6 **
D.McGimpsey, A.Nisbet, J.Preston   17 Dec 2006

Sustained climbing up the centre of the wall, but well protected and with no desperate moves. The capping roof yields unexpectedly. Start 10m left of Fuselage Gully, where a groove leads up left to roofs below the pinnacle.

1. 25m Climb the groove to blocks, return right up a huge flake and go up a short overhanging chimney capped by a chockstone to a diagonal ledge.

2. 20m Go left up the ledge and return right over a big flake to the base of a left-facing corner which is directly above the belay. Climb the corner to a ledge below roofs.

3. 25m Go up left to a niche and pull out left on to a hanging slab between roofs. Return right above the roof and climb blocky ground to the top.

18 Fuselage Gully   400m   II **

This is the gully to the right of West Buttress. It gives probably the best easy gully climb in the corrie, assuming the left branch is taken at half-height. It contains the wreckage of a Lancaster bomber which crashed in 1952. Grade I with a good build-up.

Sàil Mhòr

(NG 938 606)   Alt 981m

When entering Coire Mhic Fhearchair from the north-west, the beetling crags and terraces of Sàil Mhòr on the right cannot fail to impress, and the gullies give sporting winter climbs. The routes are described from right to left as this is the way one would normally approach them.

Descent: Go to the summit of Sàil Mhòr and follow the ridge towards Coinneach Mhòr. At the far end of the col between these two (the lowest point), turn right and descend a shallow gully, glissading as far as possible, until easier slopes lead down to the path.

Morrison's Gully (No.1 Gully)   300m   I *
The big gully on the north face of Sàil Mhòr is obvious before reaching the corrie and presents no difficulties.

Lawson, Ling and Glover's Route   400m   II ***
Culprits as above   2 Apr 1899
A fine mountaineering route through excellent scenery with only a couple of awkward sections. The next obvious gully, starting above the north-west end of the lochan, is Jenga (No.2 Gully). Climb the gully till it turns sharply left then break out up easy slopes on the right to gain the crest. This is followed to the top over rocky steps and pinnacles to the summit of Sàil Mhòr.

Jenga (No.2 Gully)   300m   VI,7 ***
B.Davison, D.McGimpsey, A.Nisbet, D.Wilkinson   4 Mar 2000
An impressive deep gully with a fierce headwall. Named after an earlier attempt when removal of a crucial block caused a pile to collapse, Davison flying with them. On the helicopter flight out, Nisbet spotted Spring Gully (Liathach) which he climbed three days later. The gully is easy until it turns left. Soon there is a chockstone pitch which can bank out and leads to the headwall. Continue up the back of the gully until forced to traverse left. Either climb ice in the left corner or a pile of blocks just to the right until steep ground forces a return traverse to near the gully bed (45m). Climb the gully into a small cave (25m). Chimney out the top of the cave to the final groove which finishes on a flat platform on the crest of the buttress, here joining Lawson, Ling and Glover's Route (25m). Follow this to the top.

White's Gully (No.3 Gully)   120m   II *
S.White and party · 26 Apr 1910
A broad gully running up from the head of the lochan is joined a third of the way up by a narrow gully whose foot is a quarter of the way down the lochan. The route follows this narrow gully and is easy up to the final 30m, which is a chimney with three chockstones. This final section is sometimes banked out and provides steep snow.

LIATHACH

(NG 929 579)   Alt 1054m   Map p327

Liathach comprises a range of seven tops forming an 8km chain running east to west on the north side of Glen Torridon, towering directly above the road. The highest point on Liathach is Spidean a' Choire Leith at alt 1054m, mid-way between Stuc a' Choire Dhuibh Bhig, alt 913m, guarding the east end of the chain, and Mullach an Rathain alt 1023m, at the west end above Torridon village. A broad shoulder extends west for 2km from Mullach an Rathain rising slightly to Sgorr a' Chadail before dropping steeply, but easily, down to Coire Mhic Nòbuil and the footpath.

In winter the mountain is transformed to produce some of the best icefall climbing in Britain. The traverse of the mountain gives one of the classic ridge expeditions of the mainland, with sensationally exposed views onto the surrounding prehistoric hills of the Torridon area.

Weather and Conditions: The described routes are almost all on snow and ice. Those wanting mixed climbing are better going to Coire Mhic Fhearchair from the same car park. Good ice may form at any time between January and April. A warm weather system may strip the buttresses and thin icefalls, but the ice will re-form quickly on a return to colder conditions. The most reliable climbs will be found in Coire Dubh Mòr and high up in Coire na Caime. With heavy snowfalls, or late in the season, many of the bigger, easier gullies will bank out with snow.

Liathach Main Ridge Traverse   4km   II ***

A superb expedition with continually interesting walking and spectacular mountain and loch scenery. It is usually traversed from east to west. Leave the Coire Dubh path at about NG 954 582 and climb steep slopes towards Stuc a' Choire Dhuibh Bhig. On reaching a high rock band, traverse right to reach its north-east ridge. Go up a short tricky section and the bouldery ridge to the top. For convenience of transport, non-purists may start up the Allt an Doire Ghairbh path. Access Gully (Grade I) in Coire Dubh Beag is an alternative. The hardest part is the traverse of the Fasarinen Pinnacles which warrants Grade II, but all sections of the traverse involve Grade I up, down and traversing. In summer a low traverse of Am Fasarinen on the south side provides a path but this is often steeply banked in winter and more difficult than the crest, especially in bad snow conditions. Usually a mixture of traversing and the crest will be taken, the recommended route being to traverse initially (at the eastern end) round the pinnacles, but follow the crest over Am Fasarinen. The main ridge finishes at Mullach an Rathain. The quickest descent and most convenient for transport is via the Allt an Tuill Bhain (see Coire na Caime, reversing approach 2).

Approach: The climbs on the north side of Liathach are described from east to west, approaching via the Coire Dubh Mòr footpath, starting from the National Trust car park in Glen Torridon (NG 958 568). The path rises under the east buttress of Stuc a' Choire Dhuibh Bhig and round the back to give access to the three northern corries of Coire Dubh Beag, Coire Dubh Mòr and the larger spectacular Coire na Caime. Access from the footpath to each corrie, and also the descents, are described for each corrie individually.

COIRE DUBH BEAG

(NG 938 583)   Alt 750m   North facing   Map p327

This is the first of the northern corries, a classic bowl with an easy snow gully on its back left side and broad steep terraces sweeping round to the right. From a distance, the cascades of ice look discontinuous, but the lines become more apparent on closer inspection.

Approach: From the Coire Dubh footpath, the best approach is to follow the burn draining from the corrie, the chosen side depending on snow deposition, 2hrs 30mins.

Descent: The quickest descent is to go down Access Gully and return by the approach. Alternatively, continue along the ridge east beyond Access Gully to traverse Stuc a' Choire Dhuibh Bhig and descend off the east end of the ridge. The third option is to descend the opposite side of Access Gully (i.e. southwards) or from a point just to its west, then turn right (west) to traverse into Coire Liath Mhor.

1 The Snotter   40m   VI,6 **

A.Cunningham, A.Nisbet   25 Feb 1986

The very steep icicle that drools down the left wall at the start of Beag Pardon. It forms after several days below freezing, the colder the better, which is more often

LIATHACH
Coire Dubh Beag

1. The Snotter	VI,6 **	
2. Beag Pardon	III *	
3. Hidden Gully	II	
4. Access Gully	I *	
5. Footless Gully	IV,5 *	
6. Headhunter	V,5 **	
7. Headless Gully	V,5 **	
8. Brainless Fall	VI,6 *	
9. The Executioner	V,6	
10. Rambler's Rib	II *	
11. Hillwalk	II **	

Brainless Fall, VI,6. Climber Dave McGimpsey

than you might think. Descend by abseil, or continue very easily to the summit.

2 Beag Pardon   200m   III *
At the back left corner of the corrie is the easy snow gully (Access Gully). Left of its base is a snow terrace leading left, then up into a narrow cleft. Climb the cleft, requiring chimneying on steep ice. From the top of its narrows, traverse right and finish up Hidden Gully, Grade I from here.

3 Hidden Gully   210m   II
C.Rowland   1977
This climb sneaks up left, usually on ice, from the lower reaches of Access Gully, breaking into a snow gully directly above.

4 Access Gully   120m   I *
The obvious snow gully tucked into the left side at the back of the corrie. It gives a pleasant route on to the main ridge and without a cornice and not steep for the grade, may also be used as a descent.

5 Footless Gully   150m   IV,5 *
C.Rowland, A.S.Rowland   Feb 1977
The obvious line on the back wall. The first 10m is the crux, an awkward narrow

vertical chimney slow to fill with ice. The climb is often only Grade III after the first pitch. Although there are many terraces, the direct line feels natural.

6 Headhunter   200m   V,5 **
N.Kekus, S.Anderson   7 Feb 1994

An obvious chimney left of the aspect change taken by Headless Gully; more of a gully than Headless. The first ascentionists climbed it in mistake for Headless, as others may have done before. From the Coire Dubh path it appears straight up whereas Headless slants right. The route starts up a steep icefall, leftmost of several (can be the crux, easier with more build-up) to gain the first terrace. A short awkward corner gains the bottom of the chimney, which can be led in one long pitch or split. Follow the chimney for 20m before leaving on the left to gain a good ledge. Regain the continuation chimney on the right and follow it to below a steep rock wall and icy slab on the left. Climb the slab to turn the rock wall on the left and reach a final steep ice pitch leading to easy ground.

7 Headless Gully   150m   V,5 **
S.Kennedy, A.Nisbet   Feb 1984

The main line on the right (east facing) wall and the route most likely to form regularly. Start by the highest point of snow under the middle of the wall. Climb an initial short steep icefall to the first terrace. Move left into the main icefall which is steep for 25m (crux) before easing onto more terraced ground. Finish via an ice filled corner through the top tier onto the summit snowfield. The main icefall forms down a chimney-line and on the first ascent, after a long thaw, the gap between ice and rock was chimneyed at an easier grade IV; subsequent ascents gave the above grade.

8 Brainless Fall   140m   VI,6 *
V.Chelton, D.McGimpsey, A.Nisbet   12 Mar 1999

Climbs some steep ice which occasionally forms on the wall right of Headless Gully. Climb ice leftwards to reach a ledge below the ice which forms on the wall just right of overhangs which run across from Headless (10m). Climb an icefall on the wall which is just below vertical (25m). Move 5m left and climb thicker vertical ice which soon eases (30m). Go up a short wall and easier ground to the final tier (50m). Climb the tier by a groove on the left to easy ground.

9 The Executioner   140m   V,6
A.Nisbet, J.Mothersele   15 Feb 1986

A large snow ramp leads right from under the line of Headless Gully, to finish at an overhang at the base of a shallow gully. The Executioner gains the gully higher up, avoiding the overhang on the left. Start halfway up the ramp and follow a very steep ice filled corner, vertical to start, to a pinnacle belay on the right. The icefall continues right of the pinnacle in two steps to a big snow ledge. Move right into the main gully which leads to the top.

10 Rambler's Rib   350m   II *
D.Broadhead, S.Sillars   15 Feb 1987

This route follows the rib bounding the left side of a narrow curving gully (Hillwalk) and bounding the west of Coire Dubh Beag itself. Start in the gully and climb out onto the rib at the earliest opportunity. Climb the rib direct, with short technical walls above big ledges, avoiding the final rock tower on the left or right. Not a safe option in avalanche conditions, as either finish is on snow slopes.

1 Hillwalk   300m   II **
First Ascent by an unknown party in 1966

The fine curving narrow gully immediately right of Ramblers Rib is also known as Trotters Gully. It can give several short pitches through interesting scenery, but often banks out to Grade I. It opens into a bowl after its narrow section, and it is common for windslab to build up here (there have been accidents).

COIRE DUBH MÒR

(NG 931 583)   Alt 750m   North facing   Map p327

This corrie is topped by Spidean a' Choire Leith, the highest peak of Liathach, and provides the best concentration of ice climbs on the mountain. In good conditions, the icefall climbing is the equal of anywhere in Scotland and lacking only the length of season of Ben Nevis.

Weather and Conditions: This corrie is the most reliable option for ice in Torridon. During a cold winter, the thicker icefalls form readily and last well, throughout January to March, and survive most thaws. In some recent mild winters, the ice on the steeper falls, like Poachers Fall, has never formed. The normal absence of cornices means that these icefalls can sometimes be climbed during a slight thaw, accepting slushy ice and potential rockfall. The thinner icefalls require good conditions and tend to lose their first pitches during a thaw. Conditions are often good when the south (road-facing) side of the mountain is bare, common in the second half of the season. The corrie is very exposed to a northerly wind, but somewhat sheltered with a south to west wind, although this often swirls around the corrie. The slope above the routes can avalanche, particularly down Poachers Fall, but some routes are safer (see below).

Approach: Leave the Coire Dubh footpath just before the watershed and angle up to join the burn draining from the corrie itself, 2hrs 30mins.

Descents:
1. For the main face, the quickest descent is to make a rising traverse left to join and descend the east ridge of Spidean to the col between it and Stob a' Coire Liath Mhor. From the col, Way Up can be descended northwards back into the corrie, but it is quicker to descend in the opposite direction (south) down a shallow gully (Grade I) to a flat area. Go straight on from the base of the gully to the south rim and descend another gully. Continue in the same direction down a shallow continuation to cross the stream and gain the footpath. In favourable conditions much of this can be glissaded.
2. If the summit of Liathach has been visited, either as an option or after George, one can still descend the east ridge to the col, or in very good conditions glissade from near the summit, but the least steep option is to descend the south ridge (a notorious dead end) until it becomes level, then turn left (east) and descend diagonally leftwards to gain the descent gully part way down from the col.
3. From West Gully or Spidean Way, one can either go west to the col and descend as above or go east and descend as for Coire Dubh Beag ('six and two threes').

Layout: The corrie has huge rambling buttresses on the left cut by two obvious gullies, West Gully and Spidean Way, followed by a deep snow gully, Way Up, bordering the left end of the steep back wall. Way Up leads to a col on the main ridge. The 200m back wall extends rightwards to a left-curving gash, George, before merging into the north ridge of Spidean. In the centre of the back wall, and obvious from a great distance, is the magnificent ice cascade of Poachers Fall, the line that forms most readily.

1 West Gully   300m   I *
C.Rowland, R.McHardy   1978
This is the first obvious gully line in the mouth of the corrie, with a steep right wall and bounding the left side of a terraced buttress. Normally banked up, it can be very icy in lean conditions.

2 Spidean Way   300m   III *
C.Rowland, B.Griffiths   1977
The next gully line, left-slanting and formed between the first terraced buttress and a larger one in the back left corner of the corrie. Often two short steep pitches followed by a longer one, but the short pitches disappear under heavy snow.

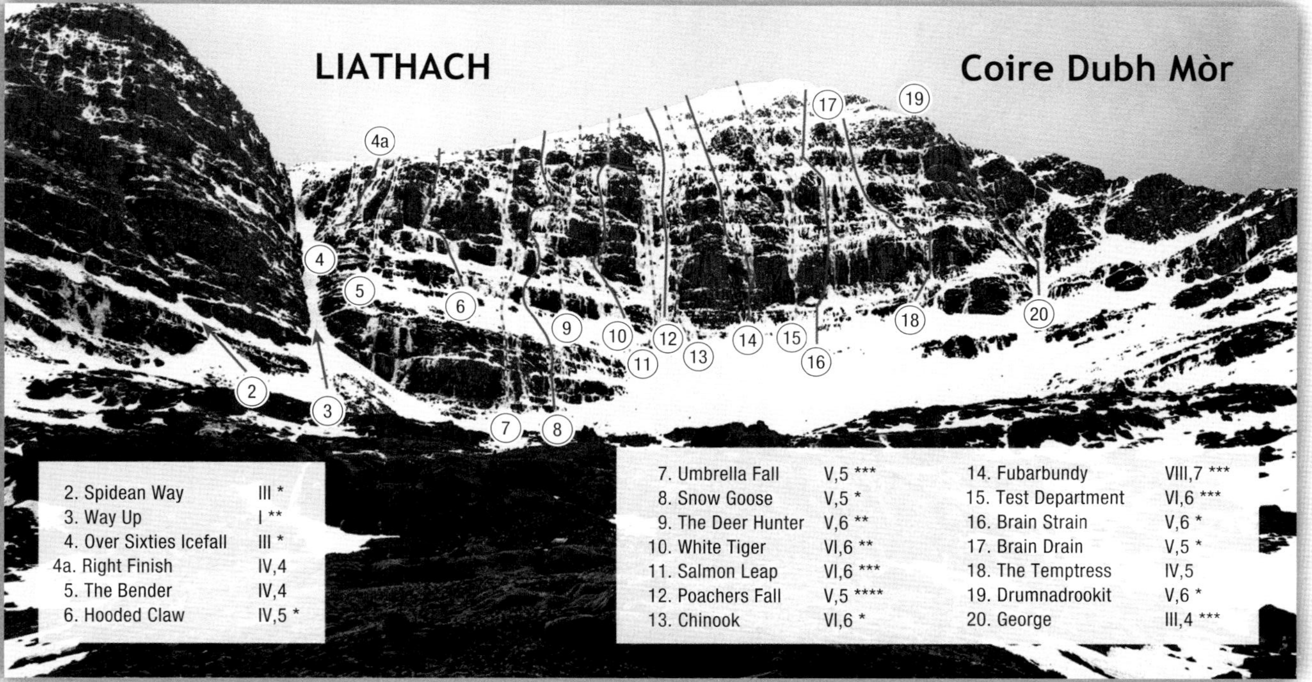

LIATHACH

Coire Dubh Mòr

2. Spidean Way   III *
3. Way Up   I **
4. Over Sixties Icefall III *
4a. Right Finish   IV,4
5. The Bender   IV,4
6. Hooded Claw   IV,5 *

7. Umbrella Fall   V,5 ***
8. Snow Goose   V,5 *
9. The Deer Hunter   V,6 **
10. White Tiger   VI,6 **
11. Salmon Leap   VI,6 ***
12. Poachers Fall   V,5 ****
13. Chinook   VI,6 *

14. Fubarbundy   VIII,7 ***
15. Test Department VI,6 ***
16. Brain Strain   V,6 *
17. Brain Drain   V,5 *
18. The Temptress   IV,5
19. Drumnadrookit   V,6 *
20. George   III,4 ***

Umbrella Fall, V,5. Climber Alan Smith

Andy Tibbs

3 Way Up   250m   I **

The straightforward snow gully leading to the bealach on the main ridge. The grade does not vary with build-up, nor does it form a significant cornice.

The next four routes finish on a slope which is too low angled for avalanches so can provide a safe option in poor snow conditions, particularly if approached by the initial icefall of Umbrella Fall.

4 Over Sixties Icefall   100m   III *

M.Johnston, A.Nisbet, D.Thompson   7 Mar 1994

A shorter and more friendly route than others in the corrie. The participants were challenged in age but not ice climbing ability. On the right wall of Way Up about halfway up is a lower angled icefall which is excellent when formed, but poor in some years. There are often two lines, a left-hand which is low in the grade and a right-hand up steeper pillars which is IV,4. The icefall leads in three pitches of largely continuous ice to a big terrace from where a rising traverse leads left to the ridge just above the col (and descent).

5 The Bender   150m   IV,4

B.Davison, A.Nisbet   6 Mar 1999

Climbs the leftmost icefall on the main face, virtually on the corner where the face bends round on to the gully wall of Way Up. The difficulties are short but useful as a second route, being accessible from the col by descending Way Up and traversing from 50m below the base of Over Sixties Icefall. Start below the icefall and climb easily to an iced corner which leads to the main icefall. Climb the icefall to a ledge at its top. Move left to slabby mixed ground leading to a big terrace. Finish easily by a choice of lines.

6 Hooded Claw   150m   IV,5 *
A.Nisbet, A.Cunningham   13 Jan 1987
The icefall towards the left edge of the main face and the next prominent ice line left of Umbrella Fall. Start from a long traverse left along the terrace above the first tier (or climb a line on the tier a bit to the right). The fine crux pitch follows a steep iced groove to an ice 'hood', bypassed on the right via a short icicle.

7 Umbrella Fall   230m   V,5 ***
M.Fowler, P.Butler   1 Apr 1984
This is the largest and most obvious icefall on the face between Way Up and Poacher's Fall. The crux pitch is much harder than the rest; it contained an ice umbrella on the first ascent, surprise, surprise. It can be Grade IV with ideal ice formations. Either start by a steep icefall on a ramp immediately right of Way Up or climb ice directly below the upper icefall to reach the first terrace. Trend right or straight up to below the main fall. The main fall steepens to its crux pitch. Often this forms a deep groove on the right of a pillar (sometimes with a big ice umbrella) which can be eased by bridging, or even chimneying. In leaner conditions a line left of the pillar may be easier. The final optional pitch is also quite steep, or escape left.

8 Snow Goose   230m   V,5 *
A.Cunningham, A.Nisbet   25 Feb 1986
The left-hand thinner icefall and just right of Umbrella Fall. The line includes a pitch up the lowest tier, which extends as far as Way Up. The ice is continuous over six tiers; the fourth a steep iced wall of a right-facing corner and the fifth tier (crux) a weave through two overhangs by a corner on the right and an icicle above.

9 The Deer Hunter   200m   V,6 **
A.Cunningham, A.Nisbet   24 Feb 1986
The middle of the thin ice lines left of The Salmon Leap. The line is obvious at mid-height as a thick ice cased right-facing corner. The first short bulging tier may be turned on the left. Again, the last tier is bare of ice and a short right traverse leads to a strenuous chimney with a difficult exit (crux).

10 White Tiger   220m   VI,6 **
A.Cunningham, A.Nisbet   14 Jan 1987
The nearest ice line to The Salmon Leap, and slow to form, but can form very thick, and then excellent. Vertical sections, but not too long, and with good belays and ledges. The first main tier, if not formed, can be avoided by a right traverse from an icy bay left of the main line. Four steep tiers lead to a final rock barrier. Follow a delicate right traverse into the final pitch of The Salmon Leap. The obvious direct finish has also been climbed in mixed conditions at technical 7.

11 The Salmon Leap   200m   VI,6 ***
A.Cunningham, A.Nisbet   23 Feb 1986
This is the left side of Poachers Fall, separated in the top half by a rock rib. It has a short vertical section when ice conditions are average, but in prime conditions this can be avoided by a groove on the right, and then it may become easier than Poachers, which can form a big ice bulge at mid-height. Good rock belays on the left wall. The line finishes naturally up a left-slanting chimney-crack, but if the ice in this has thawed, finish on the right towards Poachers.

Poachers Fall, V,5. Climber James Gordon

Pete Macpherson

12 Poachers Fall 180m V,5 ****
R.McHardy, A.Nisbet 11 Feb 1978
Take the right side of the obvious steep wide icefall draining the middle of the back
wall. The top section is in a deep groove right of the separating rib and is partially
hidden on the approach to the corrie. The route comes into condition quickly and
the top groove can be climbed even when thin. There is a good rock belay at the
right end of a ledge between the two steepest sections and about 60m from the
start; but at least one ice screw belay should be expected and most of the runners
are ice screws.

13 Chinook 160m VI,6 *
S.Anderson, M.E.Moran, M.Welch 4 Mar 2000
Climbs the ice line which sometimes forms 15m right of Poacher's; a good

independent route.

1. 50m Climb icy grooves passing a big pedestal on the right to a cramped stance under an overlap.

2. 40m Swing on to an ice fringe at the lip and follow the slab corner above to belay in a dry corner left of an icicle.

3. 25m Climb the steep icicle and move right to block belays.

4. 55m Move 5m back left, climb iced rock, an ice corner and a mixed chimney to easy ground.

The face right of Poachers Fall forms two obvious icefalls draining down a very steep first tier, giving the crux of the climbs.

14 Fubarbundy   200m   VIII,7 ***
C.Cartwright, D.Heselden   22 Feb 1994

The obvious hanging icefall right of Poacher's; it often stops at the lip of a roof 30m left of Test Department, but can form down the arete on its right. This occurred in 1993 and 1994 to produce arguably the hardest thin ice pitch in Scotland (although the ice was thicker at times in both years). A free ascent is possible in the right conditions, but they have yet to be caught. Start beneath the roof.

1. 35m Climb icy grooves trending right to belay in a small corner directly below a large left-facing corner (right of the one leading to the roof).

2. 30m Climb up to the large corner, followed for 6m, then tension left on to the hanging slab. Climb this on thin ice trending left above the large roof. The slab culminates at a small overhang; belay at its left side.

3. 30m Climb the icy groove to the left of the belay and continue up the icefall.

4. 40m Continue up the icefall trending right.

5. 45m Move right to the obvious buttress, move around its prow to belay below an icy groove.

6. Climb the groove, then easy broken ground to the top.

15 Test Department   190m   VI,6 ***
M.Fowler, C.Watts (2PA)   11 Jan 1987; FFA by the complete icicle B.Davison, A.Nisbet, S.Anderson, M.E.Moran   6 Mar 1999

The second icefall right of Poacher's, forms two distinctive consecutive ice columns (but normally seen as hanging icicles). After a 20m pitch to gain them, climb the ice columns and steep ice above (50m). On the first ascent the lower icicle did not reach the ground, so a start was made to the right and two aid pegs were used to gain a traverse line back to the icicle. The icicle was complete for the second ascent and about 20 more ascents in the following week. Take the left-hand of two ice lines, then more easily up to the final wall (50m). Mixed icy ground trending slightly left, following a shallow groove almost directly above the lower pitches, leads through a small niche to easy ground.

16 Brain Strain   180m   V,6 *
D.Wills, M.Fowler   17 Feb 1991

This takes a series of ice streaks in line with the first pitch of Brain Drain. Start up a shallow chimney-groove 15m right of Test Department (Brain Drain) – (45m). Trend slightly right to belay beneath a vertical ice smeared corner (30m). Climb the corner and continue to the next steep band (30m), which is climbed by an ice line just left of Brain Drain, or more easily further left (60m). Finish through the final tier (15m).

17 Brain Drain   180m   V,5 *
A.Nisbet, A.Cunningham   13 Jan 1987

The next main fall to the right, most obvious at mid-height, forms a thin bulging first pitch. This is avoided on the left by a hidden icy chimney-groove (crux), followed by a traverse right to join the main line. Continually interesting and varied climbing on ice leads in three or four pitches to easier ground.

18 The Temptress   220m   IV,5
A.Cunningham, A.Nisbet   16 Feb 1988
The rightmost icefall on the face, much less continuous than the others. A short steep introductory pitch leads to a steep shallow left-facing ice groove. Climb the groove (crux), step left into a shorter groove and go up to small walls (50m). Traverse left, then go up to a left-slanting icefall right of Brain Drain. Finish more easily.

19 Drumnadrookit   220m   V,6 *
E.Brunskill, A.Nisbet   27 Feb 2002
A direct finish to The Temptress, up ice which forms through a slot about 20m left of an impressive prow which sits high on the right side of the face.

20 George   230m   III,4 ***
I.G.Rowe, M.Kelsey   Feb 1967
The steep back wall of the corrie finishes at a deep gash, the next feature left of the north ridge of Spidean; this is the line. Almost always in condition, even when lean, and both forks give short but technical difficulties. The first half of the gully is easy, sometimes with short ice pitches, but then it steepens and narrows. Here is the fork, the more obvious chimney on the left being the harder Sinister Prong. For the normal route, climb rightwards out of the gully on steepish ice. One can now crawl under a big chockstone to a narrow exit (looks improbable). This through route is great fun and just possible with rucksacks as long as ski sticks are not on the outside. Climb right to left over an awkward bulge of jammed blocks, then finish up a shallow groove on the right to the crest of the north ridge. The summit of Liathach is easily visited and recommended from here. Alternatively, descend the north ridge (on which the route finishes), keeping left of the crest until a large snow shelf leads back into the base of George.
Variation: **Sinister Prong   IV,5 ***
J.Grant, J.R.Mackenzie   12 Feb 1978
This takes the left fork of George below the steep upper section. Move left into the chimney at one of two possible places. There are two difficult bulging sections (both well protected) leading to the same belay as the normal route. Finish up the continuation line, a shallow groove which is recommended when iced. Otherwise, move right to finish up the final groove of the normal route. Grade III,5 in good conditions.

COIRE NA CAIME

Map p327   Diagram p350
Walking west along the Coire Dubh path, this is the third, the most scenic and largest of the northern corries. Its relative remoteness ensures that it is less popular than the others and it will appeal to those who wish a day with a mountaineering atmosphere and an element of exploration. There is a bigger selection of lower grade routes but it lacks the steep icefalls of Coire Dubh Mòr.

Weather and Conditions: Being a little higher and more remote, better weather is recommended for a visit. Conditions are often similar to the other northern corries, although snow does last longer in the upper corrie.

Approach:
1. Leave the Coire Dubh path near the watershed as for Coire Dubh Mòr and skirt round under the north ridge of Spidean into the corrie. The exact height of approach depends on destination but all are bouldery unless there is hard snow. This takes 2hrs 30mins in good conditions but 3hrs is more normal. This is the easiest approach but returning to the car is much longer.
2. Recommended for Bell's Buttress and the Upper Corrie is an approach over the top. Park at the east end of the western of two woods and close to the river (NG 914 554). A path starts 10m east at a small cairn. It is indistinct at first over small crags but soon becomes a constructed path. Head for a stile over a deer fence. Follow the path up a shallow valley before moving right to join the Allt a' Tuill

Bhan. Continue as if heading for Mullach nan Rathain, but leave the path and climb direct up a shallow gully (first on the right) which leads towards a small top formed by Bell's Buttress (NG 916 576). For Bell's Buttress, descend the gully immediately to the west (Grade I, can be corniced) and turn right. For the Trinity Gullies, descend either this gully or one about 100m west, turning left as soon as possible into the base of the Upper Corrie.

3. Useful for Am Fasarinen and the east end of the corrie, this option is similar to number 2 but trends right on the final slopes (further right than appearances might suggest), and reaches the ridge near the west end of Am Fasarinen. The broad Gully 7 (easy Grade I) lies at a col (NG 921 574), before a 5m rise to a bump. After this the ridge starts to narrow and gently drops to another col (the top of Twisting Gully) ahead of a steep rise to Am Fasarinen. If the steep rise is reached, Gully 7 is 100m back.

Descent: See each section of the corrie.

Layout: As the name may suggest, 'crooked corrie', it is more complicated than the typical bowl shape. It is formed between the two Munros of Spidean a' Choire Leith and Mullach nan Rathain, with a long north-east ridge from the latter out to Meall Dearg forming the crooked shape. Loch Coire na Caime lurks at the entrance. The broad ridge of P.C. Buttress divides Coire na Caime into two, with the Fasarinen Pinnacles and Am Fasarinen closer to Spidean a' Choire Leith, and an upper section reaching high towards Mullach an Rathain. Right of P.C. Buttress is the Titanium Face, then the prominent Bell's Buttress, finishing in an upper corrie overshadowed by the Northern Pinnacles.

Am Fasarinen

(NG 924 576)   Alt 750m   North facing   Diagram p350

This is the largest buttress on the left of the corrie. The Fasarinen pinnacles are further left, first a small triangular buttress, then a more impressive triangular tower, The Dru.

On close inspection Am Fasarinen sports five fine looking thin ice lines, the middle three being the most obvious chimney gullies directly under the summit. Of these three, the left one (Jerbil) is the deepest, the middle one (The Andes Couloir) is essentially a right-facing corner and the right one (Echo Couloir) is only defined in its upper part.

Descent: Quickest is to traverse the ridge westwards to a col where the ground opens out to a level area (top of Gully 7). Descend south-west on steepening slopes to reach the Allt a' Tuill Bhan. Descend the path (see approach 2). If there is a good build-up, go south-south-west from the col to a gully at NG 921 573 which runs south-west towards the Allt a' Tuill Bhan (not just east of south, crucial!). This is a very quick descent if conditions are favourable for glissading, but take great care as there are drops below chockstones into which one could fall in lean or thawing conditions. It is unusual to be able to glissade all the way to easy ground but one can escape out right lower down.

1 Jerbil   120m   V,5 **
M.Fowler, B.Craig   10 Mar 1985
The deepest and often iciest of the gullies is steep. Start in a high snow bay shared by a left-slanting gully. Climb a steep ice pitch leading to a small snow amphitheatre in the deep gully (45m). Continue in the same line avoiding difficult obstacles on the left or right as necessary to an easy bay leading to the main ridge.

2 The Andes Couloir   180m   V,5 **
A.Cunningham, A.Nisbet   22 Feb 1986
A steep start up an ice curtain, quite slow to form, leads to a snow ledge under a steep iced corner. Pull into the corner over a strenuous bulge (where the ice may be thin) and take the superb right-facing ice corner above to an easing below the main ridge.

LIATHACH - Coire na Caime

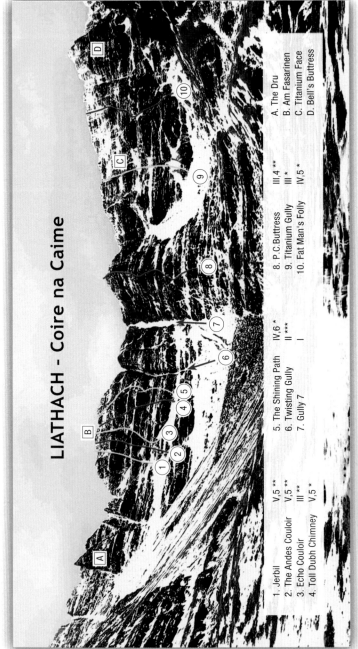

1. Jerbil — V,5 **
2. The Andes Couloir — V,5 **
3. Echo Couloir — III **
4. Toll Dubh Chimney — V,5 *
5. The Shining Path — IV,6 *
6. Twisting Gully — II ***
7. Gully 7 — I
8. P.C.Buttress — III,4 **
9. Titanium Gully — III *
10. Fat Man's Folly — IV,5 *

A. The Dru
B. Am Fasarinen
C. Titanium Face
D. Bell's Buttress

Andy Nisbet

3 Echo Couloir   250m   III **

S.Birch, C.Collin, M.E.Moran   1 Mar 1993 (with Direct Start); Left-Hand Start: A.Nisbet, G.Nisbet   19 Mar 1994

This, the fourth ice line is seen (in good conditions) as a wide slabby icefall forming below a big final corner. Start up the initial gully below Andes Couloir, then trend diagonally right on mixed ice and turf to reach the slabby icefall. Climb this and the very obvious upper gully.

Variation: **Direct Start   V,6**

The original ascent started more direct but is harder and the ice forms less readily. Climb two consecutive steep icefalls leading to the right side of the slabby icefall. Either climb the slabby icefall (if formed) or a right-facing turfy corner further right to gain the upper gully.

4 Toll Dubh Chimney   250m   V,5 *

D.Rubens, D.Broadhead   17 Jan 1987

This good route follows the left-trending chimney-line on the buttress 100m left of Twisting Gully; it is the furthest right of the five obvious chimney-lines. Climb to the foot of the deep icy chimney at one-third height in two pitches. On the first ascent, the chimney was overhung at the base and was climbed by a dry crack in the right wall until the ice was regained after 25m. The next pitch culminates in a short overhang after which difficulties eased.

5 The Shining Path   160m   IV,6 *

S.Birch, M.E.Moran   3 Mar 1993

A big icefall forms right of Toll Dubh Chimney to the left of the edge of Twisting Gully. Start just left of the gully at a slanting groove. Climb thin awkward ice up the groove, then trend more easily left up iced steps until a short steep ice corner leads to the foot of the main ice wall. The wall is normally split by a diagonal right-slanting weakness which gives a fine 40m pitch. Climb turfy corners above to the top.

6 Twisting Gully   200m   II ***

R.Urquhart, D.Stevens   31 Mar 1955

The deep snow gully on the right of Am Fasarinen is very scenic, with lovely ice formations. With a good build-up, it is easy except for a short steep ice pitch at two-thirds height. But it is perhaps a better choice when lean but frozen. Short easy ice pitches lead to the main pitch where there is a window through a screen of icicles making this crux pitch less steep.

7 Gully 7   180m   I

A wide gully which is easy for the grade and the cornice is always passable on the left.

8 P.C. Buttress   250m   III,4 **

The longest buttress, really just a long ridge at the boundary between the lower and upper corries, gives a fine mountaineering line, with some short tricky walls but not sustained. Start from a large platform on the lower part of the buttress. Climb an easy gully and move right to the crest. Thereafter, climb close to the crest, choosing the easiest line through each tier. Avoid tempting terraces leading away left. About half-height there is a 5m pinnacle on the crest. Climb up to the neck at its back (technical crux, but the devious may find a through route) and steeply above but soon becoming easier and leading to the small summit and subsequent col.

Titanium Face

(NG 918 576)   Alt 750m   North facing   Diagram p350

West of P.C. Buttress is this broad broken face cut by numerous shallow chimney-lines. These can be filled with ice or partly bank out in snowy conditions. Although escapable on to the many terraces, this is not obvious during the routes and would often only lead to another chimney of similar standard. The face ends in a large buttress of more compact rock, Bell's Buttress, situated above the entrance to upper Coire na Caime and forming a small summit on the main ridge.

Descent: Head south down steep slopes perhaps picking up the gully which descends directly from the top of Bell's Buttress (approach 2) and in ideal conditions provides a long glissade.

9 Titanium Gully   200m   III *
D.Rubens, G. Macnair, G.Cohen   21 Feb 1984
Towards the left end of the face and starting at a snow bay just above the lowest rocks is an obvious narrow ice line running virtually the height of the face. A good line in lean icy conditions, perhaps grade IV at the start, but it can fill up with snow and all but disappear.

10 Fat Man's Folly   250m   IV,5 *
D.Broadhead, D.Rubens   30 Jan 1993
In the centre of the face is a squat triangular buttress ending at half-height. This climb starts up a deep gully forming the right side of this buttress and slanting left, then breaks right to follow a slanting corner.

11 Valentine Buttress   250m   IV,4 **
D.Broadhead, W.Tring   14 Feb 1987
A fine chimney-line in the buttress at the right end of the face, left of the couloir bounding the left side of the Bell's Buttress (Vanadium Couloir). Start 30m left of Vanadium Couloir at the top of a snow bay and take the right-hand of two chimneys close together. Climb the chimney-line for about 100m, with unusual subterranean moves, until easier climbing leads out right onto the buttress. Follow a series of grooves up the rocks above leading to the ridge.

12 Vanadium Couloir   300m   III * or IV,4 Direct
A.Paul, D.Sanderson   24 Feb 1979
The obvious steep open gully line immediately left of Bell's Buttress, starting from the highest point of the snow bay. After a steep start (45m), it is then much easier with icy steps, or largely banked out. The route is Grade III, or even II in good conditions, by trending right from the base, then going back left into the upper runnel (or by traversing under Bell's Buttress into the upper runnel). There are no cornice problems, as the finish is near the top of Bell's Buttress.

Bell's Buttress

(NG 916 577)   Alt 750m   North facing   Diagrams p350, 353

Bell's Buttress is a high area of steep compact rock streaked with shallow chimney-gully lines on the left side and cut by two deep gullies on the more continuous right side; the left one is a cul-de-sac and the right one the line of Bell's Gully. All the routes merge into an easy finish up the upper crest. A snow terrace at the base of the routes can be gained from either end.

Descent: Head south down steep slopes to pick up the gully which descends directly from the top of Bell's Buttress (approach 2) and in ideal conditions provides a long glissade.

13 Bell's Buttress, Left Chimney   230m   IV,5 *
G.Cohen, D.Broadhead   11 Jan 1987
A fine route taking the furthest left chimney-line on Bell's Buttress. Start up the left of a pair of chimneys and step into the right-hand one at 10m. Where it overhangs, climb out right and up the gully above to a huge block belay on the left (30m). Continue up the chimney-line to snow ledges, turning two blocking overhangs on the right (30m). Follow the gully on the right through several narrowings past a rightwards ramp at 45m, and continue in the same line to finish.

Andy Nisbet

LIATHACH - Coire na Caime
Bell's Buttress

10. Fat Man's Folly   IV,5 *
11. Valentine Buttress   IV,4 ***
12. Vanadium Couloir   III *
12a. Vanadium Direct   IV,4
13. Left Chimney   IV,5 *
14. Last Orders   IV,6 *
15. Bell's Gully   IV,5 ***
16. The Final Gong   III *

14 Last Orders   230m   IV,6 *
S.Pearson, G.Cohen   23 Jan 1993
This is the left-hand of two gully lines on the right side of Bell's Buttress, blocked by a huge roof. Climb easy snow (40m). Climb two icy steepenings to below the large roof, then move right and climb the right wall via difficult moves to reach a crack above the overhang. Move back left into the main gully line and continue to a belay (40m). The gully gradually eases, and after 20m gives straightforward climbing to the top.

15 Bell's Gully   230m   IV,5 **
R.Anderson, M.Hamilton   22 Feb 1986
The right-hand and most obvious of the two gully lines on the right side of Bell's Buttress. Follow the increasingly difficult gully over two steepenings to a cul-de-sac at 125m. A dribble of ice may flow down from the upper gully but it looks reasonable without. Move left and take the shallow gully above to easy ground.

16 The Final Gong   200m   III *
J.Lyall, A.Nisbet   10 Jan 1995
A good easier route up the terminal buttress right of Bell's Gully. Start up an easy chimney in the lower tier, then trend slightly right to avoid slabby ground on the left. Return left to the crest between two steep tiers, climb the second, then a right-facing corner and continuing line to easy ground.

Upper Corrie

The upper corrie of Coire na Caime, Coireag Cham, feels almost alpine. It is guarded on the left by Bell's Buttress and on the right by the spectacular Northern Pinnacles of Mullach an Rathain, rising from the outrider of Meall Dearg. Mullach an Rathain itself tops the back of the corrie. Since this corrie is high and sheltered it seems to come into condition sooner and holds snow longer than elsewhere on the mountain.

Descent: From anywhere near the top of Mullach an Rathain, descend by the normal hillwalkers' route, probably down the gully heading south from the summit to the Allt a' Tuill Bhàn.

Northern Pinnacles

(NG 913 578)   Alt 850m   East facing

These are numbered ascending from right to left, One to Five. The gullies at the top of the corrie and between the upper pinnacles provide good easy winter routes and stay in condition longer than anywhere else on the mountain.

Left-Hand Trinity Gully   90m   I *
G.Sang, W.N.Ling, G.T.Glover   1928
The gully between the fifth pinnacle and Mullach an Rathain. Usually snow but icy in lean conditions.

Trinity Arete   110m   III,5 *
A.Nisbet, A.Partington   3 Mar 1996
Climbs the sharp crested buttress between Left-Hand and Central Trinity Gullies. Very helpful and well protected when necessary. Starting at the very toe, the first pitch held a barrier wall climbed by a central thin crack (crux) and higher up a steep shallow corner (40m). The easier crest (50m) led to an overhanging rock nose passed by the first groove on the right (20m).

Central Trinity Gully   105m   II *
D.Stevens, R.Urquhart   29 Mar 1955
The gully between the fourth and fifth pinnacles normally gives two ice pitches, but can bank out to Grade I.

The buttress between Central and Right-Hand Trinity Gullies is **Holy Ghost** (150m III), starting next to the base of Central Trinity Gully.

Right-Hand Trinity Gully   120m   III **
D.Stevens, R.Urquhart   29 Mar 1955
This lies between the third and fourth pinnacles. It is often the best and most difficult of the Trinity gullies, but its one steep pitch takes longer to come into condition.

The Northern Pinnacles   200m   II ***
W.W.Naismith, A.M.Mackay, H.Raeburn   16 Apr 1900
Short and sharp, the Northern Pinnacles guard the north ridge of Mullach an Rathain. Combined with a west to east traverse of Liathach's main ridge, this gives one of Scotland's finest winter round trips. With this in mind, approach via the Coire Dubh Mòr path from the National Trust car park to the base of Meall Dearg (2 to 3hrs), with grand views into the northern corries. An ascent of Meall Dearg by North Buttress (or Terminal Buttress, or Gully Obscura) seems appropriate – see below, but Meall Dearg can be bypassed by entering upper Coire na Caime (Coireag Cham), from where a short Grade I leads to the col between Meall Dearg and the first pinnacle.

There are five pinnacles in all; the first two are small and can be passed on the right (appearing to be one), the third has the longest ascent including a tricky chimney just left of the crest, and the fourth is perhaps the crux (either by flakes on the left or a chimney on the right). The fifth is passed on the right; a tempting direct line on the left has a boulder problem finish, Grade III.
Variation: A slightly shorter but still excellent circuit of the Northern Pinnacles is from the west. Starting from the Beinn Alligin car park and via the Coire Mhic Nòbuil path. Cross the first bridge as for the Beinn Alligin approach but turn right very soon (cairn) and continue round the back of Liathach. Cross the Abhainn Coire Mhic Nòbuil (no bridge!) and angle up to below the north face of Meall Dearg. Any of the routes below can be climbed to Meall Dearg but Spring Gully is the best from this direction when it holds consolidated snow.

Meall Dearg

(NG 917 582)   Alt 620m   North to East facing   Map p327

Terminal Buttress   180m   III *
G.Nicoll, J.Hotchkis   3 Jan 1983
This is the line of least resistance up the crest of the conical buttress at the base of the east ridge of Meall Dearg. Start in a bay on the left side of the east facing buttress (just inside the corrie). Climb a snowy depression up and left until a line can be taken back right to a shoulder on the ridge (100m). Interesting climbing leads up walls, towers and terraces to the top.

Gully Obscura   200m   III *
A.Bull, M.Kinsey, A.Nisbet   10 Mar 1999
The leftmost gully on the north face of Meall Dearg starting at the same point as the two diagonal shelves of North Buttress but going straight up to join Terminal Buttress at the shoulder on the crest leading up to Meall Dearg. The steepest pitch was climbed by the leftmost chimney close against the left wall, returning right to the main line immediately above.

North Buttress   200m   II
Starting at the left end of the North Face of Meall Dearg below the first gully, this route follows the upper of two right-slanting diagonal shelves crossing the face to join the easy top section of the skyline ridge. Follow this up left to the crest of Meall Dearg. The alternative is the lower shelf, which is very easy to start but you have to gain the line of the upper shelf at its end.

Rab Anderson

Pyramid Buttress (left) from the Liathach Main Ridge Traverse, II

Spring Gully   300m   II ✱✱
A.Jago, A.Nisbet, S.Watts   7 Apr 1996
The right of a set of three diverging gullies on the North Face of Meall Dearg seems to be heading directly for its summit. The gully is initially shallow then deepens and contains several short ice pitches. On the spring ascent, the gully was well frozen but the party emerged on to the summit in tee-shirt weather.

PYRAMID BUTTRESS

(NG 932 577)   Alt 800m   South-East facing   Map p327

This is the shapely buttress on the south side of Liathach and easily seen from the road. It terminates the short south-east ridge of Spidean a' Choire Leith.

Approach: From the car park at NG 935 566, follow the path on the right of the Allt an Doire Ghairbh to an easing at 370m. Cross the Allt climb a slight gully trending left and deepening to reach a plateau right of the crag. Make a leftward traverse to the buttress. This is largely reversing the descent from Coire Dubh Mòr.

Descent: The summit is optional but nearby. Return to the plateau and reverse the approach.

There are two main icefalls split by a tapering rocky rib. These are well seen from the road, the left icefall being wide while the right one is narrow. Although the ice forms readily, the buttress faces due south and is seriously affected by the sun. Even early in the season it may not be a good choice on a sunny day and is rarely in condition in March.

Pyramid Left Icefall   180m   V,5 ✱✱
K.Hopper, C.Rowland   23 Feb 1986; Direct, as described: C.Rowland, M.Antoine   1987
The wide left-hand icefall has a steep second pitch. There can be a choice of vertical icicles here; the choice and difficulty will depend on the precise formation, which will always be spectacular. Easier ice leads to an interesting final mixed section.

Pyramid Right Icefall   180m   V,4 *
D.Jenkins, C.Rowland, M.Webster   Feb 1977
The right-hand icefall is sustained and serious with little protection, but is never too steep. For an easier route (IV,4), or if the direct line is not complete, avoid the steep initial section by moving out on to the central rib for a pitch (as on the first ascent).

Busman's Holiday   120m   V,5 *
A.Nisbet, G.Nisbet   24 Feb 1995
The icefall in the depression between Pyramid Right Icefall and Pyramid Right Edge. Steep thick ice left of the depression corner (45m), the continuation in the corner on thinner ice (35m), then a thinly iced corner and right traverse into the finishing gully of Pyramid Right Edge, entering it lower than the latter (50m).

Pyramid Right Edge   180m   III *
B.Ledingham, C.Rowland   early 1980s
Follow the right ridge of the buttress, starting up a groove with a steep finish. Further turfy grooves lead logically up the crest to a final barrier which forces a traverse left into an easy finishing gully.

BEINN ALLIGIN - SGÙRR MHÒR

(NG 860 602)   Alt 986m   Map p327

Beinn Alligin is the most westerly of the three great mountains of the Torridon Forest. It is a noble mountain, well worth a visit for its winter climbs, or for the traverse of its tops, which is a convenient circuit somewhat easier than Liathach and shorter than Beinn Eighe.

Weather and Conditions: Beinn Alligin has fewer ice climbs than its neighbours and, being nearer the sea, is less often in good winter condition. The Eag Dubh always seems to be windy but the other climbs can be sheltered. Deep South and Deep North Gullies can be good options in stormy weather as the descent is quick.

Approach and Layout: Leave the road from Torridon to Diabaig at a large car park by the bridge over the Coire Mhic Nòbuil burn and follow the good path on the east side of the burn through beautiful Caledonian forest. The first corrie to be seen high on the left is Coire nan Laogh. The next corrie, Toll a' Mhadaidh Mor, between Tom na Gruagaich and Sgùrr Mhòr, is much more impressive and offers several good ice routes on the north-east face of Tom na Gruagaich. On the opposite side of this corrie is a long vertical wall angling up to form a deep cleft gully, the Eag Dubh, which reaches the ridge just south-west of the highest top, Sgùrr Mhòr. There are further winter climbs on the north side of the Horns of Alligin and in the remote Toll nam Biast. The descents are generally by reversing the traverse in the most convenient direction.

Beinn Alligin, Ridge Traverse   I **
The ridge can be traversed in either direction but anti-clockwise is easier; this goes over The Horns of Alligin first. There is a considerable path leading up towards the Horns, which involves some short and awkward, but unexposed walls. The Horns can be traversed on the crest (Grade II in very icy conditions, the hardest section being descending from the First Horn) or passed on the left (south) by a long exposed traverse. The ascent to Sgùrr Mhòr is steep but only walking. On its descent, the initial bearing will appear to lead diagonally rightwards off the ridge but thereby misses the Eag Dubh. Continue easily towards Tom na Gruagaich; on its ascent there is some easy scrambling, exposed at one point. Normally the summit of Tom na Gruagaich would be included but it can be passed on the right by traversing into a snow gully which leads up and over directly to the descent down Coire nan Laogh (a good glissade if there is sufficient snow). This leads fairly directly to the car park.

TOM NA GRUAGAICH - NORTH-EAST FACE

(NG 861 602)   Alt 600m   North-East facing

West Coast Boomer   300m   IV,4 **
D.Gardiner, N.Crawford, C.Ferguson   Feb 1973
The obvious gully on the left of the face can be recommended as a sustained and scenic route. Pass the lower crag on the right and angle up left to reach the main gully. There are numerous short pitches in the lower part and a continuous steep section in the upper part.

Eag Dubh   400m   I or II *
The diagonal vertical wall facing the road from Sgùrr Mhòr and on the opposite side of the corrie from the previous route is thought to be the sidewall of a huge rock avalanche whose debris can be seen on the corrie floor below. The wall leads up to and forms the right wall of the Eag Dubh, a deep narrow snow gully (Grade I). The gully can either be gained by a long scramble up the ramp immediately below the impressive wall or more directly up a shallow gully further left. The latter requires some consolidated snow at that level but it can have several low angled ice pitches and is a more satisfying approach (Grade II). The gully area is a windy place, susceptible to a fierce updraft (which can blow you up the route!).

THE HORNS OF ALLIGIN

(NG 877 613)   Alt 500m   North-East facing   Map p327

On the north-east face of the Horns of Alligin are the following climbs, reached by continuing along a vague path after the more obvious path to the ridge has left.

Deep South Gully   250m   I ***
This is the first gully seen on the approach towards the col between Beinn Dearg and Beinn Alligin. It curves from left to right and finishes between the first (lowest) and second Horn. In lean conditions there is a big chockstone with an easy through route followed by an easy ice pitch.

Deep North Gully   250m   II **
This gully, which finishes between the second and third Horns, requires a good build-up; otherwise an introductory pitch can be very hard.

Diamond Fire   225m   IV,4 **
S.Chadwick, G.Livingston, G.S.Strange   10 Feb 1985
This climbs a huge deep cleft on the north-west face above Toll nam Biast. It is rarely climbed but it is recommended for an adventure into the unknown. First climbed in cold but very lean conditions, it held good ice even when the surrounding buttresses had little snow. The steepest ice pitch was avoided on the left, but with a good build-up, it might not be too difficult.

SGÙRR MHÒR - NORTH FACE

(NG 868 615)   Alt 630m   North facing

Sgùrr Mhòr is the highest peak on Beinn Alligin. Approach its north face by continuing past Deep South and North Gullies and round to the north side.

Curve Stone   350m   II *
S.Chadwick, S.Gorman   Mar 1996
Left of centre on the face is a long shallow gully, initially left-trending, which ends on a shoulder of the north-west ridge of Sgùrr Mhòr. An ice pitch leads into the gully. After another 150m, the line turns right and enters the icy narrows. Two pitches lead to the exit snows.

The Fannaichs

A high group of hills central to the Northern Highlands, situated between Inverness and Ullapool, and therefore away from the west coast and its warmer climate. They can catch a lot of snow from the east, west or north. Routes are described on the two highest peaks, Sgùrr nan Clach Geala and Sgùrr Mòr.

SGÙRR NAN CLACH GEALA

(NH 184 715)   Alt 1093m   Map p364

SGÙRR NAN CLACH GEALA - MAIN CRAG

(NH 190 717)   Alt 750m   East-South-East facing   Diagram p360

The fine crag on the east face of this mountain was only marked on the most recent edition of the OS map, and named as Am Biachdaich. It is large and impressively steep, one of Scotland's best, and not as remote as rumour might have you believe.

Weather and Conditions: The approach requires a short descent which is quite hard to find and past a possibly large cornice, so good visibility is essential for a first visit. In addition, windslab can build readily below the cornice on the sheltered east facing slopes. The cliff, and particularly the buttresses, are susceptible to sun. The best conditions are normally in the first half of the season although even then the steep buttresses can be stripped of snow by thaw or sun. The gullies reliably hold sufficient ice, although even they are thawed by the sun in March.

Approach: Go via the east end of Loch a' Bhraoin, reached from a track starting at NH 162 761 on the Braemore Junction to Dundonnell road (park 100m to the north). Follow the path south from the loch along an unnamed glen, crossing the burn after 1km (about 300m after the path joins the river bank and becomes grassy). This is sometimes a boulder hop, sometimes a wade. There is a bridge a few hundred metres downstream, in case of failure to cross. Continue along the path for another 1.5km before striking up east to the col between Càrn na Criche and Sgùrr nan Clach Geala. In reasonable conditions this takes about 2hrs 30mins. A huge boulder forward and left of the lochan on the col, provides some shelter to gear-up (crampons are required for the descent) and a possible place to leave rucksacks. Go to the far end of the lochan and follow a shallow depression formed like an exit stream which forms a defined lowest point of the col. Descend from close to this lowest point of the col (usually easiest 10m north of the col, possible cornice/abseil) for about 50m to an easing in the slope. Follow the easing rightwards (facing down, a slightly descending traverse) to a bouldery terrace 25m below an obvious flattening in the near skyline.

Cross a gully, **Slanting Gully** (300m I) above its pitch to gain the terrace below the cliff. Descending too far below the col into the valley bottom forces the climbing of the lower tier (about 100m, Grade II) to reach the terrace below the cliff. An alternative descent close to Slanting Gully is steeper and harder to find in mist.

Descent: From the top of the climbs, descend the slopes northwards back to the lochan and boulder, then reverse the line of ascent back to Loch a' Bhraoin.

Layout: The main cliffs comprise a wedge like cluster of six narrow buttresses, numbered 1 to 6 from left to right, separated by five gullies, Alpha to Epsilon. From the top of these cliffs a graceful ridge leads south-west to the summit of the mountain, beneath which there is a more broken buttress.

1 Alpha Gully   120m   II
P.Baker, D.S.B.Wright   6 Mar 1965
The leftmost gully. Steep snow, particularly the finish, or it may contain two small ice pitches. The gully finishes on the crest of No.2 Buttress which gives a further 120m of easy climbing (Grade I at most).

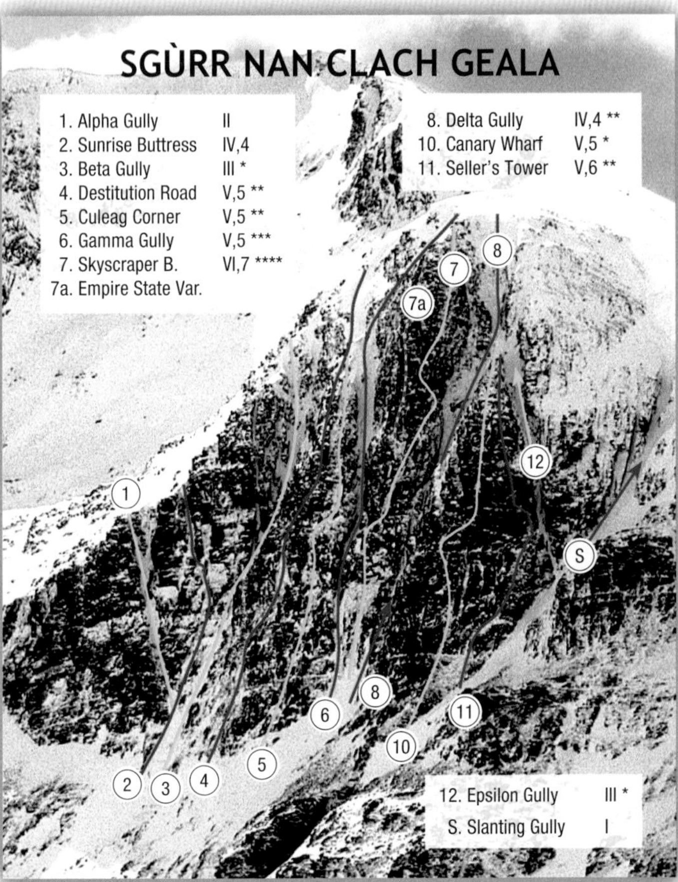

SGÙRR NAN CLACH GEALA

1. Alpha Gully   II
2. Sunrise Buttress   IV,4
3. Beta Gully   III *
4. Destitution Road   V,5 **
5. Culeag Corner   V,5 **
6. Gamma Gully   V,5 ***
7. Skyscraper B.   VI,7 ****
7a. Empire State Var.

8. Delta Gully   IV,4 **
10. Canary Wharf   V,5 *
11. Seller's Tower   V,6 **

12. Epsilon Gully   III *
S. Slanting Gully   I

Dave Broadhead

2 Sunrise Buttress (No.2 Buttress)   150m   IV,4

P.R.Baines, D.M.Nichols   18 Feb 1978

This route follows a line in the centre of the buttress. Start at the foot of Beta Gully and climb ice bulges to gain an obvious gully system. With insufficient ice, start up Beta Gully and go left on to the buttress to a turf line leading into the gully. Turn the overhang at the top of the gully on the left and continue up the arete to the top.

3 Beta Gully   200m   III *

P.F.Macdonald, J.Porteous (Centre Fork)
I.G.Rowe, W.Sproul (Right Fork)   28 Feb 1970

An icefall gives access to the gully, which is straightforward up to a trifurcation. Here a short left fork goes out to No.2 Buttress, a centre fork contains a steep pitch, and a right fork avoids this pitch and rejoins the centre fork above.

4 Destitution Road   200m   V,5 **

D.Dinwoodie, K.Murphy   19 Feb 1986

This takes the central icefall of Cuileag Buttress (No.3 Buttress). Climb directly up the middle of the buttress using the general line of a shallow corner to gain the icefall. Climb this direct past a jutting nose of rock, then traverse right to gain a blocky corner cutting through the overhangs. Climb this to the easier crest of the buttress.

5 Cuileag Corner   185m   V,5 **
C.Maclean, A.Nisbet   18 Jan 1985
This takes a line of discontinuous corners on the right side of Cuileag Buttress. The precise line depends on the amount of ice. It may well be possible with none, but no repeats have been reported.
1. 45m Climb vegetated slabs to belay under the corner system.
2. 45m Enter the corner by a thin slab and short steep wall.
3. 45m Go up the corner to a big roof. Traverse right beneath the roof and go up ice into a fault on the right edge of the buttress. Climb the fault past two steep sections.
4. 50m Continue up the fault to reach the easy ground common to all the routes on this buttress.

6 Gamma Gully   210m   V,5 ***
P.N.L.Tranter, I.G.Rowe   6 Mar 1965
This is probably the best of the gullies on the crag, only Grade IV,5 in good conditions. Climb up for 30m to enter and climb a deep narrow 30m slot. Some 20m higher is the crux, a steep 10m ice pitch with smooth rock walls on either side. Another 10m ice pitch follows, then climb steep snow and occasional rock steps to gain the large scoop above Beta Gully.

7 Skyscraper Buttress   240m   VI,7 ****
R.J.Archbold, M.Freeman, J.C.Higham, R.A.Smith   18 Feb 1978 (Original Route);
D.Dinwoodie, C.Jamieson, K.Murphy   9 Feb 1986 (Direct Start)
This magnificent sustained mixed climb is one of the finest expeditions in the Northern Highlands. Unfortunately it catches the sun and snow falls off its steep rocks, so the first half of the season is recommended for an attempt.
    The best line takes the icefall at the base of the buttress, The Direct Start. This assumes both the ice to be present and the turf to be well frozen, otherwise start by the Original Route (VI,6 overall). Climb the icefall to its capping roof and move left to where the roof is quite large, or direct if the ice allows. (With no ice but the turf frozen, a possible line is to follow a turfy corner on the right to a bay, then traverse left to the roof.). Pull up into a shallow undercut groove above the right end of the roof. Climb the groove (thin) to a turf ledge. The Original Route reaches this point by following Gamma Gully to the slot, then traversing easily right.
    Move up again (left and up looks easier, straight up more interesting) to a traverse line beneath the steep central section of the buttress. From here, go right along the traverse line to a steep 10m high iced corner. If the corner is not iced climb a thin crack on the wall just to its left. Once past the corner it is possible to follow easier ground slightly rightwards up to the obvious series of cracks and grooves on the right side of the buttress, but this avoids the final headwall - the highlight of the climb - which is now on the left. The headwall is a slightly scooped face between two crests. The right crest with the original route is in a fairly straight line with the iced corner below and the left crest with the Empire State Variation is out to the left. Other versions may have been climbed. For the original line, take the easier ground for about a rope length, then climb a short groove on the left and traverse diagonally left to gain the right crest at a good ledge. Climb the crack above then continue directly by a series of cracks and grooves for two fine pitches. The Empire State Variation traverses left lower down to climb near the left crest. All the variations finish easily along the horizontal ridge to the plateau.
Variation: **Empire State Variation   VI,6**
R.Everett, S.M.Richardson   13 Feb 1994
Climbs the left side of the headwall, very steep but the protection is excellent and

the turf is very accommodating. From the belay above the crux corner, follow the easy ground up and right for 15m to a huge flake on the left. Move left around the edge above the flake to gain a small hanging snowfield, and climb a left-slanting, shallow turfy groove which cuts into the headwall looming above (50m). Climb straight up via cracks and grooves to reach a ledge and niche overlooking Gamma Gully on the left (45m). Climb a short rib on the left edge and continue up the steep groove above to ledges, then take a turfy corner leading into the centre of the final overhanging wall. Step right one metre to enter into a second groove, then trend up and left in a spectacular position to the easy horizontal ridge (45m).

8 Delta Gully   240m   IV,4 **
D.Dinwoodie, M.Freeman   Mar 1972
After two pleasant steep pitches, often continuous ice but susceptible to sun, the gully widens and is followed more easily with impressive rock scenery on the two enclosing buttresses.

9 Sellers' Buttress (No.5 Buttress)   140m   IV,5 *
G.S.Strange, D.Stuart   19 Feb 1972
Start at the lowest rocks and climb by grooves and shallow corners always to the left of the crest. Near the top move up right to finish up the crest. About 100m of Grade I snow common to Delta and Epsilon Gullies leads to the plateau.

10 Canary Wharf   140m   V,5 *
D.McGimpsey, A.Nisbet; A.Clarke, R.McAllister   18 Nov 1998
Climbs the right-hand face (front face) of Sellers' Buttress. Start below the left end of the face and slant easily up right to below a turfy line. Climb the turfy line until about 10m below a shoulder. Go diagonally right to a projecting block and swing round it to a traverse ledge which soon leads to the central corner in the upper part of the face. Climb the corner and the wall on its left to easier ground leading to the final easy crest forming the top of the buttress.

11 Sellers' Tower   160m   V,6 **
R.McAllister, D.McGimpsey, A.Nisbet   22 Dec 1998
The right side of the front face of Sellers' Buttress gives a fine improbable route, typically steep and helpful and generally well protected. Start as for Canary Wharf but continue trending right, then curving upwards to a belay under steep ground and almost overlooking the start of Epsilon Gully (80m). Move left on to the arete of a right-facing corner and pull up to prominent turf. Traverse left along a narrow turf ledge past another corner and go up to a pedestal below the main roof system (20m). Pull through the roof (small at this point) and move left into the base of a left-facing corner, half of a pair of big corners about 5m apart and facing each other, the best indicator of the line from below. Climb this right corner, then a crack between the corners and finish up the left corner to reach easier ground. Move right and go up to a ledge below the top of the buttress (50m). Reach the final easy crest (10m).

12 Epsilon Gully   140m   III *
M.Freeman, N.Keir   16 Mar 1974
This starts somewhat higher up Slanting Gully, on the right of Sellers' Buttress. After a hard start the gully is straightforward.

SGÙRR MÒR

(NH 204 718)   Alt 900m   North-East facing   Map p364

The impressive north-east face of Sgùrr Mòr is the highest in the area, it holds snow well and can offer a winter route into April, or even May were it to freeze.

Weather and Conditions: This is a big serious face, so choose good weather and beware of windslab, cornices and warm early morning sunshine. Conditions are reliable; the better the quality of snow and ice, the easier the routes are.

Approach: Park on the A835 (there is a good place at NH 235 759) about 3km south-east of the Dundonnell turn off, where a small building is seen down by the river. This is the start of the path to Loch a' Mhadaidh, which is not obvious at first but it is easily found at the second stream crossing after 400m, where there is a bridge. Follow the path until just short of Loch a' Mhadaidh, then head up a vague spur and traverse to below the cliff (following the stream to here is rougher). Allow about 2hrs 30mins.

Descent: The most pleasant descent is to head south then east to Beinn Liath Mhòr Fannaich whose Munro summit can be traversed on the left or bagged. Then head north-east to where the track meets the stream at a bridge.

Easter Gully   240m   II *
B.Brand, O.Bruskeland   10 Apr 1967
This straightforward snow gully on the left (south) corner of the face often has a big cornice. In leaner conditions it may have an ice pitch low down but perhaps the cornice will be easier. Grade I in good conditions.

The Resurrection   320m   III ****
J.R.Mackenzie, D.Butterfield   14 Mar 1980
The central route on the face provides a serious route with a great Alpine atmosphere. The last belay is the summit cairn of Sgùrr Mòr, the highest point in the North-West Highlands. With a big build-up, the route uses no rock protection or belays (little exists anyway), so expect to use snow belays, ice screw belays and take a warthog or two for turf, particularly at the top.

Start towards the left side of the face, at the right side of a dead-end gully right of Easter Gully. Here is a large icefall, although it may have thawed away towards the end of the season. Climb the icefall, normally 45-50m but it could be longer early season and steep at the bottom (Grade IV), to reach the base of a big snowfield. Climb 45-50 degree snow for two or three pitches, then a short icefall gains a steeper snow field, climbed in one or two pitches to a scoop below the steep capping wall (no rock belay here). Go diagonally right, then continue straight up to the top (55m). This pitch is not difficult but the only protection is warthogs in the turf, the rope is too short, there may be a big cornice and it's a long way to retreat. Other than that, no problem!

Variation: **Easy Start   I**
Start by a shallow runnel just left of East Face (or East Face itself) but go left onto the lower snowfield of Resurrection. In ideal conditions, this can reduce the overall grade to II.

Resurrection Right-Hand   300m   III **
These are right-hand variations to Resurrection which can give a separate route or be used as an alternative start or finish. There are at least three icefalls in the lower wall right of the normal start, roughly Grade IV, III and II from right to left, which can be climbed to reach the big lower snowfield. Cross this to climb ice runnels in the slight buttress above the big snowfield and left of East Face to provide a more sustained line which comes directly up to finish at the same point as the normal route.

East Face   300m   III,4 *
R.Graham, R.Warrack   11 Apr 1967
The corner come shallow gully in the face right of Resurrection provides a fine route which requires some ice. Start up the right-hand of two right-slanting gullies, then a snow slope to reach the base of the shallow gully (Grade I to here). The gully has a short steep ice pitch but otherwise steep snow in ideal conditions, with an obvious finish out right.

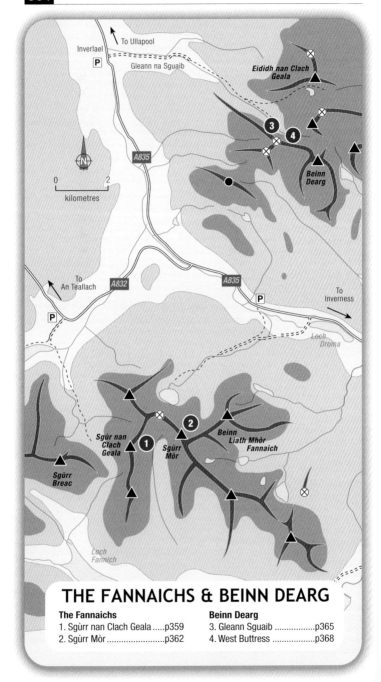

THE FANNAICHS & BEINN DEARG

Beinn Dearg & An Teallach

Beinn Dearg lies south-east of Ullapool, An Teallach to the south-west.

BEINN DEARG

(NH 259 812)   Alt 1048m

Beinn Dearg lies nearer Ullapool than the Fannaichs. This massive mountain offers excellent winter climbing in three different venues. The climbs described here are approached from the west up Gleann na Sguaib, leaving the more remote Cadha Dearg and Coire Ghrànda to the adventurous.

Weather and Conditions: The West Buttress is high and Penguin Gully is very reliable. The Gleann Sguaib gullies are less reliable, especially in recent warmer times, and have no backing plateau to collect drifting snow, but one can always continue the walk to the West Buttress. Fenian Gully, however, is the most likely.

Approach: From the Braemore to Ullapool road, at the head of Loch Broom, a forestry road runs up Gleann na Sguaib to the upper limit of the Inverlael Forest. A good path then leads up to the Bealach Coire Ghrànda, passing first below the cliffs of Gleann Sguaib (Diollaid a' Mhill Bhric), the long sloping north-west shoulder of Beinn Dearg, and then below the large West Buttress of the mountain. In heavy snow the path drifts badly but in normal conditions it gives a relatively fast approach to the lower climbs, 2hrs.

GLEANN SGUAIB

(NH 240 824)   Alt 600m   North-East facing   Map p364   Diagram p367

There are six well defined gullies and intervening buttresses on the line of cliffs under Diollaid a' Mhill Bhric.

Descent: Between these cliffs and the West Buttress is a broad gully, the Cadha Amadan, or Fool's Pass, which provides a convenient descent from many of the climbs. Alternatively, and especially with an avalanche risk in the gully, return along the ridge above the glen until the cliffs fade and allow a descent down heather slopes back to the path. The problem with this option is that the river may be hard to cross.

The climbs are described from right to left, the order reached as one approaches up the glen.

1 WhatawaytospendEaster   120m   I
W.Sproul, A.McKeith   25 Mar 1967
The first gully provides a straightforward snow climb.

2 Rev. Ian Paisley Memorial Gully   150m   I
W.Sproul, A.McKeith   25 Mar 1967
The second gully is also straightforward, uncompromisingly direct, not to be taken too lightly and prematurely named (even after 40 years!).

3 Orangeman's Gully   150m   III **
T.W.Patey   10 Mar 1968
The third gully is narrow, twisting and bow-shaped. The first pitch, which can be hard, starts up a chimney and goes left under an overhang on iced slabs. Continue up two more ice pitches to easy snow above the bend.

4 Emerald Gully   150m   IV,4 ***
B.Fuller, P.Nunn, A.Riley   Mar 1970
The fourth gully provides a highly recommended climb that can be hard in lean conditions. It usually has at least two big ice pitches. The impressive icy corner on the left wall of Emerald Gully is **Jewel in the Crown** (160m VI,6), a fine climb but requires a sustained period of frost to form.

Emerald Gully, IV,4. Climber Alan Smith

Andy Tibbs

5 Archway   250m   IV,4 **

R.D.Everett, S.M.Richardson   7 Feb 1988

This is an entertaining route which weaves through some very impressive scenery.
Start at the lowest point of the buttress left of Emerald Gully. Follow open grooves
just left of the steepest rocks to reach a prominent cave-like depression beneath
huge roofs (150m). Climb up right through the roof of the cave (40m). Follow an
interesting gully and groove system up right to finish (60m).

6 Fenian Gully   170m   IV,4 ***

T.W.Patey   11 Mar 1968

The fifth of the main gullies provides quite a sustained climb but with no particular
crux. It is recommended as it is often well iced.

BEINN DEARG - Gleann Sguaib

3. Orangeman's Gully	III **	7. Papist's Passage	II
4. Emerald Gully	IV,4 ***	8. The Tower of Babel	IV,6 **
5. Archway	IV,4 **		
6. Fenian Gully	IV,4 ***		

Penguin Gully, III,4. Climber Ian Jones

Peter Wilson

7 Papist's Passage   180m   II
T.W.Patey   10 Mar 1968
The sixth gully, just left of Fenian Gully. The main obstacle is a huge chockstone above a cave at 75m, which is climbed by the right-hand corner. Depending on the build-up, it can be Grade I or III.

8 The Tower of Babel   160m   IV,6 ★★
S.Aisthorpe, J.Lyall   22 Feb 1989
This is the imposing corner-tower right of the Cadha Amadan, the wide gully separating the climbs described above from the West Buttress. The best mixed route on the cliff by far, and the most likely to be frozen, but it does need more than just a single overnight frost. Start on an easy shelf leading out of the gully. Climb the crest of the tower as directly as possible for 60m, then take a slabby ramp on the left side of the crest (20m). A steep recess on the left leads to a promontory below a short vicious wall which is taken direct to a higher ledge (40m). Climb the final wall by a diagonal crack on the slabby left side and finish by a step left into a square-cut recess (40m).

WEST BUTTRESS

(NH 254 819)   Alt 750m   North facing   Map p364

Beyond the Cadha Amadan the cliffs rise up to their greatest height in the so-called West Buttress. In fact the cliffs have a north-west facet (well seen as one approaches up the glen), then bend round to face north and finally face north-north-east above a small lochan below the col between Beinn Dearg and Meall nan Ceapraichan. There are a couple of well defined classic lines and large areas of buttress with rather ill defined routes.

1 The Ice Hose   350m   V,4 ***
I.Dalley, D.M.Nichols, G.S.Strange   7 Apr 1979
A recommended route, but it only forms during a good winter. Climb the prominent ice ribbon directly for 140m. From its top, either follow a shallow gully easily leftwards or, better, gain the buttress on the right (with a downward-pointing toe), get onto the crest and follow this to the top.
Variation: **Right-Hand Finish   150m   V,5**
J.Currie, G.Robertson and P.Robertson   14 Jan 2001
Above the main icefall of the Ice Hose the gully forks and the right branch leads to a narrow ice cascade falling from a cul-de-sac. Climb this to a broad ledge on the right (30m). Continue up over an icy step to easier ground which is followed to the top.

2 Penguin Gully   350m   III,4 ****
T.W.Patey, W.H.Murray, N.S.Tennent   29 Mar 1964
This classic climb, concealed during the approach, provides one of the longest climbs on the mountain. It is probably one of the few ice routes where consistent conditions prevail from January to April. A steep icefall at the start can be avoided by a dog-leg gully trending right then left (the start of Eigerwanderer) to join the main gully about 75m above the start. The main gully contains several ice pitches and may occasionally have a through route behind a chockstone. In cold but lean conditions it can offer continuous ice (Grade IV,4); well worth doing.

BEINN DEARG West Buttress

| 1. The Ice Hose | V,4 *** | 2. Penguin Gully | III,4 **** |
| 1a. Right-Hand Finish | V,5 | 2a. Alternative Start | |

NORTHERN HIGHLANDS

AN TEALLACH

(NH 069 843)   Alt 1062m   Map p372

This majestic mountain is one of the most sought after in the Northern Highlands. The winter traverse of its tops ranks with Liathach as the finest in the area, although it does not quite equal its Torridonian rivals for quality snow and ice climbs. The main ridge runs in an east facing crescent from Sàil Liath in the south over the main tops of Sgùrr Fiona and Bidein a' Ghlas Thuill to Glas Mheall Mor in the north. A ridge running east from Bidein a' Ghlas Thuill separates two large east facing corries, Toll an Lochain and Glas Tholl. Both have climbs of interest, and Toll an Lochain in particular is a magnificent sight even when winter climbing conditions are poor.

Weather and Conditions: The mountain is high and holds snow well. But it doesn't get as much snow as Beinn Dearg and the Fannaichs, which can be an advantage when they are swamped in powder. Toll an Lochain is a more committing day, both in terms of longer approach and difficult descent.

Approach: The approach leaves the road (A832) from a small parking place through thickets of overgrown rhododendrons near a bridge at a point opposite Dundonnell House and about 400m on the Dundonnell side of the turn off to Badralloch. The start of the path shown on the map is no longer used due to problems crossing the burn. Start immediately right (the other side, north-west) of the burn and cross a broken fence.

A new path (not very obvious) soon leads to a log across a side branch of the burn. Cross this side branch and move right to a deer fence (the continuation path is very boggy). Follow the fence to a pine covered knoll on the left. Go round the base of this and up a little to gain the original path on the left. Follow the path until the stream from Glas Tholl joins the main burn, just before a big waterfall (30mins). Here the routes to the two corries diverge (see each corrie).

An Teallach Ridge   II ****

A long and intricate expedition with some sections of Grade II, arguably the best ridge in Scotland. The described route crosses The Pinnacles on the way to the Munros because the route finding is easier than the 'Munros first' direction, although the latter provides a good day even if discretion wins before The Pinnacles. For the purest traverse, park at Corrie Hallie (NH 114 851) and head up the Shenavall track.

Just beyond the highest point, branch right as if for Shenavall. Break off right and climb Sàil Liath, the best line varying with snow conditions but only walking. Continue over Cadha Gobhlach Buttress to a low col, then up over a slight top, more of a shoulder with a rocky crest (Corrag Bhuidhe South Buttress). The hardest section over the Corrag Bhuidhe pinnacles follows, all of which is very exposed and a slip could be disastrous unless roped. The most direct line is straight up the crest but this is Grade III in full winter conditions. The normal route is to go up the crest for about 30m to where a terrace leads left (a small path in summer). Following this line throughout misses all the difficulties but is still at least Grade I. The best and Grade II line breaks up right to the crest as soon as you dare, the sooner the harder but sooner takes in more of the pinnacles. The crest is very exposed and a real highlight, with the best line still needing some route finding.

A longer descent reaches Lord Berkley's Seat which again is spectacular but optional. From here to Sgùrr Fiona is steep but the route finding is easy. The descent from Sgùrr Fiona towards the highest top, Bidean a' Ghlas Thuill, is again steep and one has to break left off the crest to reach the col. Going up Bidean a' Ghlas Thuill should feel easier and a trig point reassures you of the summit. For a return to the car, head north to a col and descend into the corrie of Glas Tholl, from where rough sections of path on the north of the stream lead to the waterfall. Go down the path to the road (see the approach above), from where it is 700m walk up the road to the car.

Those wanting to savour the atmosphere of the magnificent Toll an Lochain can approach as described in the introduction and climb Central Gully or better, Chockstone Gully (both Grade I) to reach the crest before the start of the pinnacles.

John Biggar

An Teallach Ridge, II

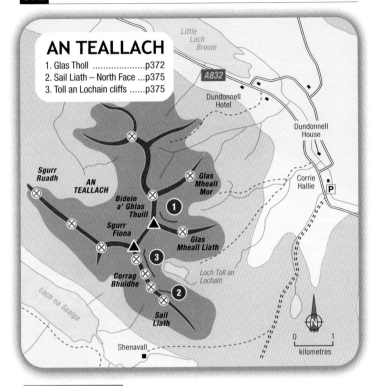

AN TEALLACH

1. Glas Tholl p372
2. Sail Liath – North Face ...p375
3. Toll an Lochain cliffs p375

Little Loch Broom

`A832`

Dundonnell Hotel

Dundonnell House

Corrie Hallie

P

Sgurr Ruadh

AN TEALLACH

Glas Mheall Mor

Bidein a' Ghlas Thuill

Sgurr Fiona

①

Glas Mheall Liath

③

Loch Toll an Lochain

Corrag Bhuidhe

②

Loch na Sealga

Sail Liath

Shenavall

0 ——— 1
kilometres

GLAS THOLL

(NH 075 845) Alt 700m North to East facing Map p372 Diagram p374

The northern of the two main corries, more accessible but less aesthetic.

Approach: For Glas Tholl, branch off up the hillside to the east after about 30mins, just before the big waterfall, 2hrs overall.

Descent: Descents can be made at a number of places. The easiest is to go to the summit, Bidean a' Ghlas Thuill. From here, follow the ridge north, then drop down the north flanks of Glas Mheall Mor to join a footpath leading to Dundonnell. Alternatively, descend into Glas Tholl from the col below Glas Mheall Mor (there is sometimes a small cornice). Hayfork Gully can also be a quick descent; climb down to the junction and in the right conditions, glissade until well below the cliff.

Layout: A prominent feature of the south side of the corrie is the bold buttress of Major Rib, with Minor Rib to the right and the clean line of The Alley in between. To the left of Major Rib are a series of parallel gullies known as the Prongs, and to the right of Minor Rib is the big Hayfork Gully leading up to an obvious notch. Right again is North Gully which leads up to the last notch left of the summit. Below and immediately right of the summit is a rather indistinct area of buttress and snowfield, but further right are a number of more definite lines, the most obvious of which is Checkmate Chimney. The climbs are described from right to left.

1 Checkmate Chimney 250m IV,5 **

T.W.Patey, C.J.S.Bonington 3 Mar 1969

A superb route unfortunately not often in condition. It is the first obvious line, a long narrow chimney, left of the easy slopes at the back of the corrie. Climb a 10m step, then 60m of snow to a fierce 30m icefall. This can be climbed on the left or right according to shape. From here on the climbing is Grade III. Climb a long enclosed chimney section with short ice pitches, and finish up an easy 60m snow channel.

**2 North Gully   300m   I ** **

The gully running up to the first notch left (east) of the summit of Bidein a' Ghlas Thuill is also known as Murdo's Gully, and is better seen on the approach than Hayfork Gully.

3 Central Buttress   350m   II
A.Nisbet   24 Dec 1999
Start where the crest just right of Hayfork Gully meets the base of the buttress. Climb just right of the crest of the buttress before moving right to climb a shallow gully which leads to the steep band. Continue in the line of the gully, which passes just left of the nose of the steep band, until the upper crest on the right can be gained by the first line of weakness. Follow the upper crest to the top. A line on the right side of the buttress has also been climbed.

4 Hayfork Gully   300m   I **

G.Sang, W.A.Morrison   26 Mar 1910
This is the deep and straightforward gully left of North Gully and right of Major and Minor Ribs. The huge vertical left wall looms over the gully which leads up to a final fork. The right branch is easier but still steep; the left branch is just grade II. The branches finish either side of a small peak which sits in the second notch down from the summit on the east ridge of Bidein a' Ghlas Thuill. No cornice. A good descent often offering a long glissade from the fork.

5 Haystack   170m   VI,7 *

D.McGimpsey, A.Nisbet   6 Jan 2000
A sensational route up the impressive left wall of Hayfork Gully. Start about a third of the way up Hayfork Gully at the first break in the left wall and where a gully runs up on to a platform on the rib on the left (the top of the steep wall of Miniscule Rib). Climb out left towards the gully to where a ramp leads right across the main wall (10m). Climb the ramp to below a chimney in the centre of the face (50m, 25m). Climb the steep chimney (20m). Go rightwards up a ramp then back left to the top of a crack which is the continuation of the chimney. Continue traversing until possible to climb through a barrier wall above by a short steep groove (important peg runner). Traverse out right, then go up, before traversing back left above the groove to the highest ledge which is above and left of the point above the continuation crack (35m). Go left round the corner past a prominent thread and climb more easily direct to the top (30m).

6 Forbidden Gully   250m   V,7 **

D.McGimpsey, A.Nisbet   24 Mar 2001
The shallow gully right of Minor Rib. Climb a low angled ice pitch and easier snow to a fork (60m). Take the left branch over a bulge to another fork. The left branch ends in an overhang. Climb the right branch, a chimney-corner to its top (50m). Traverse left to the left branch above its overhang. Climb a flared chimney (1PA, but it has been seen fully iced when the route would be V,5), then snow to another difficult bulge, over this and more snow until it is possible to move out left to easier ground (50m). Finish easily (this is also the optional final gully of Minor Rib).

7 Minor Rib   300m   IV,5 *

R.Barclay, W.D.Brooker   15 Apr 1956
The slabby rib left of Hayfork Gully. Climb the crest for 60m to a steep wall. Climb this in the centre by a crack and mantelshelf. Higher up pass a jutting fang of rock on the right. The rib now rears in a tower, climbed by a chimney on the right. Above this the ridge rises in easy steps to merge with the gully on the left (The Alley). Continue up the crest to a steep cracked wall, which may be passed by a gully on the right to reach the top.

374

AN TEALLACH - Glas Tholl

1. Checkmate Chimney   IV,5 **
2. North Gully   I **
3. Central Buttress   II
4. Hayfork Gully   I ****

6. Forbidden Gully   V,7 **
7. Minor Rib   IV,5 *
8. The Alley   II **
9. Major Rib   III,4 *

10. Fourth Prong   II *
11. Third Prong   II
12. Second Prong   II
13. First Prong   I

Andy Nisbet

8 **The Alley   300m   II ** ** **
R.Baker, A.McCord   18 Dec 1978
The gully between Minor and Major Rib, usually with some small ice pitches in the lower section, but these can disappear under heavy snow. After about 150m the gully becomes less distinct and the natural way is out right over broken rocks to the crest of Minor Rib. Continuing in the line of the gully is less interesting and can be harder.

9 **Major Rib   300m   III,4 ***
I.L.Dalley, J.Grant   Feb 1979
Climb an obvious break to reach a large snowfield. Climb up and trend generally left, avoiding most obstacles, to finish up a short, stiff step near the top.

10 **Fourth Prong   300m   II ***
T.M.Lawson, R.J.Tanton, J.Clarkson   15 Feb 1959
A good climb immediately left of Major Rib. There is a short pitch in the lower section. Higher up climb a narrow chimney then trend right over rocks below a large buttress. Finish rightwards up easy snow.

11 **Third Prong   250m   II**
Again easier with more snow.

12 **Second Prong   250m   II**
Short pitches but can bank out to grade I.

13 **First Prong   200m   I**
Straightforward on snow.

TOLL AN LOCHAIN

(NH 072 832)   Map p372   Diagram p377

The southern of the two corries, wild, magnificent and extensive.

Approach: From near the waterfall, continue up Coire a' Ghiubhsachain on faint paths which take a line between the two burns which lead towards the corrie, mostly following small ridges topped with bare sandstone and with occasional cairns (2hrs 30mins). The paths would be impossible to find under snow. The best path follows a rising rocky crest come escarpment which forms the left bank of the right burn. There is another path with a more obvious line of cairns which takes a more gently rising line but this peters out; it is however only marginally slower.

Layout: At the south end of the corrie and the first cliffs seen on the approach are the three buttresses of Sàil Liath, the south peak of the An Teallach ridge. The next big buttress to the right is the rounded Gobhlach Buttress (no routes described), then the lowest col with a snow gully below (Central Gully), before the triangular Corrag Bhuidhe South Buttress whose rocks drop straight into the loch. Right of here is the face below the jagged rocky crest of the Corrag Bhuidhe pinnacles, characterised by a triangular snowfield low down. The vertical corrie face of Lord Berkeley's Seat is high on its right end, with Lord's Gully descending right below it. The right end of the face is Sgùrr Fiona, with two ramp lines slanting up right.

Descent: May be complex and depends where the route finishes. It is always possible (but steep) to descend back into the corrie from the col between Sgùrr Fiona and Bidein a' Ghlas Thuill or from the southern of two adjacent cols between Corrag Bhuidhe and Sàil Liath (Cadha Gobhlach; this is the one nearest Sàil Liath). Central Gully descends from the main central col, also steep snow with no pitches but much more likely to be corniced. Otherwise, traverse the ridge in either direction and descend off Sàil Liath to the Shenavall path or descend from Bidean a' Ghlas Thuill as above.

Sàil Liath

(NH 077 825)   Alt 750m   North facing   Map p372

The Sàil Liath crags can be divided into three buttresses, a large dome-shaped left or frontal buttress separated from the others by a large easy snow gully. The central buttress is separated from the right by a prominent snow ramp which runs up from right to left. Near the top of the ramp three deep-cut gullies cleave the steep walls on the right, well seen on the approach to the corrie.

1 Kumbh Mela 130m V,6 **
D.McGimpsey, A.Nisbet 7 Jan 2001
The left-hand and highest of the three gullies on the right-hand buttress, the central gully being Sulphur Gully. Much deeper, longer and more impressive than it looks. Start at the same place as Sulphur Gully but go left up a ramp to reach the gully. An initial chokestone was the crux, climbed on the left wall and probably technical 7, but would become quite easy with a big build up. Thereafter it was deep and a good width for chimneying.

2 Sulphur Gully 100m IV,6 **
M.Fowler, C.Watts 12 Apr 1987
This fine central gully appears to be similar to a climb mentioned in the 1946 SMC Journal. In deference to the pioneers the original name is preserved although the modern description is given. The original description mentions jammed ice axe belays and other exotica.
1. 15m Climb a very steep iced corner to the base of the gully. This is avoidable by starting up Kumbh Mela, then traversing right.
2. 40m Follow deceptively steep iced chimneys to an easier angled section.
3. 45m Steep snow leads to a steep icy section climbing underneath a prominent chockstone. Finish up easier ground. Another 100m of easy ground leads to open slopes.

3 Bottomless Gully 135m V,5 *
M.Fowler, D.Wilkinson 13 Mar 1988
This is the furthest right of the three gullies. It is protected by an overhanging wall which necessitates a start 45m down the approach ramp.
1. 45m Zigzag with surprising difficulty, trending generally left, towards the base of the gully.
2. 20m Climb more easily to the gully, which is deep and narrow.
3. 30m Go up easy snow in the gully.
4. 40m A fine pitch leads out on to easy ground.

4 Monumental Chimney 115m V,7 **
J.Lyall, J.Preston 15 Dec 2000
The right face of the right buttress is slabby and has some good mixed climbing (routes not described). The top right end of this face is bounded by a gully. Forking left from below the second ice pitch of the gully is a very steep chockstoned chimney. It looks impossibly overhanging, but like the best routes, it isn't!
1. 60m Climb the gully up a smooth corner on thin ice, then go up easy snow to the chimney.
2. 20m Go deep into the chimney and up to jammed blocks. Cut loose under these to gain the hanging chimney which is followed by a tight squeeze and awkward bulge to a ledge.
3. 35m Follow the bulging fault and gully to the top.

5 Elemental Gully 100m II
J.Lyall 18 Jan 2001
Follow the smooth corner and easy snow of Monumental Chimney, then continue up the gully on the right. The grade varies with the build up, can be Grade III.

Corrag Bhuidhe South Buttress
(NH 068 832) Alt 650m North-East facing

6 Central Gully 300m I
A wide gully which allows an easy route up or down from the ridge, cornice permitting. It leads to the lowest point of the ridge. The section below the cornice is the only steep section and is usually easiest on the right (going upwards).

Martin Moran

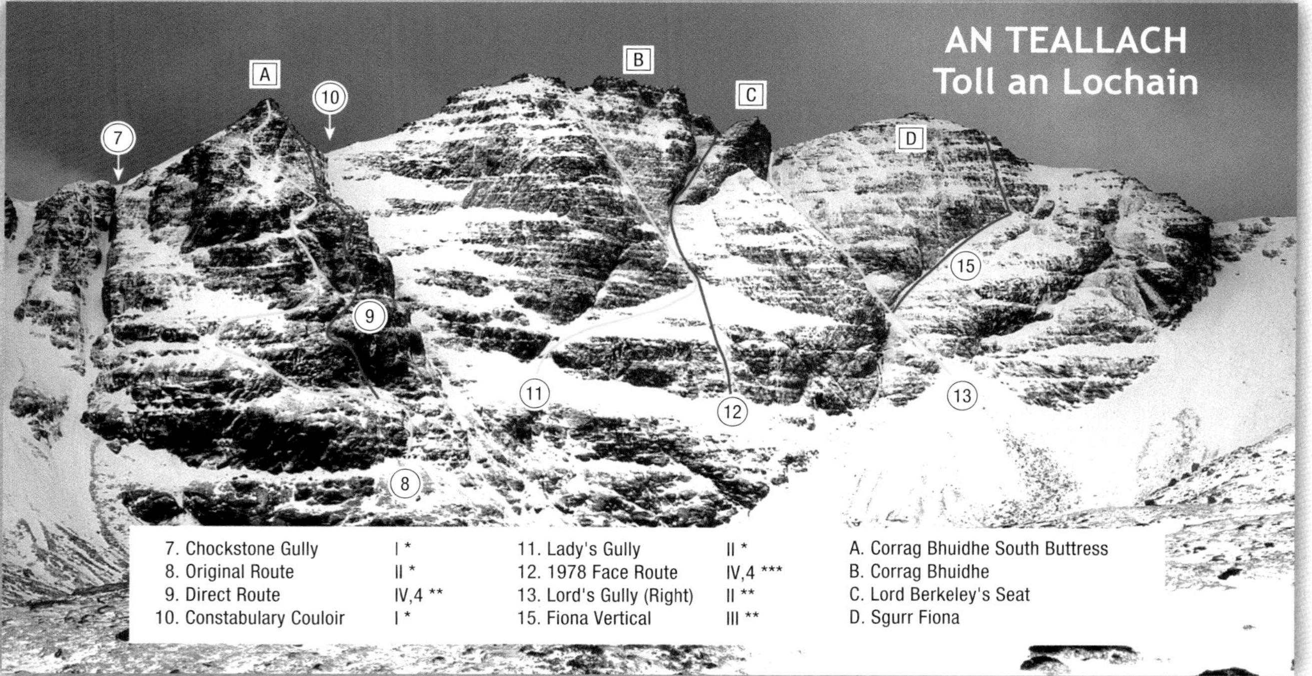

AN TEALLACH
Toll an Lochain

7. Chockstone Gully	I *	11. Lady's Gully	II *
8. Original Route	II *	12. 1978 Face Route	IV,4 ***
9. Direct Route	IV,4 **	13. Lord's Gully (Right)	II **
10. Constabulary Couloir	I *	15. Fiona Vertical	III **

A. Corrag Bhuidhe South Buttress
B. Corrag Bhuidhe
C. Lord Berkeley's Seat
D. Sgurr Fiona

NORTHERN HIGHLANDS

7 Chockstone Gully   300m   I *
A narrow gully parallel and right of Central Gully. The chockstone is near the top and the deep gully underneath it is well seen from the ridge. The gully collects a lot of snow which normally buries the chockstone. If the direct finish is corniced, a left branch may not be.

8 Corrag Bhuidhe South Buttress, Original Route   350m   II *
V.Chelton, R.McAllister, D.McGimpsey, S.Mearns   24 Feb 1999
Climbs the east face of the buttress overlooking Loch Toll an Lochain. A long and devious line through some fine scenery. Start up a shallow gully just right of the barrier wall at the base (which drops into the lochan). Climb this and trend easily left towards a very steep wall with a ramp and obvious icefall. Make a long traverse left until it is possible to climb up mixed ground to a snowfield below the main rock barrier on the face. Traverse back right towards the crest until turfy steps lead up to a left-trending ramp come gully breaching the barrier wall. At its top, climb up left into a small basin. A short turfy groove on the left (crux) leads to easier ground. Either climb straight up to the final crest or up and left across snow to the top.

9 Corrag Bhuidhe, South Buttress Direct   350m   IV,4 **
D.McGimpsey, A.Nisbet   26 Feb 1999
A varied line up a big buttress, even if not truly direct. Start up the gully as for the original route and trend easily left to the steep wall and icefall. Start up the icefall but soon go up a prominent diagonal line leftwards with a through route to reach a terrace. Gain the next terrace below the main rock barrier. Climb a turfy groove just left of the crest, breaking out left at half-height and returning right above. Follow the crest to the top.

10 Constabulary Couloir   350m   I *
The long shallow couloir separating the South Buttress from the main crags of Corrag Bhuidhe. It may have an avoidable icefall near the bottom.

Corrag Bhuidhe

(NH 066 833)   Alt 700m   North-East facing   Map p372

Near its base, the main face has a large triangular snowfield above a short rock barrier.

11 Lady's Gully   350m   II *
F.Fotheringham, J.R.R.Fowler   30 Dec 1974
Gain the triangular snowfield at its lower left corner and go up to the apex. Follow a left-trending gully from there to the top.

12 1978 Face Route   400m   IV,4 ***
M.Freeman, N.D.Keir   19 Feb 1978
This atmospheric route finds a way through serious open terrain. Gain the triangular snowfield. The best start is by a central icefall leading directly into its centre, but this needs cold conditions. Alternatively, gain its left end by a short gully. From its apex start up Lady's Gully, then turn rightwards under a wall until below a right-sloping gully-ramp (crux) and follow it for about 80m until it is easy to trend right to the crest of the buttress overlooking Lord's Gully. Either follow the crest to the top or stay in the gully and finish up it.

13 Lord's Gully   400m   III ***
J.H.B.Bell, E.E.Roberts   Easter 1923 (Right Branch). A.Borthwick, F.Fotheringham   17 Feb 1973 (Left Branch)
This is the long left-slanting gully between Corrag Bhuidhe and Sgùrr Fiona. The long initial section is usually straightforward snow (and has been skied). At its top it has two branches going either side of the huge tower of Lord Berkeley's Seat. The left branch is better defined with more interest but harder climbing.
Variation: **Right Branch   II** **
Difficulties in the right branch are often circumvented by a traverse right onto the face of Sgùrr Fiona which involves some low angled ice.

Colin Wells

Lord's Gully, III

14 Lord Berkeley's Seat   130m   VI,6 **
S.Jenkins, A.Nisbet   28 Jan 1991
This spectacular route up the face of the Seat is not as hard as it looks, possibly V,5 with well frozen turf and not too much snow. Start just left of the toe of the buttress.
1. 45m Climb the crest, trending slightly right until stopped by a barrier wall.
2. 35m Traverse right and climb a short slab overlooking the right branch of Lord's Gully. A series of walls leads to another barrier.
3. 25m Traverse left and climb corners just right of the crest.
4. 25m A short turfy ramp leads diagonally right to the final wall, which is finished to the right of the summit.

Sgùrr Fiona

(NH 066 837)   Alt 750m   East facing   Map p372
The corrie face of Sgùrr Fiona gives some long ice climbs in good conditions. The face is crossed by two big ramp systems which rise to the right. The higher and larger ramp starts near the base of Lord's Gully with the most obvious and regularly forming icefall above this ramp and right of centre. The distinctive features of the ice lines lie above this ramp although they have lower continuations to the base of the face.

15 Fiona Verticale   250m   III **
M.E.Moran, D.Litherland   13 Apr 1994
Climbs the obvious icefall in the upper right sector of the face. Start where Lord's Gully becomes narrow and well defined. Strike off rightwards up the ramp and follow this to where it becomes two ramps, one set close above the other. Follow the upper ramp to its end at a large and prominent icefall covering the cliffs above. Follow the easiest line up the ice and continue up a chimney-line to finish by a narrow cleft at the north ridge of Sgùrr Fiona about 70m below the summit.

NORTHERN HIGHLANDS

SCOTTISH
WINTER CLIMBS

Belfast